GREEK TRAGEDY
IN NEW TRANSLATIONS

GENERAL EDITORS
Peter Burian and Alan Shapiro

FOUNDING GENERAL EDITOR
William Arrowsmith

FORMER GENERAL EDITOR
Herbert Golder

THE COMPLETE EURIPIDES, VOLUME V

The Complete Euripides Volume V

Medea and Other Plays

Edited by
PETER BURIAN
and
ALAN SHAPIRO

OXFORD
UNIVERSITY PRESS

2011

OXFORD
UNIVERSITY PRESS

Oxford University Press, Inc., publishes works that further
Oxford University's objective of excellence
in research, scholarship, and education.

Oxford New York
Auckland Cape Town Dar es Salaam Hong Kong Karachi
Kuala Lumpur Madrid Melbourne Mexico City Nairobi
New Delhi Shanghai Taipei Toronto

With offices in
Argentina Austria Brazil Chile Czech Republic France Greece
Guatemala Hungary Italy Japan Poland Portugal Singapore
South Korea Switzerland Thailand Turkey Ukraine Vietnam

Published by Oxford University Press, Inc.
198 Madison Avenue, New York, New York 10016

www.oup.com

Oxford is a registered trademark of Oxford University Press.

Library of Congress Cataloging-in-Publication Data
Euripides.
  [Selections. English. 2011]
  Medea and other plays / [Euripides]; edited by Peter Burian and Alan Shapiro.
     p.   cm.—(The complete Euripides; v. 5) (Greek tragedy in new translations)
  ISBN 978-0-19-538870-1—ISBN 978-0-19-538871-8
  1. Euripides—Translations into English. 2. Greek drama (Tragedy)—Translations into
English. I. Burian, Peter, 1943– II. Shapiro, Alan, 1952– III. Title.
  PA3975.A2 2011
  882'.01—dc22   2010044566

EDITORS' FOREWORD

"*The Greek Tragedy in New Translations* is based on the conviction that poets like Aeschylus, Sophocles, and Euripides can only be properly rendered by translators who are themselves poets. Scholars may, it is true, produce useful and perceptive versions. But our most urgent present need is for a *re-creation* of these plays—as though they had been written, freshly and greatly, by masters fully at home in the English of our own times."

With these words, the late William Arrowsmith announced the purpose of this series, and we intend to honor that purpose. As was true of most of the volumes that began to appear in the 1970s—first under Arrowsmith's editorship, later in association with Herbert Golder—those for which we bear editorial responsibility are products of close collaborations between poets and scholars. We believe (as Arrowsmith did) that the skills of both are required for the difficult and delicate task of transplanting these magnificent specimens of another culture into the soil of our own place and time, to do justice both to their deep differences from our patterns of thought and expression and to their palpable closeness to our most intimate concerns. Above all, we are eager to offer contemporary readers dramatic poems that convey as vividly and directly as possible the splendor of language, the complexity of image and idea, and the intensity of emotion and originals. This entails, among much else, the recognition that the tragedies were meant for performance—as scripts for actors—to be sung and danced as well as spoken. It demands writing of inventiveness, clarity, musicality, and dramatic power. By such standards, we ask that these translations be judged.

This series is also distinguished by its recognition of the need of nonspecialist readers for a critical Introduction informed by the best recent scholarship, but written clearly and without condescension. Each play is followed by notes designed not only to elucidate obscure references but also to mediate the conventions of the Athenian stage as well as those features of the Greek text that might otherwise go unnoticed. The notes are supplemented by a glossary of mythical and geographical terms that should make it possible to read the play without turning elsewhere for basic information. Stage directions are sufficiently ample to aid readers in imagining the action as they read. Our fondest hope, of course, is that these versions will be staged not only in the minds of their readers but also in the theaters to which, after so many centuries, they still belong.

A NOTE ON THE SERIES FORMAT

A series such as this requires a consistent format. Different translators, with individual voices and approaches to the material at hand, cannot be expected to develop a single coherent style for each of the three tragedians, much less make clear to modern readers that, despite the differences among the tragedians themselves, the plays share many conventions and a generic, or period, style. But they can at least share a common format and provide similar forms of guidance to the reader.

1. *Spelling of Greek Names*

Orthography is one area of difference among the translations that requires a brief explanation. Historically, it has been common practice to use Latinized forms of Greek names when bringing them into English. Thus, for example, Oedipus (not Oidipous) and Clytemnestra (not Klutaimestra) are customary in English. Recently, however, many translators have moved toward more precise transliteration, which has the advantage of presenting the names as both Greek and new, instead of Roman and neoclassical importations into English. In the case of so familiar a name as Oedipus, however, transliteration risks the appearance of pedantry or affectation. And in any case, perfect consistency cannot be expected in such matters. Readers will feel the same discomfort with "Athenai" as the chief city of Greece as they would with "Platon" as the author of the *Republic*.

The earlier volumes in this series adopted as a rule a "mixed" orthography in accordance with the considerations outlined above. The most familiar names retain their Latinate forms, while the rest are transliterated; -os rather than Latin -us is adopted for the termination of masculine names, and Greek diphthongs (as in Iphigen*eia* for Latin Iphigenia) are retained. Some of the later volumes continue this practice, but where translators have preferred to use a more consistent practice of transliteration or Latinization, we have honored their wishes.

2. *Stage Directions*

The ancient manuscripts of the Greek plays do not supply stage directions (though the ancient commentators often provide information relevant to staging, delivery, "blocking," etc.). Hence stage directions must be inferred from words and situations and our knowledge of Greek theatrical conventions. At best this is a ticklish and uncertain procedure. But it is surely preferable that good stage directions should be provided by the translator than that readers should be left to their own devices in visualizing action, gesture, and spectacle. Ancient tragedy was austere and "distanced" by means of masks, which means that the reader must not expect the detailed intimacy ("He shrugs and turns wearily away," "She speaks with deliberate slowness, as though to emphasize the point," etc.) that characterizes stage directions in modern naturalistic drama.

3. *Numbering of Lines*

For the convenience of the reader who may wish to check the translation against the original, or vice versa, the lines have been numbered according to both the Greek and English texts. The lines of the translation have been numbered in multiples of ten, and these numbers have been set in the right-hand margin. The (inclusive) Greek numeration will be found bracketed at the top of the page. The Notes that follow the text have been keyed to both numerations, the line numbers of the translation in **bold**, followed by the Greek lines in regular type, and the same convention is used for all references to specific passages (of the translated plays only) in both the Notes and the Introduction.

Readers will doubtless note that in many plays the English lines outnumber the Greek, but they should not therefore conclude that the translator has been unduly prolix. In most cases the reason is simply that the translator has adopted the free-flowing norms of modern Anglo-American prosody, with its brief-breath-and-emphasis-determined lines, and its habit of indicating cadence and caesuras by line length and setting rather than by conventional punctuation. Even where translators have preferred to cast dialogue in more regular five-beat or six-beat lines, the greater compactness of Greek diction is likely to result in a substantial disparity in Greek and English numerations.

ABOUT THE TRANSLATIONS

The translations in this series were written over a period of roughly forty years. No attempt has been made to update references to the scholarly literature in the Introductions and Notes, but each volume offers a brief For Further Reading list that will provide some initial orientation to contemporary critical thinking about the tragedies it contains.

THIS VOLUME

The plays included in this fifth and final volume of the Complete Euripides give remarkable evidence of the playwright's range. *Medea* is one of the starkest and most disturbing of Euripidean tragedies. *Helen*, on the other hand, is a drama of rescue and escape often described as closer to being a romantic comedy than a tragedy. *Alcestis* is enigmatic in tone, its plot involving both the pathos of the heroine's voluntary death in place of her husband and her fablelike restoration to life by her husband's guest-friend Herakles. These three plays offer a trio of striking, and strikingly different, female protagonists, whereas the fourth, *Cyclops*, has no women characters at all. This drama is the only complete example to survive of the satyr-plays with which tragic tetralogies characteristically concluded. Its genre, however, links it to *Alcestis*, which we know to have been "prosatyric" (i.e., a drama without satyrs presented in place of a satyr-play).

Alcestis is also Euripides' earliest surviving play, unless (as some scholars believe) *Rhesus* is not the work of a fourth-century tragedian, but an early drama by the master. *Alcestis* was first produced at the Great Dionysia of 438 B.C., following three tragedies (*Cretan Women*, *Alcmaeon in Psophis*, and *Telephus*), all now lost. Scholars occasionally suggest that this or that play of Euripides may have occupied the same position in another tetralogy, but *Alcestis* is the only prosatyric drama for which we have any direct evidence. It is entirely possible, indeed, that it was a one-time experiment made under the influence of some particular circumstance. It remains a unique and fascinating mixture of legend and fairy tale, high tragic drama, and (particularly in a scene that features the drunken Herakles) something close to farce.

Not surprisingly, the play opens itself to a wide range of divergent interpretations. On the one hand, Alcestis', dutiful but autonomous decision to take her husband's place in death and her devotion to family have attracted much admiration. On the other, her return as a mute figure (explained in the play as a sort of ritual silence imposed by her sojourn among the dead) has seemed to many to rob her of agency and subjectivity. Admetos rewins his wife, Herakles tells him, because of the generosity of his guest-friendship, and this has been seen as his redeeming virtue by some critics as well. Others have wondered whether the accommodation of his boisterous guest in the midst of the mourning for Alcestis does not make of the virtue a weakness, especially when he yields to Herakles' insistence that he take into his house the veiled woman with whom the hero returns. Not to mention his reproach of his father, in a bitter and unseemly debate, for not dying in his wife's stead, or indeed his remorseful reproach of Alcestis herself for abandoning him after complying with her sacrifice in order to save his own life.

However one judges Admetos' worthiness of Alcestis' sacrifice, whatever one makes of the mute figure in whom he comes to recognize his beloved wife restored to life, the exploit that Herakles accomplishes on his behalf brings about the restoration of family and social order. In the process, Admetos has presumably come to understand that his wife, far from being an expendable substitute for himself, is utterly irreplaceable. And the final scene reveals that the apparent treatment of women as tokens of exchange among men is just the opposite: the return of Alcestis to life stops the cycle of exchange and insists that she is not fungible, but priceless and unique.

Medea, securely dated to 431, is a family drama of a very different sort, and its heroine could hardly be less like Alcestis. She is one of the most fascinating (and terrifying) of characters in Greek tragedy, in part because she contains within herself so many identities.

Though she is living in Greece and has learned Greek ways, she is not Greek but is a princess of Colchis. And she is effectively in exile: having killed her brother to ensure Jason's successful return to Greece with the Golden Fleece, she can no longer return home. She is also, and crucially, a witch. This is not a prominent feature of the text from the beginning, but would presumably be part of what the original spectators knew about Medea. In Greek literature, magic is associated with women who are expert at making and using poisons (with which Medea will kill in the most horrifying manner the Corinthian princess who is her rival, along with her father the king), invoke the goddess Hekate as patroness (as Medea does at 415 / 397), and have various uncanny powers.

Medea is married to a Greek hero, however, lives among Greeks, and has achieved a remarkable ability to argue with the subtlety and persuasiveness of a Greek man. Furthermore, she has adopted, it seems, the outlook of the heroic Greek male, for whom to be slighted or ridiculed is unbearable, to compromise with one's enemies impossible. She practices deception with success when that is needed but can also face down her husband, who appears far less resolute and "manly" than she in their debates. Indeed, throughout their relationship it has been Medea who aided and supported Jason, rather than the other way around. When Jason leaves Medea for his Corinthian princess, Medea appears desperate and helpless, but step by step she takes charge and wins what she needs to triumph over those who have now become her enemies.

But Medea is more than all these things. Most notoriously, she is the slayer of her own children, because they are Jason's, too, and she knows that this is how she can hurt him most. Euripides stages the deed in a way that shocks us with the ruthless finality of Medea's revenge. After Medea has extracted a promise of refuge from the Athenian king, Aegeus, and seen him on his way, she describes the vengeance she will take on her rival. Then, at 781–88 / 791–97, Medea announces that she must kill her children as the only way to bring down Jason's house. There have until this point been only the barest hints of danger for the children, and it shocks the Chorus of Corinthian women, who has to this point offered Medea sympathy and support, as surely as it shocks audiences today. We must understand, nevertheless, that Medea acts with the rigor and finality of an *alastôr*, an avenging spirit, even at the cause of sacrificing those nearest and dearest to her. Indeed, in the process she seems to have exchanged her humanity for something daemonic, something more than ordinary mortality. At the point where a *deus ex machina* often arrives in Euripides to resolve the loose ends of the plot, Medea herself makes a surprising appearance on the theatrical machine, in a chariot pulled by dragons given to her by her immortal grandfather, the Sun god (Helios). Jason has come to find her in the palace, reclaim the children's bodies, and seek his own revenge. Instead, Medea confronts him from above, far out of reach, in complete control and with the children firmly in her grasp. Medea escapes punishment, either from Jason or from the people of Corinth, whose royal family she has also destroyed. On her divine conveyance she stands literally above the laws of men. It is a stunning and deeply disturbing ending to a stunning and deeply disturbing tragedy.

Whether *Helen*, first produced in 412, is a tragedy at all has often been debated; it is a drama of rescue and escape that ends happily for its protagonist, and is undoubtedly the most amusing of the surviving plays written for the Greek tragic stage. It is also in many ways the most enigmatic, since its "counterfactual" premise (that Helen of Troy never went to Troy in the first place but has been waiting in Egypt for her husband to find her and take her home again, a model of fidelity under extreme duress) undercuts the usual tale of Troy at its very foundation. As I have tried to suggest in the Introduction to the translation in this volume, what Euripides does in recasting the character of Helen as the most steadfast of wives complicates her situation in intriguing ways that open up this alternate version of her story to wider philosophical and even political considerations.

Helen both is and is not what she seems to be. She has been substituted in Troy by a double made by Hera from thin air, a divine deception that all who see accept unquestioningly as the real Helen. Helen herself thus finds that her extraordinary beauty (the essential element in any telling of her tale, but by no means the essence of who she is in this play), while it makes her irresistibly attractive to the Egyptian king, whose pursuit threatens her chastity, also makes her utterly abhorrent to Greeks and Trojans alike, because they hold her responsible for all their sufferings. And Helen cannot escape guilt entirely: the beauty that her phantom imitates is after all finally hers, and it has indeed caused seemingly endless disasters. Ironic-ally, when Menelaus finds her at last, years after the end of the war, he still has the phantom in tow and at first refuses to believe that she is really Helen. Thus, the drama becomes at one level a consider-ation of the relation of appearance and reality, embodied in a figure in which the two seem to be inextricably linked.

Furthermore, the Trojan War, the *locus classicus* for Greek ideas of heroism, here becomes a war fought in vain, waged literally over nothing. Against the background of the terrible losses and uncer-tainties of an Athenian war overseas—the Sicilian Expedition—still ongoing at the time *Helen* was produced, and soon to end in catastrophe for Athens, spectators could hardly have missed the relevance of the questions *Helen* raises about what such wars mean and what can justify them. There is, however, a very Eur-ipidean irony here, too. After the reunion with Menelaus, Helen brings about their escape by deception, in effect creating a second "phantom" Menelaus, supposedly lost at sea. The success of this enterprise depends on a violent struggle against barbarians that is treated as the final vindication of the "Trojan glory" (1590 / 1603) that the play has cast in such a doubtful light. Whatever one decides about its generic category, *Helen* raises serious issues and elicits the spectator's (and the reader's) emotional and intellectual engage-ment.

Cyclops (the only one of the plays in this volume that cannot be precisely dated, although the current consensus puts it late in Euripides' career) also reworks an episode from Trojan saga. It can be thought of as a kind of parody of the episode in Homer's *Odyssey* in which Odysseus and some of his shipmates, sailing home from Troy, are trapped in the cave of the one-eyed Cyclops, Polyphemus. In the Homeric tale, Polyphemus devours several of Odysseus' men, but the resourceful hero outwits him with some of his most ingenious stratagems. When the Cyclops asks Odysseus his name, he calls himself "Nobody." He persuades Polyphemus to drink the wine he fortunately brought with him, sending the mon-ster into a drunken stupor. Then Odysseus and his remaining men put out the Cyclops' eye with a sharpened olive branch, its point made red hot in the fire. When Polyphemus screams for help from his fellow Cyclopes, and they ask him who is hurting him, and he, of course, answers "Nobody," they go away again. Odysseus and his companions escape by clinging to the bellies of Polyphemus' sheep—a kind of Trojan Horse maneuver in reverse. In the end, however, Odysseus' pride induces him to shout out his name, and the Cyclops sends him off with a large rock hurled toward his ship and a curse that extends his wanderings for years.

The plot of *Cyclops* follows roughly this outline but is remodeled to include, as any satyr-play must, a Chorus of cavorting, tippling, lusty satyrs whose interference in the action gives it an entirely new atmosphere and tone. In addition to the young satyrs of the Chorus, Silenus, their father and a boon companion of Dionysus, plays a considerable role in the Euripidean plot. Here are a couple of examples of the difference satyrs make: in the *Odyssey*, Odysseus falls afoul of Polyphemus by entering his cave in his absence; in *Cyclops*, Odysseus first meets Silenus and offers to trade his wine for food. Being a servant of Dionysus, Silenus can't resist the offer, even though the food in question belongs not to him but to the Cyclops. When Polyphemus arrives, Silenus accuses Odysseus of stealing the food, swearing by various gods and the lives of his satyr sons (who are standing beside him) that he is telling the truth. The Chorus Leader tells Polyphemus what really happened, but the Cyclops doesn't believe him, and eventually takes Odysseus and his men into the cave, where he will, as in the *Odyssey*, kill and eat some of them. As in the *Odyssey*, the hero offers wine to Polyphemus and gets him roaring drunk. Here, however, Odysseus manages to sneak out of the cave to tell us about what has happened inside. He explains his plan to Silenus and the Chorus: Polyphemus, in his drunken delight, wants to share the wine with his fellow Cyclopes. The satyrs are to stop him and keep him drinking till he falls asleep, and, when he's unconscious, to help Odysseus burn out his eye with the burning poker. The drinking scene that follows parodies the traditional symposium (wine party) at which adolescent males were courted by older men, a scenario reflected here as in a distorting mirror. The ugly, hairy, old Silenus plays junior partner to the monstrous *erastês* ("lover"), Polyphemus, who drags his unwilling partner back into the cave. There, of course, Odysseus will put his plan into action, but without the help of the satyrs; suddenly timorous, they balk at the door and offer a risible series of excuses. The binding then transpires with the help of Odysseus' men, as in the *Odyssey*.

What to make of all this foolery surrounding a gripping and serious episode from an epic? Fifty years ago, a distinguished classicist published an article specifically to suggest "that the value of the *Cyclops*, both as drama and as an illustration of Euripides' thought, is negligible, and that the illustrious name of its author has led us to look for merit where none exists." Although one no longer finds that kind of blanket dismissal, the secondary literature tends to be relatively sparse and generally makes rather limited claims on behalf of the play. Reasonably so, since *Cyclops* is primarily an amusing entertainment; there is an immediate appeal to recasting a well-known tale for the stage in a verbally witty, visually lively, and cheerfully irreverent fashion. And an important strand of recent criticism focuses (with varying degrees of approval or censure) on the appeal to Athenian men (and perhaps not only them) of satyrs as "ithyphallic men behaving badly." But we should not entirely neglect the fully human element in the drama, represented only by Odysseus (and his crew as extras). As David Konstan points out in his Introduction, Odysseus is represented in complete contrast to both the fun-loving but craven herd of satyrs and the solipsistic bully Polyphemus: living by a code of reciprocity, loyal to his friends, law abiding, in full control of his appetites, and with an appropriate reverence for the gods. This was by no means the only way Odysseus could be—and was—depicted (see, for example, the glib and malign Odysseus of Euripides' *Hecuba*). Surprisingly, then, for all its impudent fun, Euripides' *Cyclops* can be read as a commendation of civilized values and human decency.

Euripides' *Helen* appears in print for the first time here; the other works in this volume were originally published between 1974 and 2006. The late WILLIAM ARROWSMITH was the founding General Editor of this series. He taught in a number of major institutions (including the University of Texas, Boston University, and Emory University). Distinguished both as a critic and translator, Arrowsmith's published translations included Greek tragedies (in addition to *Alcestis*, Euripides' *Cyclops*, *Heracles*, *Orestes*, *Hecuba*, and *Bacchae*) and comedies (Aristophanes' *Birds* and *Clouds*); from Latin, Petronius' *Satyricon*; from Italian, several volumes of the poetry of Montale, Pavese's *Dialogues with Leucò* and *Hard Labor* (a volume of poetry), and a collection of the writings of Michelangelo Antonioni, *That Bowling Alley on the Tiber*; and from German,

Nietzsche's *Unmodern Observations*. PETER BURIAN, a coeditor of this series, is Professor of Classical and Comparative Literatures at Duke University. He previously collaborated with Alan Shapiro on Aeschylus' *Oresteia* and with Brian Swann on Euripides' *Phoenician Women*, and provided Introduction and Notes for W. S. Di Piero's *Ion*. He has also published a translation of Aeschylus' *Suppliants* and numerous essays on Greek drama.

MICHAEL COLLIER is Professor of English at the University of Maryland and Director of the Breadloaf Writers' Conference. Widely known as a poet and editor, he is the author of five volumes of poetry, including *The Neighbor* (1995), *The Ledge* (2000), and *Dark Wild Realm* (2006). *Make Us Wave Back: Essays on Poetry and Influence* appeared in 2007. HEATHER MCHUGH is the Milliman Distinguished Writer-in-Residence at the University of Washington, Seattle, and teaches in the MFA program at Warren Wilson College. The winner of numerous prizes and awards, she received a MacArthur "Genius Grant" in 2009. McHugh's poetry collections include *Hinge and Sign: Poems 1968–1993* (1994), *The Father of Predicaments* (2001), *Eyeshot* (2004), and *Upgraded to Serious* (2009). She has published a book of essays, *Broken English: Poetry and Partiality* (1993) and translations of Paul Celan (*Glottal Stops: 101 Poems of Paul Celan*, 2001), Blaga Dimitrova, and Jean Follain.

DAVID KONSTAN is the John Rowe Workman Distinguished Professor of Classics and the Humanistic Tradition at Brown University. Prodigiously productive, he has worked on a wide range of Greek and Roman literature, philosophy, and science, emphasizing in recent years the emotions as conceived in classical Greece and Rome (*Friendship in the Classical World*, 1997; *Pity Transformed*, 2001; *The Emotions of the Ancient Greeks: Studies in Aristotle and Classical Literature*, 2006; *Before Forgiveness: The Origins of a Moral Idea*, 2010). Konstan is translating Seneca's *Hercules on Mount Oeta* and *Hercules Furens* for the University of Chicago Press's Seneca Project. GEORGIA MACHEMER, a historian of ideas, has taught Greek, Latin, and a variety of classics courses at Duke University and at the University of North Carolina at Greensboro and at Chapel Hill.

CONTENTS

CONTENTS

ALCESTIS

Translated by

WILLIAM ARROWSMITH

INTRODUCTION

I

By general agreement the *Alcestis* is a spirited, puzzling, profound, and seriously light-hearted tragicomedy of human existence. But it is also, as I hope to show,[1] a peculiarly beautiful and coherent example of what, for want of a better word, I would call "model" drama (as opposed to modern "psychological" drama or the drama of our own "theater of character"). Moreover, the beauty and the difficulty of the play—its mysterious elusiveness, its puzzling texture and unfamiliar form—can only be understood, I think, by grasping, in all its complicated richness, its peculiar thought and structure.

Among extant Greek plays, there is literally nothing like it.[2] For works of similar tone and structure, we must go to the late Shakespearean "comedies," to *The Winter's Tale* or *Pericles* or *The Tempest*; or, in music, to Mozart's *Marriage of Figaro*, with its miraculous blend of wit, pathos, and farce, its *buffo* Figaro and its semi-tragic Countess Almaviva. In composition, the *Alcestis* is remarkably executed; each succeeding scene unerringly articulates and inflects the controlling theme; even for Euripides (one of the most severely economical of dramatists, despite the censures of his critics), the concentration is

---

1. For obvious reasons nothing more than a sketch is possible here. Demonstration and defense of what, in its aim and complexity, purports to be a coherent theory of Greek drama would require much lengthier treatment—in fact, a book. But a sketch, tentative and incomplete, may conceivably serve the reader's purpose (if not the scholar's requirements).

2. Presumably because it occupied, when first performed in 438 B.C., the position of a "satyr-play"; that is, rounded off a group of three tragedies. But since we know very little of "satyr-drama" (Euripides' *Cyclops* and a fragment of Sophocles' *Searchers* are the only extant examples of the genre—a quite insufficient sample), and the *Alcestis* is our only example of a "pro-satyric" play, it is impossible to describe or even identify the "genre."

extraordinary. So, too, is the shaping of the characters, each one, in his generically revealing way, embodying or at least illuminating the central idea—the process by which a man, instructed by the example of a woman's love and courage, at last comes into his own humanity, into his true human mode, and finally learns, through suffering, humiliation, and luck, to think recognizably "human (that is, *mortal*) thoughts." It is an extraordinary achievement. But that achievement cannot, I think, be properly understood unless the play is seen and experienced in the modal terms that control its structure, tone, characters, and themes. The play is complex, but its complexity is organically coherent; superbly unified even in its mercurial shifts of pace and feeling, in its criss-crossed paradox and irony, it is all of a piece. What makes it so, I believe, is mode and modal concentration.

II

By "mode" I mean simply the generic states and phases of human (and other) existence, as they revealed themselves to the Greek mind and imagination. No ancient writer, of course, anywhere speaks of "modes" nor is there any ancient Greek word for "mode." But it is a revealing modern notion that primitive cultures are "primitive" precisely to the degree that they are typically incapable of articulating assumptions that lie deeply ingrained in language and behavior. But this seems a dubious notion at best since the more coherent the culture is, the less perceptible its basic assumptions are likely to be to members of that culture.

Modern scholars of Greek drama have constantly pointed out that ancient tragedy aims at the archetypal and universal, and their grounds for so doing are, in essence, modal. Indeed "modal" analysis is really nothing more than an effort to work out, in ramifying detail, the dramatic and cultural implications of this "universalizing" tendency of Greek drama. It implies not only that ancient drama should not, and cannot, be understood in terms of modern ideas of character and psychology, but that the very aim of Greek drama is an account of human fate in a world where any order of "being" is defined by contrast with other modes of existence. Also implied is the corollary that modal aims will inevitably be trivialized by imposing modern notions. Thus, in sharp contrast to modern drama, the drama of the Greeks is *masked*; its characters make their appearances in ways which quite literally compel the audience to perceive and respond to them in a generic, not an individual, way. Further, the modal aim of ancient drama is reinforced, as we would surely expect, by the theatrical and rhetorical conventions of that theater.

A few examples. In both Greek and English the distinction between "mortal" (*thnētos*) and "immortal" (*athanatos*) is a modal distinction rooted in language. Men die by definition whereas gods qua immortals cannot die; their modes differ according to their subjection to, or exemption from, death. Man is modally unique, and his uniqueness is explicitly revealed by informing contrast with the gods (who live forever and know it) and the animals (who are mortal but are unaware of their mortality). Men suffer necessity (*anankē*) whether as death, political oppression, old age, suffering, sexuality, or slavery; the gods who impose, and often incarnate, human necessities seldom suffer them. In short, the modes of men and gods are defined by their vulnerability to *anankē* or limits generally. Necessity is the criterion which divides each "species" of existence from the other.

But between man and man there are also crucial differences of modal degree, since men differ in their powers and therefore in their value. There are slaves, peasants, nobles, and free men; cowards, men of courage, and heroes. The hero is always interesting to the Greek mind because he is a modal frontiersman; he confounds old modalities and redefines the boundaries between man and god. One thinks of Herakles and his superhuman labors, Asklepios with his partial conquest of death, Orpheus with his harrowing of Hades—or the bravery of Alcestis. Or perhaps an Achilles, the archetypal youth confronted with the necessity of an early death. Implicit, often explicit, everywhere in Greek literature is a great hierarchy of being which runs from absolute, untrammeled Olympian possibility at the top to sheer, wretched subjection to total necessity at the bottom. To this hierarchy the Greeks thought it possible and natural—indeed, almost second nature—to assign men and events. No body of thought is so overwhelmingly pervaded by such emphasis upon modal distinctions; no other literature is so concentrated upon the effort, to clarify, realize, and "place" the modes of existence. The spectrum is, of course, usually aristocratic, but the aristocracy involved is basically not that of blood but of achievement and *aretē*.[3]

This uniquely Greek concentration on the modalities has been slighted simply because it is so overwhelmingly obvious that the

---

3. In range and suggestions, *aretē* is badly cramped by the prim English word "virtue." Originally, *aretē* designated something like Latin *virtus*, i.e. "manliness" or "physical prowess." Later it became the (quite untranslatable) term indicating the chief aristocratic virtues, ranging from "physical courage" to "excellence" to "moral courage"—that is, the qualities exhibited by an "excellent" man. Women might perhaps lay claim to *aretē*, but the word is essentially reserved to men. Euripides, in sharp contrast, stresses moral courage as against conventional aristocratic virtue, and clearly includes women among its rightful claimants.

temptation is strong to dismiss it as cultural rhetoric or mere linguistic habit. This would be a mistake. For it is this modal obsession, this passion for observing the modes of men and gods, that gives Greek thought and art their characteristic coherence and clarity. Any object seems always to imply another. Individuals and details alike have a cosmic resonance. Unless one has a sense for modal composition it is, I think, very difficult to understand Greek literature. Needless to say, possession of a modal sense does not mean that the Greeks were amateur philosophers; they were rather the enthusiastic heirs of a fairly coherent culture whose values were, until the late fifth century, exceptionally coherent. Everything in their environment conspired to make them modally aware. The ordinary Greek surely had no more notion that he habitually made modal distinctions than Molière's *bourgeois gentil-homme* realized that he had been speaking prose all his life. But their audience's sensitivity to modes seems to have been assumed by Greek artists and dramatists, and their works are addressed directly to that understanding, as even a cursory examination makes clear.

Man (*thnētos*) and god (*athanatos*) are modal words, as I pointed out before. Similarly, the real force of the Delphic command to "know oneself" is modal. It means not that introspective awareness of identity and motives which moderns call "knowledge," but rather a recognition of one's place in the scheme of things: what it is to be a man, to possess a man's fate. The man who "knows himself" always knows one thing—his mortality. It is because he knows he is doomed that he will, in theory, act compassionately toward other men no less doomed than he. For this reason he avoids the dangerous adjectives, the epithets which belong to the gods—that blessed exemption from necessity that makes the Greek gods "happy," "immortal" (and also amoral). Because the gods see everything *sub specie aeternitatis*, that perspective of theirs obliterates both meaning and morality; since they do not suffer (or do so only rarely), they are seldom compassionate (that is, "fellow sufferers"). Man, who views things temporally, is defined as a transient and a suffering being; necessity for him is a way of life. Therefore, if he recognizes his fate, he will think "mortal thoughts" (*ta thnēta phronein*), and these thoughts will invariably be the facts of his condition: his fatedness, his limits, his death, even his Aphrodite. What man is not, god is: a concentration of supreme power and intensity, and in this sense god imposes man's necessity upon him. If a man is wise and thinks mortal thoughts, he will yield to god; only a great hero, a great fool, a great criminal, or a very young man (that is, a man who does not know himself because of his youth) will resist god. Why? Because he is contemptuous of the modes (like a man of *hybris*), or ignorant of them (like a young man whose *hybris* is natural), or defiant of them (like a hero), or innocent of them (like Admetos).

Everywhere in Greek literature the modes are implied in a structure of events, as the metaphysical basis of character, or as the given morality of the situation. Most Greek art—certainly Homer, Pindar, Herodots, Aeschylus, Sophocles, and Euripides—is sustained modal meditation. The structure is often exactly designed so as to emphasize and intensify the modal distinctions between the characters; and just as the characters are defined in their own modes, so their modal differences define each other. Sophocles, for instance, constantly returns to stark, revealing contrasts between the hero (a person always ignorant of his modalities) and the *sophron* (or man of *sophrosynē*, the man who knows who he is). This, after all, is the difference between Oedipus and Kreon in the *Oedipus Rex*; between Chrysothemis and Elektra; between Antigone and Ismene; between Ajax and Odysseus. The pairing of these fated foils is addressed directly to an audience that feels situations modally. I stress *feeling* here because it seems important to realize that modal distinctions run deep. The Greek dramatist is not a philosopher, but a thinking artist whose sense of composition resembles that of his audience; modal perception, modal composition, are second nature.

Modal distinction, then, implies a hierarchy of value and being. The hierarchy differs, of course, according to the artist; each poet uses the same perceptual tools, makes similar modal distinctions, but inflects them in an individual way. But the work of art requires the reader to respond by placing men and events in an ordered relationship, each defining the other. The great modal example in Greek literature is, of course, Homer; all the others are variations on that great original. At the very top is god, sheer power, intense being; the quality "possessed by what is wonderful and unique," the special radiance of the exceptional and prodigious. Thus in the *Iliad* unusual men and great events have a luminousness which declares their divinity; it is because they are exceptional that they are divine. Among their many other functions, Homer's gods are often functional descriptions of the modes of great men; a hero is a hero not because he enjoys the favor of a god but because his *aretē* requires a god's presence to account for it. The *aretē* reveals divinity, almost summoning the gods. Achilles' courage is like Odysseus' mother-wit and Paris' looks, a *charisma*. Every power a being possesses is pertinent to his place along this great gamut of being, running from the omnipotence of Zeus to the undifferentiated powers of the great feudal barons of Olympos, down to the modest particularisms of the nymphs and lesser powers, to the god-aspiring *aretē* of the hero, to the routine world of ordinary mortals, to weak women, helpless children, and chattel slaves. Each order suffers the cumulative *ananke* of the orders above it in an ascending curve of freedom and power. The hierarchy changes, needless to say, with the social period; Euripides' Athens is not Homer's Troy. In this flexible hierarchy, the man of *hybris* is dangerous not only to himself and others but to the order whose stability his *hybris* threatens. Against *hybris* the saving attitude is *sophrosyne*, which is little more than a mastery of the modes, a skill of acceptance and self-knowledge according to who one is, his powers and circumstances, according to his mortality. Some possess that skill; some do not. Most learn it naturally, but great men, men of exceptional good fortune, learn it the hard way because their greatness dislikes learning a limit.

In sum, necessity is the essential criterion of mode. For just as men are, as a species, differentiated from the gods by the *ananke* of death, so they are generically distinguished from each other by status, wealth, sex, and age. Perhaps the most obvious fact of the Greek masking convention is that it enables the audience to detect, at a glance, the generic traits of a character at the same time that it prevents his full individuation. His whole character, in fact, is little more than the sum of the possibilities contained in his "modal" presentation. We observe, for instance, that Euripides' Pentheus is a *boy*; but he is also a king; these two salient facts then combine to produce a third, his spiritual intransigence and pathetic susceptibility to Dionysos; and these "traits" are then given depth by contrast with old Teiresias and Kadmos. Hippolytos' defiant arrogance is a function not only of divine affinity— his indenture to the goddess Artemis—but of his youth, a youth sharply contrasted to the humble old age of the Huntsman. In the Greek theater, these defining traits are starkly visual; in most cases they are stressed by contrast and foil. The mask states the essentials, tells us whether its wearer is young or old or middle-aged; youth or young man; girl or matron; slave or free; prosperous or unfortunate.[4] These impressions are then amplified and "thickened" by language, plot, development of theme, and theatrical "blocking." But the essential lines by which a character is first introduced are never disturbed or distorted by intrusion of idiosyncratic detail. It does not follow in the least that the psychology

---

4. For instance, according to our best authority on ancient masks, the lexicographer Pollux, a sallow (as opposed to a white) mask indicated that its wearer was "unfortunate or in love." See note on page 97. Not all scholars, of course, believe that Pollux' account accurately represents fifth-century practice. But T. B. L. Webster has, in my opinion, made a convincing case and my remarks are based upon acceptance of his argument. Those interested should consult Webster's *Greek Theatre Production* (London 1956), 35, 73, and his "Notes on Pollux' List of Tragic Masks" in T. Dohrn, ed., *Festschrift Andreas Rumpf* (Krefeld, 1952), 141–50.

of the modal character is therefore wooden or "stereotyped." Metaphysical or modal psychology may be unfamiliar, but it is no less rich and complex than any modern "individual" psychology.

The *language* of mode, the reader should note, is unmistakably and for obvious reasons the language of *anankē*. Indeed, one of the strongest arguments for a modal interpretation of Greek literature is the astonishing coherence of the abundant idioms and vocabulary of necessity. Thus we everywhere have expressions of force and strength; persistent verbal images of pressure or constraint or binding, the well-developed vocabulary of authority, coercion, deference, and obligation. There are also the metaphors and symbols, often visual, of yoking, wrestling, etc. If the reader is attentive to these nuances of force (and if the translator does not obscure them), his attention will be drawn not only to the situations which such language naturally applies but to the theme which language and situation together develop. This saturation (no other word will quite do) of Greek tragedy (but also epic, lyric, and history) in the idiom of necessity and force is, in my judgment, the single most obvious (but quite unexplored) fact of Greek tragedy.

The language becomes more impressive if the reader keeps the presumable "blocking" constantly in mind. "Blocking"—that is, the way in which the characters move in theatrical space, in relation to each other—has received far too little scrutiny from modern scholars. However conjectural, a diagrammatic sense of the play's likely "blocking" is immensely instructive and often invaluable. The important thing is a simple awareness of theatrical space and the meaningful employment of this space. This is best achieved by asking ourselves where in the theater a given character, at any moment in the play, must have been; from what position, in what posture, he speaks; and in what relation to others. The suppliant posture, for instance, immediately reveals the relative power of two individuals; when the Chorus in *Oedipus* supplicates the hero, we see not only the Chorus's dependence but Oedipus' exemption and apparent self-sufficiency. When Euripides' Hecuba and Polymnestor scramble around the orchestra on all fours, animalized by their sufferings, the dramatist is making a crucial modal point about human skills, how they are saved and how destroyed. So, too, when Sophocles' Philoktetes enters, we see in his taut, bent posture—held erect by the "godlike" bow, pulled down by the "devouring" animal foot—who he is and how it is with him, a man in crisis, capable of standing erect as a *man* or falling forever. So, too, in *Alcestis*, Admetos' exemption is implicitly contrasted with the hand of death which literally, not merely metaphorically, pulls Alcestis down to Hades; later, when Herakles forces Admetos to take the veiled girl's hand, we are meant to glimpse the gulf that separates him from the earlier, self-sufficient Admetos.

Finally, there remain modal thought and psychology, the kind of perception and process by which character in Greek tragedy is perceived, shaped, and altered. The most convenient example is perhaps Aristotle, who (in *Rhetoric* 2, 12–15) gives a penetrating but schematic account of what I would not hesitate to call a modal phenomenology of human age and fortune. The entire section should be read, slowly and medatatively, but even a brief excerpt shows quite clearly the nature of "modal" thought and the distinctions on which it is based:

> Let us now discuss the character of men in terms of their emotions, ages, and fortunes.... The ages are youth, the prime of life, and old age. By fortune I mean nobility, wealth, power, and their opposites, and, in general, good fortune and bad.
>
> In character the young are full of desire, and capable of fulfilling their desires. Among bodily pleasures they chiefly obey those belonging to Aphrodite, uncontrollably so. Changeable and quickly surfeited, their desires are excessive but quickly cool; for their wills, like the sick man's hunger and thirst, are keen but not strong. They are passionate, quick to anger, and impulsive.... They are eager for honor, but more eager for victory; for youth wants superiority, and victory is a kind of superiority. And they desire both more than they desire money; they have no interest in money because they have not yet experienced need.... In character they are high-minded, not suspicious, because they have never seen much wickedness; trusting, because they have seldom been cheated; and hopeful, because the young are naturally as hot-blooded as those who have drunk too much wine. Besides, they have not yet encountered many failures.... They have exalted ideas because they have not yet been humbled by life or learned the power of necessity. Moreover, their hopeful disposition makes them think they are equal to great things— and that means having exalted ideas. They would rather do noble deeds than useful ones; their lives are governed more by moral consideration than calculation; it is calculation that aims at the useful, but *aretē* aims at what is noble.... All their mistakes lie in the direction of doing things excessively and vehemently. They disobey Chilon's precept by overdoing everything; they love too much and they hate too much and the same with everything else. They think they know everything and confidently assert it; and this, in fact, is why they overdo everything.... But if they do wrong, it is because of *hybris*, not wickedness....
>
> Older men ... have in most cases characters which are just the opposite....
>
> The type of character produced by wealth is visible for all to see. Wealthy men are insolent and arrogant; their possession of wealth makes them think they possess all good things; for wealth is a kind of standard of value for everything else, and so they imagine there is nothing money cannot buy. They are luxurious and ostentatious....
>
> In a word, the kind of character produced by wealth is that of a prosperous fool. At the same time there is a difference between the

character of old money and new money; the *nouveaux riches* have all the bad qualities of the type in an exaggerated form; that is, they have not been educated in the use of wealth. The wrongs they do are not caused by wickedness, but partly by *hybris* and partly by self-indulgence....

III

Almost nobody, of course, has ever missed the central modal point of the play—that Admetos learns from Alcestis' death that each man must do his own dying, that death is the ultimate and most personal of facts. Our lives and deaths, moreover, are inseparably linked to those of others: the life Admetos wins by Alcestis' death is, without Alcestis, a life not worth living. No less important, but seldom noticed, is the complementary point on which the play pivots: that human beings *do* in point of fact die for others, that, like Admetos, we permit or compel others to do our dying for us. Self-sacrifice, the voluntary offering of one's life for others or another, has no other meaning, and such sacrifice is a theme which Euripides explores almost obsessively in play after play. The operating premise of the *Alcestis*—implicit in its folktale plot of a man who defers his own death by finding a surrogate—rests upon this simple fact, that individuals and societies constantly ask, and sometimes constrain (as in the case of war or collective expiation), others to do their dying for them. Whether these surrogates are scapegoats like Oedipus, or victims like Pentheus, or volunteers like Alcestis (or Iphigeneia, Makaria, and the others) is less important than the recurrent human situations such sacrifices dramatize. No man, as Admetos learns, can escape his personal death; but we only learn how to live and die from those who, by dying for others, teach us their value, and ours, and the value of life generally. Men are defined, modally defined, by death; only in the presence of death does life reveal its value. Those who reveal that value best are the heroes—those who, like Alcestis and Herakles, knowingly confront death on behalf of others. The hero, as Nietzsche knew, is the only justification of human life.

That modes are at issue in the themes and assumptions of the plot is self-evident; a play whose immediate subject is a man's schooling in mortality is modal by definition. That everything else in the play—the complex, ramifying structure; the shaping of the characters; the imagery, rhetoric, and logic—are also modal may be less immediately obvious. Certainly the dramatic assumption of the play, on which everything else turns, involves a modal suspension of the law of Necessity (*anankē*), and the ironic consequence of this suspension is to demonstrate precisely that Necessity cannot be suspended.

For a brief time, Euripides would have us believe, the Fates, thanks to Apollo's stratagem, have become drunk, which is to say that Necessity is still in force but temporarily inoperative. Yet the thematic purpose of this suspension is, ironically, to school Admetos in mortality, the supreme necessity. But no sooner has Admetos accepted death than Necessity is once again ironically suspended in order to permit the "resurrection" of Alcestis. Through the alternating rhythm of these enforcements and suspensions of Necessity, Euripides' play moves in such a way that fabulous, almost fairy-tale, events suddenly take on tragic reality, and tragedy in turn is abruptly metamorphosed into comic fable and parable. It is this rhythm which any reader of the play immediately feels in the pointed contrasting of opposed moods, that chiaroscuro of life and death, comedy and tragedy, that characterize the play. Thus elegiac or funereal scenes are suddenly, often savagely, enjambed with farcical or angry scenes, and this patterning and rhythm are immediately established in the *agon* of Apollo and Death: the bright savior god confronting the dark lord of the dead. This confrontation is then repeated in the scene in which Pheres and Admetos quarrel before the bier of the dead Alcestis, or in the scene of Herakles' drunken braying in the house of mourning:

> There he was, roaring away over his supper . . .
> and there we were, mourning for our mistress,
> and what with the maids wailing and beating their breasts—
> well, you've never heard such a bloody medley in all
> your days. . . . (947–52 / 761–63)

Because in the first scene Apollo tells us that Alcestis will be rescued from death, we are freed from suspense. Deliberately freed, I would argue, so that we can attend to the dramatist's "blocking" of his themes and characters, the metaphysical rhythm of his reversals, and the virtuosity of the play's formal development.

If the structure is clearly modal, so, I think, are the characters. Indeed, they are dramatically shaped in such a way that, once the shaping is perceived, their functional coherence becomes immediately apparent. What Euripides gives us, I suggest, is a circle of modally defined characters whose initial focus is Admetos. Apollo, Death, Alcestis, Herakles, Pheres, and even the Chorus are dramatically defined in such a way that they all illuminate Admetos and show him for what he is: a man without knowledge of the human modes, without the slightest ability to "think mortal thoughts"; a man of complete modal ignorance and innocence. How, after all, could it possibly be otherwise? Admetos is a *king*; a king whose *wealth* and *good fortune* are painted (679–722 / 568–605) in almost Croesus-like terms; whose life has been marked by total *exemption* from all circumscribing necessity ("Your luck had been good," says the Chorus to Admetos. "High happiness and great wealth—both were yours. So when this sorrow struck so suddenly, it found you unprepared. Suffering was something you had never known before.") He is a man who possesses a god for a slave, a demigod for friend, and a wife who is willing to die for him. How could such a man, so metaphysically "spoiled," possibly think "mortal thoughts"? How could such a man accept death? Whatever the figure of Admetos may have meant or suggested in pre-Euripidean tradition, in this play he is represented, as so often in Greek literature and life, according to the meaning of his own name.[5] He is Admetos (that is, *a-dametos*, the "untamed," the "unmastered," the "unbeaten": the man unyoked, un-broken by Necessity). It is not an idle coincidence that the Chorus, at line 180 / 127, speaks of the "dead" as "death-tamed" and "broken" men (*dmathentas*), and, in the ode on Necessity, declares that *ananke* breaks or subdues (*damadzei*) even the iron of the Chalybes. Admetos, the unbroken man, the unsubdued, will be broken and subdued, forcibly subjected to *ananke*.

That we are intended to see Admetos' character and everything he does as deriving from modal ignorance is made clear, I think, in the remarkable foiling of the *dramatis personae*. We see who Admetos is through sharply schematized contrasts in the situations of all the others, including the gods. Thus Apollo, with his opening words, strikes a starkly modal note. He is that rare, indeed almost unique, thing, a god who has felt the hard stroke of Necessity:

> House of Admetos, farewell.
> Apollo takes his leave of you,
> dear house . . . though it was here that I endured
> what no god should be compelled to bear.
> Here, with serfs and laborers, I ate the bread
> of slavery . . .

5. Thus in Sophocles' *Ajax* we find Ajax punning on the meaning of his own name; so, too, Euripides' *Medea* and many others. The pun *need* not be explicit. Thus the meaning of Oedipus' name is *visually* evident in the hero's clubfoot; in the Messenger's speech of Euripides' *Hippolytos*, we hear how the hero was literally *destroyed* by his own *horses* and, in his dying, revealed the *other* (fatal) meaning of his name: (*Hippolytos* = "horse-destroyed"). In the *Alcestis* there is, admittedly, no explicit pun on Admetos' name, but the etymological sense could have been brought out at any moment simply by having the actor pronounce the name as "Adametos." At line 507 / 416 the poet—deliberately, I think, in order to reveal the meaning of Admetos' name—enjambs it with the word *ananke*.

> ... And so,
> in punishment, Zeus doomed me,
> a god, to this duress,
> constraining me to be the bond-slave
> of a death-bound man.[6] (1–16 / 1–7)

The customary order is here reversed, the god occupying the place of the serf, and the mortal Admetos playing the god's master. This modal contrast is then repeated and amplified in the subsequent debate between Apollo and Death. Gods they may be, yet each has his fixed sphere; each is subject to limits he cannot cross. Death possesses the privilege of his office, and he insists that he shall not be denied his due or his prize. Thus his words to Apollo are exemplary modal wisdom: "You cannot have your way in everything you want." True, Apollo finishes by having his way and cheating Death of his prize, but the dramatist's insistence that we should see that even gods have their limits throws Admetos' exemption into sharp relief. But such comparisons—god contrasted with god or mortal, mortal with mortal—are revealingly pervasive, inflecting what the characters say and do, indeed controlling their conception. They exist not as developed or rounded characters in the modern sense, but as masked embodiments of the play's dominant idea as that idea is worked out in the paired tales of Admetos and Alcestis.

Alcestis is initially defined according to the low value assigned to women in fifth-century Athenian society and also, presumably, in the traditional tale of Admetos. In the finale, of course, this low valuation is explicitly challenged and reversed. Her conventional value is low indeed, far below that of her husband; and it is with this conventional valuation that Euripides lulls his audience, deliberately working on its (complacent) expectations, and then startling it into perceiving the story, *his* story and Alcestis', with fresh eyes. In this respect, the modern reader should remember that Admetos' "egotism" and "selfishness" are simply a function of values he shares with the male audience—an audience which would have regarded Alcestis' sacrifice as both plausible and natural. But modally, Alcestis is characterized in terms of the necessity that is hers by virtue of her role as "wife." She is, in the poetic vocabulary of Greek tragedy, a *damar* (i.e. "wife," a word literally meaning "subdued" or "tamed"—derived, revealingly, from the same root as the name "Admetos"). Admetos, we understand, is her "lord and master"; as

---

6. See Note on lines 1–16 / 1–7.

damar, she stands in the same relation to Admetos as does the serf-god Apollo. Around her therefore, especially in her relation to the constraining power of Death, cluster all the modal words of her condition and fate, which she feels as constraint, a weight, a force, a hand pulling her inexorably down.

Herakles also, for the sake of revealing contrast with Admetos, is presented in terms of his subjection to *anankē*. Like Apollo, he, too, is portrayed as the suffering servant, constrained by his own heroic "labors" and his "lord and master" Eurystheus. In large measure, this Euripidean Herakles is a conventional classical representation; but, conventional or not, the contrast with Admetos is revealing. The hero of exceptional strength, the son of Zeus himself—surely Herakles, we think, might reasonably enjoy some degree of exemption from his fate. But, no, he, too, is persistently cast as the very type of patient, toiling, resigned courage. When he first appears, the Chorus' query strikes a modal note (literally, the Chorus asks him, "To what wandering are you yoked?" Cf. note on 571 / 481). The yoke that Herakles wears in his lifetime of labors links him closely to the serf-god Apollo and to Alcestis, yoked by marriage to Death. All in fact are yoked to *anankē*, and their collective bondage starkly sets off Admetos' modal exemption. In detail after detail Euripides drives his point home. Thus when the Chorus tells Herakles that the horses of Diomedes will not easily be broken, Herakles answers with something like "stoical" acceptance: "Fighting's what I do. / My labors are my life. I can't refuse" (581–82 / 487). Asked further questions about his labors, he replies: "There you have the story / of my labors and my life. It's a damned hard road / I'm doomed to travel, friend. Rough, uphill / all the way." The contrast with Admetos, especially with the Admetos whose godlike hospitality and good fortune are hailed by the Chorus in the subsequent ode, could hardly be more schematic.

As for Pheres, it is he who, in the coarse, brutal vigor of his speech and his resentment of his overbearing son's behavior, first forces into the open the perception toward which the action has been driving. It is *here*, in this crucial scene (the father-son relationship was peculiarly important in ancient Greek life), that all the previous contrasts, the slow, persistent accumulation of modal detail, surface and erupt. Euripides' strategy here, as I suggested earlier, is to lull his audience with its own (mythical) expectations and then, savagely, to shatter the illusion. It is in this explosive scene between father and son that the traditionally "noble" Admetos is exposed for what he is: a man so modally inexperienced that he cannot assign anyone his just, human value. *Timē* (honor) and *axia* (worth, desert) are recurrent words in this play, and for obvious reasons. Because he is modally ignorant, Admetos is incapable of giving others their due, of valuing them according to their real worth. His values, one might say, are "out of phase"; he treats everybody in the play with quite indiscriminate confusion, making slaves of his wife, father, and mother,[7] and treating Herakles with godlike hospitality but quite without the human candor of a friend (as Herakles later reminds him). Until the arrival of Pheres, however, Admetos' modal ignorance is only implicitly stated in the contrasts between himself and the others.

It is Pheres who brings the poet's purpose in these preceding contrasts into the open, into harsh, angry, public words:

> Boy,
> who in god's name do you think you are?
> Are you my master now, and I some poor, bought,
> cringing Asiatic slave that you dare dress me down
> like this? I am a free man, Thessalian born,
> a prince of Thessaly....
> I gave you life. I raised you.
> I am not obliged to die for you as well. (820–30 / 675–82; 829–30 / 681–82)

These are strong words in a violently strong speech. They are clearly meant to be strong. Indeed, the scene as a whole aims at outrage. Not because Euripides, as many of his critics would have it, is a sensationalist, interested in showing us a quarrel between two egotists for its own sake, but because the confrontation is crucial to his dramatic conception. In Pheres' words are concentrated all the passion and much of the dignity of ordinary, outraged commonsense. It is Pheres who first openly tells Admetos, with a Greek father's authority, who Admetos is: a modal maniac or simpleton who cannot distinguish between free men and slave, god and man; who does not know what human worth might be because he does not think "mortal thoughts" and who therefore has no *human* scale of value. We are not required to admire Pheres (indeed, he proves to be ignoble, but not until he has effectively stripped Admetos of all claim to *aretē*); and we cannot dismiss his words simply because they are angry or indecorous. They state, after all, the modal point of the play.

---

7. Cf. Euripides, *Frag.* 29 (Nauck), where a character says: "May I never be a friend or associate of that man who, convinced of his own self-sufficiency, regards those dear to him [*philous*] [that is, his family and friends] as his slaves."

As Admetos stands to Pheres, so he stands to Alcestis and Herakles, ignorant of their true worth, incapable of assigning them the value they clearly assign to him. For it is not only from Apollo's testimony—that Admetos treated him well, as a god deserved to be treated—that we learn of Admetos' intrinsic worth. Alcestis' love, Herakles' friendship, and the Chorus' ambivalent admiration (see 718–22 / 602–5) all testify to it. Admetos is not a man of criminal, but innocent, *hybris*. He has a basic liberality of spirit, a child's natural generosity combined with a child's equally natural selfishness. Youth, good fortune, and exemption from all human necessity and need have left him humanly undeveloped, meta-physically "untamed." All his traits of character, quite without excep-tion, derive from his modal innocence and inexperience. "The fortunate man," reads a Euripidean fragment, "must needs be wise." It is precisely wisdom—wisdom as *mortal* skill—that Admetos does not have; and the lack makes him kindred to Euripides' Hippolytos or even Pentheus, whose "godlike" arrogance of youth—their modal ignorance—is their mortal ruin.

Admetos' famous "hospitality" should be understood, I think, as a direct function of his modal ignorance, not as the "redeeming trait" by virtue of which Alcestis is returned to him. The point is fundamental. Both Admetos and the play as a whole will inevitably be "psychologized" by their critics unless we recognize that these characters are not a collection of unconnected "traits" whose only artistic necessity derives from their usefulness to the plot. Ancient dramatic character is not shaped in this random, helter-skelter modern way; rather, everything derives from a central (modal) definition which radiates outward into individual conduct and speech; yet the individual traits inevitably reveal the shaping center from which they spring. A Greek character is in some very real sense a destiny. Admetos' hospitality, like his acceptance of Alcestis' sacrifice, and his rage against Pheres, is a function of his modal exemption; we should see it not as a peculiar, individuating fact but as a direct revelation of a deeper "modal" cause deriving from exemption. Those exempt from suffering and death are, in their "happiness," un-mistakably "godlike." And Admetos' hospitality is a divine largesse, a largesse that cannot discriminate and that jumbles all the modes; a generosity matched only and exactly by the ignorance of value which could accept with something like the assurance of a "spoiled" child the offering of another's life. The typical man of *hybris* shows a wanton disregard for others and their human rights. But Admetos' disregard is neither callous nor wanton; he takes because he does not know the cost. And it is precisely the value and the cost that the play will teach him. Even in his hospitality he must learn a human scale, and so, at the end of the play, we find Herakles gently and ambiguously advising him, "in the future treat your guests and those you love as / they deserve" (1472–73 / 1148).[8]

Admetos is taught "mortal thoughts" by being made to suffer not one necessity, but two. In the *kommos* at lines 1174–83 / 915–25 he comes to recognize with overwhelming conviction, I believe—that, in losing Alcestis, he has lost his own life. This is what he actually says on several occasions, and in the *kommos* his language is intense poetry, not dialogue. He speaks like a man of sorrows, and we cannot, simply in order to accommodate our modern notions of consistent character, deny his words the dignity of contrition. He is also humiliated, forced on two separate occasions to violate his promise to the dying Alcestis. The first violation occurs in Herakles' "drunken scene," since Admetos had promised Alcestis that he would ban all festivity for the period of a year. The second occurs when Herakles forces Admetos to accept the veiled girl, even though his acceptance means taking a "new woman" into the house. If we are meant to observe the delicacy and punctilio of his scruples, his reluctance and *emotional* loyalty to Alcestis, we are also meant to note his weakness and his eventual surrender to his over-bearing friend's insistence. If he does not quite break the *letter* of his promise to Alcestis, it is only because Herakles prevents him from doing so.[9]

The poet's purpose here is the subtle and difficult one of portraying a man torn by conflicting claims—the claims of his dead wife, the claims of his friend; the claims of honor and the claims of need. Unless we can perceive *both* the honor and the need displayed by Admetos *and* his desperate effort to cope honorably with these conflicting claims, the point of the play and the beauty of its finale cannot be understood. Above all, we must be prepared to accept the reality of Admetos' *need*. For it is his *need* that tells us of his new involvement in necessity and vividly shows him at last thinking "human thoughts." In his effort to keep his word to Alcestis, to refuse the veiled girl, his honor and his weakness, his nobility and his ordinary need, are beautifully, tensely, balanced. Thus, while Herakles stands there, insistent in his stubborn silence, Admetos says:

> As for this woman here,
> I beg you, my lord, if you can somehow manage it,

---

8. See Note on lines 1472–73 / 1148.

9. The point would not be worth laboring if it were not in question. For a different—in my opinion, quite perversely "archaizing" and, to that degree, insensitive—reading of this scene and the play, cf. A. P. Burnett, *Catastrophe Survived: Euripides' Plays of Mixed Reversal.*

please, take her somewhere else.
Give her to some friend who is not in mourning.
Tell him to keep her. You have many friends in Pherai.
But please, please,
don't remind me of my loss. Seeing this woman here,
here in Alcestis' house, day in, day out,
would be more, much more, than I could bear.
I am crushed with sorrow as it is, Herakles.
Do not burden me with more.
Besides,
where in this house could a young girl stay?
I mean, she *is* young, I can see it, Herakles,
in her jewelry, in the style of clothes she wears.
How could she live here, surrounded by young men?
How could I protect her? Young men are lusty,
their desires not easily controlled.
                    —Herakles,
it is *you*, your interests, I am thinking of.
What can I do? Put her in Alcestis' room?
Take her to Alcestis' bed? . . .
Herakles,
for god's sake, take this woman away,
out of my sight! I am weak now, do not make my weakness worse. . . .
(**1324–55** / 1042–65; **1334–36** / 1064–65)

The leaps and ellipses here are revealing, clearly and economically depicting the passionate motions of Admetos' mind, as he stands there confronted by Herakles' silence and the eloquent presence of the girl who strangely resembles Alcestis. His feelings are all the more powerful because they so obviously derive from the conflicting claims he feels. He will, as his own words suggest, inevitably betray Alcestis (and Herakles), and he is transparently struggling with the foreknowledge of his own weakness, trying, as best he can, to remain loyal to those he loves, as his honor struggles with his need.

That this is Euripides' purpose here is confirmed by the famous "drunken speech" of Herakles. In the intoxicated hero's words, we are given a lively version of what might be called a drunkard's "modalities," the ruddy credo of a man whose drunken wisdom echoes the poetic thought of Archilochos and Bacchylides. *Everything* Herakles says is addressed to the thematic point of the play; it accords completely with the modal knowledge that the play teaches Admetos. Drunkard's wisdom it may be, but it is all of a piece with the play. "C'mere, fella," says Herakles to Admetos' scowling servant, "an' I'll let you in on a l'il secret. / Make a better man of you. / I mean, wise up: / we all gotta die." And the schooling, the recitation of the play's moral themes, promptly follows:

You know what it'sh like to be a man?
I mean,
d'you really unnerstan' the human condishun, fren'?
I can see you don't. How could you with a face like that?
Well, lissen, mister:
we all gotta die. An' that's a fact.
There's not a man alive who knows the odds on death.
Here today. Gone tomorrow.
Poof.
That's fate. A mystery. I mean,
There's jus' no knowin'. Man can't figger it out.
Well, that's my message. So what d'you say?
Cheer up and have a l'il drink,
huh?
Live for the day. Today is ours.
Tomorrow's fate.
Hey,
an' there's somethin' else. Yup. Aphrodite.
Don't forget Aphrodite, fren'.
'Cause thass a good l'il goddess....
I mean, we all gotta die. Right?
Well, that's why we all gotta think human thoughts,
and live while we can.... (983–1013 / 780–99)

In short, the old contrapuntal themes of the play once again contrasted; the firm, polar music of the opposed necessities—death and life, darkness and light, Thanatos and Apollo, the necessity to accept death and the necessity of living. But in this speech the two themes are related, with the force of felt connection: it is only in the presence of death that life takes on value; the recognition of mortality leads directly to the celebration of life. In the words of the poet Archilochos, "Do not exult openly in victory, nor lie at home lamenting a defeat; but take pleasure in what is pleasant; do not yield overmuch to grief, and understand the rhythm that holds mankind in its bonds." It is precisely this "rhythm-in-bonds" that Herakles' drunken speech asserts, and which Herakles will, as friend and moral instructor, impose upon Admetos in the person of the veiled girl, as a temptation and a prize. First comes the acceptance of death, then the acceptance of life (or Aphrodite) which is its "rhythmic" consequence. *Carpe diem*. Death is the starkest manifestation of *anankē*, and men are miserably mortal. Therefore alive. Aphrodite, no less than Death, is stamped into a man's nature and defines him, as a contrapuntal part of the great music of Necessity. The man who accepts death must also accept what death implies. This is how men live, "rhythmed in their bonds." Accept, accept; learn the modes by which you live.

This is the music of the play's finale, surely one of the most exquisitely constructed and controlled scenes in all Greek drama. Here we see

Admetos tempted and "tamed" by Herakles in a scene of radiantly gentle and understanding friendship. Admetos had earlier implored Herakles not to tempt him or add to his burden of grief by making his weakness worse; now he adjures him not to leave the veiled girl and make him dishonor Alcestis' memory. Of his honor and loyalty to Alcestis, there can be no doubt, just as there can be no doubt of what he has come to recognize: "I lost myself when I lost her. Lost myself— / and so much more" (1374–75 / 1082). This is quickly followed by his strong assertion of Alcestis' worth (*axia . . . sebein*) and the loyalty such merit imposes on his honor: "Wherever Alcestis is, she deserves my honor. / I owe it to her" (1386–87 / 1092).

Indebtedness means need; need implies dependence. In Admetos, the self-sufficient man, such need is especially revealing. Certainly these protestations should not be understood as rhetoric or mere exaggeration; they are felt, and felt with especial keenness in the context of Herakles' deft queries and sexual insinuations. Slowly, relentlessly, Herakles lures Admetos on, prodding him into more and more extravagant assertions of loyalty and love, but at the same time subtly tempting him with the veiled girl. His purpose is, of course, to involve Admetos in a public breach (or near-breach) of his word to Alcestis, to add weakness to his weakness in a demonstration of his final infidelity. It is all *force majeure*, beautifully complex modal psychology, whose goal is to school Admetos this time in still another *anankē*, his necessity to live. Its second purpose is friendly revenge—the loving but firmly playful and deliberate revenge of a man of *aretē* on his good friend. If Admetos lets Herakles make a fool of himself in a house of mourning, Herakles now humiliates Admetos by forcing him to welcome a new guest and, by so doing, to break the spirit, if not the letter, of his promise to Alcestis. Thus overbearing insistence and force are met with overbearing insistence and force; humiliation answers humiliation, deception answers deception; and godlike generosity repays divine largesse. It is very Greek, this precision of "poetic justice": meticulous and pointed, measure for measure. Essential to the scene's power, as I suggested earlier, is the reader's understanding that Admetos is both scrupulously loyal and manifestly tempted. Indeed, it is an index of the dramatist's skill in this scene that loyalty and temptation, strength and weakness, are so delicately balanced and fused in Admetos that we literally cannot tell them apart; they have blended into a single, wholly credible, human figure.

This "temptation" (or comic "taming") of Admetos reaches its climax when Herakles finally provokes Admetos to the point where he declares, in outraged loyalty and virtue: "She is dead. But I would rather die than betray her love!" (1393–94 / 1096). Once this is said, Herakles can, with quite disingenuous candor, say: "Nobly spoken, my good Admetos. Well, then, / make this woman welcome in your generous house" (**1395–96** / 1097). He means, of course, that Admetos has been tested and proven a loyal friend (*pistos philos*), and noble, too; that Herakles can safely entrust the veiled girl to a man of such nobility. And then, in some unmistakable way, having proven his loyalty to Alcestis—by reluctance, by yielding only to a kind of "moral" force—Admetos can rightly, warmly, and humanly weaken, surrendering to his overbearing friend and the necessity represented, as he obviously knows, in the veiled girl standing before him. At last, we see, Admetos thinks "human thoughts"—indeed, all too human thoughts—and this scene of his achieved humanity, his demonstration that he shares the real, right weakness of men and also a stubborn loyalty, is an exceptionally moving thing. Admetos' weakness, true, is ironically intensified, but his discovery of weakness is visibly the source of his human strength for the future. He accepts, as he once did not, the obligations of death and life. He is master of the modes he did not know before; he moves with the rhythm that "holds mankind in its bonds." It is presumably in recognition of this acquired humanity that Herakles relents and reveals the dead Alcestis before Admetos can break his promise by making "a new woman" welcome in his house. There are those who say that Admetos will hear strong words from Alcestis when she is at last permitted to speak. If I am right, and Alcestis understands what she has seen and the change in Admetos, she will not say a word—or nothing more than Shakespeare's knowing Mariana said:

> They say, best men are moulded out of faults,
> And, for the most, become much more the better
> For being a little bad: so may my husband.

IV

Both Alcestis herself and Alcestis' silence are crucial to Euripides' design. Mariana, in Shakespeare's *Measure for Measure*, must *speak* of her husband as she does since, until the fifth act, Shakespeare stresses Angelo's capacity for evil—the *fallen*, rather than the redeemable, Angelo. Then, in his "comic" resolution, Shakespeare deftly "corrects" his earlier emphasis by making Mariana's remarks suggest the richer possibilities of Angelo's one-sided humanity: "They say best men are moulded out of faults": *corruptio optimi pessima*. Euripides, in sharp contrast, completes his schematic but modally rounded account of Admetos (his faults deriving from the same source as his virtues; then his contrition and redemption in decent remorse) before the appearance of Alcestis in the finale. It is the fact of Admetos' remorse and self-recognition earlier that makes Alcestis' silence dramatically right and necessary.[10] Miraculously "resurrected," she crowns Admetos' despair with "comic" happiness; by returning from death she "blesses" him. Nothing else—and certainly no speech—is needed. She has died to give him life—and death. What could she possibly say that her death and his remorse have not already said?

But Alcestis is also there on her own account. She is there to be *seen*, seen for the revelation she is, and which she brings with her, along with her power as a "blessèd spirit" (*makaira daimōn*) to bless others as she has already blessed Admetos, through the challenge and example of her *aretē*. In the nobility of her death, Alcestis wins what, to the Greek mind, all exceptional human action really aims at: the immortality of memory, of memory become myth. Great human action is exemplary and therefore potentially contagious in a culture which everywhere stresses emulation. In Alcestis' "resurrection" here, if the reader is truly attending, everything culminates. That is, at this point the story of Admetos and his "schooling" is suddenly transcended, as the play turns, not so much to Alcestis herself, as to the idea of *aretē* which, through her, animates the entire action, and which here reaches its final, visual revelation. Dramatically, the movement is crucial. What we get is not merely the happy, comic resolution, but the direct, personal *epiphany* of Alcestis as hero and *daimōn*—an epiphany clearly designed, in its *actuality*, in the poet's insistence that Alcestis is, against all doubts, miraculously alive, to reveal the divinity of human *aretē*. I stress the word "epiphany" (used of course in its proper religious, rather than its borrowed literary sense).[11] This coda is, unmistakably, a revelation. And revelations, we

· 10. Unfortunately, neither Euripides' reticence nor Alcestis' silence have deterred critics from wordy speculations about what Alcestis will say when she is at last allowed to speak. "Surely Euripides meant us to be puzzled by Alcestis' strange silence," writes one scholar (obviously lost in a labyrinth of his own design), "and to ask ourselves the insistent questions his ending poses. What, we want to know, will Alcestis say to Admetos after this latest betrayal? Has Admetos really learned anything at all" etc." The very ability to ask such questions (suggesting a taste nourished on Galsworthy or Christopher Morley) indicates the degree to which naturalism and psychologizing have imposed themselves on Greek drama. Whether the *Alcestis* is "modal" or not, it deserves better than the trudging realism and cozy clichés of modern "domestic" drama which these questions suggest.

11. Comparison with Shakespeare is, again, revealing. At the close of *The Winter's Tale* Shakespeare "revives" the statue of the "dead" Hermione, makes her descend from her pedestal, and *speak*. The point is not, *pace* H. D. F. Kitto, *Greek Tragedy* (London, 1961), 320, that Euripides is "cleverer" than Shakespeare in keeping his heroine silent. Euripides is dramatizing the literal *epiphany*, as *daimōn*, of his heroine, whereas Shakespeare emphasizes the human warmth and reconciliation of a real "recognition-scene" in order that an art that emulates nature may finally be transformed into miraculous nature.

need to remember, are literally "unveilings": we see them, and the evidence of our eyes surpasses any words. So the revelation of Alcestis as hero appropriately crowns a play which tells, against men and exclusive male claims to *aretē*, of human courage revealed in a woman's action.

We moderns must, I suppose, take all this "metaphorically." But Greeks of the classical and archaic period, with their veneration for exceptional human achievement, would, I think, have experienced this coda differently. They would have recognized in it not metaphor but myth (which is to say, something more serious and true than ordinary or even symbolic reality). Death of course remains irreducibly death, and Alcestis, like her heroic predecessors, clearly goes, in person and in fact, "darkened into death." But against that real physical extinction, the power of myth and memory are strong. So strong in fact that, though physically dead, Alcestis is also, in a very real sense, alive forever: "a blessed spirit," "a shining on the lips of men." In memory and gratitude, the great dead quicken and take on the undying honors of heroes; they become myth and so acquire eternal life. Against the nearly invincible modern notion that myth is a literary conceit or fiction, the reader must make an effort to see these things freshly, with Greek eyes; to understand how events happen in mythical time, uniquely and forever, and that "hero" is the name for real presence, venerable and abiding, that survives the death of the body. If we cannot recover that Greek feeling for heroism, we must at least be prepared to acknowledge its actuality for an ancient audience. Even at the very end of the fifth century, veneration for heroism was strong enough that Sophocles could address his *Oedipus at Kolonos* directly to that understanding. The hero dies; his spirit, his *aretē*, survive him, rich with meaning and sanction for the lives of men; blessing the land that had the wisdom to acknowledge him and make him welcome.

Alcestis' "resurrection" should, I am convinced, be understood in the same way. Euripides, as certain scholars have argued, may have been too skeptical to believe in "the nonsense of physical regeneration." But the point surely is not bodily regeneration but the deathless presence of the hero, the permanance of heroic achivement. That Euripides did believe in the immortality of *aretē* seems to me quite beyond dispute; it is explicitly stated and also implied in the structure of plays like the Herakles and Hippolytos and in the poetic intensity with which he treats it here (above all in the choral "farewell" to Alcestis and, later, in the great ode on Necessity). And Euripides' intent here is, for me at least, strongly confirmed in a parallel passage in his older contemporary

Simonides.[12] The pertinent passage is a brief verse epitaph for the fallen heroes of the Persian Wars:

> These men crowned their country with glory
> and were gathered into the darkness of death.
> They died, but are not dead: their courage [*aretē*]
> brings them back in glory from the world below.

Sentiments like these have been too much abused in our own time for us to regard them as anything more than patriotic hyperbole. And the poet may of course be taking advantage of popular belief for his own literary purposes. Against this we should bear in mind the veneration, bordering on religious awe, that Greeks generally felt for the fallen heroes of Salamis and Plataea, and the telling simplicity and sobriety of the poetic epitaph. In any case, what finally matters is the strength of the religious feelings to which the poem appeals, and on which its poetic validity depends. This in fact was how classical Greeks understood heroism—in the firm belief, however paradoxical it may seem to us, that the hero in some real sense survived his own death and achieved the permanence of myth as an exemplary and abiding presence.[13] For my purposes here, that is enough.

Alcestis' resurrection as hero is clearly designed to be dramatically surprising, a stunning comic reversal (*peripeteia*) and *coup de théâtre* (all the more surprising if we take proper account of the male complacency reflected in the traditional handling of the story and presumably repre-sented in the male audience. That reversal has been subtly and elabor-ately prepared. There are, first of all, the pervasive parallels between Alcestis and the great male culture-heroes who, like her, all confront death or in some sense give their lives for others; Orpheus, Asklepios,

---

12. The ascription to Simonides may be erroneous, but there is no good reason to question the date or authenticity of the "epitaph."

13. Perikles, for instance, is reported to have said that the Athenian dead in the Samian War were "immortal as gods" (Plutarch, *Life of Pericles*, 8.5). See also the revealing remarks of Plato (*Symposium* 179 b–d) on Alcestis: "Only those who love are willing to die on behalf of others—not only men but women, too—a fact that is amply demonstrated for us Greeks by Alcestis, the daughter of Pelias. For only she was willing to die for her husband, despite the fact that he had a father and mother; yet her love so surpassed theirs that they seemed by comparison to be unrelated to their own son and bound to him in name only. But her action seemed so splendid not only to men but to gods that, in recognition of her greatness of spirit, the gods granted what has been given to only the fewest among those who have acted heroically—that her soul should return from Hades. Thus even the gods especially honor *aretē* and devotion in the service of love...." Finally, we should perhaps note the persistence of the Euripidean theme that, if the world were genuinely just and the gods truly cared for human *aretē*, goodness and heroism would be rewarded by rejuvenation and resurrection (cf. the "resurrection" of Iolaos in *The Children of Herakles* and the choral remarks of *Herakles*, 655ff.).

and Herakles. So, too, the obvious dramatic purpose of the "scene" between Admetos and Pheres is that they should disqualify each other as claimants to *aretē* and, by default, leave the dead Alcestis—*meg' ariste*—as the true "heroic" victor of the *agon*—a point tellingly made in the little valediction to Alcestis which closes the scene. Finally there is the ode to Necessity, strategically set just before Herakles' return with the veiled Alcestis.

Here, in this ode, the controlling themes and parallels all powerfully converge as the poet brings his "tragic" action to a close and shows us, unmistakably, how the "comic" finale is to be understood. At the same time, reinforcing the modal themes (and so preparing for the coming reversal, making it, by dint of contrast, more surprising), he declares, with full choral diapason, the iron law of Necessity and death—a bleak, irresistible force deaf to all human prayer and appeal. The old men of the Chorus—men who, unlike Admetos, have again and again felt the "relentless onset" of Anankē—tell that, try as they may, they can discover no remedy against Necessity. All human culture and wisdom are helpless against her; even the Orphic religions which saved men by taking them out of "the wheel of existence," even the remedies of the sons of Asklepios. They endow Necessity with the power of divinity, but a divinity of absolute, pitiless inflexibility: "Mistress, Lady without mercy, I have felt / your stroke before. May you never come again!" (1244–45 / 976–77). As it spoke these words, the Chorus, we must reasonably assume, made the veneration or genuflection which the dread power it invokes as "mistress" or "majesty" (*potnia*) requires. Necessity may not heed men's prayers, but before that invincible power men must kneel.

Then, in the second strophe, the Chorus turns to Admetos, whom "this goddess holds . . . in the bitter bondage of her grip" with this advice:

> Bear it. Be brave. Though you should mourn Alcestis always,
> You cannot bring the dead to life. Great heroes
> die. Even the sons of heaven fade, darkened
> into death.... (1250–54 / 985–87)

With this the Chorus turns to Alcestis herself:

> Alcestis, beloved on earth and in the world below for her bravery:
> To her, Admetos, you were bound by bonds of love.
> Then will you be less brave?
> Gory is her right, Admetos. Do not let Alcestis' grave be numbered
> among the ordinary dead. Make her grave a shrine;

> honor it as men would honor gods—a holy place
> beside the road where those who journey kneel and pray.
> The traveler will see her grave and, turning off,
> will say of her, "She gave her life to save another.
> She is a blessed spirit [*makaira daimōn*] now, and so may also bless."
> In homage men will kneel before her grave and pray:
> "Hail, Lady, mistress of mercy, by your bravery and love,
> bless us and be gracious." (**1259–69** / 994–1005)

And now, once again, we must imagine, the Chorus goes down on its knees in homage, in one of the loveliest examples of visual correspondence in Greek drama. The Chorus kneels, seeing in Alcestis the only power that countervails against Death and Necessity—human *aretē*, human courage and love. And in so doing the Chorus explicitly, in its own actions, add Alcestis' name to the great roster of those who, like Herakles, have confronted Death and bested it. To the audience, but above all to Admetos, Alcestis is revealed, against all male expectation, as a hero and peer of the great culture-heroes of the past.

V

The *Alcestis* was first performed in 438 B.C. as the final play of a tetralogy consisting of *The Cretan Women, Alkmaion in Psophis*, and *Telephos* (none of which has survived). Euripides won second place. If the *Cyclops* and *Rhesos* are not, as some scholars suppose, early plays, then the *Alcestis*, written when the dramatist was in his forties, is the earliest play by Euripides we possess. It is also unique of its kind. Since it does not possess the requisite chorus of satyrs (as does the *Cyclops*), it cannot be called genuine "satyr-drama." Yet it *did* occupy the place of the satyr-play which, in the dramatic festivals of Dionysos, traditionally rounded off a tragic trilogy (or trio of otherwise unconnected tragedies). And it also clearly displays some of those sportive and farcical characteristics (above all in Herakles' drunken speech and the happy resolution) which led one ancient critic to describe "satyr-drama" as "tragedy-at-play." Hence it is customary now to call the *Alcestis* a "pro-satyric" play, although this tells us very little since we possess no other example of that genre (except perhaps the *Orestes*). In the circumstances it seems best to accept Professor Dale's judgment that the *Alcestis* possesses a greater range and variety of mood than any extant work by any of the three ancient tragedians, and that it would be foolish to press the definition of genre beyond that point. It may be that Euripides invented the genre or adapted a traditional form in a new way; but we simply do not know. What we do know is that the *Alcestis* is the first Western drama that can truly be called "tragicomic"; the first work in a genre that runs from this play to the Euripidean *Ion, Iphigeneia at Tauris,* and *Helen,* to Shakespeare's *Measure for Measure* and the late "comedies," to Chekhov and, finally, in our own time, to such Euripidean "imitations" as T. S. Eliot's *The Cocktail Party* and *The Confidential Clerk.*

VI

Like every recent translator of the *Alcestis,* I am deeply indebted to the work of the late A. M. Dale, whose splendid Oxford text (and commentary) is, in my opinion, one of the very few editions of Euripides in which fine scholarship is guided and controlled by high literary intelligence. Certainly her edition is a milestone in the scholarship of this play, and, even in those instances when I have disagreed with her readings or interpretation, I have constantly found illumination and help in her work.

To my wife who made many valuable suggestions and who gently suffered through my theatrical *viva voce* renderings of successive drafts of each episode and Chorus, I owe the *charis* which her patient support and many suggestions merit. To my colleague D. S. Carne-Ross I am grateful for criticism and advice. To my students at Boston University and Brooklyn College and elsewhere, who provided me with the intelligent responses of a captive audience, I am deeply grateful. Finally, to Ann Dargis who, with unfailing good cheer and diligence beyond the call of duty, typed, and constantly retyped, the manuscript, I owe a great debt of thanks.

WILLIAM ARROWSMITH

ON THE TRANSLATION

The Greekless reader, if not the professional scholar, should perhaps be reminded that this translation is meant to be an accurate, but not slavishly accurate, rendering of the original. It is, I would like to think, an effort of truly liberal translation. That is, I have tried to translate according to the principle laid down by St. Jerome, that we should render according to the sense rather than the letter. My aim has been to realize, as best I could, the *dramatic* movement and unfolding poetry of the play; to follow, persistently but unobtrusively, in the most forceful and graceful English I could muster, the arc of feeling as it rises and falls, the growing pressures of action-inflected meaning in a complex structure. Admittedly, my notion of the play's "sense" is firmly—perhaps too firmly for those who would prefer the roominess of a more open structure—embedded in the translation. Here and there, and especially in the choral lyrics, I have been unashamedly interpretive, sometimes expanding metaphors and even intruding glosses where I thought them necessary. But my departures from the text have been deliberate, not absent-minded; and the reader who is willing to peruse the Notes in detail will find, in most cases, an explanation, if not always a systematic defense of my practice.

WILLIAM ARROWSMITH

ALCESTIS

Translated by

WILLIAM ARROWSMITH

CHARACTERS

APOLLO

DEATH

CHORUS of Old Men of Pherai

LEADER of Chorus

MAID to Alcestis

ALCESTIS wife of Admetos

ADMETOS king of Pherai

HERAKLES

PHERES father of Admetos

SERVANT

Line numbers in the right-hand margin of the text refer to the English translation only, and the Notes beginning on p. 95 are keyed to these lines. The bracketed line numbers in the running heads refer to the Greek text.

The scene is Pherai, chief city of Thessaly. The stage building represents the palace of ADMETOS, *king of Thessaly. In the center is a large double-doored entrance, flanked by two lateral doors; one door leads to the women's quarters, the other to the men's.*

Enter APOLLO, *with traditional bow and quiver, from one of the lateral doors. He walks toward the steps leading to the orchestra, then stops and makes his farewell to the house.*

APOLLO House of Admetos, farewell.
Apollo takes his leave of you,
dear house ... though it was here that I endured
what no god should ever be compelled to bear.
Here, with serfs and laborers, I ate the bread of slavery.

He turns to the audience.

I do not blame Admetos.
The author of my shame was Zeus. He killed
my son Asklepios, stabbing him through the heart
with his fatal lightning. And I in anger
retaliated. I killed the one-eyed Cyclopes   10
because they forged for Zeus those blazing bolts
in which my son died. And so,
in punishment, Zeus doomed me,
a god, to this duress,
constraining me to be the bond-slave
of a death-bound man.
He drove me here, to this country of Thessaly,
where I served as cowherd for a good and generous man—
a man who is now my friend—Admetos.
                                    Until today
I guarded this house from every evil thing,   20
loyally and well. It was I who saved Admetos

33

from sentence of death. He was doomed to die young,
but I outwitted the Fates and won him a reprieve:
Admetos' day of death might be deferred
if someone else would volunteer to take his place
below. One by one he asked them all,
all those who were bound to him by ties of love,
but no one would.
His father and mother were old, and he was theirs,
but even they refused. Everyone refused.   30
All but one: his wife Alcestis.
Only she
would volunteer to leave the sweet light of the sun
and take his place below.
                              She is dying now.
Her women are holding her, but she is sinking
in the final agony of death. This is the day,
the fatal day, and she must die.
                              And now
I take my leave of this dear house which sheltered me
and which I love. Death must not pollute
my bright divinity.
                   Look: already
the god of Death, the god who consecrates the dead   40
is here to take his victim to the world below.
He has been waiting for this day with great impatience.
And now Death is here, punctual as always,
at the appointed hour.

APOLLO *descends to the orchestra and moves toward the east-*
ward exit. From the west DEATH *appears, a grim and winged*
figure, shrouded in black and carrying a naked sword. Startled
to discover APOLLO, *he stops short, and the two gods face each*
other in tense confrontation on opposite sides of the orchestra.

DEATH   You here,
        Bright One,
        meddling with this house again?
        Have you returned

to violate again the dues and honors
of the gods below?   50
You cheated the Fates
by craft and guile.
You saved Admetos from death.
And now, bow in hand,
unsatisfied and unappeased,
you come in violence
to save Alcestis too.
Didn't she give her solemn word
to take Admetos' place?

APOLLO Don't be afraid, Death.   60
My principles are fair, and I have reason on my side.

DEATH If you have reason on your side, then why the bow,
Apollo?

APOLLO   The bow is my attribute and habit.
Where I go, it goes.

DEATH   Your habit, is it?
Like your habit of always favoring this house?
Is that your principle?

APOLLO   Admetos is my friend.
The troubles of those I love constrain me, too.

DEATH Then you mean to take Alcestis by force?

APOLLO I did not take Admetos. Not by force.

DEATH Then why is he still here, among the living,   70
when he belongs below?

APOLLO   He gave you his wife.
You came to get Alcestis, didn't you?

DEATH   I did.
And she is *mine*, Apollo. Where I go, she goes:
beneath the earth.

APOLLO   Take her then.
                                    No, wait, Death...

DEATH Wait?
To kill those doomed to die? Don't teach me my office,
Apollo.

APOLLO   Defer her death.

DEATH   Ah, I see. Go on.

APOLLO Let Alcestis grow old. Let her live,
I adjure you, Death.

DEATH   Never.
I have my dues and honors, too, Apollo,
as dear to me as yours to you.   80

APOLLO One life is all you get. Young or old,
what difference does it make?

DEATH   Honor.
The younger my victim, the more mankind fears me
and respects me.

APOLLO   Think it over, Death.
Let Alcestis die old, and her funeral will be rich.
The profit is yours.

DEATH   Spoken like a plutocrat, Apollo.
You legislate in favor of the rich.

APOLLO   Amazing.
This talent for quibbling, this shyster wit—
it's not what we expect of Death.

36

DEATH   The rich would buy immunity from dying.   90

APOLLO   Then you refuse my appeal?

DEATH   I do. Irrevocably.
         You know my stubborn nature.

APOLLO   All too well.
         Men hate you for it. The gods despise you.

DEATH   Even you must learn a limit, Apollo.
         You cannot have your way in everything you want.
         You will not have it now.

APOLLO   Death, Death, all your savagery
         is not enough to help you now.
         Today, now,
         a man is coming to Admetos' house.   100
         A *man*, I say. Man enough
         to break the wild stallions of Diomedes
         and herd them home from frozen Thrace.
         That man will find a welcome in this house.
         He will fight with you and break you, Death,
         and by brute strength bring Alcestis back.
         You shall honor my appeal against your wish.
         You shall not have my thanks.
         My hatred you shall have. You have it now.

                              Exit APOLLO *to the east.*

DEATH   Bluster away, Apollo.   110
         Words will get you nowhere.

                    *He moves toward the central door of the palace, then turns
                              and addresses the audience directly.*

         This woman must go beneath the earth.
         She is *mine.*

With this sword I now inaugurate my rite.
The head whose curls are cut by this bright blade
is consecrated to the gods below:
forever.

DEATH *enters the palace through the central door. The doors
close slowly behind him. There is a prolonged silence. Then the*
CHORUS *of old citizens of Pherai enters the orchestra, thronging
around the entrance to the palace.*

LEADER So still.... I wonder what this silence means.
Why is the great house so strangely quiet?
No one at the door, no servant here
to say the queen has died and we must mourn her.   120
Or is Alcestis still alive?
Let her live!
If bravery and love deserve the light,
no woman on this earth,
                              oh Alcestis,
ever less deserved to die!

CHORUS (*speaking individually*)
—Silence....
                    —do you hear the cry of women?
—The beating of women's hands?
—Or women keening with that cry
that says—
                —everything is over?
—Nothing.   130
          —Nothing.
—Silence still.
—And no servant stationed at the door....
—O Paian, lord of healing!
—Great Apollo,
                  come,
calm this storm of sorrow.

—But if the queen had died,
the house would shrill with grief,
the high, shrill cry of sorrow.
—Dead, dead. . . .
                    —She must be dead,
but not yet buried.   140
—What makes you so certain?
—How could Admetos bury such a wife
with no friends or mourners by?
—Surely he could not do it.
—Not a woman like this. . . .
—Not Alcestis!

—And where is the cleansing water
custom prescribes for a house of death?
—There is no water at the door. . . .
—And no locks of hair   150
hang in the courtyard
to honor the dead. . . .
—No cry of women keening. . . .
—But this is the day decreed.
—Decreed?
          —The day of death.
—Hateful word!
—It hurts, it hurts.

LEADER As it must.
        When the good are hurt, those who love them suffer, too.
        We love, and love hurts.

CHORUS —Take ship and search the world: there is   160
        no harbor, landfall, haven, hope;
        no oracle or pilgrimage a man might go
        and, going, save our lady's life.
        None:
        Not in Lykia where the shining god

sings to mortal men his convalescent song.
Not Sahara where, at holy Ammon's
healing touch, the dying desert makes
a miracle of green. But not for her,
whose death shows cruel and sheer
as crag or stone, where hope holds not,   170
and prayer no purchase has,
and god is still,
and all's despair.

—There was one hope: Asklepios, Apollo's
healing son. If *he* still saw the light;
if he were here, he might have brought her
back,
alive from Hades and the long black
home. Such was his skill and craft
he medicined to life and saved
death-tamed and -broken men,   180
redeeming all—until great Zeus,
enraged with man's contriving mind,
hurled the long white flash of fire in which
the healer perished with his art.
And now I see of hope no
sign. None. Nothing
but despair.

—All that kings might do, our king has done.
Everywhere, on all the altars of the gods,
the blood of sacrifice runs black. But
this disease is mortal. It has no cure.   190

LEADER Look:
a servant girl is coming out.
She is crying...
Now we shall know the truth.

Enter MAID *from the palace, weeping. At the sight of the*
elders of the CHORUS, *she tries to stifle her sobs.*

No need to hide your tears, child.
If anything has happened to your mistress,
your sorrow is only natural.
But tell us: is Alcestis still alive?

MAID What can I tell you? She is still alive.
And dead.

LEADER   What are you saying, child?

MAID Sir, the queen is dying…   200

LEADER   Oh, Alcestis, Alcestis!
What a loss. Poor Admetos, how I pity him…

MAID The master does not know the meaning of his loss.
He will not know, until it is too late.

LEADER Nothing can be done to save her?

MAID   Nothing.
This is the day. Her destiny is too strong,
a force she cannot fight.

LEADER   Admetos—

MAID   Did all he could.
Her women are working, preparing for the funeral.
She will be buried as we knew her and loved her
in this life: a queen.

LEADER   In dying and living both:
incomparably a queen. For courage and love   210
Alcestis has no rival among all women
on this earth.

MAID   Rival?
              What would the woman be who could rival
or surpass Alcestis? What woman ever loved a man so much?
Loved him more than herself? So much more
she gave her life to let him live? In love
she has no equal, sir: the whole world knows it.
But what she did and said, in privacy, inside—
her bravery and beauty in the face of death—
will touch your heart and amaze you even more.

                                                        Listen:
This morning, when she knew her day had come,   220
she bathed her white body in fresh running water
from the river. Then she opened the great cedar chest,
took out her richest, finest things and dressed herself
in all her loveliness—oh, sir, she was beautiful!
And then she kneeled,

(*kneeling*)
                        like this,
                                    before the hearth
and prayed:
                        "Bright goddess who guards my home,
I am going to the world below. This is the last time
I shall ever kneel at your feet. Lady, I pray you,
protect my children and be good to them.
Give my little boy a loving wife.   230
And give my girl a kind and gentle husband.
Do not let them die like me, before their time
has come. Let them live out their lives; let them be happy
here in the land of their fathers."
Then she went from altar to altar, praying at each one
and wreathing it with sprays of fresh myrtle; quietly,
not a sound, not a cry, that sweet face of hers
composed and calm, oh, as though no evil thing
could ever touch her.
                        But there in her room
she threw herself on the great bed, and the sobs   240
broke from her. "Dear bed," she cried,

42

"it was here I offered my maiden body and my love
to Admetos. Now I offer him my life ...
Sweet bed, I love you still ... even now. So much
that I would rather die than live without you
both. And now it is goodbye ...
Some other girl will sleep here in my place
perhaps—not more loving, not more loyal, than me,
but happier, much happier, I think.
Then she kneeled,   250

                    —so—

                           and kissed the bed,
smothering it with tears, crying uncontrollably,
till there were no tears left. Then she rose
and stumbled, head down, groping for the door.
On the sill she stopped and turned, hesitating,
then threw herself back on the bed again. There,
on the bed, the children found her. Sobbing,
they clung to their mother's dress, while she pulled them
to her, hugging and kissing: goodbye, goodbye.
Then the servants came crowding around, mourning.
No one there, not even the meanest, was forgotten.   260
Graciously, simply, she gave her hand to each
and said goodbye.
                    This is what
Admetos' house has lost. What has he gained but life?
If he had died, he would have lost Alcestis.
Now, as matters stand, he has lost her anyway.
As long as he lives, his life will have that taste
of pain and loss—a bitterness that lasts.

LEADER It is a great loss—a loss whose anguish
        he must be suffering now.

MAID   Yes, he is crying,
        holding his wife in his arms, imploring her   270
        not to leave him, not to die, madly
        wanting what cannot be,
        while she lies there, a dead weight

43

in his arms, all white and wasted
with that dying sickness.
She can barely breathe,
but with what little breath she has,
she is calling for the light,
the light she'll never see again.
She wants the light: 280
                    the light! the light!
a last look at the sun's sweet light.
But, sir, I'll go
and announce your presence.
It isn't everyone who cares about this house
or is ready to share our sorrows with us.
But you have always been a good and loyal friend,
and, sir, you're welcome here.

                              Exit MAID *into the palace.*

CHORUS —Is there no answer, Zeus?
        No way? Must it be disaster?

        —Answer our prayers, O Lord!   290
        Or must we put black mourning on?

        —We must, we must. But first, friends,
        pray to the gods. Their power is great.

        (kneeling)

        O Paian, power of healing, come!
        Apollo, have pity on this house!
        Lord, give us life
        as once you conquered Death
        and let Admetos live.
        Now Death has come to take his queen.

Apollo, lord,   300
            beat back this ruthless,
savage god of Death!

—I pity you, Admetos. How, without Alcestis,
can you live at all?

—O gods,
in bitterness for this,
a man might cut his throat
or twist the rope around his neck
and hang himself for grief
in heaven's holy face.

—Not for love,
but something more than love,   310
Alcestis dies for you today,
oh Admetos!

LEADER Look, here comes the queen Alcestis,
        with king Admetos at her side.

        ALCESTIS, *supported by* ADMETOS *and maids, appears from*
        the palace, followed by the two children. Attendants bring
                    on a litter, which they place near the door.

CHORUS O land of Pherai mourn
        and let the wounded Earth cry sorrow;
        no nobler woman ever lived
        and yet she goes   fading   dying
        wasted
                    down
                        to the world below.

LEADER Do not say that marriage has more happiness than pain.
        I have seen too many marriages.   And now I see   320

45

the torment of this house: this bravest of women
dying, and a king in agony. As long as he lives,
his life will taste of death,
all he will have is hell.

ALCESTIS (*stretching out her arms in longing to sun and sky*)
O Sun
Sweet shining light
white clouds swelling   wheeling in the blue

ADMETOS The god of light looks down and sees us suffering.
Why, why? How have we hurt the gods that you should die,
Alcestis?

ALCESTIS (*slumping down, head forward, faintly*)
Sweet earth of Iolkos   O earth   330
where I was born   O house that sheltered me
where I was a girl
in Iolkos

ADMETOS (*lifting her up and supporting her*)
Up, Alcestis. Stand. Live. Don't leave me now.
Pray. The gods are strong. What they will is done.
Implore the gods, for pity's sake, to let you, please,
let you live.

ALCESTIS I see the black water and the dead
lake   the boat beached on the sand
and look
                    Charon
                                  there at the rudder
calling me   Why are you waiting Alcestis?   340
It is time to leave   hurry Alcestis
come
              Don't you hear him calling?
So angry and impatient

ADMETOS This is a bitter crossing. It is bitter for us both,

Alcestis. O gods, what have we done that we should suffer
so?

ALCESTIS No!   a hand   *someone*   *something*
          holding me hard, forcing me down
                                            down
          to the dead world—
                              So dark   And look
          those black eyes glowing   those great black wings
          beating over me   350
                          it is Death!   Death!
          how terribly he frowns   No no
          please   no   let me go   I won't
          let me go   the road is dark
          I am so afraid

ADMETOS For all who love you, dear, for the children and me,
         this is a dreadful journey. We are afraid for you,
         afraid for us all.

ALCESTIS Admetos let me down   let me lie
          down   I am too weak to stand
          Death is closing in   my eyes are going   360
          dark
                  A *silence. Then she clutches the children to her.*
          O children
          goodbye
          you have no mother any more
          I love you   the light is yours   children
          be happy in the light

ADMETOS Goodbye—
         Oh, gods in heaven, I would rather die
         than hear you say that dreadful word!
         Oh, if you could find the strength to speak that hard and bitter
                 word to me,
         then find the strength to stay!
         Oh Alcestis

47

for our children's sake   for me
be strong   be hard   stand   370
fight it   live
your dying is my death
in you we live in you we die
by your love we pray you

(*kneeling*)

live

ALCESTIS Admetos, I am dying.
This is my last request of you, so listen well.
Of my own free will I gave my life
to let you live. I am dying for you, Admetos,
but I did not have to die.
I could have chosen otherwise. As your widow   380
I might have married any man in Thessaly
and lived with him here and ruled this royal house.
But without you, with these children fatherless,
I could not live. I am young, Admetos,
but I have given you my youth—the good years,
the happy years. All the others failed you.
Your father and your mother would have let you die,
though they had lived good lives and reached an age
when death comes naturally and right. There was glory, too,
for them, in giving up their lives to save their son.   390
For they had no other sons, and no hope of any
after you. They could have died for you,
and you and I would still have lives to live.
You would not be left alone to mourn for me,
and our children would have a mother...
                                        Why?
Who knows? Some god has brought these things to pass.
Let it be.
            Now, Admetos, I want your promise.
It is a little thing I ask you, nothing much—
oh, nothing like the gift of life I gave you,

48

since that's a gift that has no price. No,   400
a small request, but one I have a mother's right to ask,
and you, I think, a father's heart to grant. Surely
you love these children, Admetos, as much as I.
Oh, if you love them, make them masters in this house;
do not take a second wife and make her mistress here
where she may do our children harm because they're mine,
and she is jealous.
                    Oh promise me, Admetos, promise me.
Swear to me no woman will ever enter
through that door again. A new wife hates the children
of the old, hates them with a viper's poison.   410
The boy will have his father to protect him.
                                        —But you,
poor girl, what will your childhood be like,
if your father marries a second wife? Will she be kind
while you are growing up? Or will she make up stories
out of spite and spoil your hopes of marriage, spoil
your wedding day when I will not be there
to take your side? Not be there to hold your hand and help
in childbirth, when a girl most needs her mother's love
and help . . .
              I will not be there. I have to die.
Oh, not tomorrow, not the next day, not this month,   420
but now, in just a minute, I will not be here
with you at all.
                    Goodbye   I love you very much
Be happy
                Admetos   be proud of me   you can.
Children   remember your mother   remember my example
be brave

LEADER I will vouch for Admetos.
        He is a noble man. He will keep his promise.

ADMETOS You have my word, my solemn promise.

        (*solemnly raising his right hand*)

49

I swear it.
                    Oh Alcestis,
living or dead you are my wife.
I love you, I will always love you.   430
Only you.
No other woman will ever live with me again.
There is no woman in this world of Thessaly
by birth so noble or in looks so lovely,
none, none who could ever take your place
in my home or heart.
Your children are ours; I want no more.
I only pray the gods will let them live
for me to cherish and enjoy:
they are all I have of you.
I will mourn you, not the customary year,   440
but all my life.
Those whose cowardice has caused your death,
my father and mother, will have my hatred, always.
Their love was only words: a lie.
You were loyal in love. You alone, Alcestis.
You loved me so you gave your life, your only life,
to let me live.
                    I know what I have lost, how much,
and I will mourn you as your love and mine deserve.
Here and now I banish from this house
all festivity. The happiness that filled these rooms—   450
good cheer and gaiety, the table where I sat and drank with
        friends,
the joy of music, flowers—all of them I banish now
forever. I used to play the lute, but I will never
touch its strings again. Let the flute I loved
be still.
            Oh, Alcestis, all my joy in life is gone
with you!
            How can I hold you here, a little of you, still?
Listen:
            I'll have an artisan of cunning skill
contrive your likeness for our bed, and at night

I'll lie beside it, dreaming you are there
and whispering your name ...   460
                        Cold comfort, I know,
but I have nothing else. Even seeming helps.
You would come to me at night, often, in dreams,
and I would have, if only for a while,
the satisfaction of the love I used to have
in life.
              In life ...
                        Oh, Alcestis,
if I had the song and poetry of Orpheus
so I could charm the god of Hell, bewitch his queen
and, by my singing, spell you back from death,
I'd go beneath the ground. Nothing would stop me,
not Kerberos himself or Charon bending   470
at his fatal oar could stop me from bringing you back
to life.

          Wait for me below. Wait until I die.
Make a house for us, where we can be together.
I'll have our bodies buried in a cedar coffin,
side by side. In death I will never
leave your side, since only you were true in life.
You stood beside me to the bitter end.

LEADER   Admetos,
I will stand beside you now, as friends should stand,
and we will mourn your wife together.
All our grief combined is less than she deserves.   480

ALCESTIS Children, you have heard your father give his word.
He will never make another woman welcome in this house.
He will honor my memory.

ADMETOS I promised.

              (*raising his right hand*)

                    And I will keep my promise.
    I swear it.

ALCESTIS   Then give me your hand.

    She takes his right hand and formally delivers the children to
                                            his keeping.

    Now take these children and love them

ADMETOS   I do.
    I love the gift as I love the giver.

ALCESTIS Love them as their mother loved them

ADMETOS   I must.
    I will love them as their mother would have loved them,
    had she lived.   490

ALCESTIS   Oh   I should have lived   not died.
    My poor children

ADMETOS   How can I live without you?

ALCESTIS Time will dull your grief   the dead are nothing

ADMETOS Take me with you, Alcestis! For god's sake,
    let me die ...

ALCESTIS   My dying is enough   Admetos
    I am dying for you.

ADMETOS   Stay with me.... Stay ...

ALCESTIS Darkness now   so heavy   my eyes are closing

ADMETOS What am I, Alcestis, without you? Nothing.

ALCESTIS I am nothing now   the dead are nothing

ADMETOS Lift your head, Alcestis. Look at your children.
How can you bear to leave them?   500

ALCESTIS *(raising her head with a final effort)*
                                                    I have to leave them
        Goodbye   children

ADMETOS   Look at them! *Look!*

ALCESTIS Ahh
                            She sinks down on the litter, dead.

ADMETOS What are you doing? No...no...no...

LEADER She is dead, Admetos.

        (to the CHORUS *and audience)*

                            —The queen is dead.

        *Sobbing and crying, the children throw themselves on the
        body of their mother, while* ADMETOS *tries to comfort them.*

ADMETOS She cannot hear you, she cannot see you.
Poor motherless children...
                                    O gods in heaven,
        this is beyond bearing...

        Crumbling in grief, he joins his children beside the bier.

LEADER It had to be, Admetos. All we can do with death
is bear it patiently. Be brave. You are not the first
to lose a loving wife; you will not be the last.
We were born to die.   510

ADMETOS   I know.... Day after day
I saw it coming on, those great wings like a black shadow
swooping down. And waiting, just waiting—
oh, if you knew the agony of it.

(*with an effort controlling himself*)

                                        But no more.
I must give orders for the funeral.

(*to the* CHORUS)

                                —Good friends,
I need your presence and support. Help me
by remaining here. Raise a song in honor of Alcestis,
and by the beauty and the power of your singing,
cry defiance to this hard and bitter god
whom nothing will appease but death.

(*to audience*)

                                —To my subjects
I now proclaim a period of solemn public mourning   520
for your queen. Shear your hair in sign of sorrow,
put on mourning black. Let my cavalry and guard
crop their horses' manes. Throughout this city
let the lyre be still; let no one touch a flute
until twelve moons have waxed and waned and brought
the year full circle.
            I shall never bury anyone I loved
so much, nor anyone who loved me more. Only she
would take my place in death, and she shall have from me
the honor she deserves.

The servants raise the litter holding the body of ALCESTIS *and
carry it inside the palace, followed by* ADMETOS *and the two
children.*

54

CHORUS   Farewell, Alcestis. Our love goes with you now   530
         beneath the earth to your long home among the tribes
         of those on whom the sweet light never shines: unseeing
         and unseen. We shall not see your like again.
         O Death, in that dark tangle of your mind, if you have
         eyes to see, look among the herded dead who go
         with Charon in his long slow crossing over Acheron;
         look and you will see, blazing in that crowd of ordinary
         dead, the noblest life the sunlight ever shone upon!

         You shine in memory. And mortal men, remembering
         you, will praise your death: a song that does not die.   540
         Each year, unaccompanied, your song shall rise,
         a shining on the lips of men; or sometimes chanted
         to the rude and simple lyre, at Sparta when the year
         has come full circle, and the moon, a splendor, rides
         the livelong night; or there in Athens' blazing noon.
         Wherever there is light, wherever men remember love,
         Death shall not eclipse the glory of your shining.

         I am old, too old. Oh, if the strength were mine
         to bring you back, I'd go below and break the stubborn
         grip of Hell, where Charon, toiling, bends his body   550
         to the dead stroke of the sad oar slowly beating
         over Acheron. So beautiful in love, so strong
         and brave, you gave your life to take his place in death!
         For love you went below. Rest peacefully, Alcestis.
         Earth, lie gently on her grave, for she was gentle always.

LEADER   Lady, if Admetos ever loves again,
         he will have your children's hate and mine. He will have it
         always.

CHORUS   They were old, so old, his father and his mother, both
         blanched with age, both in the winter of their years.
         Old, so very old. But still they grudged their bodies   560

to the grave. Old cowards, grasping at the light,
so greedy still to live! Though he was theirs, their own,
those old ones would not die. But you, Alcestis, you,
in the fresh morning of your days, you gave your life
and took Admetos' place below. You died for love.
For such a love as yours, I would give my very life!

LEADER Unselfish love, like hers, is rare. So rare
that I would want her at my side, alive. I would love her
always.

Enter HERAKLES *from the left. Dressed in his familiar lionskin
and armed with his bow, he is immediately recognized by the*
CHORUS.

HERAKLES I give you greetings, elders of Pherai.

(to LEADER)

—Old sir,

is King Admetos here?   570

LEADER   He is, Herakles. But tell me:
what business brings you to Thessaly?

HERAKLES   Obligation, friend.
I have a labor to perform. Eurystheus is my master.
He commands, and I obey.

LEADER   What is your mission?
And where are you bound?

HERAKLES   A long, hard journey.
My destination's Thrace. My orders are to capture
Diomedes' horses.

LEADER   *Diomedes' horses?* It can't be done,
Herakles. Surely you've heard of Diomedes?

HERAKLES No. Nothing. I've never been in Thrace before.

LEADER Those horses are wild. They can't be broken.

HERAKLES *Can't* be broken?   580

LEADER   Not without a fight, they can't.

HERAKLES Fighting's what I do.
My labors are my life. I can't refuse.

LEADER But with Diomedes, it's kill or be killed.

HERAKLES I've confronted Death before.

LEADER   Suppose you kill him:
what will it get you?

HERAKLES   Why, I get his horses.
And what I get, Eurystheus gets.

LEADER   It won't be easy
to put a bridle on those jaws and curb those teeth.

HERAKLES What's so hard? Are they fire-breathing monsters,
or just plain horses?

LEADER   Wild horses, Herakles. Killers.
Cannibal horses, with teeth so sharp and fast   590
they can slice a man to ribbons.

HERAKLES   To hear you tell it,
they sound like tigers, not a team of horses.

LEADER You should see their mangers. Caked with human blood.

HERAKLES So Diomedes bred these pretties, did he?
And who does Diomedes claim to be? Who bred *him*?

LEARED His father was the war-god Ares, or so he boasts.
He commands, as king, the golden cavalry of Thrace.

HERAKLES Ares' son, is he? There you have the story
of my labors and my life. It's a damned hard road
I'm doomed to travel, friend. Rough, uphill   600
all the way. One after another
I've had to fight every bastard son the war-god ever had.
First it was Lykaon. Then Kyknos. And now
this confrontation with the master of this pack
of killer horses. But no man on this earth
has ever seen the son of Alkmene flinch from a fight.
No one ever will.

LEADER   Here comes King Admetos now
to welcome you in person.

Enter ADMETOS *from the palace. His hair is cropped and he
is dressed in mourning black.*

ADMETOS   Welcome, Herakles.
Son of Zeus, welcome to my house.

HERAKLES   Heaven smile
on you and yours, Admetos!   610

ADMETOS   If only it had ...
But thank you, Herakles. I know you mean well.

HERAKLES Why is your hair cut? Are you in mourning?

ADMETOS There has been a death in my house, Herakles.
The funeral is today.

HERAKLES   I hope nothing has happened
to your children.

ADMETOS   No, thanks be to heaven,
my children are alive and well.

HERAKLES   Your father then?
If so, he lived a long, full life, Admetos.

ADMETOS My father is well. My mother, too.

HERAKLES   Not Alcestis?
Surely not Alcestis?

(*a long pause*)

ADMETOS Yes ...   620

(*a short pause, then quickly*)

No.

HERAKLES   What in god's name are you saying,
Admetos? Is she alive or is she dead? Which?

ADMETOS Both. Both. I am in agony, Herakles ...

HERAKLES   Alive
and dead? But these are riddles, Admetos.
Make sense.

ADMETOS   You know that she was doomed to die?

HERAKLES I know she promised to take your place below.

ADMETOS Knowing what she promised, knowing she is doomed,
how can I think of her as still alive?

HERAKLES   Ah ...
Wait until she dies, Admetos. Don't mourn her yet.

ADMETOS Those who are doomed are as good as dead.
And the dead are nothing.   630

59

HERAKLES   There is a difference
             between life and death. Or so men think, Admetos.

ADMETOS That is your opinion, Herakles. Not mine.

HERAKLES Then why are you in mourning? Clearly
             someone has died, someone you loved, Admetos.
             Who?

ADMETOS   A woman, Herakles. A woman has died.

HERAKLES Was she related to you?

ADMETOS   Not by blood.
             But there were bonds . . . The attachment was strong.
             We loved her very much.

HERAKLES   Why was she living here?

ADMETOS After her father's death, she was left an orphan.
             We took her in.   640

HERAKLES   I am sorry for you, Admetos.
             I have come at a bad time, it seems.

                          He shoulders his bow and turns to leave.

ADMETOS What are you doing, Herakles?

HERAKLES   Leaving, Admetos.
             I have other friends in these parts. I'll stay with them.

ADMETOS Impossible, my lord. I won't have it.
             I won't hear of it.

HERAKLES   Your house is in mourning.
             A guest would only be a burden.

ADMETOS   The dead are dead.

(*taking* HERAKLES *by the arm and forcibly detaining him*)

I insist.
          You must stay.

HERAKLES   It wouldn't be right, Admetos.
          This is a time for mourning, not entertaining friends.
          You cannot do both at once.

ADMETOS   The guest rooms are separate.
          I'll put you there.   650

HERAKLES   Let me go to someone else,
          Admetos. Please. I ask it as a favor.

ADMETOS   Impossible.
          You must stay.

          (*to a servant*)

                              —You there. Take our guest inside.
          Open up the guest rooms on the east wing
          of the house. Then serve him dinner and wine.
          Be generous. And shut the doors on the courtyard.
          I do not want our guest to be disturbed at dinner
          by the sounds of mourning.

                              HERAKLES *is escorted inside.*

LEADER   Are you mad, Admetos?
          Your wife not dead an hour, and you can bear the thought
          of entertaining guests?

ADMETOS   This man is my friend.
          What would your answer be if I turned my friend away   660
          from my home and city? That I deserved your admiration?

61

Surely not. And what would I gain?
My wife would still be dead.
My loss would be exactly what it is,
neither more nor less. But I would lose a friend.
I have pain enough without the pain
of having my house called inhospitable and rude.
I am his host; he is my friend and guest.
His hospitality to me is lavish, unsurpassed
in generosity and love, when I stay with him in Argos.   670
And Argos is a thirsty place.

LEADER   Your friend, you say.
Then why conceal your sorrow from your friend?

ADMETOS If he suspected what had happened here,
I do not think he would have stayed. Some, I know
will shake their heads and say that what I did
was wrong. But this house of mine has yet to learn
discourtesy to guests or less than due regard
for those with claims upon my honor and my love.

Exit ADMETOS *into the palace.*

CHORUS
Hospitality is here.
What house could be more gracious or more generous   680
than this? Open-handed, always prodigal and free,
its master gives such lavish welcoming
that one might think his guests were gods.
Great gods have sheltered here.
Here Apollo, god of Delphi, condescending,
came, his high divinity constrained to serve
as shepherd for a year. And down these blessèd hills,
to mating flocks the god of music sang the season's song,
O Hymen Hymenaios O!

So powerful Apollo's song   690
that spotted lynxes crouching in the mountain rocks

were drawn by joy, no longer wild, to stray like browsing sheep
beside the shepherd god. And here, compelled
from Orthrys' shaggy glens, the golden lions came.
Bright god, so sweet your clarity of song,
the fawn came shivering from the darkened wood,
and there, beside the forest edge, shyly stepping
from the arbor of the pines, the strong light caught her—
dappled, on delicate legs, dancing as Apollo sang:
O Hymen Hymenaios O!   700

Your guest was god, Admetos. And so,
by grace, your house is now beyond all mortal houses
blest in wealth of flocks beside the clear blue waters
of Boibias. Westward, mile on mile
across the greening plain, your tilth and pastures range
to far Molossos where the lord of light drops down
to ford his horses in the Adriatic night;
and eastward, too, your kingdom goes, across the peaks
where Pelion takes its headlong plunge, harborless and sheer,
down to the green Aegean. Admetos, all   710
this blessèd land is yours, by grace of god.

And now, again, this gracious man
has opened wide the doors and welcomed in this house
another guest. Another—even though the wife he loved
was newly dead, and the agony of grief
lay freshly on him ... Noble man, his courtesy
and grace exceed all human scale. But who can say?
Greatness of soul is all that human wisdom knows;
all philosophy is in it. I stand in awe,
Admetos. And somehow I have faith, a growing hope   720
that for this noble, heaven-minded man,
all, by grace of god, may still be well.

Enter ADMETOS *from the palace.*

ADMETOS My friends, I appreciate your kindness and support.

Thank you for remaining. The funeral is ready now
and my men are bringing out the bier.

Enter Attendants slowly and solemnly, with the bier of
ALCESTIS *on their shoulders. Reverently, they set it down*
directly before the great central doors of the palace.

                                        But first,
before we take her body to the grave,
I would like you, friends, to speak the customary words:
the last farewell. We shall not see her in this life again.

LEADER Wait, Admetos.
I see your father Pheres on his way, and servants with him
bringing gifts to offer to the gods below.   730

Enter PHERES *dressed in mourning black. His shorn hair is*
white and he is stooped with age; he walks slowly up the
ramp to the bier of ALCESTIS; ADMETOS *faces him on the*
                                        other side of the bier.

PHERES   Son,
I have come to help you bear the burden of your grief.
You have lost a good wife: a decent, loving,
humble wife. A hard and bitter loss, but bear it
you must.

                        He motions to his servants to come forward
                                    with the funeral gifts.

            Accept these tokens of my respect,
and let her take them with her to the world below.
We must honor her in death as she deserves;
she gave her life to let you keep the light. No,
she would not let this poor old man drag out
his dying years deprived of all he had—his one,   740
his only, son. And by her bravery in death,
she has been a credit—no, a glory—to her sex.

64

(formally addressing the body on the bier)

—Lady,
rest in peace.
By your courage you have been the savior of my son.
Your generosity restored the fortunes
of my broken house, when it was down. Alcestis,
fare you well, even in the world below.
And rest in peace.
              —Mark my words, son.
Marriage is for most of us a losing proposition.
But this wife of yours was pure gold, and no mistake.
And gold is what I give her now.   750

He signals to his servants to lay their gifts upon the bier,
while ADMETOS *angrily steps forward to intercept them.*

ADMETOS Who asked *you* to come? Who invited *you*?
Not I. Not her.
Love? *What* love? Your love's a lie: all words.
So keep your gold. She'll never wear your trinket
love.
She'll be buried as she is. Without your gifts.
Or you. Leave. Who needs you anyway?
Who needs you now?
You came, you say, to bring me sympathy and help.
The time for you to help was when I had to die
or find a substitute. Where were you *then*?   760
Vanished. Nowhere. Like your love. You disappeared
and let another take your place in death.
You were old, and she was young.
And now you have the gall to come here with your mock
sorrow and your hypocrisy of love!
You never gave a damn for me!
Where was your love when I needed you? Why,
for all you cared, I might have been some slave's bastard
smuggled in the house and set to suckle at the breast
of that barren bitch who calls herself my mother.   770

No, when courage was required,
when dying was the issue and the test,
you showed us what you really are.
Not my father, but a cheap coward!
Gods, is there any coward in this world like you?
There you were, a withered bag of bones, tottering
into eternity. But still you wouldn't die! Not you.
You didn't dare to die. So you let a woman,
no blood of yours, do your duty for you.
To her and her alone I owe the tenderness and love   780
I would have lavished on my parents in their age,
had they loved me like a son.
If I were you,
I would have fought—*yes, fought!*—for the privilege
of dying for my son. Besides,
your time was short. A few brief years at best.
So what had you to lose?
Every happiness a man could have, you had.
You inherited a kingdom when you were still a boy.
You had a son, so your succession was secure   790
and you could die in peace, knowing there would be
no rival claimants for your throne, no wars.
You cannot say that you abandoned me
because of my neglect: I showed you all the honor
a son could give. I was always good to you
in your old age. And how have you repaid my love?
You would have let me die.
Well, now your time is running out, old man.
So hurry. Use what little time you've got to breed
another son to care for you in your old age and stuff you   800
in the ground.

(*raising his hand*)

                    So help me gods,
I will never lift a hand to bury you!
You refused to lift a finger for my life.
I disown you both.

If I still live and see the light,
everything I might have owed to you as son,
I pledge to her who gave me life.

Gods, how I hate them,
all these aging hypocrites, tottering around,
telling you how much they want to die,   810
stuffed with self-pity, whining about old age
and its indignities, their long, slow, crawling passage
to the grave.
But let them get the slightest glimpse of Death
and suddenly they stick like leeches to the light
and tell you life is not so bad.

LEADER Stop it, both of you.
Haven't you sorrows enough without this, too?
                                                        Boy,
why must you exasperate your father?

PHERES Boy,
who in god's name do you think you are?   820
Are you my master now, and I some poor, bought,
cringing Asiatic slave that you dare dress me down
like this? I am a free man, Thessalian born,
a prince of Thessaly. And I will not be bullied
by the likes of you, arrogant boy.

                        ADMETOS *turns angrily away.*

                                Hear me out.
Don't think you'll pelt me, boy, with your abuse
and then just turn your back.

Damn you, boy,
I made you lord and master of this house of mine.
I gave you life, I raised you.

I am not obliged to die for you as well.   830
Or do you think my father died for me?
There is no law, no precedent, in Greece
that children have a claim upon their fathers' lives.
A man is born to happiness, or otherwise.
He is born for himself.
Everything you had the right to get from me, you got.
I made you ruler of a rich and populous country.
And I intend to leave you all the vast domain
my father left to me.   840
So how have I hurt you? What more do I owe you?
Life?
No. You live yours, and I'll live mine.
Do your own dying. I'll do mine.
You love the light.
What makes you think your father doesn't love it, too?
The time we spend beneath the earth, I think, is very long.
And life is short, but what there is of it is good,
good and sweet.
                    As for fighting, boy, you fought all right.
You fought like hell to live—life at any price!—
beyond your destined time. You only live   850
because you took her life. You *murdered* her.
And you dare talk about my cowardice—
you, who let a woman outdo you in bravery,
let her give her life to keep her gigolo
alive?
But you're clever, I admit.
Immortality is yours, yours for the asking.
All you have to do is wheedle your latest wife
into dying in your place.
And then, like the cheap coward that you are,
you accuse the rest of us of failing in our duty!   860

ADMETOS Listen—

PHERES   You listen, boy. Remember this.
            You love your life. Well, so does every man alive.

68

And if you call us names for that,
worse things will be said of you. They won't be pretty,
and they'll all be true.

LEADER There have been too many ugly words, too much abuse,
already.
　　　　—Old man, stop provoking your son.

ADMETOS Let him talk, and then I'll have my say.
　　　　　　　　　　　　　　　　—You see?
The truth hurts. Your cowardice was your mistake.
You didn't dare to die.   870

PHERES　　　　　　　　　That was no mistake.
The mistake would have been dying for you.

ADMETOS And dying young is just the same as dying old?

PHERES One life is all we have. Not two.

ADMETOS The way you clutch at that one life of yours,
you'll outlive Zeus.

PHERES　　　　　　　　How have I hurt you
that you should hate me so?

ADMETOS　　　　　　　　　　　　Old age
has made you greedy. Greedy to live!

PHERES Greedy, am I?
Who killed that girl whose corpse you're burying?
And you talk to me of greed!   880

ADMETOS It was *your* cowardice that killed her.

PHERES *You* took her life. *You* killed her.

ADMETOS O gods, I hope

I live to see the day when you come crawling to me
for help!

PHERES That's your style, not mine.
Find some woman to help you live. Marry her,
then let her die.

ADMETOS Your fault. You wouldn't die.

PHERES No, I wouldn't.
This god's light is sweet, I tell you, sweet.   890

ADMETOS You cheap coward, you don't deserve to live!

PHERES Go bury your dead.
Whether you like it or not, *I'm* still alive.
You won't gloat over my dead body. Not today,
boy.

ADMETOS Don't expect the world to praise you when you die—
if you ever do.

PHERES What the hell do I care what people say of me
after I'm dead?

ADMETOS Gods,
what shabby, shameless cowards these old men are!

PHERES *She* wasn't shabby, was she? No, she was *brave*.   900
Brave enough—stupid enough—to die for *you*.

ADMETOS Leave. Let me bury my dead.

PHERES I'm leaving.
Let the murderer bury his victim in peace.

Exit PHERES, *followed by his servants with the rejected gifts.*

ADMETOS Go and be damned to you,
              you and that woman I used to call my mother.
              You have no son.
              Grow old, both of you, as you deserve—
              childless, heirless, alone.
              Never let me see you in this house again.   910
              So help me god,
              if I had heralds here to proclaim
              that I disown you both and ban you from my house,
              I'd do it.

              A long silence ensues as PHERES *slowly makes his exit, and*
                  ADMETOS' *attendants take up their position by the bier.*

              (*to* CHORUS)

              And now, friends, let us perform our sad task,
              and take Alcestis' body to the grave.

              The Attendants lift the bier of ALCESTIS *to their shoulders and
              the funeral cortege moves slowly and solemnly toward the
              right. Leading the procession is the bier, which is followed by*
              ADMETOS *and the children, and finally the entire* CHORUS.

LEADER Fare you well, Alcestis.
              Let Hermes of the unseen world receive his honored guest,
              and the Dark Lord welcome you below as your nobility and
                       love deserve.
              For if the good fare best, and courage has its due   920
              even in that pale democracy below,
              the Queen herself of all the dead will rise in homage,
              seeing you, Alcestis.
              No braver mortal ever lived.

              *Exeunt omnes in slow, funeral procession. For a while
              the stage is empty and silent. Then an old* SERVANT, *wearing
              a scowling mask, appears from the palace. He speaks directly
              to the audience. Now and then, as he speaks, the voice of*

HERAKLES *can be heard singing, off-key and indistinctly, the*
snatches of a familiar drinking-song.

SERVANT   I've seen a lot of strangers in my time,
guests traipsing in here from all over the world,
and we put 'em all up, bed 'em, and feed 'em
food. But this newest guest is the worst damned
guest this house and I have ever seen. Right away,
anyone could have seen Admetos was in mourning.   930
So what does this dull clod do? Barges in,
big as life and bold as brass. I mean,
any man with a grain of decency or ordinary common sense
would have seen Admetos was in trouble
and accepted what we had to give without a lot of noise
and fuss. But not this fellow. Nossirree,
if we don't fetch him what he wants, he yells at us
to shake a leg. "Hurry up!" he bellows. "Dammit. *Move!*"
Then he picks up a great big wooden bowl of wine—
both hands at once, just like a peasant—   940
and swills it down, straight, unwatered, strong,
and reddish black like the ground that grew it.
Well, before you could say Dionysos,
he was heated up, half-crocked, high
as a kite. Then he slaps a wreath of myrtle on his head,
and starts in murdering some bawdy song.
Listen . . .

From within is heard the bray of a drunken voice, singing.

There *he* was, roaring away over his supper,
without a thought for poor Admetos and his troubles,
and there we were, mourning for our mistress,
and what with the maids wailing and beating their breasts—   950
well, you've never heard such a bloody medley in all
your days. And of course we couldn't tell him we were
     mourning
because king Admetos had given orders forbidding it.
Anyway, here I am, left
behind at home to entertain this so-called guest

(though, if you ask me, burglar or highwayman
or just plain pirate is closer to the mark).
And meanwhile they've taken our lady to the grave,
and I didn't get to follow her body or hold out my hand
and say goodbye to her the way I wanted.   960
Because she was good to us all, a good, kind mistress,
more like a mother than a mistress, always
calming the master down when he went off in one of his fits
of rage. Anyway, that's why I hate the sight
of this guest who came barging in on our troubles.
Guest or no guest, I detest the man
and, god knows, I've got the right to hate him.

Enter HERAKLES, *tipsy and reeling, from the palace. On his
head he wears a wreath of flowers; in one hand he carries
a flask of wine, in the other a large cup which he periodically
drains and refills. His speech is punctuated by periodic
hiccups and emphatic belching.*

HERAKLES Hey, you there!
          Yeah, I mean you, with the big frown on your face!
          What'sh your problem, sourpuss?   970
          Butler'sh oughtta be polite, goddamit.
          Servish with a smile.
          An' none of those goddam killjoy looksh either.
          Here I am, your mashter's bes' fren',
          an' all you can do is glower at me with that goddam
          miserable mug. An' why?
          'Cause someone you barely knew dropped dead.
          Dead . . .
          C'mere, fella,
          an' I'll let you in on a l'il secret.
          Make a better man of you.   980
          I mean, wise up:
          we all gotta die.
          You know what it'sh like to be a man?
          I mean,
          d'you really unnerstan' the human condishun, fren'?

73

I can see you don't. How could you, with a face like that?
Well, lissen, mister:
we all gotta die. An' that's a fact.
There's not a man alive who knows the odds on death.
Here today. Gone tomorrow.
Poof.
That's fate. A mystery. I mean,   990
there's jus' no knowin'. Man can't figger it out.
Well,
that's my message. So what d'you say?
Cheer up and have a l'il drink,
huh?
Live for the day. Today is ours.
Tomorrow's fate.
Hey,
an' there's somethin' else, Yessir. Aphrodite.
Don't forget Aphrodite, fren'.
'Cause thass a good l'il goddess.
They just don' come any sweeter than Aphrodite.
Take my advice, fella, an' forget your troubles.   1000
Well, what d'you say?
Am I talkin' sense? Damn right I am.
So forget whatever it is thass makin' you so goddam
glum. Come on, man,
have a drink. Drown your troubles.
Here, put these flowers on your head,
and bottoms up!

                              He drains his glass and refills it.

Lissen:
you hear that wine purling and gurgling in the cup?
Well, a swallow of this will do wonders, friend,
for whatever's ailing you.   1010
I mean, we all gotta die. Right?
Well, that's why we all gotta think human thoughts,
and live while we can.
Eat, drink, and be merry.

Take it from me,
the way those gloomy, bellyachin' tragedians gripe,
life isn't life at all, it's just a goddam
funeral.

SERVANT   Quite, sir. I understand.
But, sir, this happens to be a house of mourning.
Your drunken revelry is grossly out of place.   1020
Sir.

HERAKLES Izzat so?
Jus' because a woman's dead? Stranger, too, I hear.
Sure, it's sad, but what's the tragedy? Look,
the family's alive and well.

SERVANT   *Alive and well?*
You mean you still don't know what happened here?

HERAKLES Of course I know. Admetos told me when I came.

(*pulling himself together, more soberly*)

Wait.
Are you saying that Admetos lied to me?

SERVANT You know the master, sir. He is hospitable to a fault.
Sometimes his kindness goes too far.

HERAKLES   I know his kindness well.   1030
Is that the reason I must go without my supper?
Because of some dead stranger?

SERVANT   *Stranger,* you say?
Oh, sir, what stranger could ever be as close as she?

HERAKLES (*soberly now, with genuine concern*)
What has happened here?
What is Admetos hiding from me?

SERVANT Sir, let it be.
             She belonged to us.
             Go, and let us mourn our dead in peace.

HERAKLES So it wasn't a stranger who died?

SERVANT If it were,
             nobody would have minded your getting drunk.   1040

HERAKLES Then Admetos lied to me? Deceived his friend?

SERVANT Sir, you couldn't have come at a worse time.
             This is a house of mourning. Our hair is shorn;
             we are dressed in black. You can see for yourself.

HERAKLES Who died, man?
             One of the children? Old Pheres? Who?

SERVANT Admetos' queen, sir. Alcestis. Alcestis is dead.

HERAKLES Alcestis *dead?*
             And you were entertaining me when she lay dead?

SERVANT Sir, Admetos honors you.   1050
             He could not bear the thought of turning you away.

HERAKLES What husband ever lost a wife like this?
             Oh, Alcestis, Alcestis . . .

SERVANT When she died, sir,
             it seemed as though the whole house, every one of us,
             died with her.

HERAKLES Oh, I knew it, I knew it
             when I saw his face all red with weeping,
             and his hair shorn, and the bitter anguish in his eyes!
             And, like a bloody fool, I believed his story   1060
             that he was burying some stranger.

A stranger!
And then he made me enter, forced me to come in,
against my will, and accept the welcome of his house.
And then, while he was suffering, mourning his wife,
there I was, his dearest friend,
—gods!—
feasting and carousing like some stupid, drunken clod,
wreathing my head with these damned flowers!

He rips off his wreath and dashes it to the ground.

And you let me do it!
The whole house was throbbing with this sorrow,   1070
and you never said a word!

Quick, man.
Where is the funeral being held?
Where can I find Admetos?

SERVANT   Go straight that way, on the road to Larisa.
Just outside the walls, sir, you'll see the place,
a tomb of polished marble.

Exit into palace.

HERAKLES   Now, Herakles,
your great ordeal begins.
Come, o my tough spirit, you hard, enduring hands
calloused with my many labors,
come and prove what man I am.
Prove me Herakles,   1080
the hero son my mortal mother bore to Zeus almighty!

Alcestis is dead,
and I must bring her back to the fields of light,
home, safe, to Admetos' arms, and so discharge my debt

of gratitude and love. Admetos' love to me was great,
and it deserves—and it will get—no ordinary kindness
in return.

Soon, I think,
the god of Death, those black wings beating overhead,
will come swooping down and settle by the grave
to drink the sacrificial blood. I'll lie in ambush   1090
there beside the tomb, and when the Dark Lord comes,
I'll break from hiding, seize him with my arms,
and clamp him in a hold so hard he cannot break it,
god though he is. Let him struggle.
I'll crush him in my mortal grip until he does my will
and lets Alcestis go.

But if Death fails to come,
if the blood stays there untasted on the ground,
I'll go beneath the earth, down to the unseen world
            below,
confront the god of Hell and his Persephone,   1100
and demand Alcestis back. Make no mistake:
I'll force my way below and bring Alcestis home,
and consign her to Admetos' care.
For he deserves this thanks from me:
His house was overwhelmed with grief,
but even so, he took me in, he made me welcome here.
Kind and noble to a fault, he hid his loss
to do me honor as a friend. Where in all Thessaly,
where in all the world, could I find a friend
as generous as this? I could not do it.   1110
And it will not be said of me
that this good and noble man conferred his kindness
on a friend
unworthy of his love.

Exit HERAKLES *to stage right. There is a brief silence. Then the*

CHORUS *re-enters from the left, followed by the forlorn and*
grief-stricken ADMETOS.

ADMETOS O home no home
        emptiness   silence   pain   loss
        going in or coming out   O
        walls of pain: I cannot leave   cannot stay
        Hurt   has no words
        Hurt   will not be still
        O   1120
           let me die
        better never have been born
        I envy the dead   the dead are beautiful
        not here my home
                      down   down
        my home is with the dead
        I hate the light   I hate this earth
        O Earth, come over me
        and let me die
        so lovely is the hostage that I gave to Death
        my life is all below

CHORUS (*individually, while* ADMETOS *sobs helplessly in response*)
        —Take your grief inside, Admetos. Hide, hide   1130
        from the light.
                    —You have cause for grief.
        —You have suffered, heaven knows.
        —But grief will never bring her back.
        —The truth is hard.
                    —Accept it, Admetos:
        —You will not see her in this life again.

ADMETOS Good friends, the wound is fresh,
        and you have opened it again . . . Better,
        better by far, it would have been
        if we had never married, she and I, never loved,
        never lived here in this house together!   1140
        How I envy them, those men who never marry,

men who have no children, who live for themselves,
alone. Then each would have one life to live.
That pain would be his, nothing more.
He does not live to see his children sicken,
his wife dying in childbirth...
Who that had a heart to love would choose such pain
if he could live alone and never know
how much he had to lose?

CHORUS —It had to be. We cannot choose our fates.   1150
    —A man can fight. But not with life,
not with death.
                  —Accept it like a man.
    —Hard, hard, I know.
                      —Be brave, Admetos.
    —Courage. Others, too, have lost their wives.
    —Some soon, some late, every man is curbed
by suffering or fate.
                  —Now it is your turn.

ADMETOS This sorrow lasts forever. There is no end to pain
when those we love go into that eternal night
beneath the earth. Why, why, in the name of heaven,
friends, did you stop me when I tried to die   1160
with her? There, in one grave, she and I,
we could have been together always. Always.
And then the lord of Death would have us both,
two lives instead of one. Loyal in love,
we would have crossed that dead water together.

LEADER (*with the utmost simplicity*)
    Admetos, a friend of mine once lost his son, a fine young
boy of exceptional promise, and an only child. His father was
an old man, white with age, and in the last years of his life. But
he bore his loss with dignity, as bravely as he could.

ADMETOS This house, how can I call it home? How can I go in,   1170
remembering how happy I once was here, and how, of

all that happiness, nothing now is left? Then and now:
a gulf so great it seems two wholly different unconnected
worlds. I remember then. It was dusk on our wedding day.
All around us the pine torches were blazing, and she and
I were coming home to bed, escorted by a noisy crowd of
happy friends and guests, singing and dancing. I remember
how they congratulated me, and how they wished Alcestis
happiness and long life (oh, my dead Alcestis!). In our
marriage, they told us, high nobilities on either side had
merged and met. And now? Now the only song is the cry   1180
of mourning. And the friends who bring me home wear
black instead of white. And the bed is there, the bed is
there . . . I sleep alone.

LEADER   Your luck had been good, Admetos. High happiness and
great wealth—both were yours. So when this sorrow struck
so suddenly, it found you unprepared. Suffering was
something you had never known.

    Still, your life is yours; you still have wealth. True,
you have lost your wife and the comfort of her love.
So have other men. Is it so strange, really, that human
marriages should end in this divorce of Death?

ADMETOS Dear friends,
    strange as it may seem,
    I think my wife in death is happier than I am now.
    No pain, no hurt, will touch her anymore.   1190
    She rests in peace, free at last from all
    the endless agony of life. And fame is hers
    forever.

    As for me,
    I should not be alive. I should be dead.
    The life I have is not worth living. I know it now.
    Too late.

    How can I bear to go on living in this house?
    What happiness is there in coming home, home to this
        dead house,

with its sound of absence, its echo of a voice
that greeted me when I came home? And now nothing,
    nothing
but this dead silence.   1200
When I go in, the emptiness inside will drive me out.
The empty rooms, the empty bed, the chair she used
to sit on, and the shining floor all dark with dust,
and the children sobbing, huddling at my knees
wherever I go, crying for their mother,
and the servants mourning their dead mistress,
remembering a gentle presence that my house has lost
forever...
        I cannot stay here.
                But in the city
I will see my married friends, friends with wives;
the girls and women thronging to their festivals and
        dances...   1210
The very sight of it would drive me home. All
Alcestis' friends, the girls she used to know—
I could not *bear* to see them now. Not now.

And I have enemies. Behind my back,
they'll point me out, whispering, "Look there,
look at Admetos,
the man who was afraid of death,
the coward who let his wife go down to Hades
in his place? Do you call *that* a man?
What kind of man would curse his father and mother   1220
because he was afraid of dying?
Who but a coward?"

Friends, you say my life is still mine.
But what's the good of living,
when everything I valued in this world is gone,
when I have lost my honor with my wife?

       He stands motionless, head down, in silent despair.

CHORUS Necessity is stone.
          Call her death, compulsion, fate: against
          what man her cruelty comes, that man is doomed.
          If poets know, if scholars speak the truth,   1230
          nothing stronger, nothing more resistless,
          is.
          O Man,
          against her hard, relentless coming on,
          all your craft and intellect are weak.
          There is no power in your spells and Orphic songs;
          no virtue in your herbs, your healing lore. Nothing,
          nothing can resist her coming on. Only patience.
          Suffer and submit.

          Necessity is stone,
          implacable. She has no face
          but rock; no human shape or likeness owns,   1240
          no cult, nor shrine. She heeds no sacrifice.
          She is force, and flint; no feeling has, no
          pity. None.

          (*kneeling, all together*)

          Mistress, Lady without mercy, I have felt
          your stroke before. May you never come again!
          Only by your hard strength the will of Zeus is done.
          By sheer force you break the iron of the Chalybes.
          Your will is granite, cruel. Nothing helps. Only patience.
          Suffer and submit.

          The CHORUS *now turns and addresses* ADMETOS *directly.*

          Admetos, now
          this goddess holds you in the bitter bondage of her grip.   1250
          Bear it. Be brave. Though you should mourn Alcestis always,
          you cannot bring the dead to life. Great heroes
          die. Even the sons of heaven fade, darkened

into death, though they were dear, dear as life
to the grieving gods. Alive, Alcestis had our love;
love will be her portion in the world below, for she was
brave. To her, Admetos, you were bound by bonds of love.
Then will you be less brave?

Glory is her right,
Admetos. Do not let Alcestis' grave be numbered   1260
among the ordinary dead. Make her grave a shrine;
honor it as men would honor gods—a holy place
beside the road where those who journey kneel and pray.
The traveler will see her grave and, turning off,
will say of her, "She gave her life to save another.
She is a blessèd spirit now, and so may also bless.
In homage men will kneel before her grave and pray:

(*all together, kneeling*)

"Hail, Lady, mistress of mercy, by your bravery and love,
bless us and be gracious."

                              Enter HERAKLES, *followed by a veiled girl.*

HERAKLES Admetos,
                    when a man is angry with his friend,   1270
              he should speak his mind frankly and freely;
              not keep his feelings smouldering inside.
              As your friend, I thought I had the right
              to stand beside you in your hour of need
              and prove my loyalty.
              But you misled me;
              you deliberately concealed the truth:
              instead of telling me that Alcestis was dead,
              you let me think that you were burying a stranger.
              Then you made me welcome in your unhappy house,   1280
              you gave me food and drink, as though nothing
              had happened here, nothing at all.

There you were, in mourning for your wife,
while I, like a clod, was wreathing my head with flowers,
pouring long libations to the happy gods, getting
drunk. *Drunk* at a time like this!
But how was I to know?
It was *wrong* of you, Admetos, wrong, I tell you,
to treat a friend this way. But let it pass.
You have sorrows enough, old friend.   1290

Listen: I have a reason for returning.

(*indicating the veiled girl standing behind him*)

You see this woman?
Do me a favor: Keep her here for me,
in your care, until I finish with my mission
in Thrace. I will come for her on my return,
after I have killed Diomedes, and captured his horses.
But if I don't come back—Heaven avert the omen!—
then keep the girl as a servant in your house:
my gift to you. And no small gift, either.
This woman wasn't easily won, Admetos.   1300

ADMETOS Where did you win her, Herakles?

HERAKLES Not far from your house, I happened to pass by a place
where athletic games were being held, contests
open to all comers. And the prizes offered
were very tempting. Well, in a word,
I entered the contest and I won the prize—
this woman here.
The winners in the minor events won horses.
But in boxing and wrestling the prizes were oxen—
and they threw in the girl as a bonus   1310
Well, as luck would have it, there I was,
and it seemed a shame to lose such splendid prizes.

So here she is. Now, as I said, Admetos,
I'd like you to keep her. Take care of her. She's worth it.
And she's not stolen either, if that's what you're thinking.
I won her fair and square in a damned hard fight.
Someday, Admetos, you may be glad I did.

ADMETOS   Herakles,
            my reason for concealing my wife's death from you
            was neither disrespect nor any lack of love.
            God knows,
            I had troubles enough without driving you away   1320
            to look for shelter somewhere else.
            Alcestis' death is mine to mourn. Mine alone.
            My sorrow is enough.

            As for this woman here,
            I beg you, my lord, if you can somehow manage it,
            please, take her somewhere else.
            Give her to some friend who is not in mourning.
            Tell him to keep her. You have many friends in Pherai.
            But please, please,
            don't remind me of my loss. Seeing this woman here,   1330
            here in Alcestis' house, day in, day out,
            would be more, much more, than I could bear.
            I am crushed with sorrow as it is, Herakles.
            Do not burden me with more.

            Besides,
            where in this house could a young girl stay?
            I mean, she *is* young. I can see it, Herakles,
            in her jewelry, in the style of clothes she wears.
            How could she live here, surrounded by young men?
            How could I protect her? Young men are lusty,
            their desires not easily controlled.   1340
                                            —Herakles,
            it is you, your interests, I am thinking of.

What can I do? Put her in Alcestis' room?
Take her to Alcestis' bed?
I can hear the gossip now, people in the city
saying I ran to some other woman's bed,
and betrayed the wife who died to save me.
Worse, I can hear Alcestis' voice, reproaching me
from underground. And where Alcestis is concerned,
I cannot be too scrupulous. She and she alone
deserves my love.   1350

(*turning to the veiled woman*)

       —Woman, whoever you are,
I tell you this, you look like my Alcestis,
so much like her: the same figure, the same height...
You are beautiful, too...

                              He hides his head.

Herakles,
for god's sake, take this woman away,
out of my sight! I am weak now, do not make my weakness
         worse...
Oh, looking at this girl, I seem to see
my lost Alcestis... And my heart starts churning,
and the tears—

                          He sobs unashamedly.

O gods, gods in heaven,
now, now, for the first time, I know the anguish of my life... 1360

LEADER   Sorrow: there is nothing more to say.
         It does not matter who or what we are.
         The gods do with us what they will. We must bear it.

HERAKLES   If only I had the strength, Admetos, to bring your wife
         back from the world below, back to the light,
         I would have done it.

ADMETOS   I know. But why speak of it?
The dead are dead. They never come back.
Never...

HERAKLES   Control yourself. Bear it like a man.

ADMETOS Bear it like a man? Easier said than done, Herakles.

HERAKLES Suppose you mourned her all your life, Admetos?   1370
What good would it do?

ADMETOS   No good at all.
I mourn because I must. I loved her...

HERAKLES I know:
Nothing hurts like losing those we love.

ADMETOS I lost myself when I lost her. Lost myself—
and so much more.

HERAKLES She was a beautiful woman, worthy of your love.

ADMETOS I loved her so much I do not want to live.

HERAKLES Your loss is still fresh. Time will dull the pain.

ADMETOS If time is death. Death will dull it.

HERAKLES A new wife, a new bride, will help you to forget,   1380
Admetos.

ADMETOS Silence, Herakles. Not another word.
How could you suggest such a thing?

HERAKLES   You won't remarry?
No woman, ever?

ADMETOS No woman will ever share my bed again.

HERAKLES Alcestis is dead. How does this help her?

ADMETOS Wherever Alcestis is, she deserves my honor.
I owe it to her.

HERAKLES   And I respect your feelings.
There are some, of course, who would call you foolish.

ADMETOS Let them call me anything they want.
Anything but bridegroom.   1390

HERAKLES   I admire you, Admetos.
You are loyal in love.

ADMETOS She is dead.
But I would rather die than betray her love!

HERAKLES Nobly spoken, my good Admetos.
                                        Well, then,

(*taking the veiled girl by the hand and bringing her forward*)

make this woman welcome in your generous house.

ADMETOS By your father Zeus,
I beg you, please, *no*! Anything but that.

HERAKLES You will be making a mistake, if you say No.

ADMETOS I would never forgive myself, if I said Yes.

HERAKLES Obey, Admetos.   1400
Let me have my way. The courtesy you show this girl
may serve you in your time of need.

ADMETOS   O gods,
how I wish you'd never won her in those games of yours!

89

HERAKLES Friends share and share alike.
          When I am winner, you are winner, too, Admetos.

ADMETOS   Splendid, Herakles.
          Then make this woman leave. Immediately.

HERAKLES If she must. But *look* at her first, Admetos.
          See if she should go.

ADMETOS   (*not looking*)   She *must go*.
          You won't be angry with me, will you, Herakles?

HERAKLES I have my reasons for insisting, Admetos.   1410

ADMETOS   I surrender. You win.
          But I disapprove. Your insistence displeases me.

HERAKLES You may forgive me soon. Humor me for now.

ADMETOS   If I must, I must.

          (*to Attendants*)

                    —Servants, take this woman inside.

HERAKLES Slaves?
          No, I will not surrender this girl to slaves.

ADMETOS   Then take her in yourself.

HERAKLES   No, she is yours,
          Admetos. I will not give this woman to anyone but you.

ADMETOS   And I refuse to touch that woman's hand.
          Let her go inside by herself.

HERAKLES (*taking* ADMETOS *by the right arm*)
                              No, Admetos.

I have faith in your right hand—and yours alone.   1420

ADMETOS (*unsuccessfully attempting to withdraw his arm from*
        HERAKLES' *grip*)
        My lord,
        I protest: you are forcing me against my wish.

HERAKLES Courage, Admetos. Welcome your guest.
        Here, reach out your hand. Now take her hand
        in yours.

ADMETOS (*reluctantly stretching out his hand, but carefully*
        averting his face)
             Here is my hand.

HERAKLES   Good gods, man,
        the way you act you'd think she were some Gorgon
        to turn you to stone.

        (*gently and ceremoniously, he joins the hands of* ADMETOS
            and ALCESTIS)

        You have her?

ADMETOS   I do.

HERAKLES   Then keep her, Admetos.
        She is yours, to have and to hold.
        Someday, Admetos,
        you will know your kindness was not wasted
        on the son of Zeus, your good friend and grateful guest.   1430

                He raises ALCESTIS' *veil.*

        Now, Admetos, look. Look at her.
        Doesn't she look a little like your own lost Alcestis?

           ADMETOS *stares in silent disbelief.*

Rejoice, old friend.
Be happy. Your day of mourning is over.

ADMETOS O god, gods in heaven!
This is some miracle I see, impossible, incredible!
Oh, is it you? You, Alcestis? Is it *really* you?
Or is this just some mockery, some sweet illusion
sent me by the gods?

HERAKLES No mockery, Admetos,   1440
but your own wife, in flesh and blood, your own
lost Alcestis!

ADMETOS How do I know this is not some ghost from underground?

HERAKLES I am your friend, Admetos,
not some vulgar trafficker in sorcery and ghosts.

ADMETOS But I buried her today... How can this be?
Is it really Alcestis?

HERAKLES   The very same Alcestis.
I am not surprised you find it strange.

ADMETOS Can I touch her? Speak to her?
Can she breathe? Does she feel and hear?

HERAKLES Speak to her, Admetos.   1450
You have what you wanted. You have it all.
Take it.

ADMETOS Alcestis!   O Alcestis
eyes I love   o sweetest face
these dear hands I never thought to hold again!
You are mine   so incredibly   mine
again   again!

HERAKLES Again, Admetos. And may no jealous god envy you
your happiness.

ADMETOS   O my noblest, kindest friend!
                Dear son of great Zeus, may Heaven bless you.
                May the great god who fathered you guard you
                and keep you safe, as you saved me,   1460
                you alone, and gave me back my life.

                But tell me:
                how did you bring Alcestis back to the light?

HERAKLES I fought with the god who had her in his power.

ADMETOS Death!
                Where did you find the god?

HERAKLES   Beside the grave.
                I took him by surprise, then threw him to the ground.

ADMETOS Ah.
                But why is Alcestis so still? Why can't she speak?

HERAKLES Until three days have passed,
                and the bitter stain of death has disappeared,
                she is forbidden to speak.   1470

                Now, Admetos, take her in.
                And in the future treat your guests and those you love
                as they deserve.

                And so, goodbye.
                My master Eurystheus is waiting in Argos,
                and I have labors to perform.

ADMETOS Stay with us, Herakles. My house is yours.

HERAKLES Another time, Admetos.
                I have work to do. Work that cannot wait.

ADMETOS Success go with you, friend.   1480
         But when your work is done, come back and be
         our guest.

                                        Exit HERAKLES.

         —To all my subjects and fellow citizens,
         I here and now proclaim a feast of thanks and praise
         to celebrate the happiness of this great event.
         Let the high altars blaze and smoke with sacrifice.
         From this day forth we must remake our lives,
         and make them better than they were before.

         Happiness is mine, and now I know it.

                         Exit ADMETOS, *with* ALCESTIS, *into the palace.*

CHORUS   The gods have many forms.
         The gods bring many things   1490
         to their accomplishment.
         And what was most expected
         has not been accomplished.
         But god has found his way
         for what no man expected.
         So ends the play.

                                        Exeunt omnes.

NOTES

Greek plays are not, like modern plays, divided into a given number of acts. Their effective structural unit is the *episode*, which contains everything lying between the choral lyrics (*stasima*). The *prologue* contains not only the initial expository speech but all the action prior to the entrance of the Chorus. The first choral song is called the *parodos* (from the "entrance" of the Chorus). A monody is the lyric song (sometimes recitative) of a single character; the lyric exchange between a character and the Chorus is called a *kommos*. The last episode, called the *exodos* (from the "exit" of the Chorus), contains everything after the final *stasimon*. There was no fixed or even customary number of episodes and *stasima*. Characteristic of ancient drama, and especially of Euripides, is the *agon*, a carefully structured (often schematically elaborated and counterpointed) confrontation between characters, frequently of an adversary nature. (Examples of the *agon* in *Alcestis* are the delicate "deathbed" exchange between Alcestis and Admetos and the angry debate between Admetos and his father Pheres.)

It is important for the modern reader to remember that Greek drama was a *masked* drama, and that the masks not only "distanced" both characters and action but mediated the character's condition and psychology and even the "generic" quality of the action. In the vast space of the Greek theater, masks—supported by costume, stylized gesture, and metrical and rhetorical conventions—made it possible for the dramatist, at one blow, to identify his characters and "place" them—in their condition, ago, and sex—vis-à-vis one another. If we can trust ancient (though late) sources, the masks were devices of "modal" inflection, means of stating the crucial generic facts. Thus a "sallow" mask indicated that its wearer was "in love or unfortunate"; other masks—masks with squalid features, matted or disheveled hair—indicated extreme suffering or derangement; an old man was instantly identified by his white beard, a youth or ephebe by his beardlessness, etc. Women's headgear (coifs, fillets, etc.), adornment, clothing (cf. *Alcestis* 1337 / 1050) indicated whether the wearer was young or old, rich or poor, married or unmarried. By these means the age, condition, and sex of a character were at all times theatrically *visible*. This generic visibility is crucial, since it both excludes intimate naturalism and imposes a generic account of human existence. This generic account, we should note, is quite compatible with a rich, complex psychology; the psychology, however, is not individualistic, but generic and even metaphysical. Since intimate expression and gesture—winks, nods, frowns, "body language"—were not theatrically visible, they had to be indicated verbally, by means of dramatic speech. The language and diction of Greek drama are, of course, highly rhetorical (as well as incredibly rich in metrical and syntactical nuance), and this rhetoric is designed to support the masking convention both by reinforcing its generic aspirations and also compensating for the loss of expressive means imposed by it. For this reason—its uncolloquial "elevation" and its complexity of nuance and metrical complexity—it is the despair of translators. We simply do not possess the apposite modern poetics.

A word of caution. Too much has been said, especially in theatrical handbooks, of the "hieratic" qualities of Greek drama. Elevated it clearly was; but priestly and hieratic, surely not. Increasingly, scholars now regard the familiar notion of Greek drama—with its stiff, "ritualistic" mannikins, its high shoes, and grimacing Halloween masks—as a stereotype based, not on fifth-century, but Hellenistic and Graeco-Roman, theatrical practice. As far as can be ascertained, fifth-century actors did not wear high buskins, grotesque masks, or stiffly ornate clothing. That is, fifth-century practice, though clearly "elevated" by modern or even Elizabethan standards, was based upon a dignified—but essentially representational—realism. As so often, the practice of the "great age" is distorted by the reverence accorded it by epigones, and this reverence is then passed on as an authentic account of "classical" practice.

Finally, the modern reader should constantly bear in mind the immense complexity of Greek drama—a complexity that sharply differentiates it from almost any other drama we know of. He should remember, for instance, that Greek drama is, in terms of its metrics, quite incredibly subtle, supple, and rich (and, further, that these subtleties were evidently appreciated by an audience whose aural sophistication, wholly eartrained, must have been astonishing). We should also remember that these metrics are constantly involved with dance movements (of which, unfortunately, we know almost nothing); and, further, that these dances were visual embodiments of feelings which, precisely because *kinetically* embodied, could reinforce words and also move beyond the words and so express what words could not. To dance we must also add the presumably crucial—but irreparably lost—dimension of music. If we cannot even imagine now what this music sounded like, we should at least be aware that Greek drama tends—increasingly, as the fifth century drew to a close—toward the condition of music; that, in a very real sense, this was operatic drama. Moreover, if Euripidean practice can be taken as representative, music, like dance, was used not as a decorative add-ition to language, but to express what language could not. We can tolerate quite incredible silliness in a libretto or an aria simply because the music, in the hands of a great composer, transcends the words it pretends to mediate; becomes, as we like to say, pure feeling. We shall never know what Greek drama was like at the ultimate verge of feelings, at the point (cf. the Note on the stage direction following 503 / 393–403) when words fail altogether; but we should never read a monody or choral lyric or *kommos* without remembering that these pieces were written to be *sung*. We should also perhaps remember that they were sung, not only by the actor, but later, after the performance, by the audiences who heard them (like those Athenian sailors who, accord-ing to tradition, spent the night before a dreaded battle, singing songs from Euripides' *Andromeda*); in short, that Greek drama was not a Mandarin drama but, like Shakespeare or nineteenth-century Italian opera, one of the few truly great popular art forms the world has ever known.

1–116 / 1–76 *Prologue*

1–16 / 1–7 *Apollo's prologue* I have deliberately pointed up and expanded Apollo's language here, and the literal-minded reader may reasonably wish to know why.

If I am right in my view of the play, Apollo's language and condition here (a *god compelled* to be a *slave*) are meant to be starkly contrasted with the case of Admetos (a *mortal* man *exempted* from *death*). The contrasting is, I believe, too vivid and schematic to be anything but deliberate. In large part the vividness of the contrasting depends upon our understanding that, to the Greek mind, god is defined as a being that does not suffer; man, in contrast, is a suffering thing. Here, for effect, Euripides deliberately reverses the common situation: Apollo is the "suffering servant," Admetos the "deathless mortal." The apparent para-dox is of course a device of emphasis.

The contrasting here is essentially a contrast *a fortiori*; the man and the god, so different in powers and condition, define each other in opposed weakness and strength, doom and exemption. Such contrasting is commonplace in Greek literature, as we should expect; in an aristocratic culture, the weak are instructed, exampled, in their modalities and fates, by those stronger than themselves. In the *Iliad* Achilles tries to accept his own death by arguing that "even Herakles"—a stronger hero than Achilles—had to die; later, Achilles urges his victim Lykaon to accept *his death* without fuss because better men than Lykaon have died. To a Greek audience such modal contrasts were, I believe, accepted easily and naturally. Moderns still employ—and can still respond to—moral argument *a fortiori*, but it is hardly second nature. Tolstoy's Ivan Ilych, for instance, convinces himself of his mortality, not by the power of example, but by the force of a syllogism: "Caius is a man, men are mortal, therefore..."

Unless verbally stressed and pointed up, this kind of contrast is apt to be lost in a modern dramatic performance. Not only is it unfamiliar, but in performance we cannot, as in a poem or a novel, return to the words; they must do their work now or not at all. And in a play like this—a modal play, I would argue, which appropriately begins with a violent modal contrast—the emphasis seemed to me too important to be lost to worries about excessively "interpretative" translation. The evidence is *there*, in the actual language, in the shaping of the thought. We will *hear* it, in the Greek, in the unmistakable humiliation and indignation of Apollo; in the constant language of service, compulsion, doom, endurance: "I endured [*etlēn*]...although a god [*theos per ōn*]...a serf's table [*thēssan trapedzan*]...for Zeus compelled [*ēnangkasen*] me...to serve a mortal man [*thēteuein...thnētoi*]...." And, if we hear it, we are likelier to hear the obsessive modal language of the play elsewhere, and to note the recurrent modal contrasting, all designed to throw Admetos' crucial exemption into the sharpest relief.

7–8 / 3–4 *The author of my shame was Zeus. He killed / my son Asklepios*... According to Pindar (*Pythian* 3), Asklepios had offended Zeus by restoring the dead to life, thereby threatening the gods' prerogative of immortality. In the thematic structure of the play, Asklepios' "conquest of death" provides a parallel to Herakles' contest with Death and, ultimately, to Alcestis' *aretē* in confronting Death by dying for her husband.

23 / 12 *I outwitted the Fates* By getting them drunk, according to Aeschylus (*Eum.*, 723ff.).

60 / 38 *Don't be afraid, Death* The ironic note is unmistakable, and typically Euripidean. So, too, is the abrupt transition from Death's appropriately portentous style to Apollo's delicate banter and sophistic legalisms. The director who wants to produce Euripides must be prepared to cope with a dramatic master who, like Chekhov, delights in mixing modes usually kept distinct, in flickering, lambent irony, in transparent parody; who constantly crosses tragedy with comedy, and undercuts his own solemnity with self-mockery. And nowhere is this pleasure more in evidence than in this play.

83 / 55 *the younger my victim* The preference of Death for a younger victim is a common motif of folklore. Underlying this belief (and the ritual of human sacrifice) is the conviction in primitive agricultural communities that the Earth (which includes the spirits of the dead and "the old ones") can only be fertilized by the blood of the living. The Earth is thought of as a womb which is quickened or renewed by the spermatic action of blood. The younger and fresher the blood, the more potent its fertilizing effect, as can be glimpsed in an Aztec poem on a feast of human sacrifice: "The youth chosen was of radiant countenance / of good understanding / quick and clean of body / slender like a reed . . . / He who was chosen was entirely without defect" (William Brandon, *The Magic World, American Indian Songs and Poems*, pp. 15ff.). So, too, in Euripides' *Hecuba*, Achilles' ghost cannot be laid until it receives fresh blood; and it characteristically wants the vigorous blood of the young Polyxena, not that of old Hecuba. Indeed, the persistent theme of *youthful* sacrifice in Euripides rests not only upon the notorious idealism of the young but upon the refusal of the chthonic powers to be appeased by anything less vital. Hence Death here regards it as detrimental to his honor (*geras*) that Alcestis' death should be deferred until she is old; and Death is in this respect an aristocrat of the old school, quite untempted by the mercenary bribe of the plutocratic Apollo. (We may assume that Death would have grumbled had Admetos' mother or father offered to make the supreme sacrifice.)

In later times, with the progress of morality and the eclipse of the old chthonic religion, the human sacrifice became, it would seem, first a crippled or deformed victim, and finally an animal. In modern times Death himself has been eclipsed and his office transferred to (old) politicians. See, for instance, John Peale Bishop's "And When the Net Was Unwound Venus Was Found Ravelled with Mars":

> This was in the time of the long war
> when the old deliberated and always rose
> to the same decision: More of the young
> must die.

117–190 / 77–135 *Parodos*

147 / 99–100 *where is the cleansing water . . .*   In a house of mourning it was customary to set a basin of pure spring-water at the door so that visitors could, when leaving, purify themselves from the pollution of death. Presumably for the same reason Apollo must leave Admetos' house, lest his divinity be "stained" by death.

150 / 101–2 Custom also prescribed that mourners should place a lock of their hair on the tomb of the departed (as in the recognition-scene in Aeschylus' *Choephoroe*, 167ff.). The present passage is the only one indicating that it was also the practice to dedicate a lock of hair in the house of the deceased.

166–68 / 115–16 *at holy Ammon's / healing touch, the dying desert makes / a miracle of green*   The Greek gives merely "at the waterless shrine of Ammon." Expansion is required to make the underlying religious and pictorial sense effectively vivid. The great oracular shrine of the Egyptian god Amen-Ra (Ammon) lay in the Libyan desert at the oasis of Siwah. W. S. Hadley cites what is probably an early Baedeker account of the place: "Siwah is a little paradise: round the dark blue mirror of its lakes there are luxurious palm-woods, and orchards full of oranges, figs and olives." To a traveler approaching the shrine from the bleak, waterless desert, the green oasis must have seemed the miraculous revelation of a life-giving god—the very image, to despairing eyes, of sudden life and hope. A Greek audience would have known about the site and work of the shrine either from the Greek inhabitants of Cyrenaica or the temple attendants in (Greek) Thebes, where Ammon had a statue and a cult.

180 / 127 *death-tamed and -broken men*   My effort to get the sense of the Greek phrase *dmathentas* (literally, those who have been "tamed" or "subdued," a metaphor or euphemism for "the dead"). The name "Admetos," as noted in the Introduction, means "the untamed one"—i.e. the man exempted from death. (Cf. Bacchylides, *fr.* 47 Ed., who, speaking of the gods, says that they are, unlike men, "untamed," "unbroken," by cruel diseases.) So, too, at 1247 / 980–81, the Chorus says that Necessity "tames" or "breaks" (*damadzei*) the iron of the Chalybes.

194–287 / 141–212 *First episode*

208–9 / 149 *She will be buried as we knew her . . . a queen*   Literally: "The adornments [*kosmos*] are ready in which her husband will bury her." *Kosmos* means both "beauty" and "adornment" (i.e. funeral adornments, the expensive gold-stitched robes, jewelry, perfumes, etc. customarily buried with the dead). It is the idea of beauty *and* costliness that makes the Leader exclaim, literally: "Let her know then that she dies with all *glory...*". The custom of burying the dead in golden splendor caused ancient legislators to pass laws against excessive funeral expenditure—the ancient equivalent of "conspicuous consumption." Both in ancient times and now, *kosmos* was, to the Greek mind, very much the concern of the living. In nineteenth-century Smyrna the traveler A. W. Kinglake observed, "A Greek woman wears her whole fortune upon her person, in the shape of jewels, or gold coin... enabling a suitor to *reckon*, as well as to admire, the objects of his affection" (*Eothen*, ch. v).

226 / 162-63 *"Bright goddess who guards my home"* That is, Hestia, goddess and incarnation of the domestic hearth.

288-324 / 213-43 *First stasimon*

313 / 233 *Alcestis, supported by Admetos...* It is of course impossible to ascertain the appearance of Admetos and Alcestis: their clothing, masks, etc. But they should not, for want of consideration, be allowed to fade into that indeterminate life reserved for the characters of a theater whose acting conventions and traditions have not survived and can only be conjecturally restored. The director who confronts the task of staging the *Alcestis* simply cannot avoid making a decision; and it would be better for him and for audiences alike if scholars could be trained to visualize performance.

Can we, in fact, visualize Admetos and Alcestis? What kinds of masks did they wear? How old are they? In a modal theater—i.e. a theater based upon the generic—such questions are crucial. It makes, for instance, all the difference in the world whether we see Antigone as a young woman or (as I believe) a very young girl; the age of Pentheus very seriously affects our understanding of the *Bacchae*. Obviously certainty is impossible, but there are reasonably strong hints.

Alcestis, for instance, seems to be young, quite young. Admetos at line 1336 / 1049 calls her *nea* (young); and, although she has two small children, it is also true that Greek girls, especially of noble family, married early, around the age of fourteen. That is, Alcestis may be no older than eighteen or nineteen; she would be, in that case, the "young matron." Admetos, I believe, is also young. Pheres (at line 854 / 698) ironically calls him a *kalos neanias* (i.e. "handsome youth"—with a sarcastic suggestion of ephebic beauty), and one can reasonably ask how such description could have been meaningfully applied unless it tallied with the mask and appearance. Admetos is twice called "boy" (*pais*), by the Chorus in remonstrance, and by Pheres in scorn. There may also be visual evidence of actual repertory practice. In portraying scenes from Greek drama, fourth-century Apulian vase painters, according to T. B. L. Webster, probably conveyed the general ideas and outlines of a repertory practice. Thus in the earliest extant portrayal of the play, on an Apulian loutrophoros of the late fourth century, we see, standing beside a buxom, seated Alcestis, the sorrowful figure of Admetos, depicted as a handsome and *beardless* young man. (For illustration and comment, see A. D. Trendall and T. B. L. Webster, *Illustrations of Greek Drama*, London, 1971, p. 75.) Finally, there is the suggestive fact of Admetos' general inexperience (the Chorus at line 1183 / 927 calls him *apeirokakos*, "inexperienced in suffering")—an inexperience that in Greek thought is insistently associated with youth and that, in my opinion, mediates the portrayal of Admetos throughout the play.

312–529 / 234–434 *Second episode*

325–64 / 244–72 *O Sun / Sweet shining light . . .* Alcestis' words here are in lyric meters and spoken (or sung) with the poetic intensity of the dying. Admetos, in sharp contrast, responds in the more banal iambics of dialogue. Later (365 / 273), as he begins to realize what he is losing, he, too, will turn to lyric anapests and a new level of intensity. Ultimately, in the *kommos* (1114–1269 / 861–1005), when he finally and fully comprehends his own anguish, there will be no mistaking the intensity of his language and feelings.

374–75 / 279 *by your love we pray you / live* An effort to get the full sense of the concentrated (but quite elusive) Greek. Literally, Admetos says, "For we reverence [*seboumetha*] your love [*philian*]." While it is true, as Dale points out, that *sebein* need not mean "to revere or worship [as a god]," the utter dependence stated by Admetos in the previous line ("in you we live in you we die") suggests that the strong (i.e. worshipful) sense of *sebein* is being employed here. And this seems in part vindicated by the Chorus's recognition of Alcestis as a "blessèd spirit" (*makaira daimōn*) at line 1266 / 1003.

375–424 / 280–325 *Admetos, I am dying* The abrupt tonal shift from the intensity of Alcestis' lyrics to this comparatively controlled and reasoned deathbed dialogue with Admetos is understandably disconcerting to modern readers (and directors) of Greek plays. We can only say, with Dale, that Greek tragedy, and Euripides in particular, has "many scenes where a situation is realized first in its lyric, then in its iambic aspect, that is to say, first emotionally, then in its reasoned form." This alternation of lyric and reasoned dimensions—as though we were shown *seriatim* the facets of the situation—must be regarded as a convention which, however difficult it may be for moderns to accept, apparently did not trouble ancient audiences.

503 / 393–403 *Sobbing and crying, the children throw themselves . . .* At this point in the Greek text there is a monody assigned to Alcestis' little boy, Eumelos. I have excised this song in its entirety, not because the passage is spurious or doubtful, but because, to modern taste, and, without music, it is intolerably maudlin. For those readers who might wish to know the words actually *sung* by little Eumelos, I offer the following literal rendering:

Alas for my fate! Mother has gone below. She is no longer in the light, Father. She has left me, poor woman, and orphaned my life. Look, look to her eyelids, at her arms hanging limp. Listen to me, Mother, listen. It is I, Mother, who call to you—your little fledgling, pressing my lips to yours. I am young, Father, left alone and forsaken by my dear mother. I have suffered pitifully, and you, dear, sister, have suffered with me. Ah, Father, your marriage was all in vain. You failed to reach the goal of old age with her. She died before you died. Now, Mother, with your going away, our house has been destroyed.

Euripides' purpose in this monody is clearly pathos, a *musical* resolution designed to stress the final poignance of Alcestis' death, as well as its impact upon Admetos' whole house. Pathos of this kind and degree, we must assume, was emotionally satisfying to Greek audiences. Athenian juries, for instance, expected, and evidently enjoyed, highly pathetic appeals from defendants; indeed, plaintiffs often capped their formal defenses by bringing into court their wives and children, sobbing and wailing, in order to work upon the feelings of the jurors.

Here, unmistakably, ancient and modern taste diverge. It is revealing, for instance, to compare Eumelos' baroque grief with a terse and tight-lipped sequence in Kurosawa's great film *Ikiru*. The camera shows us a car in which a small boy and his father are following a black hearse; the hearse holds the body of the boy's mother. As the hearse suddenly turns a corner, momentarily disappearing, the boy says, solemnly and matter-of-factly, "Daddy, Mother's leaving us behind." Elliptic and low-keyed, this is presumably as much as modern audiences are prepared to tolerate in the ticklish genre of childish grief (as opposed, say, to sentiment in romantic love, where Greek taste was positively chaste and severe in comparison).

Readers should also bear in mind that Eumelos' monody, like all monodies, was meant to be sung; and that in these monodies Greek drama is much closer to Italian opera than to Shakespeare or poetic drama. Given good music and virtuosity in the singer, Eumelos could have overcome the limitations of his actual words as easily as Handel's Julius Caesar succeeds in overcoming the feeble libretto and the absurdity of a castrated imperator. Indeed, one has merely to transcribe Eumelos' words into conventional operatic Italian (*Ahimé, il mio crudel destin! . . . Giovin son' o padre mio, sconsolato ed abbandonato*," etc.) to realize that the words are in fact librettist's Greek; that they belong essentially to music and are effective only insofar as their expression is finally musical. To poetry they have no pretension.

530–68 / 435–75 Second stasimon

Farewell, Alcestis . . . My translation of this lovely ode is admittedly "interpretative," designed to point up the enabling conceit and the poetic implications of details the Greekless reader could not be expected to glean from a literal translation. Thus I have stressed what I believe to be the central poetic figure of the ode—the bright image of Alcestis, whom Death would have "extinguished" in the sunless world of Hades, but whose *aretē*, in its deathlessness, cannot be eclipsed; then, again, in the second strophe, Alcestis merges with the moon which, like Alcestis, carries through the darkness the recurrent reflection of the sun's "light." Such stress may seem to some a trespass against the reader's rights: a tendentious turning. But I am concerned less with readers here than with audiences—audiences who cannot for obvious reasons be expected to cope with conventions which, because unfamiliar, tend to be elusive, especially in "theatrical time." The choral dances and the music which presumably mediated the meaning of the words are gone, and the translator must, if he can, compensate for their loss. There is, in any case, no lack of literal versions of the ode; the dissatisfied reader is invited to consult one of those.

The three notes immediately following are designed to demonstrate to the skeptical that the strategies adopted here are considered, even meditated, techniques.

532–33 / 436–37 *those on whom the sweet light never shines: unseeing / and unseen* An example of translation by expansion or intruded gloss. Literally, the Greek reads: "May you be happy in the sunless house, in the halls of Hades." The modern reader without Greek is unlikely to know that Hades was commonly derived from the word meaning "unseen" (*a-idēs*). The dead are those who do not "see the light" (the common idiom for "life"); and when the living die, they are extinguished in every sense: neither seeing nor seen. That this play on the meaning of Hades is present in the ode is confirmed not only by the persistent light imagery,

but by the word "sunless" in apposition with "Hades." None of this word-play, so crucial to our understanding of the ode, is visible in a literal version; to relegate such explanations to footnotes and commentary seems, at least in this case, a counsel of pointless despair.

533 *We shall not see your like again* This line is my own contribution, but it is not, I think, gratuitous, since it is implied in the *valedictory* quality of the preceding lines—a quality conveyed by a rich conventional language of valediction—a language quite lost to us.

534 / 37–38 *O Death, in that dark tangle of your mind* An effort, obviously conjectural and risky, to *think* my way *beneath* the poet's description of Hades here as "black-haired" (*melangehaitas*). Clearly, the epithet reinforces the etymological meaning of Hades (see Note on 532–33 / 436–37), but it also seemed to advance the conceit. Hades (or Death), it struck me was "black-haired" not only because of his dusky kingdom, but because of the apparent obscurity, to men, of his purpose. Why, after all, *should* Alcestis die? Since the point of the ode as a whole, and of this sentence in particular, is to "cry defiance to Death," it seems appropriate that the Chorus should ask Hades, bent on his obscure purpose, to *recognize* the distinction and (shining) *aretē* of Alcestis. The "dark tangle" of Death's mind is, I should confess, the trouvaille, uprooted from a very different context, of a great English religious writer.

569–678 / 476–567 *Third episode*

571 / 481 *Obligation, friend* I have rearranged in order to get the sense of "compulsion" at which the dramatist is aiming. Literally, the Chorus asks Herakles, "To what wandering are you yoked?" (The yoke, in Greek drama, is a persistent image or metaphor of necessity.) There is no way of conveying this is English without clumsiness or muting the point ("Where are you bound?" conveys the proper sense, but the metaphorical sense of "bound" is dead). For this reason I have transferred the statement of necessity to Herakles' reply.

As in the opening speech of Apollo, so here, too, Euripides moves swiftly to strike the important, thematic note. Like Apollo, and despite the paternity of Zeus and his great physical strength, Herakles is bound to a life of labor and toil for a master, Eurystheus of Tiryns.

600–1 / 500 *Rough, uphill / all the way* The depiction of Herakles' life as one of arduous, patient struggle and obstinate fortitude (*tlēmosynē*) is a commonplace of classical myth and art. On the metopes of the great temple of Zeus at Olympia, Herakles' labors were portrayed as a parable of the ordeals imposed upon civilized (and civilizing) men. Plato speaks admiringly of the (fifth-century) sophist Prodikos because he had presented Herakles as the hero who had chosen the arduous "road" of moral action as opposed to a life of pleasure and ease.

622 / 519 *Both. Both. I am in agony, Herakles...* With characteristic economy, Euripides makes Admetos' deception of Herakles here do double duty. Not only does he persuade Herakles to accept hospitality in a house of mourning, but in the process of deception we see him already acting out, exploring, the remorse and loss he is beginning to feel. His own loss is vivid enough that it brings him, for the first time, face to face with the transcience and "dreamlike" quality of human existence; death and life seem to converge. So, too, he anticipates his own later discovery that, in Alcestis' death, he lost his own life.

636 / 532 *Was she related to you?* Herakles' question and Admetos' answer provide a good example of Euripides' skill in achieving emotional tension and economy by means of ambiguity. Asked whether the dead woman was related (*sungenēs*) or a stranger (*othneios*), Admetos answers that she was a stranger, but then, quickly and equivocally, adds, "But she was connected [*anankaia*] with my house." The noun *anankē* (of which *anankaia* is the adjectival form) means, in fifth-century usage, both "necessity" and "kinship." (The ambiguity is not accidental, of course; "kinship," because it expresses a *natural bond*, and because the language of social organization precedes philosophical language, is presumably the root-meaning; cf. Latin *necessetudo*, which exhibits the same ambiguity. Durkheimians would not be surprised.) Thus while ostensibly deceiving Herakles, Admetos reveals, through dramatic irony, his own, fresh awareness of his dependence upon Alcestis: the anguish of his newly found need. Admetos, we realize, is beginning to speak the language of necessity—to "think mortal thoughts."

651–52 / 545 *Impossible / You must stay* The overbearing quality of Admetos' language should be stressed. A few lines earlier Admetos exhibited a new awareness; now, confronted by a problem touching his honor as host—i.e. with traditional *noblesse oblige*—he begins to talk in the imperious, overbearing way of a man who has never known a check upon his will; who (unlike Herakles) commands but does not obey. In the finale Herakles will, in a spirit of strict (but friendly) "poetic" justice, overbearingly impose upon Admetos the duty of hospitality to a new "guest," the veiled woman who is Alcestis.

Modal psychology can be, I am convinced, no less complex and sophisticated than modern individual psychology. Here, in Admetos' veering between two metaphysical attitudes, between the new mortal knowledge of **626–27** / 525 and the old mortal ignorance shown here, we have a modal version of what would now be called "simultaneously conflicting attitudes." Medea's famous soliloquy in which she debates with (and within) herself whether she should kill her children is often hailed as a psychological novelty; but it is only novel because scholars think they see in it the advent of our psychology. In point of fact, the psychology involved is at least as old as Homer, but its antiquity should not blind us to the sophistication of Euripides' application, the *individual* genius with which an old psychology is here inflected and employed.

671 / 560 *And Argos is a thirsty place* "Thirsty Argos"—thirsty because the land was parched and often drought-stricken—is an epic usage. Given Herakles' fondness for wine, especially in this play, it may not be amiss to suggest, as I have, that Herakles' "thirsty Argos" was more related to Dionysos than Demeter.

679–722 / 568–605 *Third stasimon*

Hospitality is here . . . My strategy with this lovely ode is less radical than in the first *stasimon* (see note on **530–68** / 435–75). Here and there I have heightened, but in order to provide the links and stresses that, in my opinion, any likely modern audience would require. The scale of Admetos' hospitality—imposed in part by timeless aristocratic practice—may be accessible to us as a kind of grand-seigneurial *largesse* (though *le grand seigneur* is hardly a flourishing species). We are much less familiar with the notion of houses (and hosts) that have gods as their gardeners, and even less familiar with the religious implications of such arrangements. In its final stanza, this Chorus expresses its fear of, and admiration for, Admetos' magnificently excessive hospitality (as does the Servant at **1028** / 809). But *structurally* this hospitality is, in this ode, profoundly linked to the fact that a *man*, Admetos, had a *god* for guest (and servant); and also that Apollo's presence *blessed* the land, enriching its fertility and, indeed, imposing upon the countryside a kind of Saturnalia in which predator and prey, wild and civil, man and nature, are miraculously reconciled. The god's presence also affects Admetos by conferring upon him the attributes of the gods: happiness, wealth, deathlessness (or deferrable mortality); and we see these divine effects in the hospitality (as well as the lordliness and "high" generosity) of the prospering Admetos. To the Greeks, such prosperity was enviable but also dangerous, since heaven is jealous of human happiness. Hence the ambivalence of the Chorus here; it fears for Admetos' excessiveness, but recognizes in it the exaggeration of a *noble* trait and the *explicit* favor of heaven.

703–4 / 589–90 *the clear blue waters / of Boibias* Both now and in ancient times, Boibias (or Boibeis) was a stagnant body of water. The conventional epithet *kallinaon* ("clear-flowing," "limpid") here applied to it has troubled commentators for obvious reasons. But the point is surely not some vague "poetic effect," but the miraculous results of Apollo's presence: marshes become limpid lakes, lynx and lamb lie down together, etc.

718 / 601 *Greatness of soul* . . . An attempt to render the quite untranslatable Greek word *aidōs*. In its full range *aidōs* means "self-respect," "respect for others," and, ultimately, "compassion." The man of *aidōs* respects, as we would say, "the rights" of others. But *aidōs* is essentially an aristocratic virtue; the man of *aidōs* is usually a man from whom, because he is powerful and wealthy (as well as noble), the weak (e.g., the suppliant) can claim compassion; the guest, hospitality; the oppressed, protection, etc. It is because he is a man of *aidōs*—scrupulously and proudly so—that Admetos is so insistent that Herakles should accept his hospitality—and so vulnerable later to Herakles' insistence that Admetos should accept the "veiled girl," even though he knows that the likely result will be a violation of the *aidōs* he owes to Alcestis. "Greatness of soul" seemed to me to have the necessary "openness," as well as to provide a link to the aristocratic "greatness" that is its common prerequisite.

719 / 603 *all philosophy is in it* The Greek word is *sophia*. Only partly intellectual in content, it is also an aristocratic virtue and suggests *fineness* of feeling or perception, broadening at its widest into the *skill* of mortality, especially compassion. "Philosophy" may be too intellectual and perhaps even anachronistic; but it has, except perhaps in academic circles, the necessary breadth.

723–1226 / 606–1005 *Fourth episode* and *kommos* (1114–1187 / 861–934)

730 / 614 *Enter* PHERES *dressed in mourning black* I have transferred to the stage direction the Leader's description of Pheres' entrance: "with aged gait." In the Greek theater, even an old man's halting gait would have been hard to see; accordingly the dramatist obligingly writes the stage direction into the text.

The solemnity of Pheres' appearance—still another of those painterly groupings for which Euripides was famous in antiquity—should be stressed. Through the funereal dignity of Pheres' entrance, Euripides enhances the indecorousness of the subsequent "scene" between father and son. The purpose is not to shock, but to emphasize, through violence, the *content* of Pheres' words and, ultimately, to reveal, by contrast, the heroic dignity of Alcestis.

The ceremonial gifts would have included such things as gold or silver mirrors, vials of perfume, and other articles of a noble lady's toilette deemed useful in "the life below."

748 / 627–28 *Marriage is for most of us a losing proposition* Mercenary and tactless, especially after Pheres' expression of "sorrow," these words are designed to be jarring. The translator may mute the effect to suit the modern taste for a single, smoothly modulated texture, but it seems a mistake to distort the dramatist's intent. In the Greek, Pheres' words are as unexpected as they are mercenary. And their very coarseness gives some tincture of provocation to Admetos' violent reply.

Modern readers should realize that Euripides' delineation of Pheres seems based upon a standard classical phenomenology of old age. Pheres, that is, is typical; *generically* old. In his *Rhetoric* (2, 12–13), Aristotle gives an account of the old which comes uncannily close to Euripides' portrayal of Pheres: "They are mean-spirited, because they have been humbled by life ... They are not generous ... and they are cowardly ... and they are fond of life, especially in their declining years, since desire is directed toward what is missing and men particularly want what they do not have. And they are unduly selfish, for this, too, is meanness of spirit. And they live, not for the noble, but the expedient, and more than they should, because they are selfish. And they are more inclined to shamelessness than the opposite ... for they pay little attention to what people think. ..."

751–816 / 629–72 By any ancient standards, Admetos' speech here is shockingly violent. But its violence is largely a function of the Greek audience's strong sense of filial piety and respect for age. Admetos' anger reaches its peak when, at line 802 / 665, he says he will not assist at Pheres' funeral. Athenian law stipulated that even a father who had prostituted his son was legally entitled to be buried by that son; since Admetos' case against Pheres is less grievous, the refusal is meant to be outrageous.

There is also violence in Admetos' language. Thus we have constant anacolouthon, the choppiness of structure indicative of strong feeling, and the "abrupt asyndeton of rising passion" (Dale). The function of this verbal violence is not sensationalism or the prospect of "an interesting conflict between two egotists," but a careful effort by the dramatist to confront the audience with the conflict in its own values: on one hand, its actual (contemporary) values; on the other, the "ideal" values embodied in myth (as a residue of older cultural values). Through violence in language and structure, Euripides' tactic is to compel his audience to consider critically the quality of Admetos' traditional, mythical "heroism." He therefore hits precisely at the point—filial piety—where the audience's own operative values can be effectively enlisted against Admetos. Obviously doubts created by Admetos' conduct toward Pheres must tend to create doubts about Admetos' treatment of Alcestis (a subject on which both the received version of the myth and the "chauvinism" of the Greek male audience were either silent or complacent). Certainly the *dramatic* effect of Pheres' vigorous denunciation of Admetos' selfishness is to make it possible for the audience to see Admetos' conduct and Alcestis' sacrifice with fresh eyes.

In order to compensate for the absence of modern audiences of anything remotely resembling Greek pietas and respect for the old, I have heightened the violence of Admetos' words. What we cannot experience as an outrage to our values (because we lack the values which might be outraged) must be experienced as an affront to decorum and taste—"aesthetically," as we like to say.

768–70 / 638–40 The text is somewhat doubtful, but Admetos' point is clearly that Pheres was lacking in paternal love. He manages, ironically, thereby to raise doubts about his own legitimacy and nobility. The irony is less grotesque if the reader is aware that, for a Greek woman, the failure to produce children was grounds for divorce; hence it seems to have been fairly common for a barren woman to foist off a slave's child as her own. (cf. Aristophanes, *Thesmophoriazousae*, 502ff. and Euripides, *Phoenissae*, 31ff.).

789 / 654 *You inherited a kingdom when you were still a boy* Since almost all of Admetos' charges against Pheres ultimately rebound on Admetos, one may wonder why he taunts Pheres with this particular piece of good fortune. The likeliest explanation, I suggest, is that Admetos had himself experienced the same good fortune. If so, it would be an additional hint of Admetos' youth. In the *Bacchae*, again, old Kadmos voluntarily abdicates the throne to his young grandson, Pentheus.

854 / 698 *her gigolo* The phrase is admittedly strong, coarser than the Greek. Pheres is scornfully suggesting that Alcestis was infatuated with the sheer physical beauty of her "handsome young lover" (*kalou...neaniou*). A more accurate rendering perhaps would have been "your little Romeo" (or "Lothario"); but moderns are intolerant of anachronisms which Euripides and his audience would have accepted without qualms. Pheres' insinuations may be coarse, but their coarseness is Euripides' means of giving Pheres' words the gritty realism that his character and the situation require.

897–98 / 726 *What the hell do I care what people say of me / after I'm dead?* By fifth-century standards and the implicit values of the *Alcestis*, these are ignoble words: no man of *aretē* could have uttered them. In a very real sense Alcestis regains the light because her *aretē* makes her, at least in terms of the human memory embodied in myth and literature, immortal. Pheres' words here are, in their baseness, an obvious foil to Alcestis' nobility. But Euripides' revelation of Pheres' baseness, we should note, is carefully delayed until *after* Pheres has demolished Admetos' claims to *aretē*. In this way the two male antagonists, father and son, are allowed to damage each other, with the result that Alcestis—against all male expectation—emerges as the sole surviving victor of this *agon*. For this reason, I think, Euripides concludes the scene with a brief funeral dirge in which the Chorus praises Alcestis' heroic endurance (*schetlia*), patient bravery (*tolmēs*), nobility and generosity (*gennaia*), and *aretē* (*meg' aristē*).

904 / 731–33 Deletion of lines from a Greek play requires extreme caution. Right or wrong, I have deleted three lines from Pheres' speech here as probable interpolations, though they are metrically and lexically correct (as educated interpolations usually are). The reader may wish to judge for himself, however. In the text, Pheres goes on to say: "But you will be brought to book by her [Alcestis'] kinsmen. / If Akastos is still a man of courage, / he will avenge his sister's death." In my judgment, the threat of Akastos' vengeance is gratuitous, the kind of tidying up of minor details commonly exhibited by pedants, but rarely by great dramatists. A revenge-motif would be at odds with Euripides' clear dramatic interest in having Admetos recognize his own selfishness and guilt. Finally, the lines seem an intolerable interruption of the arc of rising violence, so visible in Pheres' words at line 881 / 717 and the matching violence of Admetos' reply.

967–1026 / 773–807 *Enter* HERAKLES, *tipsy and reeling...* My translation of Herakles' famous "drunken speech" may raise eyebrows among those who expect dignity and decorum from their Greek tragedians (if not always from Herakles). But Herakles' drunkenness here (tipsiness is a euphemism) is a dramatic fact, and too important a fact to be played down. Certainly there is no point in translating as though Herakles had taken one sherry too many and was beginning to "unwind." In details of diction but especially in its sentiments, the speech is unmistakably spoken by a drunken Herakles; if Herakles were not in fact drunk, his acute embarrassment later would be unmotivated. I have translated accordingly. Admittedly, Herakles' Greek is more correct and "sober" than my translation; but I assume that ancient dramaturgical conventions were in this respect different from ours. The ancient tragedian wrote his words and left it to the actor to inflect them; modern conventions—designed for a reading audience—tend to be rather more explicit.

1086 / 842 *Admetos' love...* The entire sentence is an intruded gloss, designed to sharpen, for the Greekless reader, what an ancient audience would have understood without being told—that is, the aristocratic punctilio involved in Herakles' promise here to restore Alcestis to Admetos. Aristocratic *aretē* is always competitive, and Herakles is determined not to be outdone by his friend and rival (in *aretē*), Admetos. If Admetos has treated Herakles with the hospitality one might give a god (and thereby failed to treat him with candor as a friend), Herakles in return proposes to respond with an even grander and more "godlike" gesture. The entire last scene clearly illustrates Herakles' friendly and aristocratic determination to force upon Admetos the same extravagant generosity (and also humiliation) that Admetos had earlier imposed upon him.

1088 / 843 *those black wings beating overhead* The MSS. reading here is *melampeplon* ("black-garbed"), but the scholiast's comment makes it clear that *his* text read "black-winged." This seems appropriate since it echoes Alcestis' image of "winged" Death at line 350 / 262. But the point goes deeper than poetic detail. Throughout the play Euripides stresses the parallelism between Alcestis and Herakles; they share the courage (*tlēmosynē*) required to confront Death—Death in person. (For the same reason I would suppose that Death's wings should be seen beating with agitation in the *agon* with Apollo.)

1130–35 / 872–77 *Take your grief inside, Admetos...* In the Greek, each of these choral lines is followed by a cry of anguish (*aiai* e e, *pheu pheu*, etc.) from Admetos. Since modern English possesses no such stylized language of grief, translation is impossible. But the reader who doubts the sincerity of Admetos' grief should be aware that here and at 1150–56 / 889–94 Admetos, in ancient performance, was reduced to inarticulate cries of grief (hence the efforts of the Chorus to rally him from excessive mourning).

1166–1187 / 903–34 *Admetos, a friend of mine once lost his son...* In the Greek, these lines are lyrical. I have resorted to prose for two reasons. First, it seemed to me important to vary a *kommos* which, without music, cannot be sustained as poetry for a stretch of nearly seventy-five lines. Second, the words spoken by the Leader at 1166 / 903 are, at least in sentiment, in their anecdotal simplicity, extremely unusual in Greek drama. In English they simply work better in simple, cadenced prose than as formal poetry. Once begun, such a style cannot be simply abandoned, so I have made Admetos answer in a similar vein.

1227–69 / 962–1005 *Fourth stasimon*

1227–69 / 962–1005 *Necessity is stone...* The culmination, in reflective, almost philosophical, choral song, of the play's crucial language of constraint and the corresponding themes of human suffering and endurance (*tlē-mosynē*) and courage (*aretē*). "Necessity" (*anankē*) is in some real sense a learned word; originally borrowed from ordinary usage, it would seem to have been applied by pre-Socratics and early sophists to phenomena—e.g., scientific causality—felt to be somehow at odds with older and more religious concepts of Fate. My translation deliberately skirts and occludes the highly self-conscious Euripidean beginning. (Literally: "I have lived with the Muses and I have soared into lofty regions and explored many learned writings, but I have discovered nothing stronger than Necessity....") Euripides' beginning is self-conscious, I think, because he is aware of the risks of introducing legislated (and possibly controversial) "intellectual" language into a work presented to a popular audience. His own modernity and honesty forbid him to use a concept which, like the older word for Fate, Moira, was freighted with unwanted or obsolete religious meaning.

    And though he speaks of Moira earlier in the play, he seems anxious here to subsume or bypass the older word in the more neutral and impersonal Anankē. For *his* purposes what mattered, I believe, is that the Chorus should express, in a striking and comprehensive way, the essential feel of the Euripidean universe: a world dominated by the operation of relentless "laws"; the loom of an ultimate Force, beyond the power of the gods themselves to change (even Zeus, according to the Chorus, must harmonize *his* will with Necessity); a Force wholly, incomprehensibly, removed from human concerns, and utterly indifferent to them as well. The gods—and perhaps dramatists—may delay or modestly obstruct the operation of this relentless and irresistible Force; but they do not in any real way affect its workings. Only against the looming of such a Force do human love, endurance, and courage become what they are here, in the close of this ode: the saving mortal skills of tragic (and also comic) survival. I do not expect all readers (or scholars) will agree with my conviction. But it is mine, and the ode, and the play, have been translated accordingly.

1253–54 / 988–90 *Even the sons of heaven fade, darkened* / *into death* The Greek for "darkened" is *skotioi*, a word which explicitly picks up the imagery of light and darkness that clusters around Alcestis' death and descent to Hades (where, the metaphors suggest, even Hades cannot eclipse the bright glory of her courage). See notes on **530–68** / 435–75,

532–33 / 436–37, and 534 / 437–38. The suggestion of the scholiast on this line, with its suggestion that we are meant to understand *skotioi paides* as equivalent to "bastard sons of heaven" should be, I think, firmly rejected.

Euripides, I should perhaps add, does compare Anankē to a sheer crag or cliff where compassion has no purchase. But the phrase "Necessity is stone," which begins the first two stanzas, is my effort to move directly to the key word and to do so in a way conducive to a feeling of formal statement. In the same way and for the same reason I have tried to resolve the first two stanzas with the terse iteration of the Chorus's later advice to Admetos: "Be patient. / Suffer and submit." Lacking music and the metrical wealth and precision available to the ancient poet, I could see no other way of making these strophes work as poetry.

1269 / 1006–7 *Enter Herakles* I have omitted as theatrically clumsy (at least in modern production) the Leader's two lines announcing Herakles' return. Literally: "Admetos, here, I think, comes Alkmene's son on his way to your hearth." The size of the Greek theater may require such "cue" lines, but in this case the lines, I think, come from the poet's need to modulate between the preceding lyrics and the resumption of the dialogue.

1270–1488 / 1008–1163 *Exodos*

1427 / 1119 *You have her?* We have here, it has been held—persuasively, I think—a deliberate echo, indeed a parody, of the ceremony of betrothal (*enguē*, literally a giving of one's hand in pledge or troth). According to the formula, the bride's father (or nymphagogue perhaps) places the bride's hand in the groom's, then asks the groom, as here, *echeis?* ("Do you take her?"). The groom replies, as here, *echō* ("I take her hand"), and the father responds: *soidze nun* ("then keep it"). The parody is of course aimed directly, with gentle malice, at Admetos' promise earlier never to take another woman (or wife) into his house.

1444 / 1128 *not some vulgar trafficker in sorcery and ghosts* Words designed to lay to rest the audience's fear—frighteningly real in the fifth century—of ghosts and the Underworld. Alcestis, Euripides assures us, is not some bloodless revenant from Hades; so, too, Admetos' house is only metaphorically Hades (insofar as Admetos' life has become a "living hell"). Unless explicitly dealt with, the spectator's fear might jeopardize the wit and delicacy of the finale as well as Euripides' serious dramatic purpose here. Shakespeare in *The Winter's Tale*, a play tantalizingly close to *Alcestis* in mood and beauty, for similar reasons warns his audience, through Paulina, that the "miraculous" resurrection of Hermione has not been accomplished by devilish arts:

> I'll make the statue move indeed, descend
> And take you by the hand: but then you'll think,
> Which I protest against, I am assisted
> By wicked powers...

1472–73 / 1147–48 *treat your guests and those you love / as they deserve* A key passage, whose translation is crucial to interpretation. Literally, Herakles says: "For the future, Admetos, be just [*dikaios*] and act with reverence [*eusebei*] toward strangers and guest-friends [*xenous*]." To my mind, the words are playfully, and importantly, ambiguous and "open." The injunction to "be just" we should understand in the usual classical sense, i.e. distributively: to treat others according to their *just merits*, to assign others their true *value*. The injunction would have little meaning if Admetos, by treating his *xenous* with *indiscriminate* regard (and also disregard), had not violated the spirit of *dikē*. The word *xenos* is of course ambiguous—and nowhere more so than in this play—ranging from "stranger" (as "enemy") to "guest" and thence "friend" and, finally, to anyone bound by claims of friendship or love (a sense nearly synonymous with *philos*). At line 1423 / 1117 Herakles bids Admetos, ironically, to take the hand of the veiled girl (*xenēs*), who is both stranger and guest but also wife (earlier in the play Admetos claims that his house does not know how to reject or dishonor its *xenous*—though Admetos clearly dishonors the dead Alcestis when he welcomes his guest Herakles to his house). At line 1444 / 1128 Herakles assures Admetos that, as *xenos* (i.e. as friend and guest), he is incapable of vulgar necromancy. By line 1472 / 1147–48, thanks to these progressive inflections, the word can be applied to *both* Herakles and Alcestis (my translation "those you love" is designed so that it can include the application to Alcestis, as "friend" would not). Herakles, I am saying, is delicately (but also forcefully, in a world where delicacies of language and refined behavior were still understood) telling Admetos to discard his old grand-seigneurial habit of hospitality *à l'outrance* and to discriminate according to value and worth. Similarly, in the same spirit of true human justice, the Duke, in Shakespeare's *Measure for Measure*, advises the erring (but redeemable) Angelo:

> Well, Angelo, your evil quits you well.
> Look that you love your wife; her worth yours.

1489–96 / 1159–63 Modern readers, accustomed to stress the concluding lines of a play, should perhaps be aware that this brief coda also concludes the *Bacchae*, *Helen*, *Andromache*, and *Medea*. Admittedly, the sentiment seems strikingly appropriate here; but it would be unwise to press a stylized exit-song for profound meanings.

MEDEA

Translated by

MICHAEL COLLIER

With Introduction and Notes by

GEORGIA MACHEMER

INTRODUCTION

As the sun, rising above Mount Hymettus, lights up the packed wooden bleachers on the south slope of the Acropolis, some fifteen thousand Athenian citizens and resident aliens, their retinues and guests from abroad,[1] revived by warming wine, readjust their cushions, pull their cloaks around their shoulders against the early morning chill, and gaze down at the wide circle of the deserted dance floor (*orchestra*). A short while before, just after dawn, it had been abustle with purifications, libations poured by generals—chief among them Pericles—announcements of gold chaplets (*stephanoi*) awarded to the city's benefactors, panoplied war orphans eligible for the first time to bear arms against the foe, and buckets of gold and silver tribute from subject states. But now the tribute has been removed and all the VIPs have taken their seats at the foot of the hill. In the front row, toes to the orchestra's rim, the year's

---

1. Were women present? There is no good evidence one way or the other, but my guess is no, not so much because of demographics, as because of Greek attitudes toward their wives and daughters appearing in public at all and because I suspect that the satyr plays and old comedies performed along with the tragedies at this festival would have been considered too lewd for proper women to see and hear. Demographics support this conclusion: Thucydides gives figures for the number of troops, both citizen and foreign, available to Athens in 431 B.C. for the conduct of the war (*Peloponnesian War* 2.13), which, though hotly disputed by modern scholars, suggest that even if only half of these men (numbering in excess of 90,000) were in the city at the time of the festival and that if even fewer than a third of these attended the theatrical performances that spring day, along with their sons, others exempt from service or disabled, numerous resident aliens not serving, and foreign guests (and their servants?), there would have been scant room on that crowded hillside for proper ladies. Even the performers were men. It was almost a men-only political club at play. If women were there, they would probably not have been the chaste wives and daughters of upstanding citizens. For a good discussion of the Athenian audience at the City Dionysia, see Simon Goldhill, "The Audience of Athenian Tragedy," in P. E. Easterling, ed., *Cambridge Companion to Greek Tragedy* (Cambridge, 1997), 54–68.

most prominent office holders and other notables flank the Priest of Dionysus at the center and the ten judges, just chosen by lot, who will soon cast their votes for this year's winning poet (not destined to be Euripides, who will come in third or dead last). Nearby stands the old wooden statue of the wine god, brought in procession to the festival and thought to be as eager as the human spectators to watch the show. The trumpets have sounded. Anticipation has settled into stillness. In the backdrop spanning the rear of the dance space, palace doors open. The *Medea*, a new play by the notorious Euripides, is about to begin.

What did the audience expect that morning in mid-March 431 B.C., as they watched a solitary man wearing the mask of an old woman shamble toward them, and were their expectations met or frustrated? How might they have interpreted the actions and the words of the masked actors and dancers—fellow citizens all—who came before them that day to sing, to dance, to gesture, to declaim, and to honor the wine god who mingled his spirits with theirs? What circumstances impinged on their consciousness? How would their assumptions and reactions have differed from ours as they witnessed the drama from whose script our Greek text, corrupted over time, is derived, a sometimes uncertain remnant of that first performance?

For months they had known that Euripides, already in midcareer, would be one of the three tragic poets exhibiting that spring at the annual city festival of Dionysus. He, Sophocles (Euripides' senior by at least a dozen years and a frequent favorite with the judges), and Euphorion (son of the great playwright Aeschylus and destined to be this year's victor), along with their respective chorus masters, the *choregoi*, had been chosen the summer before, shortly after the highest ranking city official, the *eponymous archon*, whose duties included oversight of the great festival of Dionysus, had taken office. Whatever shows the other two poets might put on, Euripides' were sure to rattle the audience, for he had been schooled by the sophists—those foreign-born, self-promoting, self-styled wise men who, with Pericles' encouragement, had arrived in boomtown Athens to peddle their newfangled, high-priced higher education to any with the leisure and means to become conversant with its confounding techniques of arguing the pros and cons of any issue and its unnerving theories about the nature of things—and he often made his characters act as though they had received the same indoctrination.

His fellow Athenians must have had mixed reactions to his characters' more extravagant sophistries. To those who were less than sanguine about the new ideas floating around Athens, who feared for the future of Athens and for their own, and who saw in Euripides' dramatic style a sign of the city's corruption, they must have been painful. How large this group was and who belonged to it we do not know. We can guess that it included those whose power and prestige was tied (or so they thought) to inherited landed estates (large and small) and who despised the manners and pretensions of newly "sophisticated" youths and their teachers and were opposed to Pericles' aggressive, populist, imperial policies; or, for that matter, just about any fathers or guardians who at home were scandalized by back-talking, rebellious sons and wards or who in the courts had been bested by captious arguments. The list was probably as long as the motives for disliking Euripides were many. Yet, despite his poor showing with the judges, the list of Euripides' fans was even longer. He fascinated those among the upper classes, especially the leisured, city-dwelling younger generation, who had imbibed the new learning at its source and were more than ready to applaud characters who thought and talked like, or more cleverly than, themselves. Even the as-yet unenlightened, less well-to-do majority, who were either too busy or too poor to pay the sophists' exorbitant fees, must have been easily seduced by rousing displays of spellbinding rhetoric unavailable to them by any other means. They were regaled by characters who might at any time begin to wax philosophical and question the veracity, worth, even the existence of the Homeric gods and whether men ought to be worshiping them, and, if not them, who or what.

But to these working men, better than all the logic-chopping and philosophizing was the way Euripides brought the imposing presences from Greek myth—those lofty alter egos of Athens' proud, Spartan-loving oligarchs—on stage in, shall we say, debasing circumstances. His characters, less remote, more human, delighted the newly enriched and newly empowered lower classes—city-dwelling, landless traders and artisans who had prospered from the manning and maintenance of Athens' large navy and from the new markets Athens' supremacy at sea had opened up. Thanks to Pericles, who for the last dozen years or so had been the undisputed master of Athens, and much to the chagrin of the so-called few (*oligoi*), aristocrats who thought themselves more qualified by birth and upbringing to rule, these vulgar many (*demos*), whom Pericles had flattered, rewarded, and led, now dominated the assembly and the courts. It must have been they most of all who a few years back had applauded so wildly when, dressed in rags, the great and noble son of Heracles, the Mysian Telephus (in a lost Euripidean play of that name) had hobbled before ancestral Argive peers to beg for aid. Surely there would be more outrageous surprises of this kind from Euripides' fertile mental store, something everyone could love hating.

They will not be disappointed. In the play they are about to see, the wondrous, magical, triumphant marriage of two matchless heroes—Jason, captain of the Argonauts, and Medea, his trophy wife—will enter the divorce court. To an audience raised on Aeschylus' larger-than-life personages, the leading characters of the *Medea* will seem disturbingly like the chattering high-folk of imperial Athens, whose dirty linen, though washed, has been hung out to dry. Under Euripides' tutelage, the art of masking is being transformed from a ritual putting-on of the real presence of a god or antique hero into the presentation of a familiar type confronted with familiar situations. As exotic as Medea is, she is still a woman; as unusual as her story is, it is nevertheless the story of a marriage; as assimilated to the divine nature as her sorcery is, for an ancient Athenian it still rings true to the real-life activities of lady herbalists or "root-cutters." Yet, although Euripides' protagonists will suddenly seem a bit too uncomfortably familiar, the play will be no *Who's Afraid of Virginia Woolf.* The action will remain public—there will be no displays of unseemly misconduct in the women's quarters— and, by our standards, the diction will seem grave, discreet, and declamatory, though the question of carnal attraction, in keeping with the mythical tradition, will not be altogether avoided. It is mentioned in the prologue (7–8 / 8) and emerges prominently as an issue in several of the choral odes and in Jason's caviling.

Not only have the spectators that morning long been expecting something shockingly sophisticated from Euripides, they have also been primed for a "Medea in Corinth." On the day preceding the grand procession that inaugurated the five-day festival, at a preliminary ceremony in the Odeion, the new auditorium flanking the Theater of Dionysus on the audience's left, each competing producer had first presented his poet, his chorus of fifteen men, his actors—also men, usually limited to three, the number necessary to play all the roles throughout the play by assuming different masks—and then announced the subjects and settings of the four plays his team would soon present— as a rule three tragedies, followed by a ribald satyr play (a burlesque of heroic myth in tragic style). Though they held celebratory garlands, the performers were maskless and wore ordinary dress in place of the elaborately embroidered "royal" robes or lewd satyr costumes they would don for their performances. That year Euripides would be offering the *Medea*, along with three other plays now lost: a *Philoctetes*, a *Diktys*, and a satyr play called *Theristai.*

LEGENDARY BACKGROUND

Ancient Greek myths tend to coalesce around ancestral dynasties, in this case, around one known as the Aeolidae, descendants of Aeolus, Jason's great-grandfather, who had originally ruled in the plains of Thessaly in northern Greece. One of Aeolus' seven sons, Athamas, had two famous wives. The first, Nephele, bore him a son, Phrixus, and a daughter, Helle; the second, Ino, attempted to kill Phrixus. In fifth-century accounts of this wicked stepmother's plot and its thwarting—we know of at least three plays of Sophocles and three of Euripides that touch upon it—there seems to have been an abortive sacrifice of Phrixus, after which he and his sister fly off toward the East on the back of a golden ram, sent either by their mother, Nephele, or by a god. Helle falls off, giving her name to Helle's sea (the Hellespont), but Phrixus arrives safely in the land of the Colchians at the eastern end of the Black Sea. Here he sacrifices the golden ram and gives its fleece to Aeëtes, son of the Titan Helios (the Sun) and king of Aia, a city on the Phasis River. In return, Aeëtes welcomes him into his household and gives him the hand of a daughter (Medea's sister) in marriage. After fathering a number of sons, Phrixus dies in Colchis. All this time the unearthly fleece hangs in a sacred grove, safeguarded by a huge serpent.

Meanwhile, back in Thessaly, the scene has shifted to the harbor town of Iolcus, at the foot of Mount Pelion. Athamas is no longer in the picture, and his nephew Aeson, the father of Jason, has been overthrown by Aeson's half brother Pelias. At the time of the coup, Aeson's supporters entrust the boy Jason to the wise centaur Chiron, who raises him far from town in a cave near Pelion's peak. Years pass. Pelias, though tormented by a prophecy to beware of a man wearing a single sandal, rules without opposition. Then, one fine day just such a one-sandaled man arrives in Iolcus: a heroic figure, indeed, in Pindar, who a generation earlier wrote:

> a man terrible with twin javelins; and a twofold guise was on him.
> A tunic of Magnesian fashion fitted close his magnificent limbs,
> and across it a panther's hide held off the shivering rains.
> Nor did the glory of his streaming locks go shorn,
> but blazed the length of his back. Striding apace
> he stood, and tested his unfaltering will
> in the market place that filled with people.
>
> They knew him not; yet awe-struck one man would say to another:
> "This cannot be Apollo, surely, nor Aphrodite's lord,
> he of the brazen chariot...." (*Fourth Pythian Ode*, 78–88, tr.
> Richmond Lattimore)

The man is Jason, come home at last to claim his royal birthright. Along the way he has lost one of his sandals. The lines from Pindar, representative of a tradition familiar to Euripides' audience, allow us to see what that audience would have realized at once: just how far Euripides' Jason has fallen compared to Pindar's godlike warrior.

When King Pelias learns the identity of this awesome, one-shoed stranger, the wily usurper is ready with a deft proposal: The ghost of Phrixus has been haunting his dreams and has called upon him to bring the fleece of the golden ram back to Iolcus. Would Jason be enterprising enough to wrest it from the formidable Aeëtes? Jason, a hero to his core, accepts Pelias' challenge and calls upon most of the heroes of the age to go with him to the world's eastern edge, a mysterious, potent, sacred spot, charged with danger, where the Sun rises from his Underworld home, and where no Greek had gone before. They come from all over, these brave adventurers. With Athena's help, they build the world's first man-of-war, the Argo, and from Iolcus they sail (and row) into untested waters beyond the Bosporus. On the way, they encounter many obstacles, all of which they overcome, only to find the greatest obstacles of all in Colchis.

As soon as the purpose of the Argonauts' mission is made plain to Aeëtes, the ungracious and devious king sets tasks for Jason to perform in order to win the Golden Fleece—tasks that Aeëtes believes will be impossible. The hero must plow a field with fire-breathing bulls, sow dragon's teeth in the furrows, and kill the fully armed warriors that will sprout from this sinister seed. The gods, however, are on Jason's side. Aphrodite makes the king's daughter Medea fall so madly in love with the beautiful Greek stranger that she, a priestess of Hecate and therefore accomplished in the secret arts of magic, gives him potions to protect him from the bulls' fire and sound advice on how to set his new-grown adversaries to fighting among themselves. When her father does not keep his side of the bargain and refuses to grant Jason the Golden Fleece, she helps her lover seize the prize from under the watchful eye of its guardian dragon and then escapes with him aboard the Argo. Along the way, she and Jason kill her brother and, according to at least one fifth-century account (though not attested by Euripides), chop up his corpse and scatter his limbs behind them as they flee, in order to delay her father's pursuit.[2]

At some point in these adventures, in return for her aid and to protect her from her father's vengeance, Jason solemnly swears to make Medea his lawful wife. This marriage—one of the great marriages of myth, in

2. Michael Collier incorporates some details of this version at lines 160–62. Euripides, however, tells us nothing about the cause or the manner of this murder, only that it was shameful (160 / 166–67) and that it took place at Medea's father's hearth (1308 / 1334).

which the human and the divine worlds come together to celebrate an extraordinary union—is accomplished either on the homeward voyage, during which Medea's magical powers often come to the aid of Jason and his crew, or upon the couple's triumphal return to Iolcus. In Apollonius of Rhodes' *Argonautica*, an epic written about a century and a half after Euripides' *Medea*, it forms a highlight of the last, culminating book. Significantly, Apollonius has it take place in Phaeacia, the enchanted land where Odysseus in Homer's *Odyssey* was finally rescued from the sea and sent home to Ithaca. The marriage bed of the god-blessed couple—so often referred to in the play—was, we are told, set up in a sacred cave and covered with the Golden Fleece itself:

> Nymphs gathered flowers for them, and as they brought the many-coloured bunches into the cave in their white arms the fiery splendour of the fleece played on them all, so bright was the glitter of its golden wool. It kindled in their eyes a sweet desire. They longed to lay their hands on it, and yet they were afraid to touch it.... As for his bride, the place where the pair were brought together when the fragrant linen had been spread is still called the Sacred Cave of Medea.[3] (Apollonius, *Argonautica*, lines 1143–48, 1153–55, tr. E. V. Rieu)

The quest for the Golden Fleece had many sequels. The oldest and most famous was the murder of King Pelias by his daughters, who were tricked by cunning Medea into killing their own father, a tale that is introduced as background in the prologue of the *Medea* to account for Jason's and Medea's status as exiles from Iolcus (see note on 8–9). Another sequel, her stint in Athens with King Aegeus, which is anticipated in the third episode of the play (**658–815** / 663–823; see pp. 12–14) and set after Medea's flight from Corinth, may well have been devised only in classical times. Both Euripides and Sophocles are known to have written undatable lost plays called *Aegeus*. But even if one of them included Medea in its plot, and that play was produced before our *Medea*, it is unlikely that the Athens episode, in contrast to the murder of Pelias, would have formed a part of the audience's assumptions or expectations.

HISTORICAL BACKGROUND

Because the dates of most of Euripides' surviving plays are unknown, and because those that are known do not always belong to moments in Athenian history as well documented as the spring of 431 B.C., we are not

---

3. For a complete account of this and related legends, see Timothy Gantz, *Early Greek Myth* (Baltimore, 1993) where a valiant attempt is made to sort out the many competing versions.

usually in a position, as we are with the *Medea*, to explore the relationship between the action of the play and the events of the world. The *Medea* was produced during the incidents described in the first two books of Thucydides' history of the great Peloponnesian War. Of course, that proud morning the audience did not know what the future would bring or that the war upon which they were embarking would be twenty-seven years long and ultimately disastrous for Athens. They did know, however, that it had already begun, for the previous summer Sparta had declared war, and as soon as the campaigning season got under way in earnest, efficient, ruthless Spartan phalanxes would be marching toward Athenian territory.

Anxious though the majority in the audience must have been about this anticipated invasion, chances are at least one of them, the leader of the anti-Spartan, prowar, expansionist, democratic faction, was outwardly calm, for he had already decided that such an incursion would be of little long-term consequence. Pericles had always aimed for Athens' preeminence in Greece at Sparta's expense, wanting to pit his city's young sea power against the other's venerable land power. Now his efforts were paying off. On his advice, Attic farmers, the mainstay of the heavily armed infantry (the hoplites), would soon send their livestock to neighboring islands and, abandoning their holdings in the countryside, reluctantly take up temporary residence inside the city walls, along with their women and children, their servants, and, we are told, their household furniture. Let the invincible Spartans and their Dorian allies do their worst. What had Athenians to fear, so long as they stayed behind the ramparts? With Athens' coffers bursting and her fleet unchallenged from Corcyra to Colchis, they could count on war supplies and other resources being shipped in from overseas. Meanwhile, their war fleet, manned by the best-trained rowers in the world, would make surprise raids on the inadequately guarded territories of Sparta and her allies.

In this perfervid atmosphere, names like "Argo," "Clashing Rocks," and "Corinth" were laden with implications they can scarcely have for us. Had not the citizens of Athens, like the Argonauts of old, "forced every sea and land to be the highway of [their] daring" (Thucydides 2.41, tr. R. Crawley)? Not only had they sounded the farthest reaches of the Black Sea, but with their own garrisons, settlers, and naval patrols, they had turned its once formidable waters into a large lake, from which big-bellied merchantmen, laden with grain and salt fish, made their swift, unobstructed way past the Clashing Rocks, through the Bosporus and the Hellespont, to Athens.

Athens' new prosperity and sudden power, however, had brought many problems. Foreigners, both Greek and non-Greek, had flooded the city. Many of those involved in trade, native and foreigner alike, had become newly rich and influential. As the use of ships and money increased, the land holdings in Attica that supported the hoplite army no longer counted for as much, and the room and board once supplied to farmhands and servants had given way, in the city at least, to wages. With wages came the possibility of freedom and, to the ambitious, hardworking, and lucky, social and political advancement. Old distinctions no longer applied. No one knew anymore who was who. Political allegiances shifted like sand as each man sought his own advantage.

Because tragedy by definition deals with heroes' hard times, it goes without saying that the audience that morning did not expect to see either Jason or Medea as the exultant figures portrayed in early epic or in Pindar's epinician odes from thirty years before. But what would this audience at this time have felt when they saw an old slave woman—and, as they soon learned, the slave of a barbarian princess to boot—emerge from the scene building to speak the prologue of this play? By her very appearance on stage, she immediately reoriented their expectations toward the background of the action about to unfold, toward the immigrant population growth and mixing up of peoples and status that maritime supremacy had brought in its wake. If the surviving Euripidean tragedies are any guide to the common practice of this most "democratic" of the fifth-century tragedians, then the Nurse is indeed unusual. Almost always, a god or hero speaks his prologues; she is an immigrant's slave. Oh yes, she is an aristocrat among servants (see notes on 1–39 and 40), but a servant nonetheless, and there she stands in that great circle of empty space and, like any free Athenian citizen, addresses the rulers of the sea, a symbol perhaps of the recognizable confusion of daily life in democratic Athens, where the base-born lord it over their betters and slaves and foreigners cannot be distinguished from freemen (cf. Ps. Xenophon, *Constitution of Athens*, 1.4–12).

Already nonplussed by her appearance, what must their astonishment have been when the first words out of her mouth wished the Argo and its triumphs away—the Argo, whose voyage was a mythical emblem of their own sea power—and along with it the whole turmoil of domestic and public life that its sudden success had brought. Who in that audience would not have felt the pull of what she said? Even the overseas clients and the immigrants in Athens (the metics), who had prospered beyond their wildest imaginings, would have felt the anxiety of life in the fast lane, far from home and the old familiar ways evoked by this old servant's lament. But perhaps none there that day would have felt her words more strongly than the slaves, some from as far away as Colchis, who perhaps were waiting on the edges of the crowd for the signal between plays to bring more refreshments to their masters. They, too, saw the veil of literary convention raised just enough to reveal a cynical reality with which they and those around them were all too familiar. Underneath the heavy veneer of the ennobling past, the commonplace was peeping through. The Argo was beached.

Then there was Corinth. Ready to pit their seamanship against that of any of Sparta's allies, how could this audience not have reacted to the drama's being set in Corinth? Although we usually say that the Peloponnesian War was between Athens and Sparta, this is merely a neat formula for a far messier reality. In reality the war arose between Athens and her allies—that is, all the subject cities of the Delian League, the maritime federation over which she ruled—and Sparta and her allies, largely the cities of the Peloponnesus, the south Greek peninsula. Of this region the chief naval power was Corinth, the northernmost city of the Peloponnesus. Straddling the neck of the peninsula, she not only controlled the north-south land route, but had once been the busiest port in Greece, until Athens challenged her ascendancy. Indeed, it was actually with Corinth, not Sparta, that the disagreements leading up to the final breach of the Thirty Years' Truce had started. Corinth was the real enemy, her fleet the real threat, her jealousy of upstart Athens the driving cause. In the months leading up to the war, Athens, already first in the Aegean and the Black Sea to the east, had deliberately challenged Corinth's control of the sea lanes between mainland Greece and the prosperous Greek colonies in South Italy and Sicily to the west. Corinth had retaliated. By the time Corinth, during the previous summer, had finally convinced Sparta, with her invincible elite land forces, to join the fight, Athens and Corinth were already fully engaged.

So, whatever his motives, Euripides had picked a myth and a setting that fit the hour. His audience, he well knew, was made up of the same citizens who had voted to aid the city of Corcyra in her rebellion against Corinth and to reject outright the last blunt, impossible Spartan ultimatum that, to keep the peace, the Athenians should give up their empire. Now, on the brink of a war they had asked for, they sat, elated and afraid, and watched Medea wreak havoc upon hostile Corinth's ruler and his new ally, the great Thessalian seaman Jason, who, fool that he was, had suddenly switched his allegiance from her to the Corinthian king Creon.

If the dramatic action had been confined to Corinth, Medea's vengeance would have been riveting, but it would have lacked the frisson generated by the sudden appearance on stage of ancient Athens' King Aegeus offering asylum to the calculating, yet persuasive Medea (658–815 / 663–823). Since ancient audiences were used to etiologies in tragedy, like the one at the end of the play that accounts for the historical cult of Medea's children at Corinth, they would doubtless have been alert to the ominous etiological implications of Aegeus' ill-considered promise. Here before their eyes was a myth to explain how Corinth and Athens had become enemies. The scene thus reached out to them in several ways not obvious to us. We have no emotional commitment to Athens' founding hero Theseus, the son Aegeus is going to beget on Pittheus' daughter when he leaves Corinth; not so the Athenians, whose fathers and grandfathers had gone to great trouble and expense to bring this man's bones back from the island of Scyros to Athens and to inaugurate a festival in his honor, replete with a grand procession, sacrifices, and athletic contests. We do not sense the extent of Aegeus' blunder when, needlessly, in exchange for an heir, he welcomes Medea into his home and commits his city to her defense against her new enemies, ipso facto making them his and Athens' own, not for a single generation, but for many generations to come. We do not anticipate, as they did, that Medea will bear to Aegeus a child named Medus, who will become the founder of the everthreatening Persian kingdom (Media), or that she will attempt to murder the noble Theseus,[4] nor suspect that the child-destroying taint clinging to her uncanny powers might still be at work in Athens in the shape of her latter-day, root-brewing disciples (see p. 135). Nor do we fear the endless inheritability of blood guilt feared by the Athenians, who, close upon Aegeus' exit from the stage in Euripides' play, discovered from Medea's own lips[5] that he and hence their shining city had made a commitment to a woman who would murder her own children, an act of pollution so dire that they might have exclaimed along with the Chorus that no ritual cleansing imaginable could make her fit to reside among them (830–39 / 846–55). With the full extent of Medea's plans revealed, their foreboding at the outcome of her compact with Aegeus is registered musically by the contrast the Chorus draws between Athens' glorious, god-blessed, true wisdom–engendering purity and Medea's depravity (816ff. / 824ff.). Future generations found Euripides' lyrics the most moving parts of his plays. Was this also true at their premieres? Did the savvy Athenians, unconquered children of the gods and Earth, exult

---

4. We know of two undated tragedies that probably dealt with Medea's attempted murder of Theseus, one by Sophocles, one by Euripides. That one of them antedates the *Medea* is suggested by "a series of Red-Figure pots starting about 450 B.C. and showing Aigeus, Theseus, the Bull [of Marathon], and a woman who must be Medeia..." (Gantz [see note 3], vol. 1, p. 255).

5. It has been concluded by many Euripidean scholars that Euripides did not inherit the myth of Medea's murdering her own children but invented it.

unabashedly in the glory of their city and yet fear for the danger that lay ahead? I cannot help but think so.

The audience's sense of unease at the sinister quality of the Athens-Corinth connection would have been heightened by the way in which Euripides locates the familiar political machinations of the play not in a public space but deep inside a noble house, where the destabilizing quest for personal power, honor, and glory, and for the honor of one's house, began and ended. For ancient Greek politics, as will become clearer when we look more closely at the topic of Medea's honor, was not distant like ours, representative and televised, but immediate, direct, and personal, oftentimes played out among participants who had known each other since childhood. Wheeling and dealing could not be left behind when an ancient Athenian or Corinthian went home, because his home and its nexus of alliances with kin and peers constituted his faction, his party. Unstable marriage alliances and bloody vendettas (which Athenian court procedure reflected and often was powerless to replace), coups and countercoups, betrayals and counter-betrayals were the very stuff of political life throughout Greece and often undermined the common good. Not only is Euripides' play centered on one of these explosive political marriages; the maneuvering between husband and wife is brought down from the royal, public heights on which it had been displayed in other tragedies (e.g., Aeschylus' *Oresteia*) into the bathos of a domestic tug-of-war between a husband and his no-longer-convenient, unrestrained, foreign wife, who refuses to go quietly into the limbo to which she has been consigned and instead, unassisted, outsmarts all her pantywaist foes.

MEDEA'S CHARACTER

In developing Medea's character, Euripides plays the received tradition off contemporary situations and prejudices. Her fierce, mantic nature, to Pindar a sign of her prophetic powers (*Pythian* 4.10), is now a symptom of a defective character type: the aloof, intractable, uncontrollable, uncompromising, stubborn *authades*, who, when crossed, is given to inordinate rage and resentment and resists all attempts on the part of friends at mollification or amelioration. The Greek word is fairly new[6] and belongs to the emerging discourse of medicine, rhetoric, and ethics, and, although rare in Euripides, is used four times to describe Medea.

---

6. Significantly, the word first appears in the *Prometheus Bound*, which, in my opinion, is neither by Aeschylus nor much earlier in date than the 430s B.C. But this is a controversial topic out of place here.

Up until Jason's betrayal and her unjust abasement, she had managed to conceal her true nature behind a facade of restrained solicitousness, obliging her husband and his friends when necessary (9–12 / 11–15) and like a true lady, showing just the right amount of reserve and dignity to make others, like the Corinthian women who have extended their friendship to her (131 / 138; 177–80 / 178–79), think that she is a perfect wife—modest, chaste, and temperate (*sophrosyne*, or "soundness of mind / integrity of heart," includes all these attributes of a woman capable of controlling her passions). But as soon as her anger is unleashed by Jason's betrayal, she starts to behave differently. Instead of passively enduring her fate, or in shame committing suicide like some wilting Madame Butterfly, she becomes totally resistant to moderation, indifferent to the propriety of her actions, incapable of bowing to the will of her betters, much less of her equals. "She is deaf to friends' advice, like a stone, like a wave" (24–25 / 28–29), the Nurse explains early on to the audience; and later to the Tutor, "She came into the world fierce and stubborn" (94–95 / 93–94); and still later to the Chorus, "She'll growl and snarl when I approach, like a lioness shielding her cubs. She'll snort like a bull. I doubt I'll lure her out" (190–94 / 184–89). For it is not just the violence and intensity of Medea's wrath that is at issue in the play, but its utter relentlessness, its unappeasability. Inside the house, she reveals to all her familiars that she has the reach and temper of a thwarted tyrant or of one like an Ajax or a Prometheus, who, though used to high honors, has been suddenly and unendurably shamed; except, unlike them, she has at hand the means to avenge herself upon her tormentors. Outside, before the Chorus and her other interlocutors, like a true sophist, she can play whatever role is necessary to obtain her ends, including, when it serves her purpose, that of a reserved and dignified noblewoman (*semnos*, cf. 222–32 / 214–24).[7]

Of Medea's great intellectual acumen and professional skill, Euripides' audience had no doubt. Her powers of prophecy and sorcery were essential to her mythic persona. But just as Euripides has disconnected Medea's passionate nature from her noble art and turned it from a virtue into a vice, so he makes his audience view her "profession," her *sophia*,

---

7. Even though the meaning of the opening lines of this speech remains doubtful, the underlying argument can be shown to be a ploy familiar to us from Plato and Aristotle. Wishing to disguise her true nature and forestall the accusation of *authadeia*, Medea insinuates that she is not really self-willed and recalcitrant as some people think but rather virtuously reserved and worthy of respect, a claim that is convincing because the simulated virtue (*semnotēs*) is known by qualities similar to those by which the concealed vice (*authadeia*) is known. Thus anticipated censure is turned into apparent praise. (Cf. Plato, *Phaedrus* 267A; Aristotle, *Rhetoric* 1.9.28–32 1367a33–b27 and *Eudemian Ethics* 2.3.4 1221a; 3.7.5 1233b 35–38, *Nichomachean Ethics* 4.3.26–34 1124b17–1125a16)

in nontraditional ways. By moving her into a situation in which her political power and prestige as Jason's wife are at risk, he exposes the dark, destructive side of her talent. Like other sophists (professors, wise men) of Euripides' day, we see her arguing any side of any case that will at any given point best serve her interests. If she needs the Chorus's complicity, she obtains its goodwill in specious appeals for sympathy and solidarity. When her arguments fail to convince Creon that he should give her a reprieve from instant banishment, she begs abjectly for pity (abject begging was a ploy often used in Athenian courts to arouse the pity of the jurors). Confronted by the one who has wronged her, she mounts a strong prosecution. Presented with a chance for asylum, she engages in the question and answer of cross-examination, a technique from the courts that provides the backbone of Socrates' famous method of philosophical interrogation. If upon stepping through the palace doors, she appears by turns calm and dignified, abject, confident, or contrite, she is only doing what other heroes before her had done—what loyal Greeks always still did—when confronted with an enemy. She schemes, she tricks, she deceives. Only, in this play, the enemy is her husband and his friends, and the arguments she uses are taken from the latest instruction manuals for speech-making. Thus, those watching her proficient duplicity must confront not only the power of the new rhetoric but also a familiar truth, that when allegiances change—as they so frequently did in city politics—duplicity is a two-edged sword. Everything depends on who the true enemy—or friend—is.

Just as her transparent sophistry strips her of her inherited grandeur, so it strips her interlocutors of theirs. Thus, as she accuses or feigns submission or gloats, and Jason offers disingenuous (though, as we shall see, in real life often convincing) excuses or condescending approbation or a last, pathetic retort, he is demoted from a great hero and daring explorer to an exiled and humbled former first citizen scheming to better his lot. By the end of the play he has made such a complete mess of things and is so bested by his wife that her prediction—that he will end his life shamefully, one of the lowest of the low, a childless wretch accidentally done to death by a fragment of his old ship—is utterly believable. Nor is Jason the only character who succumbs to Medea's up-to-date tactics and cunning, although he alone exhibits no obvious, compensating virtue. By matching arguments or answering her far-from-innocent questions, both Creon and Aegeus diminish their kingly stature. Creon is less a king because, though he has taken accurate measure of his enemy, he nevertheless succumbs to her pleading and out of misplaced pity fails to make the right decision. The kings in traditional epics made mistakes, but it was the gods who befuddled their wits, not clever women and their own yielding natures. In a different situation, Creon's mildness and mercy might even be deemed princely virtues; but when his kingdom is at stake, succumbing to this side of his nature is folly; it is what Aristotle would call missing the mark most tragically.

As already indicated above, Aegeus' character is more of a puzzle, partly, I think, because, in his encounter with Medea, the techniques of forensic oratory are not being employed, and it was from the argumentative techniques of this kind of rhetoric which were being systematized in the courts that Euripides derived his technique of revealing character through dialogue. Furthermore, true to the politeness of this simpler question-and-answer dialogue, the poet chooses to make neither character say anything by way of praise or blame to the other, nor does he use a third party—a servant, a messenger, a Chorus—to introduce Aegeus as he introduces Medea in the prologue. Only Medea, the prevaricator—who in the audience would take anything she says without evident rancor for Jason at face value?—has any opportunity to characterize him, and she doesn't. So Aegeus seems just, generous, and a fool; not grand but tragicomic.

Much has been made in recent times of Medea's exotic nature as a barbarian witch. Of her lack of Greek culture, considering how many important Athenians at the time were the sons or grandsons of non-Greek mothers (see p. 138), too much, I believe, has been made. The only character in the play who denigrates Medea for being a barbarian is Jason, and he, like any aristocratic student of the sophists, will use whatever convenient ploy against her he can find to justify his own actions. But nowhere else in the play does her ignorance of Greek manners or speech stigmatize her socially—in her dealings with Creon, Aegeus, or the Chorus, nor in the servants' comments—although her status as an outsider of a different kind is often at issue: as a woman who does not belong by blood to her husband's family or as the wife of a political exile who is not a citizen of the city in which he finds himself. These categories were quite distinct in the Greek mind, and in the play they are regularly signified by different words, *barbaroi* for non-Greeks, *thuraioi* or *allotrioi* for nonfamily members, and *xenoi* for noncitizens.

But of Medea's proficient barbarian witchcraft, so central to the dramatic action, moderns have made too little, or, rather, they have tended to misjudge its import. To the Athenians of Euripides' day, witchcraft was not the fantastic, pagan, sci-fi art portrayed in today's movies or on TV; it was regarded as an integral part of the latest scientific research and regularly used by proficient healers and salvific priests, whose knowledge of the demonic world allowed them to harness its forces, either to cure or destroy. Even in its most rational or materialist forms, ancient Greek science never completely separated the divine nature from the world it investigated. Essential to Aristotle's biology, developed almost a century after Euripides, was the belief that the gods are living beings and that the soul, as the vital principle governing all life forms from gods to worms, not only encompasses all our physical and mental functions but is also the very stuff—the DNA, if you will—that determines our individual natures and links us to other members of our species, both those of us now dead and those yet to be born (cf., e.g., *On the Soul* 1.1 402a ff., and *On the Generation of Animals* 1.18 724b14ff.). To the Stoics, who came after Aristotle, the universe itself was a living creature suffused by the controlling fiery, pneumatic material they called Reason and God, and they claimed that a wise man's reason was actually a piece of this divine Pneuma. Such philosophizings merely rationalized an earlier, widely held, Classical belief that the human soul contains a measure of the divine, the unsullied intellect, and because of it we are in some sense akin to the gods. The greater the intellect, the more godly its possessor, and those with the most powerful, most agile, most refined minds[8] were deemed to be gods, not necessarily gods of the highest order, not the Olympic or heavenly gods who dwell in perpetual bliss, but powerful, almost indestructible beings nonetheless, the kind called *daimones*, those invisible natures proficient for good or evil who, with countless companions, travel in the soul-rich air around us, or inhabit the flowers, trees, and rivers that spring from the immortal earth, or, indeed, who themselves arise from the earth out of the corpses of previous generations or descend from on high into this miserable, tainted, mortal sphere of war, disease, decay, and death to mediate between us wretches and those glorious, uncontaminated souls above.

Although in Euripides' day this vision of the world and the role of the divine nature in it lacked the coherence of later philosophical systems, it was, nevertheless, already present in embryonic or, as late Platonists would insist, oracular form; and Euripides himself was caught up in the early stages of the great intellectual task of its articulation. He was, by all accounts, associated with the most advanced thinkers in Athens, in particular with Socrates, who was periodically accused on the comic stage of helping him write his innovative and disturbing plays. Whatever one may think of Aristophanes' historicity, his unforgettable portrayal of Socrates in the *Clouds* (produced within a decade of the *Medea*) as the

---

8. Though only implicit in Collier's translation ("And you, yes, you have a mind for plots and treachery," 537–38), in the Greek text Jason explicitly refers to Medea's mind as subtle (or finely threshed, *leptos*, 529), a word that in the late fifth century was often associated with sophistry and in Aristophanes, specifically with Socrates (and Euripides).

archetypal priestly sophist, swinging aloft in his basket and mingling his finely threshed, elevated thought with the ever-flowing numinous Air, clearly relies on a popular conception of contemporary wise men, who were laying claim to an intelligence above that of ordinary mortals and to direct contact with divine. Even Plato, Socrates' greatest apologist, depicts him in a similar state of intellectual communion with the divine nature. What is more, in the *Symposium*, he makes the young Socrates the disciple not of a sage but of a sage-ess, the plague-diverting priestess Diotima (*Symposium* 201D).

To this seldom-witnessed distaff side of the new schools of the learned, Euripides' Medea, priestess of Hecate and sharer in the goddess's most secret treasury of transforming drugs and charms, surely belongs. She is, to be more specific, a professional healer (and harmer) trained in the art of gathering, preparing, and applying drugs. Because this art depended upon knowledge of certain divine rites and charms, some of which were revealed only to women, women held a secure place in this branch of knowledge. They were thought to be particularly capable in the nocturnal collection of roots, leaves, flowers, and bark and in turning their finds into efficacious salves and potions, which they must have supplied to physicians like Hippocrates (a contemporary of Socrates and Euripides) or to less reputable healers, and which they themselves must have prescribed, particularly in their duties as midwives.

Like the sophists remembered in our ancient sources, holy wise women must have wielded sufficient power through their arts to have been labeled dangerous, *deinai*, an adjective that can describe anything alarming but in the fifth century came to be attached to those ingenious few who were possessed of intimidating new intellectual and persuasive powers. It cannot be accidental that this adjective is often predicated of Medea in the rising action of the play, where she is presented both as the awe-inspiring, semidivine ancestress of female pharmacists—a being that is *deine* in the old sense of the term—and also as her own glib, modern incarnation. She has, as it were, a split personality, and it is this unresolved tension between the exalted, awful being who can do what her modern counterparts claimed to be able to do—control nature—and a more mundane, more desperate, more human reality that makes her endlessly fascinating. She is both a steward of sacred magic and a purveyor of marvels, an emblem of the times.

There are many clues throughout the play that Euripides means his audience to see Medea and her wisdom in this way, but these will not be obvious to Michael Collier's readers, because, in order to make Euripides' difficult Greek accessible to contemporary, English-speaking readers, he necessarily recasts the passages that most reveal

the scientific-sophistic issues: the first three choral odes and the prologues to Medea's first two speeches. Since it is impossible in a general
introduction to examine all of these, I will consider but one example,
Medea's second speech (**313ff.** / 292ff.). Modern philologists steeped in
Socratic lore have long recognized the similarity between Medea's
answer to Creon's indictment (**303–12** / 282–91) and Socrates' protestations in Plato's *Apology* that he is misunderstood and not really so wise;
but not seeing its appropriateness to her character, they have treated this
point of the play as a rather undramatic intrusion of Euripides'
own voice, laden with frustration at the uneducated obtuseness of his
audiences.

In her speech, Medea's aim is to blunt Creon's fear that she will inflict
some irremediable harm upon his daughter, but rather than try to deny
the truth of the inflammatory and now public fact that she is, as he
alleges (and here I give a more literal version of the Greek text),
"distressed at being deprived of [her] man's bed" (286) and has been
"threatening . . . to take action [*drasein ti*] against [all three parties to
Jason's new marriage contract], the grantor, the groom, and the bride"
(287–89), she astutely prefers to answer the less pressing charge that she
is "by nature [*pephukas*] wise / skilled [*sophê*] and versed [*idris*, an
unusual, poetic word] in many evils [*kakôn pollôn*]" (285). Even in
these few lines, the directness, imagistic force, and colloquial smooth-
ness of Michael Collier's translation are self-evident. Instead of imped-
ing his verses with Euripides' awkward legal formalities quoted above, he
encapsulates in one or two image-laden words the gist of Creon's
accusations: Medea "sting[s] with loss" (**305**); she makes "the darkest
threats . . . against his house" (**307–8**); her "nature, clever and vindictive,
thrives on evil" (**304–5**). Since the last of these three charges is the one
Medea answers, but is the first to be uttered by Creon, in order to
preserve continuity, the phrase "a woman like you," which echoes the
idea of Medea's nature, is added to Creon's last sentence (**311**) as a
convenient thread for Medea to pick up at the beginning of her rebuttal,
when she exclaims "A woman like me!" (**313**). The transition is seamless,
but the original line of argument is lost. The issue is no longer the
frightening effectiveness of Medea's talent for and skill in the art (*sophia*)
of black magic, but a more modern issue, the denigration of a clever
women. Yet it was Medea's science, not just her intellectual agility, that
concerned Creon, and it is this objective reality, in the guise of the new
learning and its practitioners, that Medea addresses in her rebuttal.
Here, with true sophistry, she turns herself into a victim of the prejudice
widely incurred (in Athens) by the *sophoi*. Again, in a more literal
translation:

Not now for the first time, but often, Creon, has my reputation harmed me and caused great evils. A sensible man [*artiphrôn pephukas*] ought never to have his children too highly educated [in the new sciences] [*perissôs ekdidaskesthai sophous*], for, apart from fecklessness,[9] their only profit is the ill will and envy of their fellow townsmen. For, if you proffer new discoveries [*kaina sopha*] to benighted bunglers [literally "left-handed," *skaiois*], [by them] you will be thought ineffectual and not really competent [*sophos*].[10] But if in the city you are thought superior to those who think they are experts [know something abstruse, *eidenai ti poikilon*], [to these] you will seem offensive. I, too, share in this misfortune. Being skilled [*sophê*] [in my art/science], I am envied by the latter and deemed too steep by the former. (292–305 = **313–24** in Collier's version)

Instead of calling attention to her proven and therefore dangerous skill in witchcraft and its possible application to the case at hand, Medea shrewdly speaks of the *sophoi* in general, claiming, with a wonderfully personalized and, under the circumstances, apt rhetorical ploy (I wouldn't want my children to be wise), that experts and scientists like her are misunderstood. Since the majority of citizens don't know what to make of them and cannot use their advice, they are in effect useless to the city (and therefore not dangerous); at the same time they arouse envy in those who think that they too know something worth attending to or paying for. Either way, out of envy or misunderstanding, their skill is (unjustly) condemned as dangerous and deemed a potential source of trouble to the well-being of the city.

Although the Greek is not entirely clear here and the passage has in fact proved a stumbling block to commentators, it is obvious from this rendition that Medea's arguments have nothing to do with the distinction between men and women that resonates so forcefully with us moderns and upon which Michael Collier's translation depends; rather, they aim first at the conflict between newfangled science and received wisdom; then at disparities between those who are both gifted and educated and the stupid and ignorant—or, as students of Classical rhetoric know, between the upper and lower classes; and, finally, at the sometimes vicious rivalries among those competing for political prominence. All three motifs are at work here.

MEDEA'S HONOR

As telling to Euripides' audience as her sophisticated learning (*sophia*) and her unbending refusal to be placated (*authadeia*) was

9. Cf., e.g., Aristophanes, *Clouds* 334.

10. Twenty years later in the *Thesmophoriazousae*, Aristophanes makes a pretend-Euripides parody these lines ("For if you proffer new insights [*kaina sopha*] to the benighted, you expend them in vain

Medea's "divorce" from Jason and consequent reduction in legal standing from wife to concubine. The topic had been rendered thorny for many in Euripides' audience by a restrictive citizenship law ushered through the assembly twenty years earlier by Pericles himself. Previously, a child was considered legitimate if he was the offspring of a legitimate marriage and if his father had citizen status. Even many highborn, celebrated Athenians had non-Athenian mothers. Cimon and Themistocles, heroes of the Persian wars, had Thracian mothers, and Pericles himself was the great-grandson of Agariste, daughter of Cleisthenes, tyrant of Sicyon. Now both parents, no matter how well born, had to be able to prove their citizen status.

For many Athenians this law must have had grave consequences. Despite its not being retroactively applied to citizens already registered with their precincts (*demes*), it must have immediately affected young men eighteen years of age who were just then applying for citizenship. Children of Athenian fathers who were declared illegitimate lost not only their citizens' rights but their inheritances as well, which would go instead to the nearest legitimate relative and his heirs. A poor man who had little to leave his sons would not have had to defend his own or his heirs' legitimacy in court against would-be heirs or beneficiaries; a rich man an easy target, so like most of the legislation of the Periclean age, as a rule this law punished the propertied classes more than the working man.

Another of the law's consequences must have been that Athenians who had married foreign women now had to replace them with Athenian wives if they did not want their future sons and daughters to be bastards. These divorces would have created a class of newly disfranchised, but still free, foreign-born grass widows, who, Medea-like, either had to stay in a reduced condition as concubines in their former husbands' households—the option Jason seems to envision for Medea—or find new partners and legal protectors (*kyrioi*) among the foreigners who resided in Athens or, like Aegeus in Corinth, who were just passing through.

If these independent, foreign women happened to be beautiful, rich, well-connected at home, or highly educated, they might have been seen

[lines 1130–31]), only in the comedy the unspecified benighted being referred to here is made flesh and blood on stage in the shape of an uneducated policeman, a Scythian archer and public slave, whose pidgin Greek (in the preceding dialogue) has already assured the audience that Euripides' clever arguments will be lost on him.

by many powerful men as desirable additions to their households. Pericles himself might have married his notorious Milesian mistress, Aspasia, had he been able. But ironically, because of his own citizenship law, unlike the noblemen of preceding generations, he was forced to make other arrangements. What he did might seem shocking to modern sensibilities, but makes good sense in light of Athenian custom. As his Athenian wife's guardian in law, he divorced her by arranging a new marriage for her with an acceptable new husband—one wonders how much this unnamed woman suffered from the humiliation of being transferred from Pericles to someone else—and then lived openly with Aspasia as his legal concubine. Under this arrangement, their children would be free but not citizens, a fact that would not have been a hindrance to Pericles since he already had two legitimate sons by his former Athenian wife.

As for Aspasia, concubinage with Pericles brought her as much honor as she could hope to claim in Athens. As a foreigner, she had none of the public religious duties and enjoyed none of the privileges accorded great Athenian ladies. Even though within Pericles' house hold she might have been in charge of the domestic servants and the storeroom, as the mother of a bastard (she had one son, named after his father), she was second-class, not the equal of the proud mothers of Athenian boys. Philosophers may have admired her, but from the moment she caught her man, this influential, unconventional woman became a lightning rod for Pericles' political enemies and grist for the comic poets' mills, a convenient instigator of all his blunders and hated policies. Like Medea, she was a liability if she proved to be too much for the man who had put his honor on the line to win her.

At the time Euripides was composing the *Medea*, general awareness of the effects of Pericles' marriage law must have been quite acute, because first sons of marriages made immediately subsequent to its passage were just now applying to their precincts for entrance onto the citizen rolls. It is not surprising then to find traces of its impact in Euripides' dramatization of the appalling end of Medea's fairy-tale marriage. Has not Jason, like so many Athenians, set aside his marriage oaths and dishonored his wife for his own political convenience, apparently believing that, under altered circumstances, the gods would allow his new arrangements to override old oaths (**494–96** / 492–94)? Does he not believe that unrestrained rulers—like Creon and himself or, in democratic Athens, the majority of the citizens' assembly—could with their decrees, newly inscribed on mere wood and stone, override old unwritten marriage settlements, sanctioned not just by mouthed formulas but by oaths spoken directly from the heart to the ears of the gods?"[11] To the extent that the *Medea* engaged such issues, it offered its audience small consolation that there might be satisfactory solutions. Indeed, one of the things that is so disturbing about this play is that Medea refuses to go along with the little arrangement between Jason and Creon to sustain Creon's family's rule in Corinth and to return Jason to power in Iolcus, managing instead to enforce divine justice within a single day.

The audience that morning in the Theater of Dionysus must have begun to squirm in their seats when Medea and Jason finally confronted each other in the great debate (*agon*) that supplies the climax to the first part of the play. In the course of her argument, Medea reviles her former husband for his contempt of their marriage contract, his willingness to trample her honor, and his desertion of their friendship, not in the emotional sense so much as in the sense of an alliance of interests. To satisfy his lust, a man had other places to go, but for the raising of chaste and strong children and harmony within the house, tranquil friendship (*philia*, the word Aristotle uses to describe the relationship between man and wife) was best. Medea's lust, her succumbing from the outset to the strong and wrong Aphrodite (cf. *Medea* 634ff. / 627ff.) in her relationship with Jason, was a sure sign of something gone awry in the marriage she had forged in defiance, ironically, of all the old unwritten laws of the family she now invokes; it is a sure sign of a force that might in the end tear a friendship apart (cause civil war), rather than cement it for all time. For in this society, where all friendships were understood to entail a mutual exchange of benefits, not just goodwill rooted in affection, and every party to a friendship was publicly judged according to the amount of honor he had gained in forging it, a dishonoring misstep could lead to disaster.

When Medea says to Jason, "Or have the gods allowed you / to make new rules that govern oaths?" (495–96 / 494), her meaning for the ancient audience was far more pointed than it is for us modern readers. When she says, "Come then, if you want, I'll speak to you as a friend and ask the questions a friend would ask" (502–4 / 499), she means what she says not just in an intimate, personal sense but in the wider political sense upon which their union was founded, as a wartime alliance between herself and Jason. In fact, however, she had been willing to betray her father's house, not for gain—as Jason liked to think—but for love. She was so maddened by love, so innocent of Jason's true character,

11. Cf. Sophocles, *Antigone* 453–55; Plato, *Phaedrus* 274b ff.

that she told herself it did not matter that she was marrying him for the wrong reasons and in the wrong way. But, of course, in the delicate balance of honor gained and given, it did matter. She gave up the rights that she held under her father's rule for other rights, secured, she thought, by oaths; but as it has turned out they were rights that could be overridden as soon as the political winds shifted.

Although Jason's arguments in his defense may seem lame and chauvinistic to us, who feel the justice of Medea's charges, they were probably familiar to Euripides' audience and would have had more force with them than they have with us, because Athenians had both used them themselves and believed them implicitly. Like Jason, Athenians might have argued that, since emotions did not count, according to the public honor code, a foreign "wife" actually got more out of her friendship with her Greek husband than she had put into it. Just the chance to live in Greece so far exceeded her investment that she would have no grounds for complaint. Through her Greek spouse, she, like Medea, would have achieved celebrity and the privilege of submitting to Greek "laws" rather than barbarian force. The irony of this latter claim would probably have been felt by Euripides' audience, who were increasingly aware of the way Athenian laws, not least the marriage law, could be imposed on others, both individuals and subject city-states, by whoever at the moment ruled the assembly. The decrees they voted upon every month seemed to undermine the ideal of inherited law and to serve convenience rather than justice. Thus, in the play, when Jason alludes to the privilege of living under Greek laws,[12] which kind did they think he meant, the sacrosanct traditional laws that Greeks were willing to die honoring, as the noble Three Hundred Spartans had done at Thermopylae, or these latter-day contingent laws passed by men proficient in the new techniques of oratory, who were able to gain ascendancy over the many by securing for them the privileges and wealth that were once enjoyed only by the noble and able few? Instinctively, they would have said that he means the former; but they could see that, by his actions, it is the latter, the laws that guaranteed the Greeks their honor as free men and the aristocracy its greatness, that he is flouting and that Medea, the barbarian, is upholding as she defends her own and her children's honor. Paradoxically, she, not Jason, seems to be the one making the stand at Thermopylae and obeying the unwritten, divine law of oaths and the inviolability of an honorable man's word: "Whatever it

12. *Medea*, 545–46 / 537–38. "Justice, not force" in Collier's lapidary phrase, but the run of the Greek, "You . . . are acquainted with justice and enjoy laws without having to gratify force," implies not so much the rule of force as the need to do favors to the powerful or submit to their will.

commands [she does]; and its commandment is always the same: it...
requires [her] to stand firm, and either to conquer or die" (Herodotus,
Persian Wars 7.104, tr. George Rawlinson). If along with Aegeus (cf. **690** /
695) the audience found themselves agreeing with Medea's stronger
case—if they found themselves censuring Jason—they would logically be
obliged to censure themselves, too.

But Jason in his argument with Medea does not stop with pointing
out the benefits she has reaped by having the privilege of learning
Greek laws and being lauded by Greek poets. He goes on to maintain
how very advantageous, despite appearances, his new marriage arrangements are to Medea and her children, how they do not really represent
the dissolving of an old friendship but its expansion. With Creon as a
near connection by marriage and with future royal half brothers as kin,
they will be so much safer, wealthier, and better placed politically than
they would have been on their own. Truly, he had not acted out of lust;
he had acted the way a savvy Greek vying for a place at the head of the
table always acted, to satisfy ambition and the constraints of altered
political circumstances. In other words, he makes a lame excuse to
justify an arrangement that increased his own honor but destroyed
Medea's.

Much that is strange in this play can be made more intelligible if we
remember how crucial honor was to the calculations of all the Greeks.
In our society nonconformity, independence, and self-reliance are
prized, even in women. But this kind of individualism (a nineteenth-
century word) is alien to the ancient world, not just in women, who were
praised when compliant and invisible, but even in men, whose duty it
was always to be striving to promote their honor and the honor of their
family. The leadings of conscience meant nothing to them. Their very
being, their selfhood was bound up in the opinion others had of them. In
their small world of virulent family feuding, especially the privileged
upper-class part of it, honor—the respect due to position and achievement, openly acknowledged every hour of every day—was everything.
Breeding (high birth and the right education), wealth, talent, physical
presence, offices won and successfully administered, above all prowess
in war, both as a strategist and as a fighter in the front lines—these were
the things that counted most, these and the fact that they were known to
and approved of by others, especially one's peers and betters. "Fame," as
Jason so pointedly observes (**548** / **542–44**), "is the important thing," for it
was the measure of a man's greatness. Being top dog on a desert island or
in faraway Colchis was tantamount to not being at all. A man who had
lost his honor, whom no one feared or respected, had nothing left to fall
back on, nothing to make life meaningful.

To such men as these, there was nothing more glorious to be sought than to die in battle, fighting for the city of one's fathers and the honor of one's house. The Three Hundred Spartans who fell at Thermopylae against an overwhelmingly superior Persian force reached the pinnacle of honor and had for their reward lasting glory, because they had subordinated all their personal desires for the salvation of Greece and to uphold the honor of their ancestors. Conversely, to have survived the battle by some incalculable misfortune, like being behind the lines on sick leave, was a disgrace worse than dying unburied on a desert shore, for living in Sparta after Thermopylae meant enduring day after day the open contempt and open laughter of those who had once feared, respected, and praised you. You had gone from being a Somebody to being less than a Nobody, and there was no place to hide from this fact. "When Aristodemus [who had survived Thermopylae because he had been ill and unable to fight] returned to Lacedaemon [Sparta], reproach and disgrace awaited him; disgrace inasmuch as no Spartan would give him a light to kindle his fire, or so much as address a word to him; and reproach, since all spoke of him as the craven" (Herodotus, *Persian Wars* 7.231, tr. George Rawlinson).

In the honor game women, too, had a strategic part to play, and they knew it. Though subordinate, they were essential to their husbands and fathers, not just biologically as mothers of their children and grand-children, but as keepers of their own and their houses' reputations as well. How large a dowry and how much political influence they brought to their husbands' houses, how well they managed the household staffs and the storerooms, how modestly they comported themselves inside and outside the home, even how good they looked (for beauty adds grace to virtue and enlarges praise)—these things really mattered. But what mattered most, the thing that brought them the greatest personal honor, because by its means they proved themselves capable of bearing noble, purebred offspring, was their chastity—before marriage their virginity and after marriage the sanctity and purity and, indeed, the discreet privacy of the marriage bed.

In honor due a woman, as the Nurse tells us at the beginning of the play, Medea stood at the top, and her unmerited demotion from a proud and revered legitimate wife to the exposed, degraded position of a concubine had destroyed her honor as surely as illness had destroyed the honor of the Spartan Aristodemus, with this important exception: misfortune was not the cause of her disgrace; Jason was. She had never been at fault in their marriage, but he had treated her as though she had been, and, as far as she was concerned, he had done this for no good reason. If she had been barren or had crossed him in his public or private life, her fall would have been hard but understandable. As it was, he had acted just to aggrandize himself, to serve his own pleasure, for lust (as she saw it) and convenience and apparent, not true, honor. The Greeks had a good word for this kind of transgression, *hybris*: intentional and arrogant insult, any action that purposely depreciates or shows too little respect for another worthy of respect.

If the marriage of Jason and Medea had been in any way ordinary, his arrogant trampling underfoot of the just pride of a weak woman whose protector he was supposed to be would have been wrong but perhaps pardonable, since in the ancient honor code, his honor trumped hers. Regrettable as such divorces might be, they were some-times necessary. The man, the stronger, ultimately determined the right. But as Euripides' audience well knew and as Medea herself reminds her women friends (**271ff.** / 251ff.), theirs was no ordinary marriage. She had been no meek bride obedient to her father's will, but Jason's companion in arms, who had more than once given him tangible aid against his mortal enemies. Her reward for her help in his foreign and domestic wars had been her marriage. Under such circum-stances their union could not be deemed a mere alliance between two families, but something more electric, a blood pact between fellow conspirators, who were honor bound to harm each other's enemies and do good to each other's friends.

In the computation and retention of honor, harming one's enemies was not just a duty, it was a coveted mark of success. By contrast, to hurt one's friends without cause, to disrespect them, was despicable. The trick lay in being able to distinguish between them, in order not to do the wrong things to or with the wrong people. Feelings, especially strong feelings, were better ignored or muted, for they could easily lead one astray, as they did Medea, whose passion for Jason had deluded her into thinking him a worthy ally. Of course, affection, even love, played a cementing role, especially among close friends, but in the ancient city, where no higher impersonal corporate authority as yet defined or pro-vided for the common good, friendships were too important to be left to affection. They involved careful, reasoned deal making, for a friend was not necessarily someone you liked, but someone to whom you owed tangible benefits and who owed you benefits in return. Friendships not formed for pleasure's sake, though pleasure might indeed result, but for honor's, for visible political gain and prestige, were negotiated in many ways, marriage alliances being but one of them—albeit an extremely important one because they stood at the intersection of two basic kinds of friendships, those determined by blood and those based on agreement. Although marriage was, of course, intended to enlarge and perpetuate the former, in origin it belonged to the latter, those freely made, which were designed to advance family honor and the honor of the participants and their kin. When peacefully negotiated between responsible, rational parties—like Creon and Jason—they might indeed lead to unforeseen political calamities, especially if the contracting parties were leaders in their cities, but they were not calamitous in themselves, like the one Medea, *in loco patris*, forged with the desperate Jason.

Among voluntary friendships, the purest, most emotionally intense were not marriages, but those made by the young among their peers. The Greeks termed such friends *hetairoi*, that is, the friends of the shield or comrades with whom one marched in battle, engaged in politics, did business, formed a cult or even a cabal. Although they might include kin, and often did, kinship was incidental to their basic conception. Indeed, such friendships might even include former enemies. In large cities, just as the assembly was a meeting of the army and veterans, this model of comradeship defined many nonfamilial associations, the sworn alliances called *hetairiai*. Such friendships might be formed, for example, to forward a public concern or commercial enterprise. But sometimes they had the force of life and death alliances formed in times of extreme danger for the purpose of overthrowing a common enemy by force of arms. Of this latter kind was Medea's marriage pact, a joining of forces by two natural enemies under such duress that, like other life and death pacts, it was sealed by an oath, taken "over a [blood] sacrifice without blemish," whereby the two parties swore to "pray that he who observes this oath may be blessed abundantly: but that he who observes it not may perish from the earth, both he and his house."[13]

Thus, it was under constraints of this kind of oath that Medea avenged herself upon Jason to restore the honor his *hybris* had taken away. We can measure its putative binding power by the way in which the gods themselves fail to censure Medea's vengeance. To fulfill its terms and avoid the humiliation she might endure if she tried to attack Jason in person and failed, she made his life a living death and destroyed his house, rather than him, by slaughtering his new wife and her own darling boys, the latter an act so terrible, so polluting to the Greeks that it required annual rites of expiation for all time to come (**1353–57** / 1378–83) as compensation. Yet despite her palpable grief, she remains utterly unrepentant; nor is she punished for her crime. Instead she flies off to the temple of Hera and thence to Athens, in a conveyance

---

13. After a law of Solon, decreed by the democratic Assembly in 410, concerning slaying with impunity any enemy of the Athenians: quoted in Andocides' speech, "On the Mysteries," paragraphs 97–98, tr. K. J. Maidment.

provided by her ancestor, the Sun, the very god appointed to be the eye of the world's all-powerful enforcer and judge, Zeus. It is as if only the destruction of Jason's whole house, including his children (106–9 / 112–14), would satisfy the bloodthirsty Underworld avengers, set loose upon the earth by his breaking of the mighty wartime oath by which he had bound himself to this superhuman woman (163–66 / 160–63).

What we see at work here is a merciless, more primitive kind of justice, far removed from our abstract, carefully defined notions of law and order and closer to the kind of sublegal justice portrayed in *The Godfather*. Jason's sons' were necessary victims, whose death completed the punishment exacted by the Underworld; the annihilation of his house was guaranteed by the oath he had sworn and sealed by blood offerings poured into the earth and by the curses he had himself invoked. Although in this instance retribution was swift, it need not have been. Indeed, Jason himself, blindly trusting in the genuineness of his goodwill toward Medea and his own innocence—after all, under the pressure of circumstance he had done nothing more than other honor-seeking, realistic Athenians would have done with impunity—believes that the death of his boys must be delayed retaliation for the earlier death of Medea's brother back in Colchis (1306–7 / 1333). His line of reasoning was familiar to and accepted by many in Euripides' audience.

Although most in that audience would have readily acknowledged the power of animate blood and of the Underworld gods who drank it eventually to punish Jason for his wrongdoing, even by the killing of his sons, to judge by the Chorus, they would have found it difficult to justify Medea's making herself their instrument. While the compensation demanded by the gods for the violation of a powerful, sacred oath might explain the bloody outcome of the plot, it does not explain how Medea, who knew what she was doing—she was no "deranged housewife"—was able to force herself to commit what amounted to self-murder, the spilling of her own blood. Looked at from one perspective, the demonic, she was justified; from another, the ethical, she was not: hence the emphasis in the play upon her corrosive anger and how deeply she felt the insult of the blow Jason had dealt her. Repeatedly she expresses her horror at the derisive laughter of those she now considers her enemies (787–88 / 797), aimed not just against herself (1328–30 / 1354–57) but also against her children, if they were to remain in Jason's house (771–72 / 781–82, 1035–37 / 1059–61) or be buried by Jason (1353–55 / 1378–81). This horror of insult was something Euripides' audience with their explosive, Mafia-like contentiousness, would have understood, even if we do not. For them as for Medea, it was an irresistible motivating force. Medea had risked everything for Jason, not just the undying enmity and disgrace of her father's house but her own life and honor as well. Her reward was a marriage bed shared with Greece's greatest captain and the head of one of Greece's richest, most powerful, and lordly houses, to whose welfare she contributed unstintingly, for she was more than Jason's Mamma Corleone; she was his loyal, irreproachable *consigliere*. No wonder then that Jason's betrayal cut so deep. Euripides' audience would have understood the depths of Medea's uncontrollable anger, her dread of public shaming, and her thirst for the sweet honey of revenge. When wronged in the privileges of the marriage bed, even ordinary women become bloody minded (281–83 / 263–66). But would they have thought that Medea's fear of imagined future insults against her boys justified her, their nourisher and ally, in killing them? Drama with its many voices and diverse points of view shuns easy answers. But in this instance I think not, and not for sentimental reasons so much as for the fact that in killing them she had violated not just another unwritten law but one as strong as nature itself, the bond between mother and child.

Beyond the wildest imaginings of even the most callous Athenian, Medea had succeeded in wreaking total vengeance on her betrayer, but in so doing she had betrayed herself. In the grip of this palpable paradox, chances are that the audience, as they marveled at Medea rising in her chariot with the sun, sat in dumb silence, afraid not just for themselves and their own precarious honor—what man in that audience did not fear the power of women, especially able women they could not control, to undo them behind their backs—but for mankind's inability to fathom the Underworld's—and Zeus'—inexorable logic.

GEORGIA MACHEMER

ON THE TRANSLATION

The story of Medea is one of the best known from ancient Greece and the play is one of the most widely translated Greek tragedies. As a result readers come to *Medea* knowing in some detail what will happen. Unlike other Greek tragedies there are no strong reversals and few surprises. When the play begins events have already reached a crisis. The Nurse tells us that Medea is starving "herself, except from grief / and endless hours of crying / ... she loathes her children" (**21-32** / 24-26). Medea, Jason, and their children are on a fast track to murder and destruction. There will be no veering. Added to this is the fact that for a modern reader or audience inured to the public flaunting of unhappy relationships between celebrities, Medea's sacrifice of her two sons to avenge Jason's divorce and remarriage is an act of such enormity that it seems excessive and unbelievable. All of this pushes the play in the direction of melodrama. One of my biggest concerns as a translator was to find a way to control the almost hysterical emotional energy of the play so that it avoided becoming shrill with anger and blame or claustrophobic with revenge. This is a problem that modern actors and directors can partially solve through setting, pacing, gesture, and tone. I wanted, however, to make the text itself capable of controlling and releasing this emotional energy so as not to exhaust the reader too soon as well as to make the tragic events more plausible. In the end, I wanted the play to read with the force and clarity of a dramatic poem.

Uncertain of how to solve the problem of melodrama, I began by tightening and compressing the language. I found that a fairly regular iambic rhythm might control the play's emotional urgency—somewhat—and that if the diction remained plain and direct, the characters might begin to speak in distinct ways. The range of diction I had in mind was that in Robert Frost's "A Servant to Servants," "The Death of the

Hired Man," and other of his dramatic narratives. It is my hope that the meter and diction of the translation, along with the voice of the speakers rising from these elements, offer the reader and dramatist a version of *Medea* that approximates the tonal shifts and emotional tensions in Euripides' incomparable play.

A great part of the pleasure of working on this project has been in the collaboration with Georgia Machemer. Her line-by-line and often word-by-word translation guided me through the controversies and uncertainties that inhabit the original text. The suggestions and corrections she has given me have been invaluable as has been her support. David Kovacs's 1994 Loeb *Medea* provided an extremely useful starting point as did translations by Philip Vellacott, Frederic Raphael and Kenneth MacLeish, and John Harrison. Many discussions with Tom Sleigh, who had finished a translation of Euripides' *Herakles* as I was beginning *Medea*, helped to steady and encourage me.

MICHAEL COLLIER

MEDEA

Translated by

MICHAEL COLLIER

With Introduction and Notes by

GEORGIA MACHEMER

CHARACTERS

NURSE of Medea

TUTOR to Jason and Medea's children

MEDEA daughter of Aietes, king of Colchis

CHORUS of Corinthian women with their leader

CREON king of Corinth

JASON leader of the Argonauts

AEGEUS king of Athens

MESSENGER servant in Jason's household

CHILDREN Jason and Medea's two sons

Line numbers in the right-hand margin of the text refer to the English translation only, and the Notes beginning at p. 199 are keyed to these lines. The bracketed line numbers in the running heads refer to the Greek text.

Enter NURSE *from the house.*

NURSE   If only the Argo had not tricked the sea,
           had not flown on its wings past the Clashing Rocks
           to Colchis! If only the pines of Mount Pelion
           had not been hewn for the heroes' oars,
           who rowed for Pelias to win the Golden Fleece!
           Then my mistress Medea would not have sailed
           to the walls of Iolcus, her heart broken
           with love for Jason, or have persuaded the daughters
           of Pelias to kill their father or be living now
           in Corinth with her husband and children,   10
           a refugee who's won respect, admired—stable,
           domestic—supporting her husband as she should.

           But now she hates all things. What love remains
           is sick. Jason has left his sons and my mistress
           for a royal bed and bride—the daughter
           of Creon, the king who rules this land.
                                    Medea,
           enraged, recites the list of Jason's vows,
           mocks the way he raised his hand as pledge
           and demands the gods stand witness to what
           her faithful love's produced.   20
           Now she starves herself, except from grief
           and endless hours of crying since she learned
           her husband's wrongs.
                              She won't look up.
           Her eyes fixed to the floor. She is deaf
           to friends' advice, like a stone, like a wave.
           The only thing she does is turn away
           her lovely face to grieve in solitude—
           her father, land and home—what she abandoned
           to come here with the man who's now dishonored her.
           Poor woman, misfortune's taught her what it means   30
           to live without a country.

She loathes her children. They bring no pleasure
when she sees them. I'm afraid of what she's
thinking—fueled by her vengeful temper
to some new plot. She is dangerous.
I know how she responds to treachery.
No one who goes against her can win.
                                    But now
her sons return from play unaware of trouble.
Innocence protects itself from grief.

TUTOR   Old slave of my mistress's house, why are you   40
        alone outside the entrance, filling up
        your ears with your own complaints?
        Can Medea afford idleness like yours?

NURSE   Old tutor to Jason's sons, if servants
        are loyal, they take on their master's misfortune
        as if it were their own, deep and heartfelt.
        So great is my grief I've come outside
        to make the earth and sky listen to Medea's troubles.

TUTOR   And still she moans and grieves?

NURSE   What do you know? Her pain has just begun.   50
        Its pitch rising.

TUTOR   I shouldn't say this, but she's a fool
        and worse for what she doesn't know.

NURSE   What's that? What she doesn't know?

TUTOR   No, I was wrong to bring it up.

NURSE   Surely you can trust me with your secret.
        I'm a slave like you.

TUTOR   I was passing near the sacred water of Peirene,
        where old men throw dice, when I heard one of them
        mention Creon. I slowed down, pretending not
                to listen,   60

and overheard that the King would soon exile
        these children
and their mother. Drive them out of Corinth.
Don't ask if it's true. I don't know.

NURSE Jason will be a party to this? Exile his sons?
His argument is with Medea.

TUTOR That marriage is finished. He has a new wife.
He's no longer bound to honor Medea.

NURSE Doom follows evil and the sea rushes in
to fill a sinking boat.

TUTOR Why talk of doom. Hold your tongue.   70
Now is not the time to incite Medea more.

NURSE But children, now you know about your father.
I'd like to see him die! Yes, I would! But he's
        my master.
And yet his faithlessness is too awful, unheard of.

TUTOR That a man, a hero, abandons his wife and children,
bestows his love on someone new,
and at the same time keeps his self-regard—
        unheard of?
What world have you been living in?

NURSE That's enough!
Children, go inside. I promise, nothing
        will happen.   80
And you, keep them from Medea.
When they are near, her eyes are fierce, savage like
        a bull
as if she'd trample them with anger.
When she breaks out, let's hope the children aren't
        around.
Let's hope her enemies receive this wrath instead.

155

MEDEA   *Sung from within.*

My hope is death!
Death's sorrow my gift!
My gift...my wretchedness!

NURSE   Quickly! Didn't I predict this?
Your mother's fuming anger—   90
despair at its boil.
Hide from her.
Rage must not find its target.
She came into the world fierce
and stubborn and then she learned
to hate. Go inside,
don't look back!

                    Exit TUTOR *and* CHILDREN *into house.*

Her cries are nothing now.
But when she learns about her exile?
We'll see how the sky   100
catches fire. We'll see
how she feeds those flames
with her implacable hate.

MEDEA   I suffer!
Nothing can answer it.

I want my children dead.
I want his house destroyed,
to crush my sons
and their father beneath it.

NURSE   She'll make the children pay   110
for their father's treachery.
Reason and moderation is what's needed.
Time to think. What else can I do?
Her power makes her dangerous.
Privilege provides a license
for her violent moods. If she
were more like me, more like others,

that would tame her.
I aim for dignity in old age
to bring a modest honor   120
and enough money for my needs.
It's no good if your means
exceed your grasp.
The gods will notice
and then your fortune
pays for ruin.

Enter CHORUS.

CHORUS   I heard her voice. I heard
the desolate cry of the Colchian.
Her lamentation called me out
from deep inside my house—   130
a neighbor whom I befriended—
and so the misfortunes
of her house are mine.
Nurse, what will soothe her?

NURSE   How do you soothe utter desolation?
How do you say, "Climb out
from your abyss, reach up
to your friends. They'll help
you stand among the ruins
of your home?
                    Oh, yes,   140
and that man who's looking on,
the one who married Creon's daughter?
He used to be your husband."

MEDEA   Zeus' thunderbolts kill!
Cleave my head!
      Peace will then
spill out!

That's a cure.

CHORUS   Listen, Zeus, and Earth and the Light!
She sings a dark destructive song.

Medea, why lie down with death?   150
Why let desire have fatal sway?
Death is always near.
Don't pray for it.
Don't kill yourself with grief.
Trust in Zeus. His justice
is the way to settle scores.
Grief is what the newly married Jason
feeds you. Spit it out!

MEDEA Before I betrayed my father,
before I butchered my brother at home   160
then dropped him from the Argo,
piece by piece, like bait,
I made Jason swear to love
and honor me, for after my shameful treason,
I thought only great oaths would keep
him bound to me.

Themis and Artemis, brave goddesses,
enforce those vows—or let me see Jason
and his princess buried
beneath the rubble of their house.   170

NURSE Do you hear her terrible prayers?
How she begs Themis and Zeus
the guardian of oaths
to revenge the broken vows?
All along I've feared she needs
cruelty to soothe her rage.

CHORUS Then, go, Nurse, tell Medea
we are outside, faithful friends,
women who can bear the worst
of what she feels.
                    When she sees us,   180
our voices will be a song
that calms her anger.
Do this quickly, no excuses.
Time is all she needs

to carry out cruel plans.
Who knows, her cries,
already come too late...

NURSE   I'll go. I can't refuse orders.
I'll make duty the pleasure
that hides my fears.
                    She'll growl   190
and snarl when I approach,
like a lioness shielding
her cubs. She'll snort like a bull.
I doubt I'll lure her out.
But I'll go.

        NURSE *starts to leave, then turns back to* CHORUS.

I know a servant shouldn't talk
like this, but your singing voices
won't heal Medea.
When men invented song,
they had in mind decoration
for festivals and banquets,   200
pretty tunes.
Think how much better off
we would be if music
like a magic spell could reverse
the bitter histories of our lives
or cure human sorrow.
As it is I wouldn't bother
with the twanging lyre,
let the gorged and drunken
fall asleep happily   210
in their cups
that's enough satisfaction...

CHORUS   Again we hear the lamentations,
her fury rehearsing
Jason's grotesque betrayal.
Again she invokes Themis' help,
the goddess of oaths,
who guided Medea

over the haunted sea
and through the impassable maw   220
that guards the way to Greece.

MEDEA Women of Corinth, here I am, as you wish
and not as you might think, uncaring.
                                              All of us
know women who no matter the occasion
remain decorous, or because they stay at home
are thought to be cold and implacable,
indifferent to their neighbors' needs.
All of us judge by sight and not by knowledge.
Because I'm an outsider I know this better than most,
and have worked hard to fit in,   230
but not, like some, I hope,
in a prideful or aggressive way—
even so I'm a target of suspicion,
especially since Jason, yes, my faithless husband,
tore out the threads I'd stitched to hold
our life together. So quickly and suddenly
was it done, I wasn't given time to console
myself or build alliances with friends.
A brutal man whom I once loved has smashed me
in the face so hard I wear the face of death.   240

What other creatures are bred so exquisitely
and purposefully for mistreatment as women are?
Think of how we buy ourselves husbands,
power and alliances for them, slavery
and conquest over us. Bad enough
to have no choice in servitude—
but to pay for it and then celebrate
a wedding feast adds salt to the wound.
Try refusing the arrangement, or later
petition for divorce—the first is impossible   250
while the second is like admitting
you're a whore.
                      And who ever warned us
of a husband's rough hands,
breath aflame on our neck, or the inscrutable

customs of his house?
Some of you will say, "It's not
that bad"; and with work can learn the rules
and maybe find a meager happiness.
But as hard as we try to do the pleasing thing,
it usually leads to resentment,   260
complaints about our moods.
That's why when they seek out friends
for entertainment, death looks so good to us,
much better than our husbands who think
we adore only them, grateful that they,
not us, go off to war. But they're wrong!
deluded by soldier fantasies.
If they like pain and danger let them take
a turn at bearing children and for every birth
I'll fight three wars.   270

But I've been talking as if our lives
are the same. They're not. You are Corinthians
with ancestral homes, childhood friends,
while I, stripped of that already,
am now even more exposed by Jason's cruelties.
Remember how I came here, a war bride,
plundered from my country, an orphan?
Now who's obligated to shelter me? Not you,
I know. As you watch my plans for justice unfold,
keep them secret, that's all I ask. I've never felt   280
this threatened nor fearless: men win their battles
on the field but women are ruthless when the bed
becomes the battleground. We've lain
in our own blood before . . . and have survived.

CHORUS   Medea, now I understand your grief
         and why your husband's treachery
         must be revenged. Go ahead, I won't tell.

Enter CREON.

But, look, our king approaches.
He's come to listen and advise.

CREON   I've decreed your immediate exile   290
         from Corinth, Medea. This includes
         your children. Get your things together.
         An escort's waiting to take you to the border.
         Hurry up!
         Later you can twist your face like that
         and rage against your husband all you want.

MEDEA   You, too, will drown me in the storm
         unleashed by my husband?
         Did he send you to cut away the sails,
         and clear the decks of my last hope?   300
         If not, then why this "Hurry Up!"—
         this unseemly rush to exile?

CREON   The truth is I fear you'll harm my daughter.
         Why? Because your nature, clever and vindictive,
         thrives on evil and because you sting with loss.

         A king has many ears;
         through them he hears the darkest threats
         made against his house.
                                        I've heard yours.
         I know about your plans, so why should I wait?
         Exiling you now is my best protection.   310
         If I let you stay, a woman like you
         will only hate me more for my weakness.

MEDEA   A woman like me! What am I like
         that's different from you or any man,
         except I'm a woman who is clever ...
         and that's my reputation? Then no one,
         man or woman, should be encouraged
         to be clever. Stay dumb!
         It's easier to fit in with fools.
         Fools, educated or not, will resent   320
         you for what you know. A woman like me
         is mistrusted and despised for her cleverness,
         feared by you because your fear's misplaced.
         Creon, I'm not so clever. Don't fear me.

I haven't the power to kill a king.
Besides what harm have you done me?
Like any father you arranged your daughter's
marriage to make the best match.
I respect that.
        It's my husband I hate.
Yet I wish your alliance well.   330
From now on I'll be quiet about my wrongs
and respect the judgment of my betters.
That's difficult for me to say. All I want
is for you to let us stay in Corinth!

CREON You'd do better persuading me
with a fit of rage. A woman like you
keeps planning harm no matter
what she says. Meekness
is more dangerous than guile. Even if you
silenced your hate I would never believe it.   340
I won't be tricked by an enemy.
Exile is what I've decreed.
Immediate! Irrevocable!

MEDEA A woman like me never begs. But look. . . .
I beg you.

CREON So don't try. You can't convince me.

MEDEA But you are bound by my plea to listen.

CREON No: I'm bound to protect my family and home first.

MEDEA I need my birthplace more than ever now.

CREON I love my children first and then my home.

MEDEA Yes, but what we love too much is dangerous.   350

CREON That depends; sometimes it's dangerous not to love.

MEDEA Zeus, you won't forget who caused our pain.

CREON Go, the longer you stay the more trouble you bring.

MEDEA No: my trouble starts when I go.

CREON If you don't go, my men will throw you out.

MEDEA Creon, I told you I never beg, but look I'm begging!

CREON I don't call this begging! You're defying my decree!

MEDEA No, I accept exile.

CREON Then let go of my hand, stand up!
       What do you want?   360

MEDEA A day's reprieve to prepare for exile
       gracefully. And since my husband loves
       his new home more than his children
       I need to plan their future carefully.
       Put yourself in my place. You'll feel differently.
       As a father you can see the children
       aren't to blame. Exile is not new to me,
       but it will crush my sons.

CREON I'm not a rigid tyrant. Mercy
       has undermined my resolve before.   370
       I'll regret my wavering. Nevertheless
       you can have one day on one condition:
       When the sun comes up tomorrow
       if you and your children have not crossed
       the border, you die.
       Stay if you must.
       One day won't give you time
       to work the wicked plans I fear. Ask no more.

                                          Exit CREON.

CHORUS Medea, you're doomed!
        An exile needs help and protection,
        a destination and shelter.   380

Where will you go?
To whom will you turn?

MEDEA You're right! My situation's bad,
exile's made it dire but don't think
there isn't time to settle the score
with the newlyweds and their procurer.
When I kissed Creon's leprous hands,
when I got on my knees and begged,
it was not for pity but for a brief reprieve.
If he had stood his ground I'd have no hope,   390
but foolish as he is, now I have a day,
and a day is long enough to make of him,
his daughter, and the one I used to love
a heap of bones.

So, friends, what method should we use?
Hard to choose. I could torch them
in their love nest or butcher them sleeping
in their fragrant bed. These require stealth,
luck more than nerve and style.
Nothing could be worse if I were caught   400
lurking in their house. They'd mock and laugh
at me intolerably before putting me to death.
Better to reach them directly without detection.
I'll do what I do best. I'll poison them.

See how easy it is to kill!
But when they're dead where will I go?
What country or household will welcome
and protect me? None.
If someone should arrive to rescue me,
though time is short, then I'll use silence   410
and trickery to carry out the murder,
but if no protector comes then I'll attack
directly with an unmistakable sword
and die along with those I kill.

Hecate, dearest of my household gods,
by your dark magic I will repay

the pain and ridicule I've suffered.
Bitter with grief will be their marriage.
Bitter will be what Creon tastes
for his part in this alliance.   420
Bitter for me my banishment.

Come, I must be Medea, Hecate's servant,
artist of potions and spells of guile.
Listen to the voice of her suffering.
Hear what others hear, that Jason's
absurd marriage was made by outwitting you,
daughter of a king, granddaughter of the Sun!
Remember, you're a woman and it's useless
to compete with men like Jason.
Speak courage to yourself!   430
Be Medea, invent their grotesque murders.

CHORUS   Now sacred waters flow uphill
and the world where men
once honored oaths is parched.
Look, at last, women embody truth!

No longer will the ancient songs
that sing our faithlessness be sung.
If Apollo allowed us to carry a tune,
we'd write the epic of men's worst frailties.

We'd sing, Medea, of your inspired love,   440
how it guided you through the Black Sea.
We'd sing of what you lost, your fatherland,
a husband's love, and now your children's home.

The spell of trust is broken, and shame,
like you, is banished. Past and future hold
no welcome, while the present is a princess—
younger, stronger—who sleeps where you once slept.

Enter JASON.

JASON   Even before I met you, I knew rage
        and anger were their own worst enemies.
        Generous terms were offered you: the house,   450
        protection, and privileges, but could you bear
        these gifts without complaint? Now exile
        is your reward. Keep railing at me.
        Call me vile and disgusting. It doesn't matter.
        But keep it up about Creon and his family
        and exile will be a kindness.
        And just so you know—I've been your advocate
        with him because I wanted you to stay.
        But could you stop your rant against the king?
        You've bought your exile with your foolish mouth.   460

        Still, after all the trouble you've caused
        I won't be accused of neglect. I'm here
        to do the right thing, to ensure the children
        and you have the means and money to endure
        the worst exile will bring. For this I'm sure
        you'll hate me, but it's a hate I won't return.

MEDEA   How can I say what you are! Curses
        won't answer your vileness and names
        don't exist for your cowardice. In fact,
        I doubt you're real. What real man,   470
        so offensive to everyone, would think it
        courageous to face the family
        he's betrayed, and lie to them again?
        But I'm glad you're here. I'll catalog your sins
        and feel better for it while you feel worse.

        I'll start at the beginning, and if you don't
        remember, ask any Argonaut—they
        saw how I saved your life when my father
        challenged you to harness the fire-breathing bulls,
        plough the field of death, and sow the monster seeds.   480
        I killed the insomniac serpent coiled
        inseparably around the Golden Fleece,
        whose light and shimmer raised by me
        brought your success instead of death.

More eager than wise, I abandoned
my country and father to follow you
to Iolcus where I engineered your uncle's
murder, wasting that house, too, with grief
and death. All this I did for you!
And in return you honored me   490
with contempt, betrayal, a replacement wife.
I might understand your disappointment
if I'd been barren but I gave you sons!

Now your promises are worthless.
Or have the gods allowed you
to make new rules that govern oaths?
See my right hand, how often you spoke
in pledge to it, how often you bowed
your head—an earnest supplicant.
You lied then as you lie now,   500
a thief of all my better hopes.

Come then, if you want, I'll speak to you
as a friend and ask the questions a friend
would ask. And when you can't respond,
I'll have shown what kind of friend you are.
So, as an exile where should I go? Home
to my father whom I betrayed for you?
To the cousins who stewed your uncle
with my recipe? I'm sure they'd set
an extra place so I could eat with them.   510
That's how things stand, friend.
For you, I became my family's worst enemy.
For you, I set my fatal traps
and in return you made a spectacle of me
for all of Greece to see. What do they imagine
as I'm sent from my home, alone, except
with the children you've abandoned? That Jason
is a faithful, honest husband? Surely
your new wife is reassured to see
your sons poor and homeless, and me—   520
the *former* wife—who betrayed herself
to save you, destroyed again.

Why has Zeus given us the alchemy
that detects true gold from false
and yet withheld the means
to expose evil in men?

CHORUS Stronger than lover's love is lover's hate.
Incurable, in each, the wounds they make.

JASON I suppose I should stand here
and ride out the tiresome storm   530
of your complaint, put on my captain's hat,
reef sail, and drag anchor to your mood.
But I can't bear how you exaggerate
your selfless role in my success.
I know how I was saved. Powerful Aphrodite!
She led me to the Golden Fleece and back.
And you, yes, you have a mind for plots
and treachery, but Cupid had to wound you
with his darts before you moved. Go ahead,
remind me I'm ungrateful.
                       I won't say   540
your passion wasn't real. I won't say
you didn't help, you did. And for it
you've been paid more than you deserve. Listen,
and I'll prove it.
                Now, you live in Greece—
the center of the world. Justice, not force,
rules here. Here your cleverness has brought you
fame. Out beyond the Black Sea, no one sings
in praise of you.
                To me, fame is the important thing.
I'd give up all I owned for it.
What good is a voice like Orpheus'   550
if no one knows it belongs to you?
Remember who started this war of words.
That's all I'll say to counter your account.

As for my royal marriage, if your reproaches
weren't so blind, you'd see it as a plan—

ingenious, disciplined, farsighted—
to support you and the children.

MEDEA: *furious.*

If you'd just listen, for once, maybe you'd
remember we fled Iolcus and washed up here,
broken refugees. So what better reversal   560
than to marry the daughter of a king?
                                          That I
grew bored with you in bed and wanted
a younger wife? These thoughts drive your anger.
Or that I want to father more sons?
The ones I have—yours and mine—
are more than adequate.
                              I remarried
so we might prosper and live in the comfort
we deserve, surrounded by true friends.
If I should have more sons, they'll be
brothers to ours, not rivals.   570
I've forged an alliance that protects
and elevates us all. Children are more important
to fathers than to mothers. My unborn sons
will save our living ones.
                              Is this plan bad?
No, you'd admire what I've done if sex
wasn't your obsession.
                              It's folly
that women measure their happiness
with the pleasures of the bed, but they do.
And when the pleasure cools or their man goes
        missing,
all they once lived for turns dark and hateful.   580
If I could remake the world, I'd banish women,
send them away with all their trouble.
Then children would come from a purer source.

CHORUS Jason, reasonable words make reasonable arguments
        and I could believe them but truth lies in deeds
        and, I'm sorry to say, you left Medea.

MEDEA A reasonable argument? Am I the only one alive
       who hears lies made reasonable by this liar?
       Shouldn't truth twisters be punished
       instead of listened to? Not, apparently, if they deceive   590
       as brazenly as Jason does. Where will he stop?
       But he's not so clever. Watch how my words
       will pin him to the mat.
                              If this marriage
       was part of such a selfless scheme, why hide it
       until now? Why not ask me for help?

JASON Help? If I'd mentioned marriage, divulged my plan,
       what part of your hateful, broken heart
       would have come to my assistance?

MEDEA The part that knows your shame to live
       the rest of your days with a barbarian like me   600
       was greater than your honor.

JASON I'll say this one more time! I didn't need
       another woman. The marriage was strategic,
       a defensive ploy to protect you—to give our sons
       brothers connected to the throne.

MEDEA I don't need fortune's gifts if they're made from pain
       or wealth derived from the heart's torture.

JASON Wake up, Medea! Good fortune isn't painful.
       Be thankful for the chance to prosper.

MEDEA Don't mock me! Fortune sends me wounded   610
       into exile, while the palace is your home.

JASON Exile was your choice; don't blame fortune.

MEDEA My choice? Did I abandon you?

JASON No, you chose to curse the king.

MEDEA Of course I did, just as I curse you.

JASON   I won't argue with you any longer.
        My offer of help stands: money to ease
        exile for the children and you. Also,
        I have friends who can arrange to take you in.
        Say the word. What's mine is yours.   620
        It does no good to harden yourself
        to charity. Leave behind your destructive anger.

MEDEA   I won't take help from you. Besides, your friends
        are now my enemies and gifts from
        a faithless man like you are bribes.

JASON   Then let the gods judge me. They see
        my plan for you and the children is good.
        They see this obstinate refusal of my help.
        Remember, the gods can still make life worse for you.

MEDEA   Leave me, your impatience stinks of lust   630
        for the new bride. Go and be the groom!
        But listen well, your skill at marrying
        will bring you a dowry of tears.

                                                      Exit JASON.

CHORUS See, how strong love overwhelms us.
        See, how it wounds and destroys
        and yet when Aphrodite wants to soothe,
        nothing cures as love cures.
        So, my love, shoot me gently,
        barely break my skin with your terrible arrows.

        Then I'll know happiness in life.   640
        Then Aphrodite's urgings will enflame
        my heart, but love will keep me faithful, far
        from the wildness of a stranger's bed.
        Then I'll know that when she chooses lovers,
        it means that love will never fail.

        O, and this sweet city, Corinth,
        may I never be its poor exile.

May I never wander in realms
where pity is my name. Kill me
first, spare me life's worst torment   650
to lose your true home and native land.

This is no invented grief.
In Medea I have seen
the friendless suffering exile breeds.
Let those who promise love
and then defile it, die unloved
and never ask to be my friend.

                    Enter AEGEUS *in traveling clothes.*

AEGEUS Medea, greetings, happiness!
       What better hopes can friends express.

MEDEA Happiness to you, Aegeus. Welcome.   660
      What brings you to Corinth?

AEGEUS I come from Delphi—Apollo's oracle.

MEDEA The world's most potent seer. Why?

AEGEUS To ask how I might father a child.

MEDEA Childless? How can that be?

AEGEUS I think by a god's curse.

MEDEA Are you married? Do you have a wife?

AEGEUS Yes and we find pleasure in our bed.

MEDEA What advice did Apollo have?

AEGEUS A riddle to confuse the most clever.   670

MEDEA Can you say it? Or have you been forbidden?

AEGEUS No, it begs for cleverness like yours.

MEDEA Then tell me. Don't hold back.

AEGEUS "Choke off the wineskin's spout," he warned.

MEDEA What else? For how long?

AEGEUS Until my journey ends at home.

MEDEA Yet by sailing here you're far from home.

AEGEUS I've come to speak with Pittheus, the Troezen king.

MEDEA Pelops' son, he's known for piety and wisdom.

AEGEUS I'll tell him what the oracle declared.   680

MEDEA He's nimble enough to solve the riddle.

AEGEUS And there's no better friend. A brave man in the ranks.

MEDEA Good luck and may you obtain all you desire.

AEGEUS But, Medea, I see your face is etched by tears. Why?

MEDEA Aegeus, my husband is vile. There's no one worse.

AEGEUS How? Tell me what darkness haunts you.

MEDEA It's his fault. He's wronged me. I'm blameless.

AEGEUS Fault? Blame? There's more, I can tell. Go on.

MEDEA He's thrown me out. Installed a new wife.

AEGEUS What's compelled him to act so shamelessly?   690

MEDEA His promises are lies. His love false.

AEGEUS Perhaps he's confused a brief passion for love.

MEDEA His passion is for faithlessness . . .

AEGEUS Then it's your duty to forget him.

MEDEA . . . and ambition. He's married the king's daughter.

AEGEUS What king consents to this?

MEDEA The Corinthian, Creon, who rules this land.

AEGEUS I understand your torment.

MEDEA And my exile? I've been sent away to die.

AEGEUS By whom? I see how trouble overwhelms you.   700

MEDEA Creon. My sentence starts tomorrow.

AEGEUS Where's Jason? He won't allow this.

MEDEA He acts appalled but won't do anything to help.

MEDEA *kneels before* AEGEUS *in supplication.*

By all that's honorable and wise in you,
you who recognize the shameful wrongs
I've endured, save me from friendless exile.
I need refuge in your country, protection in your home.
Do this and the gods may give you children.
Help me and you'll die a happy death.
Seize this moment that fortune brings.   710
I know recipes and spells to quicken men.
Let Medea end your quest for children.

AEGEUS Noble Medea, I'm ready to help.
        I know the gods want justice.
        I trust your magic will produce my sons.
        Already I feel the burden lifting.

        Listen and I'll lay out our plan:
        The Corinthians honor me as their guest.
        I won't insult them by stealing you away.
        Instead you must reach Athens on your own.   720
        There you'll be my guest. Do this
        and Creon can't come demanding
        that I give you up. My home will be
        your best protection. I promise.

MEDEA   I understand these obligations. Now restate your
                promise
        as an oath. Only then will I feel secure.

AEGEUS Is it the plan or me you don't trust?

MEDEA   Aegeus, you I trust but not my many enemies:
        Pelias' sons, Creon . . .
                      An oath
        Will keep your promises safe against   730
        their powerful inducements to give me up.
        I'm weak and need the gods to help.

AEGEUS Your argument, wise and measured,
        is convincing. An oath provides me cover
        from my enemies and gives you peace of mind.
        Tell me which gods to swear by. I'll do it.

MEDEA   Start with Gaia, then Helios, my grandfather,
        and as usual, all the gods no matter where they be.

AEGEUS Yes, but what am I obliged to do? You've left that out.

MEDEA   Swear never to exile me from Athens.   740
        Never, on your life, no matter what they say,
        agree to my enemies' demands to hand me over.

AEGEUS Gaia, Helios, and all the gods,
I swear by Medea's spoken oath.

MEDEA Exactly. And if you break this pledge?

AEGEUS May the gods punish me like others who renounce them.

MEDEA Dear friend, go now, you have your happiness.
Mine follows once I've carried out my plans.
Then I'll come to Athens.

Exit AEGEUS.

CHORUS LEADER May Hermes, protector of travelers,   750
lead you safely home
and may your eager wish for children
be granted. Aegeus, a noble heart
like yours deserves reward.

MEDEA Zeus, your justice shines brightly under
Helios' light. Look into that light, my friends,
and you'll see victory lies ahead. What else
could Aegeus' sudden appearance mean—
his offer of safe harbor, but certain punishment
for my enemies. Yes, and afterwards,   760
I'll ride out the storm my vengeance has caused,
securely docked in Athens.

Listen, now it's time to unfold my plans,
though what I say is certain to displease.

I'll send a servant to summon Jason
and when he comes, I'll tell him
what he wants to hear: yes, his marriage,
my abandonment—two parts of a brilliant plan.

And since this concerns the children's fate,
not mine, I'll suggest they remain with him.   770

But don't think for a moment I'd leave my sons
in this unfriendly land, targets for my enemies.

No,
            the children are the bait I'll use to trap
and kill the princess bride.
Each will bear a gift to her—
one a priceless gown,
the other a diadem of supple gold.
She needs only to unwrap and touch
the precious things to die painfully,
and any one who touches her
infected corpse will die as well.   780

That's the easy part, all thought out
and what follows is more than unspeakable.
I must kill my children.
Only their deaths will bring down Jason's house.
Quickly I'll go into exile, guilty
forever of my sons' ungodly murders.
But this is easier to bear than my enemies
who mock me. Why should I care anymore?
And what's the good of living?
                            I can't restore   790
my home and country; no spell will release
misfortune's hold. I was wrong to leave
my father, wrong to let a Greek
seduce me with his promises.
But the gods will assist me. Jason
will pay for mistreating me.
                        The next time
he sees his sons, he'll see them dead
and his hideous bride—meant to bear
new sons—destroyed by my fatal potions.
Who then will dare to say I'm weak or timid?   800
No, they'll say I'm loyal as a friend, ruthless
as a foe, so much like a hero destined for glory.

CHORUS LEADER We've listened to you. We want to help.
                But the laws of man demand we urge you
                not to carry out your plan.

       MEDEA The plan is set. Advice like yours lacks nerve
                and my experience with grief and suffering.

CHORUS LEADER Suffering so great you'll kill your sons?

       MEDEA Yes, anything to make Jason's suffering worse than mine.

CHORUS LEADER And turn your grief into wretchedness and misery?   810

       MEDEA Who can say? The time for talk has ended.

                                    To the NURSE.

                Go, find Jason. Invite him here.
                There's no one else I'd trust with this mission.
                If you are a woman truly loyal to me,
                you'll tell him nothing of my plans.

                                    Exit NURSE.

      CHORUS Children of the gods, of sacred Earth,
                since ancient times, Athenians
                have flourished, unconquered, nourished
                by the vivid air that brings them
                grace and wisdom, a residue   820
                from when the muses once combined
                to fashion Harmony, their perfect child.

                A time, we're told, when Aphrodite
                drinking from the sweet Cephisus
                would fill the river valley with her breath,
                fragrant as roses that bind her hair,
                a scent that guides her Loves to wit,
                where side by side they invent
                beauty and excellence in every art.

How then can Athens   830
with its sacred river,
its land where gods find refuge
admit a murderer, fouled
by her children's slaughter,
to live among its citizens?
Consider the knife, the innocent throats,
the slit and cry and blood!
By all we know, we beg and plead:
Do not kill your sons!

And at that terrible moment   840
how do you know your heart
won't fail, hand not tremble
when you see the blade flash
in your children's eyes?
When it's your own sons
begging for their lives
then not even you—cold
hearted—will drench your hand
in their warm blood.

Enter JASON *accompanied by the* NURSE.

JASON As you command, I'm here, once more,   850
ready to listen, though your enmity for me
is clear. . . .
           Tell me, what's your new demand?

MEDEA I want, Jason, your forgiveness for all
I've said, to understand that my anger
is the other side of love provoked
by years of happy marriage.
                           I've taken stock,
talked to myself—and it's stubbornness,
fed by rage, that blinds me to these preparations.
Why should I oppose you and Corinth?
You've conspired to make me more secure,   860
to give our sons princes for brothers.
Why not trade anger for peace? Give up suffering

and recognize the gods offer hope.
The truth is, the boys and I are exiles. We need
    friends.
I've come to realize calmness and steadiness
are what's required, a partner in your plan,
a proud bridesmaid to the nuptial
you've generously devised.

Women are not dumb and wicked by nature
but we are what we are. Knowing this,   870
you should avoid treating me the way
I treated you, answering a fool with foolishness.
Now that I've brought myself to this understanding
I can admit how wrong I was. Clear thinking
is all I needed to join your undertaking.

Children, come out, it's safe! Greet your father.
Speak to him with love. Our feud is over.
We've called a truce. Our hate has vanished.
Grip his right hand like men. . . .
                        Now the future
lies ahead, its troubles hidden.
                    . . . Children,   880
promise all life long you'll embrace me, too.
Here's wretchedness, fear, foreboding, sorrow
I can't hold back. The quarrel with your father
made up and yet I'm moved to tears.

CHORUS LEADER My eyes, too, are soft from crying.
            Let misfortune stop here where these tears fall.

JASON Good, you've got the right attitude now.
        I'll let pass the earlier tantrums.
        Women aren't made to share their husbands.
        And though it took awhile for you to change   890
        your mind about my triumphant plan . . .
        Well, I'm glad that reason has returned.

        My sons, your father's careful deliberations,
        blessed by the gods, guarantee a better life

for you. Someday with your future brothers
you'll help to govern Corinth. Only now,
grow into men. Let your father
and a favoring god fashion your destiny.
Once you've reached your prime—strong,
    irrepressible—
I'll watch with satisfaction as you crush my enemies.   900

> MEDEA *turns away from the scene, weeping.*

Why keep crying? Why the downcast face?
Have my words again disturbed you?

MEDEA I'm fine. My concern is for the children.

JASON Why prolong this torture with your fears for them?

MEDEA I'm their mother! And when you begin to speak
about their futures, doubt and pity rush in.

JASON Their futures are safe, sealed. Give up your worries!

MEDEA Then I'll submit to what you say. Remember,
as a woman my nature is to cry.

But there are other reasons I summoned you: 910
I won't escape the king's decree of exile.
It's better that I'm banished. I'd be a hindrance
if I stayed, a source of suspicion
for all the threats I've made against his house.
I've reconciled myself to leaving Corinth,
and the children. In order for your plan
to work, you must raise the boys here.
Go, beg Creon not to send them into exile.

JASON He's stubborn and resolute, but I'll try.

MEDEA Start with your wife. Use her to persuade   920
her father the boys don't deserve banishment.

JASON Yes, with her I'll have success.

MEDEA That's right, if she's like other women,
       but let me help. I have a plan to send
       the children to her with gifts more beautiful
       than mortals know: a seamless gown,
       a diadem of supple gold . . .

                                              To the SERVANTS.

                                      Quickly,
       one of you go bring the treasures here.
                                              To JASON.

       Look how fortune multiplies for her:
       first, a brilliant husband fills her bed   930
       and now these adornments, heirlooms that Helios,
       my grandfather, bequeathed to his descendants.

                          The SERVANT *returns with the gifts.*

       Boys, take these presents, hold them tightly,
       hand them to her highness, your father's radiant bride.
       Gifts like these she will more than embrace.

JASON Medea, this is foolish. Keep them for yourself.
       The palace has chests filled with fine garments,
       vaults of gold. Don't give up your legacy.
       If I have any say with my wife, my words
       will persuade more than your family's wealth.   940

MEDEA Don't count on it! Even gods like gifts.
       And men always prefer gold to promises.
       Her youth and status appeal to the gods,
       so let's treat her like a goddess. Gold, yes,
       but I'd give a life to buy the children freedom.

       Now, boys, go to the king's magnificent palace,
       get on your knees and beg your father's new wife,

my mistress, to stop your exile. Give her
these rare gifts. Most importantly, put them
only in her hands. Go quickly. Good luck.   950
I'll wait for your return and the news
that all your mother wishes for is true.

> *Exit* JASON *and* CHILDREN, *accompanied*
> *by the* TUTOR *and the* NURSE.

CHORUS Abandon hope that the children will survive.
Now they walk the murderous road.
The bride will embrace the lacework of gold,
blind to its enchanting ruin.
She will lace her beautiful hair
with death's poisonous ribbon.
Heavenly charms, Helios' crown of gold
and shimmering gown, glamour   960
she can't resist, though it makes her
a bride of the dead. The snare is set.
Death waits at the center.
No power can come to her rescue.

And you, unfortunate bridegroom
who engineered a royal marriage
to shape his destiny, could you have guessed
your plan would murder your sons
and deliver your bride to a hideous death?
Unlucky man, could you have been more wrong?   970

And Medea, you're wrong, too,
in every way, sad and sadder still,
you'll kill your sons, justice too harsh
for Jason's heartless crimes—
your husband who left your marriage bed
to occupy another.

> *Enter* TUTOR *with the* CHILDREN.

TUTOR My lady, the princess took the gifts into her hands
and happily consented to give your sons reprieve.
In the House of Corinth they'll find happiness.

Medea turns away and weeps.

But why should good fortune make you sad?   980
Why turn away from my report?
Have I displeased you?

MEDEA Sadness everywhere!

TUTOR But the children are happy.

MEDEA Sadness is everywhere!

TUTOR I thought my news was good.
Tell me what I've said to upset you.

MEDEA You saw what you saw. You're not to blame.

TUTOR Then why the dark face and tears?

MEDEA Grief is all that's left. My vengeful schemes   990
and the gods' help have made it so.

TUTOR Think of the day your sons will bring you home!

MEDEA But first there are others I must carry home.

TUTOR Women lose their children frequently
so bear this sorrow as best you can.

MEDEA Yes, in time I will. But now go inside.
Get ready for the children's day. They'll follow soon.

Exit TUTOR *into the house.*

Children, my dear sons, this is your city.
Here is your home where you will start new lives,
bereft of me, your abandoned mother.   1000
I must begin my exile in a land
far from you, without the happiness
of seeing you grow and prosper, unable

185

to perfume your nuptial baths, arrange
the bridal sheets or light the wedding torches.
My unforgiving self has made me wretched.
And all I've done to raise you, the ceaseless work,
the excruciating pain of childbirth—
all count for nothing.
                          Foolishly I hoped
you'd care for me in my old age, dress my body   1010
when I died. What better fortune than to have
such sons.
                          But this sweet dream of life
has ended. Bereft of you I'll spend my days
in heart-broken grief. And you no longer
within sight of me will grow accustomed
to my absence.

Oh, children, I don't understand your looks.
Why smile as if it were your last?
I despair of what to do.
                          See, my strength
and resolve vanish in the children's   1020
lively faces. It can't be done.
Farewell to my schemes. When I leave, I'll take
my sons with me. Why should I make them
suffer to revenge their father and make
my own suffering so much worse? No, farewell.

And yet what will change? My foes
unpunished mock me.
Should I endure it? The pledges I've made
my heart have weakened me.

          The CHILDREN *begin to move toward the house.*

                          Boys, go into the house.
Now, only the sacred and pure are allowed   1030
to witness this sacrifice. My hand has strengthened.
Yet, my angry heart resists these urges.

Release the children. Spare them from my
    wretchedness.
In Athens they will bring me happiness.

But it's too late. By all of Hell's vengeful
demons I'll not leave my sons
for my enemies to ridicule.
           The children
must die. I gave them life and now
I'll take it. No more wavering. It's settled.
There, I see the princess wearing the crown   1040
and know the poisonous robe eats her flesh.
The path before me is filled with grief
but it's nothing like the dark road I'll send
my sons down.
           Let me say goodbye to them.

The CHILDREN *return to* MEDEA.

Children, give me your hands to kiss.
Sweet hands, sweet lips. Strong bodies
and noble faces. May happiness follow you
into that other place. Here your father
has stolen your happiness.
           Such tenderness,
my hand caressing your skin, your sweet breath—   1050
My sons.
       Leave me, go into the house.
I can bear no longer to look at you.
The horror of my evil overwhelms me.
Horror of what I'll do. Angry passions
have mastered me—emotions of misrule
that destroy men.

Exit the CHILDREN *into the house followed by* MEDEA.

CHORUS LEADER Many times I've joined in formal arguments
             with men whose skill in the subtle art
             of rhetoric was greater than my own
             and lost. But all women aren't strangers   1060

to Wisdom's muse. Sometimes one of us
is chosen to be guided by the inspiring daughters.
And so my thoughts have led me to believe
that childless men and women lead lives
more fortunate than those with sons and daughters.
Although they never know the joy and pain
that children bring, they avoid
a much greater sum of trouble.
Households filled with children
are slaves to the work and worry of their care.   1070
The first concern is how to raise them,
then how they'll manage once they're grown.
Yet even when they're independent,
it's still uncertain if their success
will honor you for all you've done. But heartbreak
worse than what's produced by all these
common dangers lurks and waits.
Let's say the children turn out perfect.
Does fate care if fate has other plans?
Death comes to drag our children   1080
off to the underworld no matter how beloved.
You'd think the gods might offer inducements
to men and women for bothering to bring
children into the world; instead they take it
as a chance to pile grief on top of grief.

Enter MEDEA *from the house.*

MEDEA Our long wait for palace news is over.
One of Jason's servants sprints this way.
Listen, he gasps from exertion.
When he arrives, expect to hear about disaster.

Enter servant of Jason's as MESSENGER.

MESSENGER Medea, such crimes, heinous—inhuman—   1090
You must go, now, by any means,
land or sea. Don't stay, fly!

MEDEA What's happened? Why should I escape?

MESSENGER The princess and her father, Creon,
           lie dead, victims of your poison.

MEDEA Splendid news! Let me reward you
       with my undying friendship and protection.

MESSENGER Madness speaks through you.
           How can you slaughter Creon's family
           and then rejoice so fearlessly?   1100

MEDEA There's an answer to your question—but first
       calm down, friend, and tell me
       about their deaths. Pay special attention
       to their agony so I might take some pleasure.

MESSENGER The moment your sons with their father
           entered his bride's house, all of us,
           who once served you and who mourned
           your fate, were heartened. A shout went up
           that you and Jason had called a truce.
           This was like music to our ears. Suddenly,   1110
           we wanted to kiss the children, touch their
           lovely hair. Overwhelmed by happiness
           I followed them inside the princess's chambers.
           Understand, she's the woman we must serve
           instead of you.
                          At first she saw only Jason,
           but when the children came into view,
           she veiled her eyes, and turned away.
           Impatient with this display,
           your husband scolded her, saying:
           "Look at us. Don't revile your friends.   1120
           Your job is to love those your husband loves.
           They've brought gifts. Accept them graciously
           and for my sake ask your father to release
     ·   these children from their exile."

           The gifts astonished her with their beauty.
           She agreed to what her husband asked.
           So eager was she to wear the treasures,

even before Jason and the boys had reached
the road, she put on the colorful dress,
set the gold crown on her head,   1130
and in a bright mirror arranged her hair.
She laughed with pleasure at the beautiful
but lifeless image. Then as if the gifts
had cast a spell, she stood up, dancing
through her rooms, giddy with the feel of the gown
twirling so she could see repeatedly
her shapely feet and pointed toes.

But soon her face changed color. She staggered,
legs trembling, almost collapsing
before she reached a chair. One of the older, wiser   1140
servants believed some wrathful god possessed her
and so cried out in prayer to Pan,
until she saw the mouth foaming,
eyes wild and rolling, and skin leached of blood.
Then the prayers turned shrill with horror
and we servants raced to find Creon
and Jason to tell them the piteous news,
filling the house with the sound
of our panicked feet.

All of this happened in less time   1150
than a sprinter takes to run the dash
and quicker still was the way the princess
from her terrible trance woke, eyes
wider than before, screaming
in anguish. For now a second torture
wracked her. The gold crown exploded
in a fiery ring about her head, while
the delicate gown, brought by your sons,
ate into her sweet flesh. Consumed by flames,
she stood and ran, shaking her head   1160
as if to throw the fire off, but the crown tangled
tighter in her hair and the blaze roared higher
as she fell to the floor and rolled
in the unquenchable flames.

Only her father could have known
who she was. The eyes had melted.
The face no more a face, while flaming blood
leaking from her head fueled the blaze.
But worse was how the flesh like tallow
or pitch sloughed off her bones.   1170
All of this because the viperous poison
had locked her in its invisible jaws.

Schooled by what we'd witnessed, none of us
would touch the body, but her father,
rushed to her side, not knowing what he'd find.
Nothing could prepare him for his daughter's
corpse. Misery broke from his voice.
He embraced and kissed her, lamenting,
"Unhappy child, murdered so shamefully,
why do the gods torture an old man like me?   1180
Daughter, let me die with you."
But when his sobbing ceased
and old Creon wanted to rise, he found
he was woven to the fatal dress, stitched
to it like ivy to laurel, unable
even as he wrestled furiously
to free himself. The living father,
who felt his flesh ripping from his bones,
could not match the strength of his dead daughter
and so he gave up and died, a victim   1190
of her hideous fortune. Together now they lie,
an old man and his daughter. Who wouldn't weep?

As for you, Medea, and your fate,
hear my silence. From it will come your punishment,
swift and sure. As for our brief lives, I've learned
once more we are mere shadows. No longer
do I fear to say the truth: Fine words
and clever plans breed folly.
No man can count on his happiness.
Some have luck and fortune on their side   1200
but never happiness.

Exit MESSENGER.

CHORUS Today the gods delivered the justice
        Jason deserved and seized him with calamity.
        But the princess, a victim of marriage,
        now passing through the halls of death,
        we lament her terrible misfortune.

MEDEA Nothing will undo my resolve
        to kill my children and escape
        —but it must be quick.
        If I hesitate now someone else   1210
        will murder them more cruelly.
        There's no way out. They must die.
        And I who gave them life will take it.
        Come, heart, shield yourself.
        Why doubt what must be done?
        Come, unlucky hand,
        grip the sword, carry it to where
        unhappiness begins and ends.
        Do not weaken.
        Forget you love your sons.   1220
        Forget you gave them life.
        Today, remember nothing.
        Tomorrow, mourn them.
        For even if you kill your sons,
        you once loved them dearly.
        My life has been all grief!

Exit MEDEA *into the house.*

CHORUS Earth, hear us! Bright sun, Helios,
          look down, expose Medea,
            before her sons are murdered
        by her bloody hands. Remember,   1230
          they are your radiant children. Remember,
        when men wound gods, fear and darkness rule
           over us.

Brilliant, heavenly light, burn up
   this murdering Fury. Banish her
from the house, cast out
   this servant of vengeance!

Wasted, the pain of bearing sons.
   Futile, their brief dear lives.
      Better not to have sailed the Black Sea,
escaped the Clashing Rocks. Why, Medea,   1240
   does rage cloud your mind?
      Why must murder follow murder?

When families kill their own, they spill
   no darker blood, leave no fouler stain.
And the gods drawn to its stench
   punish all who bear the family name.

CHILDREN   *Cries for help from within the house.*

CHORUS The children! Do you hear their awful pleas?
        Oh, wretched and afflicted woman!

FIRST CHILD Mother, no!
        Brother, help me!   1250

SECOND CHILD There's nothing I can do. We're trapped.

CHORUS If we went inside now we might stop the murder.

FIRST CHILD Yes, with the gods' help, save us!

SECOND CHILD Look, a knife!

CHORUS Only a stone or iron forged from ore
        is harder than your heart. If it weren't their fate
        could you bear to murder the children
        you brought into the world?

        Only Ino before you—of all women—
        killed her sons with her own hands.   1260

And she, deranged by Hera, was sent to wander
the ends of the earth in madness.
That's why she leapt into the sea.
That's why in her unholy plunge
she carried her murdered sons—and all perished.
What worse horror will we face
now that a woman's marriage bed
has bred again mortal pain and evil?

Enter JASON.

JASON You women, gathered near the door, tell me,
is Medea inside—such unspeakable crimes!
                              —or has she fled?   1270
She'll have to use the underworld to hide
or fly on wings to heaven to avoid what she deserves.
Murderess of the rulers of this land!
Does she think she'll leave this house alive?

But why should I care for her? It's the children
I'm looking for. She'll be punished.
Others will see to it, but I must protect my sons
from the revenge Creon's survivors are sworn
to make them suffer for their mother's crime.

CHORUS LEADER Jason, ignorant beyond pity, if you knew   1280
what lay ahead you'd never speak again.

JASON More treachery? Plans to murder me?

CHORUS LEADER With her own hands Medea killed your sons.

JASON What are you saying? This woman has destroyed my life!

CHORUS LEADER I'm saying that your children are dead.

JASON Where did she do it? In the house? On the street?

CHORUS LEADER Behind these doors you'll find her slaughter.

JASON   Call out the servants! Unlock the gates!
        First, I must see the murdered. Then I'll find Medea,
        the source of my disaster—   1290
        and seek revenge.

            JASON *tries to open the doors of the home.* MEDEA *appears*
                        aloft in a chariot drawn by dragons.

MEDEA   Why rattle the gates? Why open the house?
        You want the corpses? The murderer?
        Stop that banging! If it's me you're after, speak.
        Tell me what you want. Only words can reach me.
        Helios has sent his chariot to keep me from my
            enemies.

JASON   Vilest woman! Condemned, hated by the gods,
        by me, and every human creature. No one
        but you raised the knife that butchered
        your children. No one but you destroyed   1300
        my life. How can you stand there
        and speak about the sacred Sun?
                                    Guilty!
        Sentenced to die!
                            Now my mind is clear.
        How wrong I was to bring a barbarian home
        to Greece, already a dangerous betrayer
        of family and country. For this the gods have sent
        their Fury to torment me, though it was you
        who was cruel enough to kill your trusting brother,
        then leave with me aboard the noble Argo.
        That's how it started. Then we married.   1310
        Then you bore me children. The ones you've killed!
        All of this because of jealousy.
        Barbarians act like this, not Greeks.
        Yet I married a barbarian and yoked myself
        to hate and destruction.
        Compared to your brutal nature Scylla,
        with her heads and massive teeth,
        her many feet, is tame. Nothing hurts you.
        Insults and curses are praise.

Leave me, nothing worse than these murders   1320
can be done by you. My sorrowful fate
is my own: a bride's widower,
a childless father—all that I've worked
and planned for—lost.

MEDEA Why should I waste time replying to your words?
Zeus knows how I saved you and how
you repaid me with ingratitude.
Did you think that after you betrayed
our marriage you'd live a life of ease,
mocking me with Creon and his daughter,   1330
the princess he promised you before condemning me
to exile? Yes, call me fierce and vicious.
Say I'm a water fiend like Scylla—tell me,
how does it feel with my teeth in your heart!

JASON If you eat my heart, you swallow my pain.

MEDEA Pain without mockery is pleasure.

JASON My sons, you died at the hands of an evil mother.

MEDEA My sons, you died because of broken promises.

JASON My hand was not the one that raised the knife.

MEDEA No, the knife was whetted on your pride   1340
and the rails of your marriage bed.

JASON For pride and marriage you murdered sons?

MEDEA What woman would find your crime forgivable?

JASON A woman of sense, not a vengeful woman like you.

MEDEA Well, our sons are dead and that pain pierces your
              heart.

JASON No, they live on as Furies who will punish you.

MEDEA The gods understand the source of this violence.

JASON That means they fathom your gruesome heart.

MEDEA Go on, keep hating me, I detest your voice!

JASON And yours is worse. But I can end our argument.   1350

MEDEA How? Show me. I wish it, too.

JASON Let me bury our sons. Let me mourn them properly.

MEDEA Impossible! My sons will be interred by me
in the sacred ground of Hera Akraia, safe
from my enemies who'd want to dig them up.
And to expiate their murders, a solemn festival
will be performed. Once these things are done,
I'll go to Athens and live with Aegeus,
my protector. But for you, justice is approaching.
More miserable than now you'll die a coward,   1360
your head crushed beneath a beam of the great Argo.
Only then does the bitter story of our love end.

JASON May Fury and Justice, vengeful
and murderous, tear you apart.

MEDEA Don't you know, gods are deaf to oath breakers
and to those who deceive their guests.

JASON Defiled forever. Executioner!

MEDEA Go home to your wife. Go bury her.

JASON Yes, I'll go, grieving my sons.

MEDEA When you're old, grief that worsens day by day.   1370

JASON They were my beautiful boys!

MEDEA More beautiful to me, their mother.

JASON And so you murdered beauty?

MEDEA To give birth to your unending grief.

JASON If I could see them once more,
       I'd take them in my arms and kiss their mouths.

MEDEA Speak to them now?
       But you sent them away.

JASON Only to touch their soft skin, please . . .
       to hold my innocent children.   1380

MEDEA Impossible! Save your breath.

JASON Zeus, do you hear how I'm treated
       by this monster of filth and pollution
       who keeps me away from the children she murdered?
       All my life I will honor them with grief.
       I will call upon the mighty gods
       to remember how their killer denied
       my wish to lift them in my arms
       and place them in the earth. Now
       I regret their lives, for when I fathered them   1390
       I delivered them to a butcher's hands!

                MEDEA *with the corpses of her children is borne aloft*
                            away from Corinth. Exit JASON.

CHORUS LEADER The gods love surprise, so what men want
               is often denied, and yet the gods prevail
               for us. Think of the story we've just listened to:
               Who won? Who lost?
               Zeus stores our destinies in his great house,
               some glitter brightly, but most are hidden.   1397

                                              Exit Chorus.

NOTES

1–126 / 1–130 *Prologue* Unusually, in this play the prologue proper—the Nurse's introductory speech, followed by spoken dialogue between the Nurse and her fellow slave, the Tutor—ends with a duet between Medea offstage and the Nurse onstage, which begins at line 86 / 96. Into this duet the Chorus of Corinthian matrons intrudes itself as a third voice at line 127 / 131 (see notes on 86–221 and 127–221).

1–39 / 1–48 Euripides' surviving plays usually begin with a long introductory speech by a leading character or god, designed to situate the audience in the action about to unfold. Only in *Medea* is this introductory speaker a solitary servant. The Nurse's age and affiliation with Medea's household and her knowledge of the past suggest that, in accordance with ancient practice, she may have been Medea's wet nurse and personal possession (see notes on 40 / 49 and 926–27 / 949 [= 786]).

1 / 1 The opening of the play must have caught the ear and imagination of the Greeks, for twenty-five years later its first line appeared as Euripides' first entry in the verse weighing contest between himself and Aeschylus at Aristophanes' comedy *Frogs*, 1382 and was ever afterwards cemented in the ancient poetic memory (cf., e.g., Catullus 64.171ff.).

2 / 1 *wings* In ancient poetry flying metaphors were frequently used of beaked warships speeding like birds over the surface of the sea. Sometimes the billowing square-cut sails are envisioned as wings; at other times the rising and falling of the oars on either side of the hull as it cut through the water.

3 / 3–4 *the pines of Mount Pelion* The Greek refers to a pine (*peukê*)—not pines—that turned heroes into oarsmen (literally "put oars in the hands of the best men"). Since oars were not regularly made from pine—in Homer they are of silver fir (*Iliad* 7.5, *Odyssey* 12.172; cf. Theophrastus, *Enquiry into*

Plants 5.1.7), in Virgil of oak (e.g., *Aeneid* 4.399–400)—but ships' hulls were (cf. Aristophanes, *Knights*, 1300–1310 and Theophrastus, *Enquiry into Plants* 5.7.1–2), it does not seem unreasonable to suppose that Euripides' seafaring audience would have imagined either that the hull of the Argo was made from one huge primeval pine or several pines, or that a single pine became her mast (cf. Lucan, *Pharsalia* 2.695). Legend had it that Athena herself had come to lofty Mount Pelion, above Iolcus, and with her own bronze ax had cut Argo's timbers. Indeed, the construction of this remarkable warship was a tale so well known that Apollonius of Rhodes, the third-century B.C. author of the *Argonautica*, an epic in four books recounting the adventures of the Argonauts (see note on **481–82** and Introduction, "Legendary Background"; Glossary, "Orpheus"), decided to skip it (*Argonautica* 1.18–19).

4 / 5 *heroes* Greek *aristoi andres*, or "best men." One of the extraordinary things about the Argo was that it was manned entirely by ancestral *aristoi*, who now, from the point of view of Euripides' audience, were each and every one a hero, a son or grandson of immortal gods. The heroic Argonauts contrasted sharply with fifth-century Athenian rowers, who were drawn from the lowest class of citizens, the '*thêtes*' or hired hands. As the "Old Oligarch" (a fifth-century B.C. political tract preserved among Xenophon's works and considered roughly contemporary with the composition of the *Medea*) confessed, it was their contribution to Athenian power that entitled this traditionally subject working class to the new political rights and power they now enjoyed under Athens' radical democracy. Is there, then, a trace of sarcasm in the Nurse's "heroes' oars"? See Introduction, Historical Background.

8–9 / 9–10 *persuaded the daughters of Pelias to kill their father* Different literary sources give conflicting reasons as to why Jason was justified in killing Pelias; none explain why he and Medea must go into exile from Iolcus. The murder is a startling proof of Medea's frightening proficiency in sorcery. In order to convince the daughters of Pelias that she knows how to make their father young again, she puts the pieces of a dismembered old ram into a bubbling cauldron and then resurrects it whole and rejuvenated out of her potent stew. Eagerly Pelias' daughters try the same treatment on their beloved father, who, alas, fails to respond.

9–10 / 10 *living now in Corinth* The play tells us nothing about why Jason and Medea sought refuge with Creon in Corinth. Their exile status, which Euripides makes so much of, nevertheless contradicts earlier legends that connect both of them to the town. Jason's great-uncle Sisyphus was its legendary founder, but, according to Eumelus, a Corinthian poet of the eighth century B.C., who wrote an epic history of the kings of Corinth, Jason succeeded to the throne only after Medea had held it in her own right. It seems Helios (the Sun) first gave Corinth to his son Aeëtes (Medea's father), who, before leaving for Colchis, entrusted its rule to Bounus (whoever he might be), until he himself or one of his descendants should return. When one of Bounus' heirs died childless, the Corinthians bestowed the town's rule on Medea, and it was through her that Jason became king. Clearly Euripides ignores this genealogy to produce a new dramatic situation, perhaps more indicative of the political turmoil of his times. What happened to cause the death of their children is variously reported by different sources: out of hatred of her rule the Corinthians slaughter them, Medea kills them unintentionally, or she leaves them behind when she leaves Corinth and Creon's faction kills them, and so on. Common to all accounts is the fact that the children are remembered in an actual Corinthian cult. Thus, the cult of the children, also of importance to Euripides (see 1353–57 / 1378–88), seems to be a fixed element in this otherwise fluid Corinthian myth.

15–16 / 19 *the daughter of Creon* Although unnamed in the play itself, the plot summary (*hypothesis*) affixed to the beginning of the *Medea* calls Creon's daughter Glauke (blue-eyed), a name apparently memorialized by the name of a sacred spring in Corinth into which she was said to have thrown herself to quench the malignant fire that was ravaging her body (see 1138ff. / 1167ff.). The name Creon simply means ruler and is used to designate place holders in a royal succession, such as Oedipus' successor in Sophocles' Theban plays.

40 / 49 The Nurse's interlocutor in the ensuing dialogue is another trusted servant whose primary duty, like that of the Nurse, concerned the care of Jason's and Medea's boys. This Tutor or, literally, "Escorter of Children" (*paedagogos*) accompanied his charges to and from school and had general oversight of them outside the house. Just as the main characters represent the noblest of the noble, so these household servants represent servile nobility. Their power in the house among their fellow slaves and their importance to and intimacy with their masters and their children are suggested by Plutarch (*Life of Alcibiades*, c. 1) when he attests that the names of the nurse and tutor of the infamous Alcibiades were known to posterity.

44 / 53 *Old tutor* Drawing attention to old age here and in the preceding greeting may be intended not so much to enliven the servants' repartee as to flesh out what is seen. In a huge outdoor theater in which the performers are lit by the sun, the details of a mask would be less visible than the stance and

gestures of the actor, and the visuals overall are less individualizing than the clear auditory signals lodged in the dialogue.

47–48 / 56–58 The sentiment is found repeatedly in ancient drama in the mouths of characters who like the Nurse have to justify their uncustomary and often improper public appearances (before the Chorus) outside the palace.

61 / 70 *exile* Among the ancient Greeks, exile was considered almost as bad as decapitation, for an exile cut off from his family and city became almost a nonperson. Like a beggar, he was reduced to living off the benevolence of others.

68–69 / 78–79 Among these maritime peoples, the metaphor of the ship of state or, in this case, of the great household is traditional, and, not surprisingly, it is prominent in this play about the shipwreck of the Argo's commander.

86–221 / 96–212 At this point the Greek meter changes from iambic (spoken) to anapestic (sung and declaimed or chanted) verse, as Medea offstage sings of her woe and Jason's treachery, and the Nurse in response comments upon what she hears, using a more elevated vocalization to match the musicality and more insistent tempo of the anapestic meter. Later, when the Chorus adds its voice to their exchange, what seemed to be a duet is transformed into a regular antiphonal *kommos*, a lyrical interchange between the actors and Chorus. It is probable, based on Medea's use of rounded ah's (Doric dialect) instead of the Nurse's flat ay's (Athenian or Attic dialect, regularly used in the spoken iambics of Attic tragedy) that Medea sings and the Nurse declaims. The anapestic meter sets up a marching rhythm and so is a natural accompaniment to the Chorus' entrance song, or *parodos* (see note on **127–221**).

This passage and the other lyric passages of this play were accompanied by a single piper playing on *auloi*, that is, twin reed pipes (like oboes or clarinets), which were played as a pair, each of the *aulete*'s hands fingering one of the two pipes.

127–221 / 131–212 Parodos. Fifteen high-born Corinthian matrons now add their voices to those of the Nurse and Medea, first with sung anapests as they march into the orchestra (the theater's large circular dancing floor at the foot of the south slope of the Acropolis upon which the audience is sitting) and then with two matching stanzas (see note on **148–58**) in the mixed lyric meters characteristic of choral odes. After the Nurse leaves the stage to fetch Medea, they sing a third stanza to mark the end of the play's preparatory action and the beginning of the first episode.

Choruses sang a single melodic line—polyphony and harmony in our sense of these words were as yet unknown—in a one-to-one ratio between notes and syllables of text, and their range did not exceed an octave. Thus, their lyrics would have been more readily understood by the audience than those of modern choruses. Whether the male choristers sang in a falsetto when impersonating females we have no idea. Choral song was accompanied by mimetic dancing, whose movements are unrecoverable.

127 / 131, *I heard her voice* Despite the use of the first person singular, the Chorus is singing collectively as it enters from the wings. "I" and "we" seem to be used interchangeably in choral lyrics.

131–33 / 138 Lyrical lamentations sung by a distraught main character are an essential, almost ritualized feature of Attic tragedy. When the tragic Chorus participates in them and they occur at the beginning of the action, the collective Chorus often acts conventionally as comforters to the soloist. To make their exchange dramatically convincing, the playwright often highlights some plausible prior ground of allegiance between them. Here, because Medea is a foreigner and the Chorus members are natives and, consequently, their friendship cannot be taken for granted, they explain their friendly visit by referring to the goodwill they owe her in return for previous benefactions to them. Friendship, especially between strangers, is not so much a matter of affection as of a network of obligations. Medea was useful to Jason because she could perform favors for the Corinthians that made them obliged to him. Presumably the women represent their husbands' or fathers' houses in a kind of parallel "female polis"; they need not like Medea.

144 / 144 *Zeus's thunderbolts kill* An expansion of the Greek *phlox ourania* (heavenly flame or lightning), the invincible weapon by which Zeus, the king of the gods, rules the universe. The Chorus picks up this theme in its response, "O Zeus, and Earth and Light..." (line 148 / 148).

148–58 / 148–59 Choral odes in Attic tragedy commonly consist of one or more paired strophes and antistrophes. Each strophe (or "turn," a dance term in origin?) is answered by an antistrophe (counterturn), which is rhythmically—and presumably melodically—the same. Thus, the Chorus dances and sings a turn, then a matching counterturn, usually following immediately upon the turn but in this case postponed until after the Nurse's and Medea's anapests.

148 / 148 Zeus guarantees justice (see notes on 155–56 and 344ff.), Earth sends forth her avengers against the forsworn, and the Light of Day (or the Sun) sees

all wrongdoing. This divine triad is often called upon to witness oath taking.

155–56 / 157 *Trust in Zeus* Zeus is preeminently the god of Justice (Dikê; see the Glossary, "Themis" and "Zeus") who keeps watch over the right ordering of the universe, secures equitable distributions and alliances among gods and men, and punishes wrongdoers. The Greek implies that Zeus will be Medea's advocate in her just cause against Jason.

160–62 / 166–67 The Greek says simply "I departed in shame, having killed my brother." However, the story of Medea's strewing the fleeing Argo's wake with bits of her slaughtered brother Apsyrtus in order to delay her father, who piously stopped to collect each precious limb, presents such a compelling image that commentators often assume that Medea alludes to it here. This gruesome version is generally attributed to Pherecydes, a mid-fifth-century B.C. Athenian genealogist, but may actually have originated with Sophocles in a lost play, *Scythians*, which recounted the return voyage of the Argo; see H. Lloyd-Jones's comments in his Loeb *Sophocles III* (Cambridge, Mass., 1996), 274–77. We do not know, however, whether this undateable version was already circulating when Euripides wrote the *Medea*; he, in any case, seems to have another version in mind (see lines **1307–9 / 1334–35**, with note).

163–70 / 160–65 Medea takes up the theme, suggested by the Chorus, of the mighty oath that Jason once swore and now has broken. She invokes Themis, an archaic personification whose name, "Law" or "Custom" (literally, "That which has been established"), implies that she is a guardian of the prohibitions and prescriptions that regulate the affairs of men (and gods), especially those of divine or primordial origin.

Artemis, the virgin huntress leading her train of dancing nymphs through the wilds, is often depicted in myth as the slayer of young women, a reminder of the risks girls face when they become brides and new mothers. Perhaps she is called upon here to be Medea's savior, both in memory of what she once was when she first bound Jason to herself and entered upon motherhood and as the destroyer of his new wife. It may be that Artemis is also invoked here because of her association with the goddess Hecate (see note on **415**).

198–212 / 190–203 To Greeks, music as a way of forgetting cares was proverbial.

220–21 / 210–13 *through the impassable maw that guards the way to Greece* The Bosporus.

222–447 / 214–409 *First episode*

222–84 / 214–266 In sharp contrast to her previous wailing, when Medea now comes through the palace doors of the temporary scene building, her polite and politic words give to modern readers the impression of calm self-control. This sudden change from fire to ice has been rationalized in many ways, sometimes in terms of Medea's character, psyche, or personality (she is the kind of woman who under these circumstances is able with great effort to rein in her emotions), sometimes according to formal variations between impassioned lyrics and supposedly rational deliberations. Still others have called attention to the sophistical quality of her rhetoric with its indirect generalities.

285–89 / 267–70 The Chorus is now speaking (in iambics), not singing. Whenever this occurs, it is thought that only the Chorus Leader speaks.

288–89 / 269–70 Creon appears with a small retinue (cf. **355** / 335). Both Aegeus and Jason may also have retinues.

344–60 / 324–39 Formal line by line interchanges between two characters are typical of Greek tragedy, particularly in contexts of debate and cross-examination.

344ff. / 324ff. *I beg you* At this point, or, as some critics maintain, at **356** / 336, Medea kneels in a formal act of supplication and grasps Creon's knees (in the Greek) and right hand. By following these rituals, she puts herself and her claim to Creon's favor under the protection of Zeus as god of suppliants (Hikesios/Hiketesios). This is another way in which Zeus secures justice for the weak in the face of brute force.

377 / 356 This play, contrary to contemporary fashion and Euripides' usual practice, does not require the usual three actors, but like earlier tragedies could be performed throughout by just two actors. If indeed it was so performed, the actor playing Creon would exit at this point to change into the Jason mask and costume. (Only in the prologue, when Medea sings from within, is a third voice required, and that voice need not have belonged to a third actor. Any good singer would do—the poet himself, for example—and, since Medea does not sing on stage, the audience need not have noticed the difference between the unseen singer's third voice and the voice of the actor on stage intoning Medea's spoken lines.)

401–2 / 383 *They'd mock and laugh at me intolerably* It is not death per se she fears, but their gloating laughter and her degradation. See also lines **772** / 781–82, **787–88** / 797, **1026–27** / 1049–50, and **1330** /1355 and Introduction, "Medea's honor."

407–9 / 386–90 These lines prepare us for the arrival of Aegeus later in the play.

415 / 395–97 Hecate Euripides' *Medea* is our earliest evidence for Hecate in her classic role as the sinister goddess of magic and sorcery, by whose secret nocturnal rites a privileged few, her priests and priestesses, gained access to the Underworld with its disembodied souls and hidden lore. Like other purveyors of novel mysteries who were then flocking to Periclean Athens, Medea keeps a shrine to her special goddess in the innermost reaches of her home, presumably as a repository for the rare and potent drugs (*pharmaka*) that, with the goddess's help, she has harvested at times and places suitable for contact with dangerously polluting demonic powers (see Introduction, "Medea's character").

The exclusivity of Medea's mysteries contrasts with popular cult, in which both public and private shrines were placed at the entrances to cities and houses, along roadways near graves, and especially at crossroads, those dangerous points of contact between lower- and upper-world forces where triformed Hecate of the Crossroads (Enodia, Trioditis) was thought to dwell. Here, when the moon was full, her devotees would make offerings of shiny cakes. Conversely, at midnight on starlit new moon nights they would set out strange prophylactic sacrifices, called "Hecate's dinners," whose contents seem to have included kneaded cakes and puppies or fish.

Hecate appears in two forms in Greek art, as single-faced and Artemis-like with torches and hounds and, when her nature as Mistress of the Crossroads is being emphasized, in triplicate, sometimes with three heads on one body but more often with three full images facing outward from a central pole, a type immortalized in a famous statue of Alcamenes, set up in Athens about the time of the *Medea*'s first performance.

432–47 / 410–45 First stasimon This is the first of five choral odes sung and danced by the Chorus in front of the scene building. They are called *stasima* or "standing" odes, presumably because the Chorus begins and ends its movements in a standing position, possibly a squared military formation three files deep.

432 / 410 The Chorus mentions a reversal of nature that ancient magicians (like Medea) claimed to be able to effect (cf. Virgil, *Aeneid* 4.489; Ovid, *Metamorphoses* 7.199–200).

436–37 / 421–23 *ancient songs that sing our faithlessness* Commentators usually cite lines from Hesiod or the invective of Semonides as illustrations of the contumely heaped upon women, but I think the reference here is most probably to epic tales. The queen of faithlessness is Helen, but there are others, like Phaedra or Clytemnestra, and Aphrodite herself, the teacher of untrustworthy seduction. Not to be forgotten among treacherous women is, ironically, Medea.

438–39 / 424–26 *Apollo* As Lord of the Lyre, the shining god (Phoebus) Apollo leads the Chorus of the Muses, daughters of Memory (the oral tradition) and goddesses of song and choral dance. *Mousikê,* his province, embraces more than the knowledge of the tunings of the lyre, melodies, or rhythms; it embraces the winged words themselves, messengers of the divine knowledge of the past, present, and future that epic bards dispensed. That Apollo does not let this Chorus "carry a tune" (**438**, in Greek "did not grant the inspired song of the lyre," 424–25) indicates that the Chorus members have not gone to school.

448–633 / 446–626 *Second episode* The real-world analog of the explosive *agon* ("contest" of paired antagonistic set speeches) with which this episode begins is to be found in the formalities and vitriolic, highly personal atmosphere of the Athenian law courts—a speech of prosecution (Medea) spoken by or on behalf of the victim, answered by the accused's own defense (Jason)—with two notable concessions to the dramatic milieu: overwrought women did not appear in courts on their own behalf, and the introductory remarks designed to elicit the jury's sympathy and goodwill are lacking.

448–66 / 446–64 The tone of these lines is hard to fix. One can imagine them as conveying officiousness, "nauseating self-righteousness" (Elliott), or "ineffable smugness" (Morwood). One can even imagine a sympathetic rendering in which a sorrowful and frustrated husband tries to deal with a hysterical and intractable woman. Contemporary audiences, persuaded by the affecting directness of Medea's first speech whose justice they feel, find her a sympathetic character and Jason incomprehensible, if not downright reprehensible. But ancient Greeks would not have been so repelled. The citizenship law of 451 B.C., which decreed that Athenians had to prove that both their parents were citizens, made the disadvantages of a foreign marriage for one's children keenly felt. As heads of households, men legally ruled their wives and believed that a woman's greatest assets were temperance and submissiveness, virtues Medea clearly lacks. It was considered dangerous for a man to contract an alliance with a wealthier, higher class, smarter woman, since she was more likely to rule him than to be ruled. Thus, though Jason was clearly in the wrong for having broken his oath, the men in the audience would not have been as unreceptive as moderns to his excuses.

477–78 / 476 *they saw / how I saved your life when . . .* The Greek—*esôsa s' hôs isasin Hellênôn hosoi* ("I saved you, as all the Greeks know who . . .")—was famous for its (snaky, hissing) sibilants, which were designed to grate on the ear. Medea is spitting mad.

481–82 / 480–82 *I killed the . . . serpent* In Pindar's Fourth Pythian Ode, an earlier account of the legend of the Argo, Jason, not Medea, kills the dragon. Apollonius of Rhodes, writing a century and a half later, has Medea put the dragon to sleep. Such variants are typical of the fluidity of ancient myth.

481ff. / 480ff. Medea omits her brother's murder (see **160 / 167**) from this catalogue of the benefits she has conferred upon Jason. A good lawyer never brings forward facts that can have negative implications for his client, and Medea, as the audience already knows, speaks like a well-trained and effective advocate.

497–99 / 496–98 Breaking his oath is Jason's greatest offense against the gods. In the Greek, without mentioning supplication per se, Medea refers to her right hand and knees, thus immediately reminding her audience (and Jason) that Jason had knelt to her in formal supplication, just as she has just knelt to Creon. Because this custom with its symbolic gesture of submission, whereby the kneeling petitioner clasps the right hand (of honor and power) and knees of the one being petitioned, is foreign to modern English speakers, Collier substitutes another familiar act of submission, bowing the head, for "knees," and overtly names Jason as a "supplicant."

Interestingly, Apollonius makes Medea, not Jason, the suppliant; she begs that he take her away with him.

527–28 / 520–21 In formalized debates, choruses often offer neutral comment to mark the transition from one speech to the next.

533–39 / 526–31 The idea, first exampled here, that love, not the perpetrator, is the true cause of an action was a rhetorical commonplace favored by sophists in practice or display speeches, most notably in defenses of Helen of Troy. Euripides has Helen herself use it in the *Trojan Women*, 940ff. (415 B.C.), and it is also found in a famous "Encomium [Praise] of Helen" by the brilliant and influential sophist Gorgias of Leontini (in Sicily) who, we are told, came as an ambassador to Athens in 427, soon after the production of the *Medea*.

545–46 / 537–38 *Justice, not force, rules here* Barbarians who are the slaves of the Great King must serve his pleasure (cf. Herodotus 7.79 where the Colchians are part of the invading Persian army), but free Greeks obey only their city's laws. On the other hand, at the time of this play, recent decrees promulgated by a sovereign Athenian assembly were seen by many to be blatantly unjust, an irony that may extend to Jason's own claims and actions with regard to Medea. He broke his oath, and she can find no Greek law to protect her.

550 / 543 Orpheus is mentioned by Jason here not only as a fellow Argonaut, but because he, like Medea, was the proud possessor of powerful occult wisdom—knowledge of Underworld mysteries, incantation, and, indeed, the entire nature of things both human and divine. This wisdom, the know how to make things happen, not just to entertain with delightful sounds, made Orpheus' voice worth coveting. By the fifth century B.C. there was in Greece a body of oracular hexameter poetry—cosmogonies, revelations, healing spells, purifications, and so on—circulating under his name, promulgated by secret "Pythagorean" societies that practiced various forms of abstinence and held out the promise of a blessed life after death to those who had been initiated into the highest level of divine science.

569–70 / 563–64 *sons... brothers to ours, not rivals* Jason is assuring Medea that her sons will not be disinherited. Under the new Athenian marriage law (see note on **448–66** and Introduction, "Medea's honor") their legitimacy might have been questioned; but clearly under ancestral law they would have kept their rights as *his* sons and heirs to *his* lands (in Iolcus and elsewhere), though, to be sure, they would not be eligible to inherit Creon's estate and power, as would Jason's sons by the princess.

572–73 / 565 *Children are more important to fathers than to mothers* (in Greek, "Why do you need [more] children?") Since mothers were technically out-siders (*thuraioi*) to their husbands' and children's houses and could themselves own no property or be heads of households, a woman could not enlarge her own wealth or her husband's family's prosperity by marrying a second spouse and adding his sons to sons she might already have. Once a woman had borne two sons—one to care for her in her old age and to guarantee her status as a mother in his household, and one to serve as a spare, in case the first son died—then she had as many as she needed. More than two would diminish the wealth of the house in which she would eventually reside once her husband was dead. For Jason and perhaps most ancient Greeks the importance of children derived not from parental affection but from the fact that, even more than fame and glory, they (especially the males) were tangible sureties of their father's own immortality and of the enduring power and prestige of his house. Though Medea once was the cause of the success of Jason's house, she is now irrelevant to its prosperity (or so Jason supposes), since he has found a more materially rewarding alliance elsewhere.

575–83 / 568–75 That women are slaves to the pleasures of sex is a commonplace of classical literature. The protagonist of Euripides' *Hippolytus*, 616ff. makes a similar protest against the need for women in order to beget children.

584–86 / 576–78 The Chorus, like the disinterested Aegeus later on, finds Jason's deeds blameworthy, representing perhaps a naive but normative rejection of Jason's rhetoric.

600 / 591 *barbarian* The Greek '*barbaros*' means anyone who was not a Greek by language or race. Since the Persian wars, barbarian slaves, whose presence in Athens was quite noticeable—for instance, the police were Scythians—had been deemed slavish, not just in their submission to their masters but also in their lack of self-control. Without the benefit of a true Hellenic education, they could be neither good nor beautiful. Their dress, their strange manners, even their attempts to speak Greek were mocked on the comic stage.

618–19 / 612–13 These lines remind the audience of the power and high status of Jason's house throughout the Greek world and beyond. A literal translation of the Greek—"... I am ready ... to send tokens [*symbola*] to my guest-friends elsewhere in Greece, who will treat you well"—reveals a reference to a specific Greek custom: upon the completion of an agreement or contract, either unique (or rare) objects were exchanged or, more commonly, an object was broken into two (or more) dovetailing pieces and each party was given one of these unique pieces, as proof of the holder's legitimate interest in the deal. In this instance, the agreement was one of "guest-friendship" (*xenia*), a pact of mutual assistance or an alliance between two noble houses of different cities. Through such an agreement, influential exiles, though parted from their friends and denied their accumulated honors and political rights at home, could rely upon family guest-friendships to provide refuge and a base of operations.

634–57 / 627–62 *Second stasimon* The Chorus picks up the thematic thread of excessive passion from Medea's closing statement and gives it general application. By doing so, it evokes her earlier intemperate love for Jason. The first system of strophe and antistrophe (see note on 148–58) uses one complex metrical pattern, the second system another. The second strophe and antistrophe turn from intemperate Love as the cause of

Medea's betrayal of her father and city to her present situation, as one bereft of city and friends. As usual, the Chorus provides supplemental generalizing comment on the action, rather than contributing to it. With the appearance of Aegeus and his grant of asylum, we soon discover, however, that this picture of an abject Medea is false. A person with her extraordinary powers can always buy another friendship.

658–815 / 663–823 *Third episode* This scene is famously condemned by Aristotle: "It is right, however, to censure both improbability and depravity where there is no necessity and no use is made of the improbability. An example is Euripides' introduction of Aegeus or (of depravity) the character of Menelaus in the *Orestes*" (*Poetics* 1461b 19–21, tr. W. Hamilton Fyfe [Loeb]). If Aristotle is actually referring to our play and not some other lost play—we know of one called *Aegeus*—he seems to have in mind the accidental, unmotivated way in which (a less than heroic) Aegeus and Medea meet halfway through the action. The Athenian king just happens to be passing through Corinth on his way from Delphi to Troezen; she just happens to be standing there for no particular reason, a happenstance with no justification in the received tradition (*Poetics* 1461b 14–15 and cf. 60b 35–61a 3). Indeed, the received tradition seems to be altogether against it, since Theseus, not Aegeus, was considered an Argonaut and Jason's contemporary. Furthermore, the meeting might be thought to serve no vital purpose: a heroine with Medea's talents and supernatural connections hardly needs a rescuer, and her intractable anger guarantees that she will punish Jason and Creon regardless of the aftermath.

In Euripides' defense, moderns have offered compensating dramatic reasons for bringing the clueless Aegeus so unexpectedly onto the stage: His dialogue with Medea provides a sharp contrast to the preceding *agon*. Unlike Jason, he respects her, recognizes her wisdom, confirms her judgment of Jason's wickedness, and swears an honorable oath to provide her with sanctuary. She, on the other hand, is shown, less sympathetically than before, to be a woman as willing to manipulate this honest, unsuspecting man for her own ulterior devices as she is her enemies. All of these dramatic justifications are quite reasonable, especially if one takes into account the dramatic force of surprise. More provocative and anti-Aristotelian is the argument that the Aegeus scene is actually essential to the plot, on the grounds that, since Medea announces that she will kill her children only after the Aegeus scene, her decision must have been prompted by Aegeus' desire to remedy his childlessness. Before this scene she is still uncertain of her methods, and even asserts that she will kill Jason (lines **393–94** / 375); after it her plans are set. She will kill her own children, not Jason, since killing them will accomplish more than killing him: it will destroy his whole house. This logical connection between Aegeus' childlessness and Jason's is, however, completely absent from Medea's dialogue, which is the only sure evidence of her reasoning process. All that Medea says—and the Chorus offers no contrary evidence—is that Aegeus has provided her, not the children (cf. line 793), with a "safe harbor." She will kill them not just to destroy Jason's house, but because she will not leave them behind in the hands of her enemies.

Aristotelian probabilities and plot construction aside, there is another obvious reason for Aegeus' appearance: the Athens connection. Aegeus was a founding king of Athens and the father of Athens' greatest hero, Theseus. The bargain that Medea strikes with him, to the detriment of the Corinthians, has aetiological value. It explains why Corinth becomes Athens' enemy. Perhaps the generous, righteous, yet ultimately gullible Aegeus is a convenient precursor of the timely, patriotic, and cautionary "Athens Ode" (third *stasimon*, 816–49 / 824–65). In other words, the patriotic value of the Aegeus scene provided Euripides with sufficient motivation and his audience with sufficient delight to overcome its inherent improbabilities.

662 / 667 *Delphi—Apollo's oracle* Apollo alone understood the mind of Zeus and, when inquiries were made at his temple at Delphi, a sanctuary centrally located in a steep mountain pass above the north shore of the Gulf of Corinth, he transmitted bits of this complete knowledge to the Pythia, a ritually pure prophetess who in an ecstatic trance intoned messages from the beyond.

674 / 679 *Choke off the wineskin's spout* The plain meaning of the oracle, that Aegeus is not to get drunk or have sex before reaching home, seems not to accord with the legend of Theseus' birth as we know it. See next note.

677 / 682 Not necessarily on his way home to Athens from Delphi, but certainly on his way to Troezen, Aegeus would have passed through Corinth. If we can trust Medea's wishes for his success (683 / 688, 747 / 756) and the absence of any obvious clues to the contrary, undeterred by his profitable encounter with Medea, he will continue his journey to Troezen, where Pittheus, wise to the intent of the oracle, will see to it that Aegeus becomes drunk (unchokes the wineskin's spout) and, as a result, sleeps with (unchokes the wineskin's spout) Pittheus' daughter Aethra *before* he returns to Athens. Theseus, the greatest of Athens' heroic forebears, is the offspring of this union.

How is it possible, moderns ask, for Aegeus to beget an heir in Troezen when the oracle expressly forbids his having intercourse before reaching Athens? Since Euripides seems not to have invented the oracle—a presumably earlier epic version is preserved in Plutarch's *Life of Theseus*—it is likely that the Greeks did not read it as a prohibition, but as indicating that the next time Aegeus had intercourse he would beget an heir. Pittheus' wisdom lay not just in understanding this but in ensuring that Medea would not be the mother of the prophesied heir. The story of Medea in Athens and her attempt to murder Theseus was the subject of two undatable plays called *Aegeus*, one by Sophocles, the other by Euripides himself. Aethra, Theseus' mother, is a main character in Euripides' *Suppliants*.

684 / 689 *tears* By her verbal delivery or by some gesture or altered posture, Medea elicited this response. Tears would not have been visible through a mask or even on a naked face, considering the distance between the ancient audience and the actor. They were made evident by Aegeus' words.

717–24 / 725–30 If Medea comes freely as a suppliant to Aegeus, he can honor Zeus Hikesios (protector of suppliants), like the righteous man he is, and protect her, without violating his guest-friendships with Creon and Jason and the house of Pelias. But if he were to help her flee Corinth, he would be transgressing these older alliances that, like all foreign alliances, were protected by the enforcing might of Zeus Xenios (protector of hospitality). As one who had broken faith with his Corinthian hosts, he would have merited their revenge.

725–26 / 731–32 Medea says, in effect, that it's time to bring on the lawyers. The language of oath is the ancient Greek equivalent of our written contract law, a protection for all parties concerned. Since for the Greeks the enforcement of law was ultimately the responsibility of the gods, an oath, calling upon the gods as sureties, added real binding force to the proceedings. The ensuing oath taking suggests the original oath taking between Jason and Medea. As in that earlier contract, she now promises Aegeus the effective use of her drugs if he will accept her into his house as her protector (*kyrios*). Aegeus' promise to Medea (deliberately, out of politeness?) obscures what legend supplied, namely, that she would become his concubine—not marry her surely, as he already has a wife (668 / 673). See Introduction, "Medea's honor."

729 / 734 *Pelias' sons* In Greek "the house of Pelias," which would include Pelias' sons-in-law (see note on 8–9 and Introduction, "Legendary background") and grandsons, as well as his celebrated son Acastus.

737–38 / 746–47 In his daily passage across the sky, Helios, the sun, the all-seeing eye of Zeus, espies evildoers and reports their activities to his master. The whole race of gods is a conventional fail-safe in oath taking, in case whoever swears later alleges that his oath was not binding because some other god, by whom he should have been sworn, was overlooked. Such procedural mistakes could be used to invalidate an agreement, sometimes long after the fact.

740–46 / 749–55 Oaths must be specific; the vaguer they are, the more easily they are abrogated. Curses were routinely added to oaths to strengthen them.

746 / 755 *others who renounce them* Those who failed to respect the gods properly, the *dus-seboi*, were liable to prosecution for impiety under Attic law (this is what happened to Socrates), and, if convicted, they suffered severe punishments (divine and human) that had serious consequences, often beyond a single generation. Pericles' mother's family, the Alcmaeonidae (called the Accursed), were under a curse two centuries old, because an ancestor had wrongfully killed certain suppliants. (See Herodotus 5.71 and Thucydides 1.126.)

772 / 782 *targets for my enemies* The Greek for targets, *kathybrisai*, refers to the ways her enemies in Corinth will insult and degrade, even harm, her defenseless children, who are their enemies, by virtue of their kinship with her. On the ancient honor code and the power of *hybris*, see Introduction, "Medea's honor" (cf. the passages listed in the note on 401–2).

775 / 786 *one priceless gown* The Doric *peplos* was a simple overgarment, a rectangular piece of woolen cloth draped like a tunic and secured at the shoulders. The adjective *leptos*, here "priceless," indicates the fineness of the thread and the overall delicacy of the cloth.

784 / 794 *bring down Jason's house* This formula was common to curses. Medea will be the instrument of the curse that would have been placed on Jason at the time of their oath taking. Annihilation of a man's house entailed erasing its wealth, honor, and male progeny. Thus, to kill an enemy's male children was the right of an avenger. What is unusual here is that the enemy's children are the avenger's own.

787–88 / 797 *easier to bear than my enemies who mock me* We may find it incredible that Medea would kill her children to forestall her enemies' laughter at her expense, but our sensibilities are not attuned, as the Greeks' were, to the demands of a militant shame-culture in which Achilles destroys many sturdy Greek souls just to make Agamemnon pay for his bullying and Ajax kills himself because he cannot endure the disgrace of his comrades' gloating (cf. the passages listed in the note on 401–2).

803–5 / 811–13 Medea finally loses the Chorus's goodwill when she announces her decision to kill her own children (783 / 792–93).

812–15 / 820–23 The Nurse, who is addressed here, must have been a silent figure by Medea's side during the preceding action, perhaps having come out of the house with her before her first speech. It is possible that, while the Nurse goes off in another direction to look for Jason, Medea exits through the center door. Possible, but unlikely, since the second strophic pair of the next choral ode is addressed to her. Still, an exit at this point would give Medea the opportunity to ready her poisonous gifts, and she could reenter in time for the Chorus to address her in its lyrics. But if she misses the first system, how can she make sense of the second, which begins with a conclusion based on the first?

816–49 / 824–65 *Third stasimon* Referred to as the "Athens Ode" (cf. note on 658–815 and Introduction, "Historical background"). Serious ideas about Athens and the nature of things lie behind the conceits of the first strophe and antistrophe.

816–18 / 824–26 *Children of the gods, of sacred Earth, since ancient times, Athenians have flourished, unconquered* Erechtheus, from whom all Athenians claimed descent, was born from the Earth, begotten by Hephaestus (god of fire, metalworking, and other crafts), and raised by Athens' patron goddess Athena (bestower of prowess in war, wisdom, and weaving). He married the granddaughter of the River Cephisus, who like all rivers is a deity. The Athenians were proud of the fact that they were born from the earth (*autochthonoi*); that is, not immigrants. The notion was emphasized by sponsors of the democracy, because it made even lower-class citizens somehow landed nobility and worthy of rule.

818–20 / 826–30 *nourished by the vivid air that brings them grace and wisdom* The image is more concrete than we might realize, for progressive thinkers of the day believed that human intelligence comes from a tangible divine nature manifest in the air and light around us. Even in later Greek thought, *pneuma* (breath, wind, spirit) at its finest is not to be differentiated from light or intelligible fire (*aether*). The theme of purified and intelligent air is taken up in a different way in the antistrophe (see next note).

823–29 / 835–45 Since the River Cephisus, unlike the Illissus, did not dry up in summer, even at the hottest time of year it could be the source of air-tempering moisture. A climate most favorable to the good health and moral perfection of living beings was thought to depend upon the proper mixture of purifying sunlight, air, and moisture. Thus, here Aphrodite, fashioner of living things and goddess of all mixing, wreathed in roses (her signature flowers), blends air and Cephissan water, the dry and the moist, to concoct a perpetual life-giving, soul-enhancing, creativity-sustaining springtime. She does this in her cosmic breathing, which mimics human respiration.

850–952 / 866–975 *Fourth episode*

926–27 / 949 A woman's clothing and jewelry—possibly also her personal slaves—were hers to dispose of as she wished, unlike the rest of her dowry, which was controlled by her husband (see Raphael Sealey, *Women and Law in Classical Athens* [Chapel Hill, NC, 1990], 26–27).

931–32 / 954–55, *heirlooms that Helios ... bequeathed* Yet another allusion to Medea's kinship with Helios, a sign of her portentous access to potent Underworld magic. Gold, a solidified liquid (cf. Plato, *Timaeus* 59B), retains the fiery qualities of its original molten state and is emblematic of Helios' original nature.

953–76 / 976–1001 *Fourth stasimon* This song notably lacks the general utterances that predominate in the first strophic pairs of the first three Choruses. Close linkage to the action at hand complements the heightened pace and helps alter the tonal register of the proceedings as Medea implements her vengeance.

977–1056 / 1002–80 *Fifth episode*

1003–5 / 1026–27 A child's marriage was the final maternal duty, and ancient mothers exulted in the part they played in the wedding ceremonies. As heads of housekeeping, they would have had oversight of the ritual bath taken by the bride and groom before dressing for their nuptials, and, in the case of the mother of the bride, of the smooth running of the banquet at the bride's father's house, where the formal unveiling of the bride before the groom took place. The climax of the nuptials came when the groom took his bride from her father's house, and here, after the young couple, the bride's mother held pride of place. Raising torches aloft, she led the procession of well-wishers who, with song and dance and shouts of congratulations, escorted the newlyweds to the groom's house. There, at the door, she ceded her honors to the groom's mother, who with torches newly lit from her son's hearth, greeted him and welcomed her daughter-in-law to her new home. A mother's lamentations, like

Medea's here, that she will not participate in this blessed event because of her or her children's death are common to tragedy.

1006 / 1028 *My unforgiving self has made me wretched* Medea here finally confesses the fault of which she has been accused by all others in the play (save Aegeus), her *authadeia*, her unshakeable determination to carry out her will and satisfy her implacable anger. See Introduction, "Medea's character."

1026–27 / 1049–50 Medea's dread of being laughed at by her enemies again; cf. the passages listed in the note on 401–2.

1029–31 / 1053–55 Medea is sending her children into the house as sacrificial animals. The language reflects the often-heard formula warning the profane or impure to keep away from sacred rites, whose performance their presence would invalidate or corrupt.

1032–56 / 1056–80 Some critics have regarded these lines as an interpolated doublet of lines 1017–31 / 1040–55, ill-adjusted to the context. Others have disputed this radical surgery and bracketed some lines, but not others. This translation assumes the lines are genuine and makes them dramatically plausible.

1035–36 / 1059 *Hell's vengeful demons* In Greek "the netherworld avengers [*alastores*] in Hades," that is, the Furies.

1054–56 / 1078–80 *Angry passions have mastered me—emotions of misrule that destroy men* The Greek reads "I understand the kind of evil I shall bring myself to perpetrate, but my anger [*thumos*], which is the cause of the greatest evils for mortals, is stronger than my counsels [*bouleumata*]." Stoics used these lines to illustrate their belief that the rational soul acts as a unit in coming to all decisions. By their account, Medea, fully conscious of which path she is about to take and even that it is the wrong one, nevertheless deliberately chooses vengeance on Jason over saving the children. In rebuttal, Platonists, who believed the passionate part of the soul to be in conflict with the rational part, took the lines to mean that Medea's anger is stronger than her right reasoning (John M. Dillon in James J. Clauss and Sarah Iles Johnston, eds., *Medea: Essays on Medea in Myth, Literature, Philosophy, and Art* [Princeton, 1997], 211–18. Either way, the ancient debate proves that these lines were established in the Greek text by the third century B.C. and shows that the word "counsels" was taken to refer not to her plotting throughout the play (as some scholars think), but to her present advice to herself that she ought not kill her children.

1057–85 / 1081–1115 If Medea exited with the children at 1056 / 1080, then the Chorus
Leader speaks to an empty stage. These comments in declaimed anapests, similar to those uttered by the Nurse (86–221 / 96–212), mark an
interlude during which neither Chorus nor audience knows what is
happening inside. But the mention of the premature death of children
might suggest that Medea is now preparing to carry out her threat to kill
hers. Against such consonance of theme and dramatic expectation, the
philosophic quality of the discourse acts like counterpoint, thus heigh-
tening the suspense.

1086–1226 / 1116–1250 *Sixth episode*

1105–1201 / 1136–1230 Euripides was known for his vivid messenger speeches, conventionally used by tragedians to dramatize violent offstage action that
could not be shown in the theater to such great effect. This one is
among the best.

1113 / 1143 *princess's chambers* Wives and daughters in great houses occupied separate
quarters, where they worked and tended the younger children. Only
certain men—primarily family members—were permitted access.
Others, like this messenger, were deliberately kept out.

1117 / 1147 The veil is a sign of her status as a newlywed.

1118–24 / 1149–55: It was normal for husbands to be many years older than their
teenage brides. Part of a husband's duty as her new governor (*kyrios*)
was to train his young bride in how to behave as the mistress of her new
household.

1195–1201 / 1224–30 Another piece of proverbial wisdom from a servant; messenger
speeches regularly end with them.

1199–1201 / 1228–30 A striking version of the sentiment expressed here can be found in
Herodotus' tale about the reply Athenian lawgiver Solon gave to Lydia's
King Croesus, when he asked Solon whom he counted the happiest of
men, thinking his own wealth and power so great that he himself would
be deemed happiest. But Solon disappointed him by naming others, not
nearly as rich or powerful, who had led honorable lives and then ended
them in the most honorable way imaginable. According to Solon,
happiness cannot be determined until a man has lived the whole of
his life and cannot be equated with wealth and power. Even if a man is
as rich as Croesus, he is only happy in conformity with his good luck,
because at any moment his happiness can be taken away.

1227–68 / 1251–92 *Fifth stasimon* Throughout this ode, the agitated meter ("doc-hmiac") indicates an increase in the emotional intensity of the music as the play reaches its dramatic and rhetorical climax.

1227–46 / 1251–70 As witnesses to all oaths and omnipresent observers of all misdeeds, Earth and Sun are summoned to prevent an act that will activate the ineluctable Furies. In her pursuit of Jason, Medea is here depicted as one of these demonic avengers, the materialization of her own wrath which will not be appeased until she destroys his whole house, root and branch, a punishment warranted by the oath-protecting curse sworn at the time of their marriage, but one that will have grievous consequences for her, since, if she kills her children to gain the fear-some justice she seeks, she ought in turn to become the target of the new Furies awa-kened by the scent of her children's contaminating blood as it spreads over her hands and seeps into the ground. Indeed, among human crimes and pollutions, the shedding of kindred blood is the worst and demands compensation, no matter how long delayed, and the grace of grave purifications. Much worse than spilling an ordinary human's blood, however, is the spilling of the divinely infused blood of the gods' descendants, who have the gods themselves, not mere mortals, as their swift and sure avengers. With the words *your radiant children* (**1231 /** 1255), Euripides reminds us not only of Medea's and therefore her children's descent from Helios but also of the fearfulness of her act and its consequences. Had Medea just avenged herself on Creon and his daughter and Jason himself, she would only have shed the foreign blood of enemies, a justifiable, though dangerous, act; but by killing her own offspring she ought to incur unspeakable cosmic retribution. Yet, in the mythical record she never does, a problem Euripides appears to dispose of at the end of the play by having Medea declare her intention of establishing a festival and expiatory rites in Corinth for her children's murder (**1356–57 /** 1381–83).

1240 / 1263 *Clashing Rocks* The Symplegades (see line **2 /** 2 and Glossary).

1247–68 / 1270a–92 An offstage scream inaugurates the second strophe and antistrophe of this last choral ode, unique in that the cries of the children issuing from behind the scene building in spoken iambic verses are mixed with the singing voices of the Chorus in the orchestra. This contrast between singing and terrified shouting further heightens the agitation of the musical lines. The alternation is continued in the antistrophe, but this time the Chorus utters the unusual spoken iambic lines, which, though not screams, are nevertheless rhetorically intense.

1247 / 1273, 1252 / 1275 No matter how absurd we may find a do-nothing Chorus reacting ineffectually in song to murder and mayhem within, we must remember that this is a script for a musical and that song and dance numbers, even in our own theaters, tend to override absurdities in the action (or inaction). It is also possible that the choral dancers rendered the action more plausible through mime, for instance, by trying in vain to open the barred palace doors. Regardless of the original staging, however, standards of realism are relative, and ancient audiences who accepted rigid conventions of masks, three actors, and formal speeches in verse would not have been discomposed by passive choruses.

1259–65 / 1282–89 Ino's story is bound up in Medea's in two ways. She was the stepmother who, by persuading her husband Athamas (Jason's great-uncle) to sacrifice his two children by his first wife, was the instigator of the whole saga of the Golden Fleece and its return to Greece (see Introduction, "Legendary background"). More important, her murdered son Melicertes (Palaemon), like Medea's sons at the end of the play (**1353–57 / 1378–83**), became the center of a Corinthian cult. This famous "boy on a dolphin" was venerated just outside Corinth, on the shore of the isthmus, at a tomb-temple that stood within the sanctuary of Poseidon, near the race track where every fourth year the Isthmian Games were held in his honor.

After Ino's sister Semele was killed by Zeus' thunderbolt while giving birth to his son Dionysus, Ino became the infant Dionysus' wet-nurse, raising him alongside her two sons by Athamas. In so doing, she incurred the anger of Hera, who drove her mad and caused her to murder her sons. After her leap into the sea, not only was Melicertes' body rescued by Poseidon's dolphin, but Ino herself was transformed into the sea nymph Leucothea, the white goddess, worshipped all over the Mediterranean basin.

Euripides wrote a tragedy called *Ino*, which recounted her persecution and transformation and was performed prior to 425 B.C. (cf. Aristophanes, *Achamians* 434).

1267–68 / 1290–92, *a woman's marriage bed* The image is ambiguous in that it refers both to a woman's cravings and need for a man and a man's cravings and need for a woman. Either way, it is a fitting image to introduce Jason, who has won evils because he used the bed and a woman's lust for his own ends.

1269–1397 / 1293–1419 *Exodus*

1272 / 1297–98 *or fly on wings to heaven* Foreshadows Medea's final appearance.

1292 / 1317 To the surprise of the audience, who were probably expecting Medea and the children to be rolled out of the center door on the *eccyclema*, a platform on wheels regularly used in tragedies to display interior carnage, Medea appears above the roof of the scene building riding aloft on (or suspended from) the crane in a chariot drawn, as ancient comment and a number of vase paintings attest, by a pair of winged dragons (her own sorcerer's steeds), instead of the traditional horses of the Sun. The children's corpses must have been visibly draped on the chariot rail. The crane was a standard piece of stage equipment, the *machina* of *deus ex machina* fame from which high-flying gods often appeared abruptly at the end of Euripides' plays.

Medea's flight to Athens was enduringly etched on the ancient imagination. Eight centuries later, St. Augustine confesses (*Confessions*, 3.6) that in his pagan youth he used to sing a popular song called *Flying Medea*. See Edith Hall, "The Singing Actors of Antiquity," in P. E. Easterling and Edith Hall, *Greek and Roman Actors: Aspects of an Ancient Profession* (Cambridge, 2002), 3–38.

1296 / 1321–22 *Helios has sent his chariot* A reminder of how well this rescue comports with Medea's dark nature as mistress of Underworld magic. After setting, the Day Star is borne on the streams of Ocean in a golden cup from west to east, where he dwells in the domain of Night with his family (Stesichorus, fr. S17 = 185 PMG [*ap.* Ath. 469e–f]; Parmenides DK 1.9) and keeps his winged car (Mimnermus, fr. 12W [*ap.* Ath. 469f–470b]) ready to carry him aloft again at dawn through the gates of the Underworld (cf., e.g., Athenaeus, *Deipnosophistae* 469c–470d on the "cup of Heracles"). How, after a day's drive, his chariot and its steeds (whether they be horses or dragons) get back to their stalls and garage must have bothered the Greeks as well as us, for in addition to quoting earlier poets, Athenaeus 469c–d cites the fifth-century Pherecydes (see note on **160–62**) as saying that the cup carried the god *with his horses*. Be that as it may, the notion of the subterranean Sun as an occult power, known to us from post-Classical Greek sources, appears to have had a firm place in fifth-century Greek thought (e.g., Peter Kingsley, *Ancient Philosophy, Mystery, and Magic* [Oxford, 1995], 49ff.). See note on **415** and Introduction, "Medea's character."

1307 / 1333 *Fury* Jason says that the gods have let Medea's *alastôr* (literally, the unforgetter) fall on him by association only, thereby indicating that his children's death is really the handiwork of a demonic pursuer wreaking vengeance on Medea for her murder of her brother Apsyrtus. His own punishment, being purely accidental, is thus undeserved.

1307–9 / 1334–35 This version of the myth, in which Medea kills her baby brother at her father's hearth before boarding the Argo, appeared in the *Colchians*, a lost play of Sophocles. It should not be confused with the more gruesomely picturesque one attributed to Pherecydes (see note on **160–62**). Modern readers must remind themselves of the fluidity of ancient myths, which were constantly being altered to meet the varying demands of the uses to which they were put. From her father's point of view—and from the point of view of Athenian law—this is the worst charge against Medea, that she killed her baby brother, her father's seed and heir.

1330 / 1355 *mocking me* Cf. the passages listed in the note on **401–2**.

1350 / 1375 In the Greek, which literally says, "The terms of divorce [*apallagai*, cf. line **250 / 236**] are easy," Jason ends more than his and Medea's shouting match.

1353–57 / 1378–83 Much like gods at the ends of other Euripidean tragedies, semi-divine Medea now sets up a causal connection between the action of the play and a real cult, in this case one established at Corinth, as expiation for her children's murder (see notes on **9–10, 1227–46,** and **1259–65**). Inasmuch as Hera was the guiding goddess of the Argo adventure, it is fitting that in death Jason's children find sanctuary in the precinct of Hera Akraia, the Hera who dwelled (had a cult statue) in a temple "on the heights" (*akraia*). This location is perhaps to be linked to Ino's mad plunge into the sea (**1259–65 / 1282–89**). Upon what heights the historical temple was founded, however, is disputed. Earlier scholars assumed it was upon Acrocorinth, the mountain above the city: archaeologists now prefer the bluffs at Perachora overlooking the Corinthian gulf. Unfortunately Pausanias, the intrepid cataloguer of the monuments of Roman Greece, saw the sacred tomb of Medea's children not in the sanctuary of Hera Akraia but near the local Music Hall, where he tells us annual rites of mourning were observed until Corinth was laid waste by the Romans (2.3.6–7).

1359–62 / 1386–88 In addition to making Jason's humiliation complete, Medea's prophecy of his death ensures that he will never beget other sons to replace the ones he has lost. In case they had forgotten, the spectators are reminded that Jason's saga ends here.

1363–97 / 1389–1419 The Greek meter switches from spoken iambic trimeters to declaimed (i.e., Attic) anapests, a fact reflected in this translation by shorter lines. See notes on **86–221** and **127–221**.

1366 / 1392 *those who deceive their guests* Does this refer to Jason's treatment of Medea, who is a stranger and therefore a guest-friend to his house and to Greece, or to his abortive guest-friendship with Creon, or to his stealing of Aeëtes' fleece? Since Medea has just mentioned the Argo, she and the audience likely assume the last.

1370 / 1396 In Greek Medea says "Wait for old age," a statement that is not sentimental but practical. In a world without old-age pensions, children were the only means of obtaining a respectable retirement and were therefore required by Athenian law to care for their aged parents.

1392–97 / 1415–19 This is a stock choral tag found with slight variation at the end of four other Euripidean plays. It served to close the action but had little or no bearing on the particular play. Editors often feel compelled to bracket it to show that it is a later addition.

HELEN

Translated by

PETER BURIAN

INTRODUCTION

I. EURIPIDES' "NEW HELEN"

"The new *Helen*" Aristophanes called it, not only because it had been produced only a year before his brilliant parody in *Thesmophoriazusae* (*Women at the Thesmophoria*)[1] but also for its "newfangled," even shocking, presentation of a Helen unlike any seen before on the Athenian stage.[2] Helen was and remains one of the most famous—or notorious—figures of Greek legend. She was worshipped as a goddess in her Spartan homeland, but as Helen of Troy she became in the Greek world at large the figure of the faithless wife, a symbol both of surpassing

---

1. *Thesmophoriazusae* 850. A happy concatenation of references in scholia (ancient annotations) to Aristophanes' plays allows us to date *Helen* securely to the year 412: lines 1060–61 of *Thesmophoriazusae*—itself securely dated to 411 by scholia to lines 190 and 841—refer to the performance of Euripides' *Andromeda* in "last year's festival," and a scholion to line 1012 says that *Helen* was performed in the same year as *Andromeda*. Additional such references confirm this dating. We do not know the other plays that made up Euripides' tetralogy (three tragedies and a satyr play), but both *Helen* and the lost *Andromeda* are tragedies with "happy endings" that involve recognition and escape from danger, as are two other surviving dramas produced during the same period, *Ion* and *Iphigenia in Tauris*. The latter in particular has extremely close links to *Helen*, with similarities that reach into details of dramatic design and verbal expression, but are sufficiently apparent from the barest outline of their plots. In both plays, Greek princesses are being held against their will in distant lands and are reunited with a long-lost loved one, with whom they escape and return home. Each woman is being pressed to marry the king of the land in which she now lives, and each refuses the match. Each is in despair because she believes that the rescuer whom she awaits is dead, and when the men arrive, initial misunderstanding leads only painfully to recognition. In both lands, strangers are put to death as soon as they are discovered, so the arrival of Greek men is fraught with danger. Facing this challenge, both couples plan escapes based on an elaborate deception of the barbarian kings, and succeed in their flight. In each play, divine intervention settles a remaining complication and clarifies the future of the hero and heroine.

2. I borrow this word from the title of an article by W. G. Arnott, "Euripides' Newfangled *Helen*," *Antichthon* 24 (1990), 1–18. The adjective used by Aristophanes, *kainos*, has overtones of strangeness as well as novelty.

227

beauty and of dangerous sexual allure. In the traditional story, she left husband and home for a foreign prince, bore the brunt of blame for the Trojan War, and thus drew upon herself the hatred of gods and mortals, especially of all who lost loved ones in the many years of war and its aftermath. Such, by and large, is Homer's Helen and the Helen of Greek tragedy. But there is another version of Helen, which first comes to light in archaic Greek poetry and finds its most complete and complex expression in Euripides' *Helen*. This is a Helen who never went to Troy at all, but to Egypt, remained faithful to her husband Menelaus and resisted the advances of a barbarian lord, but was fought over nonetheless in her absence and for no reason, despised for what she never did and blamed for what she only seemed to be and do.[3]

Euripides' play begins seven years after the end of the Trojan War, with Helen still faithfully waiting for Menelaus. Her prologue speech gives us the necessary background. When Aphrodite won her famous "beauty contest" with Athena and Hera by promising Paris the hand of Helen in marriage, Hera, enraged, decided to deny him his prize. She arranged for Hermes to carry Helen off from Sparta to Egypt, then formed a phantom Helen out of thin air for Paris to take to Troy. Helen, entrusted to the virtuous King Proteus, was kept safe in Egypt through the war and the long years of the Greeks' homecoming. When Proteus died, however, his son Theoclymenus came to power and decided to make Helen his wife. Relying on the promise Hermes had made to her that Menelaus would one day arrive to take her home, she resisted Theoclymenus' forcible advances, taking refuge as a suppliant at his father's tomb, where the drama now unfolds.

Euripides' freedom in adapting myth for the purposes of his new plot is matched by the inventiveness with which he varies the formal conventions of tragedy to serve his new expressive ends. We are accustomed to thinking of tragic structure in Aristotelian terms (prologue, episodes divided by choral odes, *exodos*),[4] but these are manifestly inadequate to describe the larger units with which Euripides, especially in his later plays, achieves both formal coherence and a sense of forward movement. The most obvious division of the play is into somewhat unequal thirds, movements, as it were, of a large and complex dramatic symphony.

---

3. For Euripides' sources, see section 2. Norman Austin, *Helen of Troy and her Shameless Phantom* (Ithaca, NY, 1994) takes this alternative tradition as the central subject of a lively but sometimes idiosyncratic study.

4. *Poetics* 12.1452b14–27. For a general statement of the deficiency of this structural vocabulary and understanding, see Oliver Taplin, *The Stagecraft of Aeschylus* (Oxford, 1977), 44–60, 470–76.

In the first of these movements (lines 1–377 / 1–385), Helen's sorrows mount as her hope of rescue appears to recede. The prologue consists of Helen's introductory monologue, followed by a dialogue with Teucer, younger brother of the great Achaean hero Ajax and himself a warrior at Troy. Banished from home for having failed to prevent the suicide of his brother Ajax at Troy, he arrives in Egypt on his way into exile. His violent reaction to seeing someone who (as he thinks) so closely resembles Helen reminds her and us of the deep hatred in which she is held, but his chief function in the drama is to report news from Greece: Helen's mother is dead, her brothers, the Dioscuri, have disappeared, and Menelaus is presumed to have drowned on the voyage home. Helen, convinced that her husband has perished, expresses her despair in lyric dialogue with the Chorus of Greek slave women and threatens suicide. The Chorus persuades her to leave her refuge and consult Proteus' daughter, the infallible seer Theonoe, about Menelaus' fate. They all go into the palace, leaving the stage and orchestra empty for the arrival of Menelaus.

The second movement (378–1120 / 386–1106) constitutes a single, immense episode in which Helen and Menelaus are reunited and prepare for their escape. This long sequence is organized into a continuous series of scenes articulated by significant entrances and exits and usually separated by two- or three-line choral "tags." The first segment constitutes, in effect, a second prologue whose formal components replicate those of the first. Menelaus, who has survived shipwreck along with some of his companions and the phantom Helen, enters alone, dressed in tatters of sailcloth. His expository monologue tells us of his long and increasingly desperate wanderings. There follows a dialogue with an old serving woman, who brusquely refuses any aid, but warns him of the suspicious king's order to kill any Greeks found in the land and gives him the bewildering news that Helen is in Egypt. In a second monologue, Menelaus tries to make sense of what he has heard, and then goes into hiding. The second scene is introduced by a short outburst of song when the Chorus reenters the orchestra. Helen, too, returns, reassured by Theonoe's promise that Menelaus is alive and on his way to Egypt. Menelaus comes out of hiding to greet her, but because of his rough appearance she feels threatened and escapes to her refuge at Proteus' tomb. A complex recognition scene ensues, in which Helen reaches the joyous realization that this is indeed her husband, only to find that he is unwilling to accept her as his wife in place of the phantom he has brought from Troy. Just when things seem to have reached an impasse, a servant of Menelaus arrives to tell him that the phantom has disappeared from the cave where Menelaus had left her for safekeeping. Understanding at last, Menelaus embraces his wife, and the two sing a "recognition duet" that leads them to recognize also the difficulties that lie ahead as they try to escape. Helen convinces Menelaus that they must seek Theonoe's help. Theonoe tells them that their fate is at that moment being debated among the gods. They both plead their case and Theonoe consents not to tell her brother that Menelaus has arrived. With this assurance, Helen and Menelaus forge their plan for escape.

The final large-scale movement of the drama (1121–678 / 1107–692) is the only one articulated in the traditional sequence of episodes and choral odes, but it too is best understood as a single sweep of action. The fast-moving deception and escape plot is preceded by a *stasimon* that comes very late in the play and punctuated by two more in fairly rapid succession. As usual with such songs, these odes suggest both the passage of time between episodes and changes in mood as the plot progresses. They are perhaps best understood as a cycle of songs that comment in word, music, and movement on aspects of the surrounding action (and will be examined in section 5 of the Introduction).

The escape is now fully in the hands of husband and wife, and Helen suggests a clever plot: Menelaus will pretend to be the messenger of his own death, and Helen will persuade Theoclymenus to allow a funeral rite to be held for him at sea. When Theoclymenus returns, he finds Helen missing from her refuge at the tomb and suspects the worst. At that moment, however, she emerges from the palace dressed in mourning and makes easy work of convincing the king that she is ready to be his bride once due honors have been paid to Menelaus. Theoclymenus agrees to allow her to perform the rites at sea, and provides his best ship, sailors, and all the provisions required. Helen and Menelaus, aided by his companions, escape after a battle with the Egyptian crew, as we learn from the sole Egyptian to survive. The king can only vent his rage against his sister Theonoe for her betrayal, and he is on his way to kill her when he is blocked first by a servant, then by Helen's brothers, the deified Dioscuri, who appear as gods from the machine to explain the will of the gods and announce that Helen will become a goddess and Menelaus will be granted after death a life of eternal ease on the Island of the Blessed.

No summary can do justice to the variety and verve of this play, but even one as bald as this reveals that *Helen* does not offer what we have been led to expect from Greek tragedy—no downfall of a great but flawed hero, indeed no overturn from good fortune to bad at all. Rather, there is much here that might seem more at home in comedy, as when Menelaus, the conqueror of Troy, is shooed from the gate by an old woman, a slave to boot, or when Helen outwits the love-blinkered barbarian king with her feminine wiles and Greek cleverness. At the beginning of the nineteenth century, A. W. von Schlegel called *Helen* "the most entertaining of all tragedies" (not altogether approvingly),[5] and similar sentiments have often been repeated over the last two centuries. The play has been called an escapist entertainment, an amusing romantic comedy, and an effective piece of theater, always with a note of puzzlement that it is somehow not sufficiently serious. More recently, a good deal of attention has been paid to philosophical and political themes that are said to rescue the play from the charge of excessive frivolity. In truth, however, there is still no clear consensus about what kind of play this is or how to evaluate it. Before returning to this question, we must look more closely at the play itself from a number of different perspectives.

II. SOURCES OF THE MYTH

New as Euripides' *Helen* was to the tragic stage, his treatment of the story was not—nor, given the traditions of the Athenian theater, could it have been—entirely without precedent. Although a connection between Helen and Egypt is already apparent in Homer's *Odyssey*,[6] the lyric poet Stesichorus, active in the first half of the sixth century, was probably the first to recast the story with the real Helen in Egypt and a phantom Helen in Troy. Plato's *Phaedrus* preserves lines from a poem known as the "Palinode," in which Stesichorus declares: "The story is not true: you did not go on board the well-benched ships, you did not go to the citadel of Troy." Plato explains that the poet had been blinded for offending Helen with an earlier song, but regained his sight as soon as he had composed this recantation.[7] Plato also refers to Stesichorus' poem in the *Republic* calling the false pleasures that men strive for mere phantoms and comparing them to "the phantom that Stesichorus says was fought for by those at Troy, ignorant of the truth."[8] These citations show that Stesichorus sent a phantom to Troy in Helen's place, but do not tell us what happened to Helen herself. Until forty

---

5. "Die belustigenste aller Tragödien," as quoted from Schlegel's *Fünfte Vorlesung über dramatische Kunst und Literatur* in Charles Segal, "The Two Worlds of Euripides' *Helen*," *Transactions and Proceedings of the American Philological Association* 102 (1971), 553, who goes on to give a useful sampling of subsequent opinions.

6. See section 3.

7. *Phaedrus* 243a–b; thus also the roughly contemporary Isocrates, *Helen* 64.

8. *Republic* 9.586c.

years ago many scholars assumed that his Helen never sailed away at all,[9] the publication in 1963 of a papyrus fragment from an ancient commentary on lyric poems made this view untenable. It states in part that "Stesichorus himself says that the phantom went to Troy, but Helen remained [or simply "resided"] with Proteus," i.e. in Egypt.[10] Thus it is clear that, whatever differences of detail there may have been, and whatever additions to the story Euripides may have made, the basic premise of his *Helen* was already given in Stesichorus' "Palinode." That this basic story was well known to Euripides' audience can be inferred from the fact that some years before he produced *Helen*, he was able to allude to the tale in a few lines near the end of his *Electra*: "For she has left Egypt and come here from the house of Proteus, and she never went to Troy. But Zeus, in order that there should be strife and slaughter of mortals, sent a phantom of Helen to Troy" (1280–83). Interestingly, like the "Palinode," these lines constitute an apologia for the much-maligned Helen. She, along with Menelaus, is to bury her slain sister Clytemnestra (1278–80); and her brothers, the Dioscuri, wish to free her from the guilt falsely ascribed to her in order to establish her fitness to perform the rite.

Another account of Helen's sojourn in Egypt deserves attention, since it appears to have influenced Euripides and in any case will have been known to many in his audience. This is the story Herodotus claims to have heard from Egyptian priests at a temple dedicated to "the foreign Aphrodite," whom he takes to be Helen, at the precinct of Proteus in Memphis (*Histories* 2.112–9). The priests' tale brings Helen herself to Egypt but makes no mention of a phantom: Paris and Helen, blown by strong winds to the mouth of the Nile, come ashore near a temple where some of Paris' slaves, granted immunity from seizure, accuse their master of the great wrong he has done to Menelaus. Upon hearing this, Proteus demands that the foreigners be brought before him, finds the charge to be true, and (since Egyptian laws of hospitality prohibit the killing of strangers) expels Paris from the land, keeping Helen and the

9. Indeed, this view is affirmed by Dio Chrysostom, *Orationes* 11.182, but it could easily have been derived from the well-known quotation in Plato's *Phaedrus*, as Ulrich von Wilamowitz-Möllendorff, *Sappho und Simonides* (Berlin, 1913), 241 n. 1, suggested long before the new evidence compelled that conclusion.

10. P. Oxy. 2506, frag. 26, col. 1 = Stesichorus frag. 193.12–16 (*Poetae Melici Greci*). The question of whether to translate *katameinai* in this text "remained" or "resided" reflects a significant uncertainty about the Stesichorean story. Was the phantom given to Paris already in Sparta, and Helen spirited away to Egypt in secret, as in Euripides; or did Helen go with Paris as far as Egypt, where his crime was discovered and punished and her honor saved by the substitution of the phantom? There is scattered late evidence that appears to attribute to Stesichorus a version of the story in which Proteus (in Homer a master of transformations) was the source of the phantom.

treasure that Paris had taken from Menelaus safe in his own keeping. As the Egyptians later learn from Menelaus, the Greeks have sent a great expedition to Troy and asked for Helen's return. The Trojans have replied that she and Menelaus' treasure are in Egypt. Not believing this, the Greeks have laid siege to Troy, and only when they finally sack it ten years later do they discover that it must after all be true. Menelaus then goes to Egypt and collects his wife and goods, but when unfavorable winds continue to block his departure, he sacrifices two Egyptian children, and narrowly escapes the outraged Egyptians by fleeing to Libya, where they lose track of him.

Although Herodotus insists that he heard this tale directly from Egyptian priests, it is best understood as a rationalized version of the Stesichorean story. In a kind of epilogue (2.120), Herodotus adds his own grounds for believing that the tale plausibly explains the known facts in terms of an overriding divine justice, but without resorting to miracles and poetic mystification. In any case, it seems highly unlikely that Helen's sojourn in Egypt with Proteus during the Trojan War, an essential part of Stesichorus' account, could have developed independently in Egypt as well. It has been suggested that Herodotus' Egyptian informants had already heard a version of Stesichorus' story when he met them at Memphis, or that Herodotus in fact fed them relevant information in ways that invited their confirmation and elaboration. It is also entirely conceivable that the "priestly tale" is more or less a convenient fiction.[11] It is at any rate characteristically Herodotean, not least in the very favorable light in which it presents Proteus and the Egyptians in comparison to the Trojan Paris and the Greek Menelaus.[12] In Euripides' dramatic conception, on the other hand, a confrontation between Greek and barbarian from which the Greeks emerge triumphant plays an essential part,[13] and the phantom Helen is of course fundamental. Herodotus' chief influence on our play is its emphasis on the Egyptian setting of the story.[14] The pains Euripides takes to

11. For Herodotus' careful construction of credibility in this episode, see Paul Cartledge and Emily Greenwood, "Herodotus as a Critic: Truth, Fiction, Polarity," in E. J. Bakker, I. F. J. de Jong, and H. van Wees, eds., *Brill's Companion to Herodotus* (Leiden, 2002), esp. pp. 355–56.

12. For Herodotus' Helen story as the correction of Greek prejudices about the Egyptians, see Rosaria V. Munson, *Telling Wonders* (Ann Arbor, 2001), 142–44. On Herodotus' knowledge of and attitude toward Egypt in general, see A. B. Lloyd in *Brill's Companion to Herodotus* (see note 11), 415–35.

13. See sections 6 and 7.

14. It is certainly likely that Egypt plays a far more developed narrative role there than in the Stesichorean account. The real protagonist of Herodotus' story is Proteus, and, as Austin (see note 3), 136, points out, Helen is simply absent as an agent. Austin himself emphasizes the anti-Egyptian tone of the play, and sees several features as deliberately designed to redress Herodotus' mistakes by

preserve Proteus' reputation for virtue may well reflect Herodotus' picture of an enlightened Egyptian ruler. Euripides sets the play after Proteus' death in order to accommodate the theme of immediate danger to Helen, and in effect divides Proteus' inheritance between his two children. Theoclymenus, who inherits his rule, becomes Helen's pursuer and Menelaus' antagonist, and as such a kind of anti-Proteus,[15] eager to kill any Greek he catches (149–50 / .155, 437–38 / 439–40, 1178–83 / 1171–76), whereas his father scrupulously avoided killing strangers (Herodotus 2.115). Yet even Theoclymenus reveres his father's memory, making scrupulous obeisance at his tomb (1165–68) and respecting Helen's supplication there. Proteus' daughter Theonoe, on the other hand, combines the clairvoyance of the Homeric Proteus[16] with the wisdom and love of justice he shows in Herodotus.[17]

III. PATTERNS: ODYSSEUS, PENELOPE, PERSEPHONE

Euripides' play makes use of story patterns that would have been well known to his audience, often redeploying them in strikingly original ways. Perhaps the most obvious literary "intertext" of *Helen* is Homer's *Odyssey*, which tells the story of Odysseus' return to Ithaca and to his faithful but hard-pressed Penelope after the Trojan War. Even though Euripides' version of Helen and her story contrasts in almost every way with Homer's, the *Odyssey* not only shares many narrative and thematic elements with *Helen*, it also provides part of the background.[18] The *Odyssey* alludes to an Egyptian sojourn of Helen and Menelaus, pre-

---

restoring honor and glory to the Greeks and "purge the story of its unsavory foreign influences" (143). This desire to highlight Euripides' "pro-Hellenic and xenophobic bias" (144, note 11) leads to a certain overemphasis on the relation of two texts.

15. Euripides' treatment of Theoclymenus may have been inspired by a story which we know only from a stray fragment of his predecessor, the Ionian logographer Hellanicus, *FGrH* 4, frag. 153, which tells how, when Menelaus and Helen were in Egypt after the Trojan War, King Thonos tried to rape Helen, whereupon Menelaus killed him. In that case, Euripides has made both crime and punishment less extreme, by having Theoclymenus respect Helen's supplication and Menelaus only trick him to escape.

16. *Odyssey* 4.412ff.

17. On Theonoe, see section 6.

18. The parallels have long been recognized and widely discussed. Bernard Knox, *Word and Action* (Baltimore, 1979), 268–69, points to the *Odyssey* as Euripides' model for comic and satyric elements in several of his tragedies. Robert Eisner, "Echoes of the *Odyssey* in Euripides' *Helen*," *Maia* 32 (1980), 31–37, conveniently lists the main parallels; both he and Segal (see note 5), 572, properly dispute the view of Hans Steiger, "Wie Entstand die Helena des Euripides?" *Philologus* 67 (1908), 202–37, that *Helen* was intended as a burlesque of the *Odyssey*. Nevertheless, the ironic elements of the juxtaposition cannot be gainsaid, as Berndt Seidensticker, *Palintonos Harmonia* (Göttingen, 1982), 162–64, points out. For the complex relation of Euripides' Helen to Homer's, see also Ingrid E. Holmberg, "Euripides' *Helen*: Most Noble and Most Chaste," *American Journal of Philology* 116 (1995), 27–49.

sumably on their return from Troy.[19] Furthermore, both the *Odyssey* and the *Iliad* offer the device of a divinely manufactured phantom that appears to be the real person.[20] In Euripides, the phantom Helen is first of all a tool to overturn Homer's "authorized version" of her story, but it also serves as a means of harmonizing the new narrative with the old, since it explains how Helen could both be at Troy and not be there.[21] As we shall see, Euripides exploits this double function of the tale to the full.

The Odyssean echoes in *Helen* are pervasive. Seen from the familiar perspective of the *Odyssey*, Helen is a Penelope waiting chastely for her husband and beset by an importunate suitor. Menelaus is an Odysseus battered by storms as he tries to reach home. The "double prologue," with separate monologues, one spoken by Helen (1–69 / 1–67), the other later in the play by Menelaus (378–433 / 386–436), both to an empty stage and orchestra, seems to have been inspired, perhaps unconsciously, by the dual beginnings of the *Odyssey*: Telemachus leaves home to get information about the father he believes dead (Books 2–4); Helen leaves her refuge to get information about the husband she thinks dead (312–77 / 315–85). Odysseus leaves Calypso's island, is shipwrecked, and washes ashore naked and uncertain of what awaits him (Books 5 and 6); Menelaus, separated from the Greek fleet, is shipwrecked and washes ashore in rags, uncertain of what awaits him (403–9 / 408–13).

In this context, the phantom Helen might be regarded as a version of Calypso (the "Coverer"), the minor deity who tries to keep Odysseus hidden from his true destiny. Odysseus leaves her because he understands this, whereas Menelaus only realizes that the phantom is an illusion after it disappears. Menelaus must grow into his Odyssean role

19. 4.125–27 and 227–30 (gifts given to Helen in Egypt, with no mention of the occasion), and 4.351–592 (Menelaus' tale of his adventures there on the way home from Troy, but with no mention of Helen). Note also that the *Iliad* tells of Helen and Paris stopping in Phoenicia on their way to Troy (6.289–92). Aeschylus' satyr play *Proteus* was produced following the three tragedies of his *Oresteia* in 458 B.C., but unfortunately little more than its title remains, so we cannot say whether it suggested any association of Helen with Egypt.

20. In *Odyssey*, Book 4, Athena creates a phantom that looks like Penelope's sister Iphthime. The phantom appears to Penelope in a dream to save her from despair (795–801) and, having accomplished her mission, disappears into "breaths of the winds" (839). In *Iliad* 5.445–53, Apollo removes the wounded Aeneas from the battlefield to his temple on the citadel of Troy to be healed by Leto and Artemis. He then makes a phantom that looks like Aeneas. Both of these scenes are highly unusual and therefore striking (see the commentary of Stephanie West on *Odyssey* 4.795ff. in A. Heubeck, S. West, and J. B. Hainsworth, eds., *A Commentary on Homer's Odyssey*, vol. 1 [Oxford, 1988]), and that of Geoffrey Kirk on *Iliad* 5.449–50 (G. Kirk, ed., *The Iliad: A Commentary*, vol. 2 [Cambridge, 1990]). Both passages use the word *eidōlon* to denote "phantom," as does Euripides.

21. See Karen Bassi, "Helena and the Discourse of Denial in Stesichorus' Palinode," *Arethusa* 26 (1993), 51–75, esp. 51–59.

in the course of the play, until at last he is prepared to rewin his wife, not by killing suitors but by an equally bloody escape from the suitor's land. Along the way, he is cast in the role of beggar (**427–33** / 428–34, cf. **804–6** / 790–92), as Odysseus was (e.g., 15.307–24, 17.336–41), and then, again like Odysseus (23.153–63), retransformed at the proper moment by bathing and change of clothes (**1376–79** / 1382–84). Helen, in turn, plays a number of roles paralleled in the *Odyssey*. The role of a faithful, virtuous Penelope of course embodies the fundamental paradox of this Helen, but there is more to it than that. Penelope is dogged by the repeated insinuation that she might become another Helen or Clytemnestra (e.g., 11.427–46, 13.333–38),[22] and, pushed to the limits, she is clearly considering the possibility of marrying one of the ever more importunate suitors (e.g., 15.19–26, 16.73–77, 19.157–61). Similarly Helen must struggle with the reputation that the phantom has procured for her and a situation in which escape from unwanted marriage seems increasingly difficult (e.g., **294–99** / 293–97).[23] And Penelope, like Helen, employs deception and cunning to cope with her difficult situation.[24] In addition to becoming an unlikely Penelope, Helen also briefly plays Nausicaä approached by a rough and dangerous-looking stranger when Menelaus suddenly appears before her (**551–56** / 550–55, cf. *Odyssey* 6.135–44).[25] Later, she will even be cast as the Telemachus of the story, with whose help Menelaus-Odysseus defeats his rival. Beyond this kind of general similarity of roles and situations, many other parallels can be discerned, for example that both Odysseus and Menelaus hide their greatest treasures in a cave—Odysseus his Phaeacean guest-gifts (13.363–71); Menelaus the phantom Helen (**423–26** / 424–27). Penelope and Helen provide the means of defeating their suitors—the test of the bow (19.570–81) and the false funeral rites at sea (**1062–93** / 1049–80), respectively. And in both works recognition is delayed because of resistance by one of the parties—Penelope (23.97–110) and Menelaus (**590–97** / 589–96).

A second story pattern, less obviously but perhaps even more deeply embedded in the play, is one that we (and, given the importance of the Eleusinian mysteries to Athenians, presumably Euripides' audience as

---

22. Marylin Arthur Katz, *Penelope's Renown: Meaning and Indeterminacy in the Odyssey* (Princeton, 1991), 12, 26–29, 51–58, 61–63.

23. See Holmberg (note 18), esp. 28–33.

24. See, e.g., John J. Winkler, "Penelope's Cunning and Homer's," in *The Constraints of Desire* (London, 1990), 129–61.

25. More precisely, the scene plays like a parody of Odysseus' encounter with Nausicaä. The Phaeacean princess stands fast, her courage strengthened by Athena; not so Helen, who flees. Unlike Odysseus, Menelaus lacks "gentle and crafty words" (*Odyssey* 6.149) with which to reassure her.

well) most readily associate with the myth of Persephone.[26] Persephone, also known as Kore ("the Maiden"), was abducted by Hades and taken to his home in the underworld to be his bride. Her mother, Demeter, the goddess of grain, won her daughter's release, though only for part of the year. Demeter in her anguish made the earth barren while Persephone was in Hades, but when she returned to earth, it flourished once more, symbolizing the annual death and rebirth of life with the turning of the seasons. Her story also becomes paradigmatic for women's experience of marriage as a symbolic death and birth into a new life in a new family.[27] Three surviving plays of Euripides (*Alcestis*, *Iphigenia in Tauris*, and *Helen*) have plots related to this pattern, involving the abduction of a heroine into a realm of (literal or symbolic) death from which she is rescued and returned to the world of the living. In *Alcestis*, the death is literal, but chosen as the least of evils by the heroine; in *Iphigenia in Tauris* and *Helen*, the death is symbolic but unchosen.

Helen's story is explicitly made to parallel that of Persephone: The world believes that Helen was abducted by Paris, but instead she was taken away by Hermes while gathering flowers (**239–48** / 243–49), just as Persephone was by Hades in the Homeric *Hymn to Demeter* (6–8). Helen is now threatened by Theoclymenus' designs, and in an essentially comic version of the motif, at one point she even briefly believes that Menelaus has come as an attacker (**551–53** / 550–52). Persephone finds herself condemned to live in the underworld; Egypt figures in *Helen* as a symbolic land of the dead.[28] Helen finds herself in a "yonder" approached, as often in ancient lore, through water, the mouth of the Nile.[29] Helen's Egypt is a world that resounds from beginning to end

26. The fullest treatment of this pattern, with ample bibliography, is Helene P. Foley, "Anodos Dramas: Euripides' *Alcestis* and *Helen*," originally published in 1992 and revised in her *Female Acts in Greek Tragedy* (Princeton, 2001), 303–38. The presence of this pattern was briefly adumbrated in Richmond Lattimore, *Story Patterns in Greek Tragedy* (New York, 1964), 52–53, and filled out by J.-P. Guépin, *The Tragic Paradox: Myth and Ritual in Greek Tragedy* (Amsterdam, 1968), 120–33, 137–42. Other important discussions include Anne Pippin [Burnett], "Euripides' *Helen*: A Comedy of Ideas," *Classical Philology* 55 (1960), 156; Segal (see note 5), esp. 569–71 and 595–600; Christian Wolff, "On Euripides' *Helen*," *Harvard Studies in Classical Philology* 77 (1973), esp. 63–64, 70–71; D. B. Robertson, "Helen and Persephone, Sparta and Demeter," in G. W. Bowersock et al., eds., *Arktouros* (Berlin, 1979), 162–72.

27. See Helene P. Foley, ed., *The Homeric Hymn to Demeter* (Princeton, 1994), 81–82, with further bibliography.

28. See Roger Goossens, "L'Égypte dans l' *Hélène* d'Euripide," *Chronique d'Égypte* 10 (1935), 243–53; Helen Bacon, *Barbarians in Greek Tragedy* (New Haven, 1961), 137–38; F. Jesi, "L'Egitto infero nell'*Elena* di Euripide," *Aegyptus* 45 (1965), 56–69, esp. 58–59; Guépin (note 26), 128–32; Wolff (note 26), 64; Rush Rehm, *Marriage to Death* (Princeton, 1994), 121–27; Phiroze Vasunia, *The Gift of the Nile* (Berkeley, 2001), 64–65.

29. Cf., e.g., the marshy lake through which Dionysus enters the underworld in Aristophanes' *Frogs*.

with echoes of death. To fend off the King, she takes refuge at his father's tomb (65–67 / 64–65). Teucer tells Helen of the slaughter at Troy, the suicide of Helen's mother Leda, the possible death of her brothers the Dioscuri and the apparent death of Menelaus (91–138 / 94–42),[30] and when he leaves she breaks into a long dirge culminating in the threat of her own suicide (435–52 / 353–59). Helen's song begins with an invocation of the Sirens (figures associated with death)[31] and Persephone herself (161–74 / 167–78). Hearing her, the Chorus compares her pitiful lament to an outcry provoked by threatened abduction: the cry of a nymph fleeing the unwanted embrace of Pan (182–88 / 184–90).

Just after Helen has launched her plan to escape from Egypt and return to her own world and to her own daughter Hermione, the Chorus recounts Persephone's abduction and her mother's mourning (1309–62 / 1301–68). The significance of the story now appears to lodge not only in Helen's abduction but also in return, the resumption of life and the replacement of lament with laughter and joyous music (1339–50 / 1337–52). Indeed, as a model for the passage from the symbolic death of the maiden to the renewal to life in the world as a married woman, the Persephone story underscores the thematics of rescue in *Helen*. Yet it does so in a way that never leaves death far behind. If the first third of the play is dominated by Helen's fear that Menelaus is dead, the second gains much of its momentum from her terror that having recovered him she will lose him again (949–52 / 936–38). And the escape itself is of course ironically empowered by the mock funeral rite for Menelaus that Helen devises and carries out with him. In the end, however, Persephone's story combines with the play's Odyssean motifs of hardships overcome, hard-won recognition, and tenacious struggle to give a strong sense of life not just renewed but reclaimed.

IV. *HELEN* IN THE THEATER

In the original production, three actors and fifteen choristers, all men, would have performed the speaking and singing parts. This means that

---

30. Teucer makes another possible connection with the underworld when he remarks that the grandeur of the palace is worthy of Plutus, the god of wealth, who was associated with the almost identically named Pluto, king of the underworld. On this connection, see Wolff (note 26), 64. The Greek names are Ploutos and Ploutôn. Plato, *Cratylus* 403a, gives an etymology that connects the names: "Ploutôn obtained his name from the giving of wealth [*ploutou*], because wealth comes up form the earth below." Clearly, the closeness of the names was itself a reason for the association of the two gods. In addition, Plutus as a god of agricultural plenty is associated with Demeter, whose son he is said to be in Hesiod, *Theogony* 969ff. See Nicholas J. Richardson, ed., *The Homeric Hymn to Demeter* (Oxford, 1974) p. 469, and Aristophanes, *Thesmophoriazusae* 299 and *Plutus* 727. In the latter passage, Wealth (Ploutos) is called Ploutôn.

31. See note on line 162.

ten roles[32] were divided among *protagonist*, *deuteragonist*, and *tritagonist* (i.e., the first, second, and third "competitor"). There is more than one way to divide the roles in *Helen*, but the likeliest seems to be as follows: the protagonist certainly played Helen, a taxing part both in terms of length (apart from two short absences, she is on stage throughout) and of the musical challenge of its sung passages. Nevertheless, Euripides' virtuoso performer probably also took the parts of the Messenger and of Castor. The deuteragonist would have played Menelaus and in all likelihood Teucer and the second servant. The tritagonist would then have played the Old Woman, first servant, Theonoe, and Theoclymenus.[33] Extras are needed as attendants to Theonoe and servants of Theoclymenus.

In addition to the wooden building (*skênê*) at the back of the stage, which on this occasion represented the great outer wall and gate of the Egyptian royal palace, there was also a tomb in the midst of the playing area, substantial enough to conceal a person crouching to one side of it. Although Theoclymenus says that he has buried his father "at the gate" (1174 / 1165), a number of passages suggest that the tomb is located at some remove from the palace. Both Teucer and Menelaus approach and comment on the palace without apparently noticing the tomb; and when Helen returns from the palace after consulting Theonoe, she catches sight of Menelaus, decides he has been sent to waylay her, and rushes toward the tomb, Menelaus appears to block her way, and she only reaches the tomb some lines later (542–57 / 541–56). The precise location of this tomb must remain a matter of conjecture, but there are enough Aeschylean examples of substantial structures of this sort (Agamemnon's tomb in *Libation Bearers*, Darius' tomb in *Persians*—which must also be large enough for an actor who plays Darius' ghost to hide behind—and the "common altar of the gods" in *Suppliants*) for us to suppose that they have a considerable history and, in all likelihood, a conventional location in the theatrical space.[34]

32. Not counting the Chorus Leader, who engages in dialogue with the actors, and only nine if the small part of the slave who opposes Theoclymenus' decision to kill his sister is given to the Chorus Leader or, as is less likely, to the messenger; see note on 1608–30.

33. Possible alternatives: the protagonist might have played the Old Woman, the tritagonist Teucer, the deuteragonist the messenger. In the latter case, either the protagonist took the role of the second servant, leaving Castor to the deuteragonist, or the second servant's part belonged to the Chorus Leader.

34. Precisely where the tomb was is impossible to say. Graham Ley, "Scenic Notes on Euripides' *Helen*," *Eranos* 89 (1991), 25–34, makes the case for its placement in the orchestra, pointing out that there are a number of plays in which altars, tombs, or shrines are clearly represented as separated from the *skênê*, and reasonably suggesting that all had a similar location in the theater. It seems unlikely, however, that a permanent small altar of Dionysus situated in the center of the orchestra was so used here, as has been argued for other plays and as Ley seems to imply for *Helen* (26). Not only does the

The tomb, Helen's refuge, is the center of the action for the first two-thirds of the play; the great exception is Menelaus' arrival and encounter with the Old Woman at the palace gate (378–517 / 386–514), prepared by the surprising departures into the palace of both Helen and the Chorus. Once the escape plot has been laid, however, the scenic focus effectively shifts to the *skênê* with its palace gate. Interestingly, the escape plot begins with Helen in control of the gateway. At 1174 / 1165, Theoclymenus returns from a hunt and notices her absence, and at that moment Helen appears, now dressed in black, with hair shorn and face disfigured by tears. On cue, Menelaus appears from his place of hiding at the tomb (that he is the only character to conceal himself twice in the course of a single tragedy gives a measure of the playfulness of Euripides' dramaturgy here). From this point forward Helen and Menelaus are in command. The comings and goings at the palace gates mark successive steps in the successful campaign. A last exit into the palace—Theoclymenus rushing to kill Theonoe—is blocked by the opposition of the second servant on stage and the appearance of the Dioscuri, presumably swung above the stage building on the *mêchanê* (theatrical crane: see Commentary on 1642–87).

Costume plays an unusually important and emphatic part in *Helen*, more so than in any surviving Greek tragedy except Euripides' *Bacchae*, where the grotesque sight of ancient Cadmus and Teiresias dressed up as Bacchants and the terrifying robing of Pentheus for death at his mother's hands are among the effects that Euripides achieves through the contrast of Dionysiac garb and the "proper" clothing of the male citizen. Parodies in Aristophanes suggest that bringing heroes on stage in rags was a Euripidean trademark,[35] and in *Helen* much is made of the tattered piece of sail cloth in which Menelaus has wrapped himself, and for which he feels great shame (415–24). Both Helen (544–45, 554) and Theoclymenus (1204) manifest revulsion when they first see him. When, through Helen's clever planning, Menelaus is properly dressed and armed while playing someone else, it has the force of a true transformation, not a mere change of costume, and it paradoxically restores him to his true self. The same plan, on the other hand, leads the woman whose very essence is beauty to disfigure herself (1186–90). The reference to shorn head and tear-stained cheeks suggests that the

tomb need to be large, but its structure would cover an altar of the god in whose honor the festival was being held. It would also make Menelaus' question about why Helen was supplicating at a tomb rather than an altar (800) into a pointless joke.

35. See especially Aristophanes *Acharnians* 412–34.

actor who plays Helen has not only changed costume but donned a new mask.[36]

Whether the Egyptian locale was made a feature of stage setting, costumes, or props we cannot say, but certainly the Theonoe scene, with her elaborate entry preceded by attendants carrying a vessel with burning sulphur and a torch (865–72), must have had an exotic feel. In general, props play a larger part in *Helen* than in most other tragedies. In addition to Theonoe's purificatory apparatus, Teucer enters carrying a bow and wearing a quiver of arrows (76–77); Helen has some sort of bed strewn beside the tomb (798); Theoclymenus returns from the hunt with attendants carrying the requisite equipment (1169–70; whether the dogs mentioned here were actually brought on stage is a matter of speculation). Most impressively, the action at 1390ff. requires that a number of extras carry quantities of goods of various kinds to be used on the burial at sea from the palace down the side entrance of the orchestra that represented the path to the port.

V. THE CHORUS AND MUSIC

The Chorus of this play is made up of Greek captives who serve in the palace of Theoclymenus and have befriended Helen. Unique as Helen's situation is, these women share a parallel experience of exile and captivity, are sympathetic to her, and are eager to help, as is made abundantly clear in their entrance song (or *parodos*, 158–251 / 164–252), which is led off by Helen, with the Chorus entering the orchestra in answer to her cries and engaging her in a lyric dialogue of lament (*kommos*). The situation is typical for tragic choruses, who usually have a direct connection to and concern for the protagonist. A second lyric dialogue between Helen and the Chorus follows at 323–77 / 330–85, emotionally charged by Helen's threat of suicide (340–52 / 348–59) and reflections on the immense sufferings of Greeks and Trojans that have been blamed on her (355–68 / 362–74). These examples of highly stylized sung "conversations" make it clear that the primary purpose of lyrics, whether performed by a chorus or individual actor, is not to provide information or further the plot, but to raise the emotional stakes through heightened poetic language and the addition of music and movement.

What is unusual in *Helen* is the degree to which, after the Chorus' two kommatic exchanges with Helen, there are no extended choral lyrics

---

36. The mask used in the later fifth-century theater included a hair-piece and covered the entire head. For illustrations of such masks from Greek vase painting, see A. W. Pickard-Cambridge, *The Dramatic Festivals of Athens*, ed. J. Gould and D. M. Lewis (Oxford, 1988), plates 32–34.

until the three odes (stasima) clustered late in the play as part of a carefully planned cycle of three songs that punctuate the escape plot.[37] The first stasimon returns to the past to raise questions about the gods and their role in apparently endless human strife. The second stasimon does not provide a direct answer, but by offering a sacred narrative, outside of time as it were, it offers a model of resolution to seemingly endless sorrow and destruction. The third, then, looks forward to the happy outcome of the escape now under way, imagining Helen's future as a resumption of past happiness in Sparta. Like the other lyrics of this drama, these odes are written in a style that is often referred to as "ornamented" or "decorated"—terms that perhaps predispose too much to the view that late Euripidean choral odes in particular are ornaments or decorations divorced from a properly organic connection to the dramatic action. The decorated aspects of Euripides' choral lyrics include such things as richness of description, elaborate and artful development of pictorial detail, receptivity to mythological parallels and analogues, and a tendency to emphasize mood rather than narrative continuity.[38] Euripides' choral odes do not always comment directly on the action, but that does not necessarily mean that their songs are irrelevant to it.

The first stasimon (1121–72 / 1107–64) follows the planning for Helen's and Menelaus' escape, but with the end of the long struggle still hanging in the balance, the Chorus sings one more lament for all the sufferings that the war brought to Greece and Troy. Decisively distancing themselves from the forward motion of the dramatic action, the Chorus members return to Paris' abduction of Helen, "sped on his way by cruel Aphrodite" (1130 / 1121), then dwell on the deaths of both Trojans and Greeks before reminding us that it was not Helen who went to Troy, but only "the holy phantom, the Helen Hera made" (1142 / 1136). Significantly, the two phrases just quoted are, in the Greek text, the metrically equivalent last lines of the first strophic pair. This parallelism

---

37. The Chorus continues of course to participate through the Chorus Leader, who represents the entire group in dialogue passages. Unusually, this leader intervenes directly in the action by convincing Helen to leave her sanctuary at Proteus' tomb in order to consult Theonoe (312–26/ 315–33). Just as unusually, after the second kommos the Chorus goes out with Helen, leaving the scene entirely empty for Menelaus' entrance. Apart from the brief song that marks their return (515–27), they do not sing again for almost 600 lines, until the first choral ode. Music enters the central portion of the drama only in the form of a "recognition duet" performed by Helen and Menelaus in a combination of sung and spoken verse (629–713 / 625–97). The choral odes are well discussed as a cycle by Wolff (note 26), 68–77, and his comments are reflected often in the following paragraphs.
38. Walter Kranz, Stasimon (Berlin, 1933), esp. 235–45, is still fundamental; see also T. B. L. Webster, The Tragedies of Euripides (London, 1967), 283–87, as well as his comments on several of the later plays.

equates the two stories of Helen in more than one way. Waste and ruin attach to both the real and the phantom Helen, and the two goddesses who have wreaked such havoc upon and through her are pitted against each other once more.

The evocation of past sorrows leads to a general theological conclusion: if even a child of Zeus can be unjustly slandered throughout Greece, divine power is incomprehensible and unpredictable (1143–57 / 1137–50). The *stasimon* concludes with a powerful assertion that those who fight and die in battle are fools, since "if blood / is to decide" (1161–62 / 1155) strife among cities will never end. They suggest that the dispute, which led to so much death and destruction and to Helen's continuing burden of sorrows, could have been settled by words (1164–72 / 1157–64). As Wolff points out, however, the suggestion is problematic in somewhat contradictory ways. First, the play itself has shown that fatal strife has all along been part of the gods' plans, and there is nothing to justify the Chorus's faith that words could have changed the course of events. But second, the plot of the play will bring a resolution to strife only through further bloodshed, nipping in the bud the last lethal outburst of violence and fulfilling the promise made to Helen at the start of all her troubles, in accordance with the will of Zeus, whose plans set the strife in motion (see 34–48 / 36–48). The Chorus's searching questions receive no certain answers here.

The second *stasimon* (1309–62 / 1301–68) is one of a number of Euripides' odes that present a mythical narrative—usually one that is part of the background of the dramatic action but at some remove from it—in an allusive and highly pictorial style.[39] In this *stasimon*, the myth has no direct connection to Helen or the Troy tradition, and the ode has therefore often been criticized for irrelevance or even treated as an unrelated musical interlude. However, its subject—the search of Demeter (in this version conflated with the Phrygian Mother Goddess) for her lost daughter Persephone—can be understood as a parallel narrative with thematic connections both to Helen's story and to the questions about the gods raised in the first *stasimon*. Seen in that light, its place in the economy of the play seems far less uncertain than is sometimes claimed. Unfortunately, two passages crucial for the understanding the whole ode (1351–52 / 1353–54, 1361–32 / 1366–68) are as good as undecipherable. Despite that, important connections can still be traced. The first is the nexus of similarities between the myth retold in the ode and the story recounted in our play. Obviously, there is not a

39. See note on 1309–62.

simple one-to-one correspondence between the two tales, but their intersections are striking.[40]

A second strand of connection is suggested by the presence of Aphrodite in a role precisely opposed to the one she takes in Helen's own story. Helen was the unwilling "bait" (26 / 28) with which the goddess won the beauty prize from Paris, and through which Zeus brought about the Trojan War; and the enmity of Aphrodite has persisted. Here, Aphrodite instead brings comfort and consolation, and it is her music that soothes the Mother Goddess at last, brings her to laughter, and ends her anger (1346–49 / 1346–49). This can hardly be called a theodicy or regarded as answering the questions about the nature of the divine raised by the first *stasimon*. It does, however, suggest another side of divine power: through orgiastic abandon it offers ecstatic release and renewal. The questioning, doubting spirit of the earlier stasimon and the uncritical acceptance of irrational but transcendent experience in this one cannot be reconciled. Each has a place in the attempt to understand what is finally beyond human comprehension.

The third *stasimon* is the one that connects most directly with the dramatic action as a beautifully realized propitiation and imagination of Helen's return to Sparta. Formally it can be called a *propemptikon*, a poem that wishes a safe and happy journey to a departing friend. A handsomely structured and crafted song, it illustrates in many ways the beauties of the "decorated" style. The language itself seems festive, reveling in sonorous adjectival and verbal compounds. Its structure has a striking symmetry that suggests the journey the ode imagines: each of its two strophes begins far from Greece and ends in the Peloponnese; each antistrophe imagines a scene developed from the movement of the corresponding strophe (the ship brings Helen home :: the Chorus imagines her encounters there; cranes are asked to fly to Sparta to announce the homecoming :: the Dioscuri, Helen's immortal brothers, are asked to fly along with her ship to ensure safe passage and happy return).[41] Within this frame, a series of arresting vignettes filled with color, light, and movement (dolphins dancing around the ship, cranes migrating in formation behind their leader, the sea itself with its many hues) and telling allusions to local sites and legends (the daughters of Leucippus, the nightlong festival of Hyacinthus in Sparta, the towers Apollo built at Troy) fill a richly imagined canvas.

---

40. See section 3.
41. Ruth Padel, "Two Choral Odes of Euripides," *Classical Quarterly* 24 (1974), 238.

What is most striking about this *stasimon*, however, is the "imaginative projection"[42] of the journey that Helen and Menelaus will make. The participation of the dolphins and cranes, the encouragement of the sailors by the sea nymph Galaneia, the final invocation of the Dioscuri, all surround the voyage with an atmosphere of the miraculous. A characteristic Euripidean trope, the desire to fly expressed by the Chorus, is not used in the usual way to express a wish to escape,[43] but to help in the escape by meeting the cranes where they winter in North Africa. They, too, wish to participate in the success of the voyage, to be part of the imagined company that attends them. The world has not been cleansed of all its sorrows. Hyacinthus was accidentally killed by Apollo, his divine lover, just as other gods nearly destroyed Helen. But Hyacinthus has been given a festival that first mourns him and then celebrates the renewal of life and joy, and it is the joyous nightlong revels of that celebration that Helen is pictured as joining.[44] Helen's daughter Hermione is still unwed, but Helen will soon be there to see to her marriage.[45] This *stasimon*, then, creates pictorial and mythological associations that provide an imaginative projection of what the drama has led its audience to desire.[46]

Significantly, music itself—broadly understood, as the Greeks did, to include melody, rhythm, words, and dance—is not only the expressive medium of the lyrics in *Helen*, but one of their most important recurring themes. The very first song of the play begins with Helen's question, what kind of music is appropriate to such sorrows? (**157–59** / 164–66); in answer, Helen invokes the Sirens, demonic musicians connected to the world below,[47] to bring her mournful music, but it is a Chorus of Greek slave women who respond to her call. Their first words, in the ornamented style of the lyrics in this play, evoke a picture of their daily activities as palace servants washing clothes in the river, thus providing a glimpse of a more normal world in answer to Helen's cries of anguish. To the

---

42. Shirley A. Barlow, *The Imagery of Euripides*, 2nd ed.(Bristol, 1981), 39.

43. E.g., *Hippolytus* 732–41, *Andromache* 861–65, *Ion* 796–99.

44. See note on **1463–67**.

45. Traditions about Hermione's marriage vary; in Homer (*Odyssey* 4.3–9) Menelaus, while still at Troy, promises her to Achilles' son Neoptolemus, and the marriage takes place after his return. Other authors, including Euripides in *Andromache* 966–70, tell of a prior engagement to Orestes and agree that Hermione married him after Neoptolemus' death at Delphi. In *Orestes* 1653–57, however, Euripides makes Apollo explicitly deny Hermione's marriage to Neoptolemus and sanction that to Orestes.

46. Padel (note 41), 241: "The ode stands in a relation to the drama similar to that which exists between the play and the audience."

47. See note on **162** / 169.

Chorus, Helen's laments are "unlike those sung to the lyre" (184 / 185) but resemble instead the cries of a mountain nymph escaping forced mating with Pan. But her music affects them, and they soon join in the lament. Their song is metrically (and thus presumably musically) as well as thematically almost indistinguishable from Helen's own.

The first choral ode begins with an invocation of another musical mourner, the "tuneful, tearful nightingale" (1121 / 1108–10). Like Helen's summoning of the Sirens, this invocation indicates the kind of music we will hear in the ode, dominated by grieving for past sorrows. The nightingale's story is only alluded to here, but it was well known to Euripides' audience.[48] As a story of erotic betrayal (Tereus' rape of Philomela, sister of his wife Procne) and of murderous revenge (Procne's killing of Itys, her child by Tereus), it is not inappropriate to the larger themes of the *stasimon* and the play. Music plays a different role in the second *stasimon*. Here it is the ecstatic music of the *orgia* of the Mother and Dionysus that dominate, with its drums and cymbals, pipes and bull-roarers. The instruments first accompany her grief-stricken search (1316–18 / 1308–10), then the relinquishing of her anger (1346–50 / 1346–52). This music moves, like the Mother herself, from mourning to joy. Perhaps the most striking manifestation of syncretism in this *stasimon* is that Zeus responds to the grief-stricken Mother's withering of life on earth not by sending gods to win her over with promises and gifts, as in the *Hymn to Demeter*, but by sending the Muses and Graces to charm her with their joyous song and dance. In this way the *stasimon* acts as a kind of metaphor for the healing of sorrow that poetry (such as *Helen* itself) can accomplish. The third *stasimon*, far more tranquil in its depiction of calm seas, festive rites, and the flight of migrating birds, makes the ordered dance (the oars of Helen's ship beating a rhythm for the dance of the dolphins in a calm sea, 1448–51 / 1454–56; Helen joining the women's dances in Sparta, 1460–61 / 1465–68) its central musical figure. Even the flight of the cranes is figured as a kind of dance, with the flock "led by their eldest, trumpeting his orders / as he flies" (175–76 / 1482–84).

This brief look at how music itself becomes a theme of song is of course no substitute for the music itself and the choreography of *Helen*, both lost beyond all but the most schematic and abstract kind of recovery. It is salutary to remember that song and dance, accompanied by the

48. Sophocles' *Tereus*, which appears to have been the most influential Greek version of the story, was produced some years before *Helen* (perhaps as early as the 430s), but its impact was still sufficient for it to be parodied by Aristophanes in his *Birds* of 414. See Gregory W. Dobrow, *Figures of Play* (Oxford, 2001), 105–32.

aulos (an oboe-like reed instrument),[49] were an integral part of ancient tragic (and comic) performances. Reading the text of a fifth-century Athenian tragedy is in many ways like reading an opera libretto without seeing a performance, hearing the music, or even having access to a score.

VI. THEMES AND IDEAS

At the thematic level, *Helen* is built upon a series of antinomies and paradoxes. The heroine is herself a paradox, of course, since she is the antithesis of what the world believes her to be: not the proverbial betrayer of her husband, but the most faithful of wives, steadfast in defending her chastity; not guilty of causing the war at Troy, but hidden away far from its horrifying ravages. It is the phantom Helen, made by the gods, who has deceived the world and inflicted so much suffering. In Euripides' hands the myth of the phantom Helen is the starting point for the exploration of a pervasive gap between *appearance* and *reality*.[50] This is the most widely discussed of the antinomies in *Helen*, but a number of others related to it also demand our attention.

The doubling of Helen by her phantom is not an isolated plot device; it is mirrored in almost every aspect of the drama.[51] There are not only two Helens but two Menelauses, the live one and the one whose death Menelaus, playing the part of the sole survivor of his shipwreck, is said to have witnessed. Two kings of Egypt, one dead, one living, are essential to the plot, and in addition the traditional role of the ruler in receiving suppliants is divided between Theoclymenus and his sister Theonoe.

49. For this instrument and its use in the theater, see note on 164.

50. The distinction and its ontological and epistemological implications are central preoccupations of Greek philosophy from the time of the Presocratics (e.g., the antithetical positions of Parmenides and Heraclitus on what *is* and what merely *seems* to be) and found especially fitting expression in the sophistic habit of thinking in binary oppositions (e.g. *nomos* and *physis* and the much-discussed question of which has primacy). Friedrich Solmsen, "*Onoma* and *Pragma* in Euripides' *Helen*," *Classical Philology* 48 (1934), 188–90, summarizes the evidence of a specifically sophistic rhetorical background for *Helen*.

51. On doublings in the plot and their significance, see Hans Strohm, *Euripides: Interpretationen zur dramatischen Form* (Munich, 1957), 85–86; Segal (note 5), 562–63. Pietro Pucci, "The *Helen* and Euripides' Comic Art," *Colby Quarterly* 33 (1997), 42–75, elucidates this phenomenon as a "structure of substitution [that] seems to dominate the whole of the play and even its details" (47). Eric Downing, "Apate, Agon, and Literary Self-Reflexivity in Euripides' *Helen*," in M. Griffith and D. J. Mastronarde, eds., *Cabinet of the Muses* (Atlanta, 1990), 1–16, offers a subtle analysis of the ways in which "Euripides ... delights in the doubling of his language" in *Helen* (3). The technique here is in many ways characteristic of the later Euripides. For an excellent discussion of another play in which doublings and repetitions constitute "the principal means of the play's construction," see Christian Wolff, "The Design and Myth in Euripides' *Ion*," *Harvard Studies in Classical Philology* 69 (1965), 169–94.

There are two scenes of a Greek soldier's arrival in Egypt (Teucer and Menelaus), each followed by a confused encounter with Helen. There are two prologues, formally similar and both delivered to an empty orchestra. All this duplication (and much more)[52] reflects both the doubling of Helen—the springing point of the entire drama—and the confusion with which that doubling burdens "reality" as perceived by the participants.

As regards Helen herself, the dialectic of appearance and reality is closely related to themes of *guilt* and *purity*. The most striking expression of the duality of Helen is the contrast she repeatedly makes between her body (*sôma*) and her name (*onoma*).[53] As parallels in roughly contemporary plays of Euripides suggest,[54] the disjunction of name and body implies a disjunction of elements that are ordinarily felt to constitute a unitary self. In all these cases, "name" carries its common extended sense of "reputation," but in the others, the contrast puts reputation on the side of the "real" person, whereas in *Helen* the reputation is quite literally a phantom. This is of course deeply problematic, especially in terms of heroic culture, where reputation is so essential to identity and the sense of self.[55] Thus, Helen feels deep shame for what she knows she has not done, but which nevertheless adheres to her name, so that "I" and "my name" actually become synonymous for her at 194–97 / 198–99, though she elsewhere insists that they are not the same.[56] And there is irony implicit in the very use of "body" to represent Helen's true self, since her reputation always identifies her precisely with the beauty of her body, suppressing the reality of her chastity and devotion to her husband, while holding her appearance responsible for all the suffering of the Trojan War. Paris imagines (*dokei*) that he possesses her, but holds only

---

52. Menelaus is twice thought to be dead—once, by Helen to her great consternation, and a second time by Theoclymenus, to his delight, but as part of Helen's escape plot. Helen makes two requests for complicity through silence (first to Theonoe and later to the Chorus), and the deception of the king is accomplished in two separate episodes. Two stories circulate about Helen's twin brothers, the Dioscuri: that they have killed themselves for shame at their sister, or (as is confirmed at the end of the play) that they have "become gods in the likeness of stars" (140). On this, see G. S. Meltzer, " 'Where is the Glory of Troy?' Kleos in Euripides *Helen*," *Classical Antiquity* 13 (1994), 253.

53. Solmsen's brief essay (note 50) is the fundamental treatment of this aspect of the play, and its influence is seen in almost everything written about it since. Helen makes an explicit contrast of name and body at 67–69 / 66–67, 589 / 588, and 1114 / 1100; and cf. 41–42 / 42–43. Other noteworthy contrasts: *onoma* / *pragma* (name / deed), 602 / 601, 806 / 792; *onoma* / *nous* (name / mind), 746–47 / 730–31, and *sôma* / *phrenes* (body / mind or heart), 152–54 / 160–61.

54. See *Iphigenia in Tauris* 504, *Orestes* 390.

55. E.g., Achilles in Homer, *Iliad*, especially 1.148–303 or Ajax in Sophocles *Ajax*, especially 430–80.

56. See Pucci (note 51), 42–48, for a sophisticated analysis of Helen's self-identification with her phantom.

an image (*kenên dokêsin*, "an empty seeming" **33–34** / 35–36). Nevertheless, the fact that Helen's beauty was the prize awarded to Paris by
Aphrodite and that he came to Sparta to claim her (even if it was only
the phantom he took home) gives her beauty, however much she wishes
it could have been washed away (**259–65** / 260–66), a heavy burden of
guilt for all that followed, guilt from which Helen cannot completely
free herself.

Whatever the complexity of Helen's feelings regarding her identity,
the play emphasizes her exemplary purity. This is of course a fundamental fact of the plot, but it is underscored by a tendency to relegate
terms like "beauty" (*kallos*) and "form" (*morphê*) to the world of (false)
appearance. As Downing suggests, Helen's phantom is "the *kallos* that
Paris takes away,"[57] leaving the real Helen to embody the ethical opposite of the hedonistic deceit and destruction that her beauty has come to
signify. Indeed, the "new Helen" is imbued not only with the chastity of
a faithful wife, but through images and associations with an aura of
regained virginity. From the first words of the play, invoking "the lovely
virgin streams of Nile," virginity is a surprisingly pervasive theme. We
have already noted (in section 3) that Helen's description of her abduction by Hermes while gathering flowers is reminiscent of Hades,' seizure
of the maiden Persephone, and the play elsewhere offers Persephone as
a figure whose experience is parallel to Helen's. Helen's abduction
associates her not with Aphrodite, as in the usual story, but with the
virgin goddess Athena, for when Hermes sweeps her up she is gathering
flowers to take to Athena's temple (245; cf. 228, 1466–68). Most important, Helen is linked in several ways with the play's chief representative of
virginity, the prophetess Theonoe, to whom Helen appeals for help in
escaping from Theoclymenus' grasp.[58]

The first mention of Theonoe in the prologue already suggests an
important connection: in yet another instance of the play's characteristic
doublings, she has two names that suggest two natures. Named Eido
("Image," "Beauty") as a child, she receives the name Theonoe ("Divine
Wisdom") only when she reaches the age of marriage.[59] At that point
she transcends beauty (Helen's characterizing trait) by rejecting marriage in favor of a life devoted to truth and justice. Her identity as
Eido is evanescent, like Helen's phantom (*eidôlon*), the embodiment

57. Downing (note 51), 2.
58. See Segal (note 5), 589–90.
59. For these names, see note on 8–9 / 11–13.

of a merely outer beauty.[60] Helen, addressing Theonoe as *parthenos* ("maiden") at the beginning (910 / 894) and end (952 / 939) of her appeal, acknowledges that virginal purity is fundamental to her nature as a wise prophet.[61] Though sharing neither virginity nor prophetic power with Theonoe, the purified "new Helen" of this play can appeal for her help as one who (like herself) stands apart from the machinations of Aphrodite, and who will listen to claims truly based on justice and piety. And indeed, her plea is made precisely in such terms.[62] It is not least through Theonoe that Helen demonstrates that her mind and heart are indeed far different from her (supposed) body. At the end of the play, Theoclymenus associates the two women, agreeing to spare his own sister and congratulating the Dioscuri on theirs, the "best and purest" of women (1671 / 1684).

A final element that associates Helen and Theonoe is the complex figure of *aether*, the thin upper air of the heavens.[63] For Theonoe, it is a divine substance from which she draws "pure breath from heaven" (883 / 867), the repository of consciousness after death and a true and lasting object of reverence. Elsewhere in the play, it is the medium of Hermes' abduction of Helen to Egypt[64] and of other divine journeys, including Zeus' arrival "through the air" (210 / 216) for the amorous visit to Leda that led to Helen's birth, and the swift arrival of the Dioscuri, speeding their horses "down paths of air," for which the Chorus prays in order to assure Helen a safe voyage home (1487–88 / 1495–97). And of course it is the material from which the phantom Helen was fashioned (585 / 584; cf. 32 / 34) and to which it returns (606–7 / 605–6, cf. 1223 / 1218), that is, a cleverly crafted but evanescent divine deception.

---

60. George E. Dimock, *"God, or Not God, or Between the Two": Euripides' "Helen"* (Northampton, MA, 1977), 8, and David Sansone, "Theonoe and Theoclymenus, *Symbolae Osloenses* 60 (1985), 20, who point out the parallel between Theonoe's renunciation of marriage and Athena's. Sansone picks up and makes an interesting case for the suggestion of L. A. Post that Theonoe in effect substitutes for Athena in the play.

61. As Segal (note 5), 587, points out, Theonoe is called *parthenos* even before we learn her name (7 / 10). In the Greek text, she is called *parthenos* seven times, *korê* ("maiden") five, and *neanis* ("girl," "maiden") once.

62. See 915–17 / 900–904, 928–38 / 914–25, 939–43 / 940–43. Her appeal is "in striking contrast" to that of Menelaus, as Segal (note 5), 589, points out; only she, among all the characters, seems to understand and speak Theonoe's language. "In a sense," Segal concludes, "Theonoe is Helen's purer self" (590).

63. It should be noted that Euripides uses *ouranos* ("sky," "the heavens") unproblematically as a synonym for *aether*, e.g., 32 / 34.

64. 43–44 / 44–45, 243–45 / 246–47. Helen is indeed the only mortal to travel by this divine form of conveyance, at least in surviving tragedy, and it is possible that this reflects her divine origins and, in some versions of her story, her destined immortality (cf. Euripides, *Orestes* 1629–37). I owe this observation to Dr. David Banta

"Aether" is a particularly Euripidean word, occurring especially often in later plays. (There are ten occurrences apiece in *Helen* and *Bacchae*, more than in all the surviving plays and fragments of Sophocles.) Aristophanes certainly associates the word with Euripides. In *Thesmophoriazusae*, produced a year after *Helen*,[65] Euripides swears by "aether, dwelling place of Zeus" (272) and more strikingly, in the later *Frogs*, when Dionysus asks Euripides to pray to his "private gods," the playwright addresses "Aether, my nourishment" (891–92). In *Helen*, however, although aether is imbued with the divine, it makes an extraordinarily equivocal showing as the source of Theonoe's purity and truth, of Helen's rescue, and also—through the deception of the phantom—of all the death and suffering caused by the war at Troy and the destruction of Helen's reputation.[66]

The disjunction of appearance and reality is not limited, however, to the figure of Helen. Menelaus, in particular, is characterized from the moment he enters by the contrast between his fame as the great hero of Troy and the "shame" he feels (**413 / 415**) at being seen as a shipwrecked beggar. In many ways, his situation resembles Helen's, since his identity, too, is shaken by forces beyond his control. For him, however, the Trojan War is the great confirmation of his glory, whereas Helen sees it as the source only of pain and grief. Helen must somehow rid herself of the "shame" (**135**), the reputation that makes her despised of Greeks and Trojans alike; Menelaus must reclaim the heroic identity that he lost along with his "famous" army (**451 / 453**) and "splendid" clothing (**420–21 / 423–4**).[67] Helen cannot escape the guilt that rightly belongs to her phantom; Menelaus will find it hard to function as the commander he was and still believes himself to be until he receives new clothing.[68] Meanwhile, he is a figure of surprising fragility, blustering and confused by turns, given to tears and emotional outbursts, and at times edging

---

65. See note 1.

66. The ambiguity of aether reflects a larger ambiguity about the divine and its role in *Helen*. For brief consideration of these theological issues, see section 7. For discussion of the possible religious significance of aether in Euripides, see Kjeld Matthiessen, "Zur Theonoeszene der euripideischen *Helena*," *Hermes* 96 (1968), 699ff.

67. Segal (note 5), 577, points out that Helen's and Menelaus' use of words denoting "glory," "fame," "shame," "disgrace," and the like differ sharply—not surprisingly, since Helen's very name brings her grief (**196 / 199**), whereas Menelaus expects (wrongly, as it happens) that his good name will sustain him everywhere (**503–4 / 501–2**).

68. See note on **378–433 / 386–434**, and cf. Pippin [Burnett] (note 26), 152: "But just as he was made cowardly by rags, Menelaus is made strong again by princely robes; ... he walks out of the palace a hero once more, sure of his own strength. Yet Euripides has contrived that we should still be reminded that appearance can lie, for those clothes are not his own, and Menelaus is now masquerading as one of his own shipmates."

toward the ridiculous or even grotesque.[69] Helen suffers despite her innocence, Menelaus despite what he has accomplished. It is of course part of the dramatic strategy of *Helen* that the two reunite precisely when each needs the other most.

Once the reunion has been achieved and Theonoe's support assured, plot and thematics both take new turns. The plot moves from recognition to escape; the chief thematic antinomy becomes clever Greek versus slow-witted barbarian. No longer victims of deception and aggression, Helen and Menelaus employ both with cunning, successfully plotting to deceive the Egyptian king and then fighting a battle in order to effect their escape. Menelaus, instructed by his smart, resourceful wife, "plays" the shipwrecked sailor he was so ashamed to be and announces his own supposed death by drowning, thus obtaining from the unwitting king arms and the ship he claims to need for funeral rites at sea. Helen forgets the horrors of the Trojan War and throws herself into the new campaign, exhorting Menelaus' men in the thick of the battle to show "your Trojan glory" (**1590** / 1603).[70] And in the end, the barbarian king is brought to accept Greek wisdom and morality; at the bidding of the Dioscuri he gives up his plan to kill his traitorous sister Theonoe, and closes the play with praise for Helen's "noble mind" (**1672** / 1687). Evidently, appearance and reality are crucial to this segment of the play, as well, if only because of the elaborate play-acting with which Helen and Menelaus trick the Egyptian king into permitting their successful escape. Critics have variously commented on the great change in Menelaus, some attributing to him a noble, more "tragic" dimension in this part of the play[71] and others seeing in his transformation an almost parodic version of traditional heroism.[72] Similarly, Helen's leading role in the intrigue has been characterized both as a demonstration of her identity as a virtuous wife[73] and as a disturbing replication of the deceptive qualities of the phantom.[74] One can in any case see all of these transformations as further variations on the theme of

69. Thus Patrizia Mureddu, "Gli Stracci di Menelao," *Philologus* 147 (2003), 192, who reviews the thematics of Menelaus' rags and argues that it is part of a Euripidean response to Aristophanic parody.

70. On the complexity in this play of the idea of "Trojan glory," see Meltzer (note 52); Segal (note 5), 572–84, and cf. section 7.

71. E.g., Anthony J. Podlecki, "The Basic Seriousness of Euripides' *Helen*," *Transactions of the American Philological Association* 101 (1970), 405; Cedric H. Whitman, *Euripides and the Full Circle of Myth* (Cambridge, MA, 1974), 66.

72. E.g., D. Galeotti Papi, "Victories and Sufferers in Euripides' *Helen*," *American Journal of Philology* 108 (1987), 39–40; Austin (note 3), 176, 183.

73. E.g., Segal (note 5), 606–7; Holmberg (note 18), 36ff.

74. E.g., D. M. Juffras, "Helen and Other Victims in Euripides' *Helen*," *Hermes* 121 (1993), 54–56; Pucci (note 51), 66–70.

appearance and reality that in some sense acts as the master signifier for the entire drama. The central tropes return transformed: deception becomes the strategy for escape and a war against barbarians is won, like that at Troy, by trickery of Odyssean cleverness—only this time to rescue the real Helen.

VII.   *HELEN* AND HISTORY

It is significant that *Helen* was presented at a moment when Athens had suffered immense losses in battle overseas.[75] In 412, the Athenian military intervention in Sicily begun in 415 was already heading toward its disastrous conclusion. Undertaken with high hopes, it would end in a debacle that cost thousands of lives and left the city desolate.[76] The worst had not yet happened, but already in 413 Athens had been forced to mount a "rescue expedition," and it must have been clear to most Athenians that the situation was precarious at best. Those who see *Helen* as predominantly comic in tone, insofar as they consider its historical context, are inclined to label it "escapist," an entertainment aimed at distracting the Athenian spectators from the military and political realities of the moment. This characterization, however, fails to reckon with an audience that would surely have been particularly sensitive to the depiction of a war fought with immense losses and to no good purpose. Nor does it do justice to the complexity with which the play treats the Trojan War and the thematics of war more generally.

There are no direct allusions to contemporary events in *Helen*, but if one considers those events, how can they not give a certain charge to its depictions of shipwrecked sailors, soldiers lost or enslaved in foreign lands, facing death or waiting for rescue or plotting escape far from home? Several characters comment on the futility of a war fought only for a phantom—over nothing—and conclude that it was fought in vain.[77] Given the play's premises of the uncertainty of human knowledge, the deceptiveness of appearances, and the instability of fortune, it is not surprising that we find a rethinking of the meaning of the Trojan War, in at least one striking passage in terms applicable to war in general. In the first *stasimon*, the Chorus calls all who pursue glory in battle "mad" and pronounces in the most unequivocal of terms that as long as disputes are settled by violence, "fighting will never / be driven from among our

75. For the secure dating of the play to 412 B.C., see note 1.

76. See the gripping account in Thucydides' *History of the Peloponnesian War*, Books 6 and 7. For the hopes invested in the expedition and the scene of its brilliant departure, see esp. 6.24–25, 30–32; for the final debacle, 7.79–87.

77. Helen: **355–57** / 362–63; Servant: **604** / 603, **608–17** / 608–15 (quoting the phantom), **722** / 707, **733–34** / 718, **763–66** / 749–51; Theoclymenus: **1224** / 1220.

HELEN

cities" (1158–63 / 1151–7). Powerful as this reflection is, it cannot be taken straightforwardly as the "message" of so many-layered a drama, for it comes just before the entrance of Theoclymenus and the start of the escape sequence that will end with a re-enactment of the Trojan War in miniature, presented as a necessary and triumphant final stage in the restoration of Helen and Menelaus to their homes, reputations, and good fortune.[78] How typical of this paradoxical play that it shows at length and repeatedly the futility of the Trojan War, only to culminate in a battle that deliberately replicates that war!

The battle sequence pits Menelaus and the Greeks who survived shipwreck with him against the Egyptian sailors who have been put under his command. Menelaus, who has never abandoned the idea of Trojan glory,[79] evokes it again when inviting his men on board (1548–49 / 1560); his battle-plan—ambush from inside the walls of the ship against an unarmed and unsuspecting foe—bears a witty resemblance to the ruse of the Trojan horse. The battle itself (like so much else in the play) has elicited very divergent reactions, from appreciation of Menelaus' moment of glory to outrage at the undeserved slaughter of so many innocent victims.[80] There is no need to suppose that the original audience was any more unanimous than modern readers in its response to this scene (or to the play as a whole). Some may have been amused or disturbed by the reduction of the heroic struggles at Troy to "a brawl between sturdy young Greeks ... and a handful of simple Egyptians left at their mercy by a stupid king."[81] One may perhaps guess that more will have been elated by the Greeks' triumph than appalled by the Egyptians' undeserved deaths.

Nevertheless, there is much in the drama that could suggest to the attentive spectator (and to readers, as well) the hope of good will and reconciliation as alternatives to violence in settling disputes. In

78. See further note on 1158–72.
79. Even after learning about the phantom, Menelaus clings to his Trojan fame as the motivation for all he does: e.g., 820–22 / 806–8, 859–60 / 845.
80. E.g., Whitman (note 71), 66, who sees Menelaus here as a newly heroic figure "taking a bold step in a desperate hour.... Euripides seldom exploits heroic values, but if the moment of truth is to come, it calls for high-spirited effort and a drop of grace, as well as for stratagem and intrigue." For Burnett (note 78), 97, on the other hand, the contest is the only aspect of the confrontation with the Egyptians that is "anything like a confrontation of equals, and even then, though the ... ship is filled with blood ... it is only the blood of a good messenger speech," and Menelaus' victory is "far too cheaply won." Objection to the brutality of the spectacle begins with A. W. Verrall, *Essays on Four Plays of Euripides* (Cambridge, 1905), 85–86: "cold-blooded cruelty,... a hideous thing, a thing intolerable," and more recently, e.g., Galeotti Papi (note 72), 39: "The ferocity of the battle won by Menelaus over his unarmed enemy seems instead perfectly in character with his nature as a false hero."
81. Wolff (note 26), 84.

254

particular, the beautiful lyrics of the second and third *stasima*, in their different ways, strike such notes. In the second *stasimon*, Aphrodite, who caused Helen so much suffering, instead brings comfort and consolation to the Mother Goddess in the form of music that dissolves her anger at last in laughter, thus ending the famine she had caused. The final *stasimon*, looking forward to Helen's homecoming so long delayed, imagines in joyous and beautiful verses Spartan cult and festival on the banks of the lovely Eurotas. If we remember that Sparta was Athens' chief enemy in the Peloponnesian War and chief rival for hegemony in Greek lands, we might see this passage as a subtle plea for an end to the destructive (and self-destructive) enmity.[82]

VIII. IS *HELEN* A TRAGEDY?

From at least one point of view, this play cannot be anything other than a tragedy: it was presented at the festival of Dionysus, in the Theater of Dionysus, after having been awarded a chorus, as part of the tragic competition.[83] Who, then, are we to say on the basis of the small remainder we possess of the plays produced for that competition that *Helen* was not a tragedy, or that what we mean by tragic is what Euripides and his audience would have meant? It is true that the play is written in what is often called a "romantic" and/or "melodramatic" style that appears in others of the late dramas (notably *Iphigenia in Tauris* and *Ion* among surviving plays) and certainly distinguishes them from *Oedipus Tyrannus* or indeed from a number of Euripides' other plays (*Hippolytus, Trojan Women, Bacchae,* to name some of the best known) that end in misery. But tragedy, at least as practiced in the fifth century, clearly allowed for reversals of fortune from sorrow to joy. On any reading, however, *Helen* is willful, playful, self-consciously theatrical, and overflowing with intellectual energy. Parts of it are certainly amusing; some of its most memorable moments are by general consent quite funny. Furthermore, comic technique and tragic content are often combined or juxtaposed.[84] All this certainly needs to be accounted for in any understanding of this remarkable drama. And a

---

82. This notion is made more explicit in Aristophanes' *Lysistrata*, produced the following year, after the full extent of the Sicilian disaster had become known. The conclusion of *Lysistrata* imagines an alliance of Athens and Sparta, solemnized by a common meal and ritual songs and dances.

83. The speculation of D. F. Sutton, *The Date of Euripides' "Cyclops"* (Ann Arbor, 1974), 104–24, and *The Greek Satyr Play* (Meisenheim am Glan, 1980), 184–90, that *Helen* is prosatyric (i.e., was presented as place of a satyr play as the last drama in Euripides' tragic tetralogy of 412), even if accepted, would not settle the question of the play's claims to seriousness.

84. See note on 73–78 for a typical example.

long tradition of scholarship treats the play as essentially an entertainment, primarily comic in tone and technique.

More recently, however, claims for a more serious intent, and even for a degree of philosophical depth, have predominated.[85] Yet at almost every point, the significance of the features advanced to support *Helen's* claim to intellectual and emotional gravitas has been open to question. At the center of most attempts to claim a seriousness worthy of tragedy for the play has been, not surprisingly, the Theonoe scene, with its striking juxtaposition of divine machinations and a higher, more mystical reality. Theonoe's knowledge of things divine provides two incompatible pictures. The first offers the traditional Olympian deities, who act capriciously (at least from a human perspective), self-interestedly, and with little or no concern to establish a consistent relationship between human behavior and divine rewards or punishments. Indeed, Theonoe's report of the debate among the gods over Helen's fate reinforces and continues the account of divine deception that is at the core of this version of the myth. But Theonoe is also endowed with an inward source of piety she calls "a temple of Justice . . . deep in my nature" (**1015 / 1002–3**), and she explains that, although the mind does not live on as an individual entity, it somehow retains consciousness after death and, even though "it blends with the deathless air above," is subject to the requital of impious acts (**1026–30 / 1013–16**). This evidently happens apart from the gods of Olympus. The significance of Theonoe's revelation has been debated at length.[86] Whatever the precise import, it suggests that mortals cannot expect moral guidance from the gods, but must choose what is right according to the dictates of their own sense of piety, as Theonoe does in agreeing not to betray Menelaus to her brother.

The play makes no attempt to coalesce the two visions of the divine realm that coexist in Theonoe's speech. Indeed, she ends by urging Helen and Menelaus to propitiate the gods who have taken sides in

---

85. E.g., Gunther Zuntz, *"Helena*: Theology and Irony," in *Entretiens sur l'Antiquité Classique VI: Euripide* (Vandoeuvres-Genève, 1960), 201–41; Anne P. Burnett, *Catastrophe Survived: Euripides' Plays of Mixed Reversal* (Oxford, 1971); Solmsen (note 50); Pippin [Burnett] (note 26); Matthiessen (note 66); Segal (note 5); Wolff (note 26); Downing (note 51); Holmberg (note 18); Pucci (note 51).

86. For the critical response to these lines, see note on **1026–30**. Zuntz (note 78), 211–14, and Dimock, 8–14, are among those who take Theonoe's piety to provide a higher and purer moral teaching that is at the heart of Euripides' enterprise in this play. A. M. Dale crisply expresses a more skeptical view in her edition of the play (Oxford, 1967) on 1013–16: the lines represent merely "a piece of high-toned but vague mysticism appropriate to Theonoe." Pippin [Burnett], esp. 158–63; Segal (1971), 583–91; and Sansone, esp. 24–25, although differing in their approaches, all point out that one cannot simply take Theonoe's piety as the enlightened replacement of primitive superstition, as embodied in the traditional portrayal of the Olympians. The latter remain very much part of the world of the play, and upon them success or failure seems finally to depend.

their affairs (1037–40 / 1024–27); despite everything, their success depends on the Olympians' favor, or at least on appeasing their anger. The dilemma that faces the human actors of *Helen* does not stem from a simple duality, but rather from the interpenetration of two conflicting "systems" of thought and action. From the spectators' point of view, of course, the overarching shape of the plot provides reassurance of a justice over which the gods preside, punishing the Trojans for Paris' transgression, reuniting the innocent Helen with her long-suffering husband, and bringing the two safely back to Sparta. The human actors, on the other hand, must struggle to achieve their ends in a world of uncertainty and danger. The plot depends at crucial points on divine strife (Theonoe reveals that it is continuing as she speaks, and in a way which directly affects Helen's fate, 895–904 / 878–86) and divine deception (above all, of course, the phantom Helen, Hera's device to foil Aphrodite, e.g. 29–34 / 31–36, 686–97 / 673–83), with all the attendant suffering they bring, from the deaths and destruction at Troy to Helen's own struggle to bring what she appears to be into harmony with what she really is.

The escape sequence makes it clear that strife and deception are an unavoidable part of human behavior as well. Theonoe's decision has given Helen and Menelaus the chance to escape, but it is now up to them to make it happen. Menelaus' failed attempts to concoct something suitably "heroic" leave deception as the only hope, and Helen devises a plan that involves the skillful trickery that had such negative associations in the first half of the play. Like a new Hera, she creates a phantom Menelaus. The central feature of Helen's deception is the cenotaph that functions as the exact counterpart of the phantom in the first half of the play.[87] Learning from her own experience, Helen effects her salvation at last by using to her own advantage the tools and techniques of which she was so long the victim. In so doing, however, Helen also replicates the seductive and destructive role that had hitherto belonged, as she has insisted, only to her phantom, turning herself (in Helene Foley's phrase) "into a commodity to be exchanged among men by abduction."[88] She uses all the deviousness at her command (overseeing Menelaus' costume change, altering her own appearance, using artful words to deceive the king)—and thereby proves herself to be a virtuous and deserving wife. Paradoxically, to do so, she must offer herself to Theoclymenus—though only as a ruse, like the phantom made to fool Paris. And, as we have seen, the violent but triumphant

87. Downing (note 51), 11.
88. Foley (note 26), 318.

escape in which Helen participates at Menelaus' side is similarly full of mixed messages.[89]

And yet the more thoughtful spectators, at least, will have understood that *Helen* shows, even through its characteristic filter of ironic wit, how uncertainty and error, violence and suffering are inevitably part of human experience. They will also have observed that in the world of this play luck, pluck, cleverness, and deception are needed more than nobility or moral rectitude for success, and even for survival. At the same time, they will have felt the pleasure of witnessing beauty, innocence, and fidelity win the day, belatedly but with irresistible panache. It is this mixture of sensations and emotions that makes it difficult, and finally irrelevant, to decide whether *Helen* is a tragedy or something else.[90] This is a play that lives from its dichotomies and antinomies, not by resolving them but rather by making their incompatibilities and ambiguities an essential part of the experience. That it has comic elements is undeniable; that its vision is finally a comic one, far more questionable. If *Helen* is "about" anything, it is about the consequences of allowing appearance to overtake reality and the joys and pains of emerging from delusion. The world of the play is a tragic one, immersed in the brutalities and stupidities of meaningless strife, unnecessary suffering, and undeserved death. Within it, "something like comedy is at work,"[91] suggesting a renewal of life and rebirth of hope; in Gunther Zuntz's memorable phrase, *Helen* is "an ethereal dance above the abyss."[92]

PETER BURIAN

89. See section 7.
90. Cf. Segal (note 5), 613.
91. Wolff (note 26), 84.
92. Zuntz (note 78), 227.

ON THE TRANSLATION

This translation is the product of long years of engagement with a play that continues to fascinate and delight me. Having been asked by Christopher Collard to prepare an Aris and Phillips edition of *Helen*, I decided to offer a graduate seminar on the play and began by preparing as carefully literal a translation as I could, noting both problems and pleasures as I went. Reading and rereading the original convinced me that it could hold its own on stage and should be seen as well as read. I was able to persuade my colleagues in theater studies (then the Drama Program) at Duke University to give it a try, but my "pony" could hardly serve as a play text, and the translations I looked at seemed in one way or another unsuitable. At the end of spring term, I went to the North Carolina shore and spent some days divided between wandering the beach and retranslating *Helen* into the verse forms that seemed to suggest themselves: relaxed pentameter for the dialogue and rhythmic-ally varied stanza forms for the lyrics, reflecting strophic responsion where found in the Greek.

Quite differently from my usual experience of translation, the writing flowed with ease and almost unnerving speed. My long immersion in the text no doubt helped me find the tones of voice I was looking for, but more important, I think, was a sense of liberation that stemmed from having already set down a text that mirrored the letter of the Greek as closely as I could. My attention could now be directed to communicat-ing nuances of expression, to making the lines speak and sing as best I could. At the end of my week at the beach, I had a substantial sequence of scenes on paper in something like the form in which they appear here, followed the pleasure of hearing a first read-through by and for friends and family (with my step daughters in the roles of Helen and Theonoe).

Of course I had only made a beginning, and many revisions that followed benefited from the rehearsals of the Duke Players cast. These ranged from the minimal and occasionally amusing (I discovered, for example, that American college students at the turn of the millennium could not say the word "booty" without smirking or cracking up) to major revisions (particularly to the choral lyrics, to make them rhythmically more vital and more easily intelligible). The version printed here stays close to the run of the Greek, but I hope that it also gives the characters believable voices and conveys some of the music, wit, and verve I sense in Euripides' text. At this point, perhaps, an example will be more telling than further attempts to describe the processes involved. The example is admittedly not typical, but gives, I think, a clear idea of my aspirations for this translation.

Here is the first strophic pair from the third and final choral ode of the play, first in the version as published alongside the Greek text of lines 1451–77 in the Aris and Phillips volume, complete with indications of textual uncertainties [† . . . †] and a lacuna [< >]:

> Swift Phoenician galley of Sidon, whose oar-beat is dear to the loud surges of Nereus, dance-leader of the beautifully dancing dolphins when the sea is calm and free of breezes and Galaneia, the grey-green daughter of Sea, speaks thus: "Let the sails hang free, since you have left sea-breezes behind, and take up your pinewood oars, sailors, o sailors, as you bring Helen to the shores with fine harbours where Perseus made his home."

> Surely she will meet the daughters of Leucippus beside the rolling river or before the temple of Pallas, joining them in the dance after a long absence, or for the revels of Hyacinthus in their nighttime joy. He it was whom Phoebus challenged to a contest †with the wheel edge of the discus† and killed; and for †the† land of Lacedaemon the son of Zeus decreed to observe with reverence a day of bull-sacrifice. And < > the child †she left at home,† for whose marriage the pine-torches have not yet blazed.

Here is the passage as it appears in this volume (1448–71):

> Swift Phoenician galley, whose beating oars make music
>   for Nereus, leader of the dance—
>   sail home, sail home—
> leader of the lovely dance of dolphins when the sea is quiet
>   and the winds are lying low—
>   sail home, sail home—
> and Galaneia, grey-green goddess of calm seas,
>   cries: "Spread the sails—

> sail home, sail home—
> leave them to the breezes, sailors; take up your oars and bring
> Helen to harbor at home"—
> sail home, sail home!

> Beside the river, at Athena's temple, she'll meet Leucippus'
> daughters
> and join the dance again—
> at home, at home—
> after so long away, share the nighttime joy of the revels
> for Hyacinthus, the boy—
> at home, at home—
> Apollo loved and killed with a careless throw of the discus,
> and made a festival—
> at home, at home—
> to honor him. And she will meet her daughter, whose wedding
> torch has not yet blazed
> at home, at home.

In the verse translation, I was able to free myself from the fetters of fidelity to the letter of James Diggle's text, restoring the evident meaning of the damaged bits and filling in the gap. Beyond that, however, this translation recognizes (and I hope makes clear to readers and spectators) that the essence of the ode is the hopeful, joyful balm of its music. Helen and Menelaus have managed to trick King Theoclymenus into giving them a ship with which to sail home at last. The ode marks the passage of time between their departure from the stage and the arrival of the Messenger, who will describe the stealthy, then bloody seizure of the Egyptian vessel by the Greeks. It is framed as a wish for a safe journey (a subgenre of classical poetry known as *propemptikon*); its contents, however, are secondary to the mood of release and relief, the tone of anticipated joy, that give it poetic vitality. A kaleidoscopic series of vignettes is filled with color and movement, sea deities, and evocations of Spartan lore and festival. In this first strophic pair, the festive dancing of dolphins, the return of the cranes to Greece with joyous news, the encouragement of the sailors by the sea nymph Galaneia, the invocation of the tutelary gods and legendary heroes of Spartan lore surround the voyage with an atmosphere of the miraculous. Musical, pictorial, and mythological associations combine to permit us to participate in the outcome that the drama has led us to desire. Magic and music, then, are what this version attempts to convey, and the refrains of this strophic pair (developed in rehearsal with the Chorus of the Duke production as a repeated background chant over which individual singers intoned the lyrics) find in that attempt their sole—and I hope sufficient—justification.

My hope for this version as a whole is that it reflects the pleasures of the text with sufficient conviction to encourage a wider readership and more frequent performances in theaters across the English-speaking world.

ACKNOWLEDGMENTS

The Introduction and Notes are modified and abbreviated from the Introduction and Commentary to the prose translation (with accompanying Greek text) referred to above, which appeared in the Aris and Phillips Classical Texts published by Oxbow Books (Oxford, 2007). Interested readers are referred to that edition for fuller explanations and scholarly apparatus.

The memorable original production of this translation by the Duke Players was directed with great imagination by Robert Richmond, with a cast of talented students, splendid sets and costumes designed and executed by an equally talented group of faculty and students, and a very effective percussion score improvised by Ken Ray. The entire, memorable experience taught me a great deal about Greek drama and the art of translation, and I remain deeply grateful to all concerned.

Finally, I want to thank Kenneth Reckford for sharing his love of Helen and *Helen*, and for his support and encouragement at every stage of my engagement with this wonderful play.

PETER BURIAN

HELEN

Translated by

PETER BURIAN

CHARACTERS

HELEN daughter of Zeus and Leda, wife of Menelaus

TEUCER Greek warrior, son of Telamon and brother of Ajax

CHORUS of captive Greek women

MENELAUS king of Sparta, son of Atreus, husband of Helen

OLD WOMAN doorkeeper of the palace

OLD MAN loyal servant of Menelaus

THEONOË prophetess, sister of Theoclymenus

THEOCLYMENUS king of Egypt, son of Proteus

MESSENGER sailor in the service of Theoclymenus

SERVANT of Theoclymenus

DIOSCURI (CASTOR
AND POLYDEUCES) deified brothers of Helen

SERVANTS AND
ATTENDANTS of Theonoe and Theoclymenus

Line numbers in the right-hand margin of the text refer to the English translation only, and the Notes beginning at p. 327 are keyed to
these lines. The bracketed line numbers in the running heads refer
to the Greek text.

Before the palace of Theoclymenus in Egypt. One side exit leads to the sea, the other inland. At the center of the stage is the main gate to the palace precinct. Near this gate stands the tomb of Proteus, Theoclymenus' father, at which Helen takes refuge as a suppliant.

HELEN

> *(entering and gradually moving toward her place*
> *at the tomb)*

We are in Egypt. The lovely virgin streams
of Nile water the fields with snow that melted
on mountains far away. Proteus, who ruled here,
may he rest in peace, married the sea nymph
Psamathë after she broke off her wedding to Aeacus,
and she bore him two children: a son, Theoclymenus,
and a girl, her mother's joy, a virgin still,
called Eido when she was little. But when she came
to the age of marriage, they changed her name to Theonoe,
because the gods had given her knowledge of all   10
that is and is to come. This was the legacy
of Nereus, her mother's father, lord of the sea.
    As for me, my home is a place you will have heard of:
Sparta. My father's a man called Tyndareus—though
they say that Zeus disguised himself as a swan
and, pretending to flee from an eagle's attack, took refuge
with my mother Leda and made love to her—and it may
be true. My name is Helen, and I will tell you
what I have had to endure.
                            Three goddesses came
to Mount Ida—Hera, Zeus' wife, Athena,   20
his virgin daughter, and Aphrodite, goddess
of love. They wanted Paris, prince of Troy,
King Priam's son, to settle an argument for them
about which one was most beautiful. But it was my
beauty, if you can call this curse of mine beauty,
that Aphrodite dangled before Paris as bait,
with a promise of marriage—and she won the contest.
So Paris left his mountain and flocks and went
to Sparta to make me his wife. Hera, enraged

at losing, blew my new marriage to the winds   30
and gave young Paris not me, but a living image
just like me, conjured out of thin air.
Paris thinks it's me he's embracing, but he's
a fool; it isn't. Meanwhile, Zeus devised
a plan that only adds to my troubles. He stirred up
war between the Greeks and the poor Trojans
so he could lighten the load of Mother Earth,
this vast mob of mortals that overruns her,
and show the Greeks who their mightiest warrior is.
But in this combat, the Helen Troy fought for,   40
the Helen all Greece battled to claim as spoils,
was not me at all. It was just my name.
Hermes veiled the real me in a cloud,
took me up into the folds of air,
and set me down here at Proteus' palace.
For Zeus had not forgotten me. He chose
the man he considered honest above all others
to be my host and keep my marriage safe.

      So, here I am; but my hapless husband assembled
an army and marched against the towers of Troy   50
to hunt me down, his kidnapped wife. Thousands
have died by Scamander's stream because of me.
And I, who have endured these wrongs, am cursed,
slandered because it *seems* I betrayed my husband
and dragged Greece into war. Why do I go on
living? Because Hermes assured me I'll go
home again and live once more on Sparta's
famous plain with Menelaus, once
my husband finds out I never went to Troy—
and if I can escape being made to serve   60
some other man in bed. As long as Proteus
saw the light of day, I was safe from marriage,
but ever since the dark earth claimed him, his son
Theoclymenus has been setting traps to catch me.

                   (taking up her position at the tomb)

But loyal always to my husband, I sit
as a suppliant at this tomb to keep my marriage

safe from harm. Even if my name
is a byword for dishonor throughout Greece,
my body here will win me no disgrace.

TEUCER   *(entering alone, armed with a bow and wearing a quiver)*

Who is master of this mighty palace?   70
The house is worthy of the god of wealth
himself, and the circuit of its walls is kingly.
(seeing Helen) Hah! What do I see? The deadly image
of that abomination, the woman who destroyed
me and all the Greeks. My curse on you
for being so much like Helen! If I weren't
standing on foreign soil, this arrow would pay you
with death for looking like the daughter of Zeus.

HELEN Poor fellow, whoever you may be, why turn
against *me* in hate for what you say she's done?   80

TEUCER I was wrong; I let my anger get
the better of me. You see, all Greece hates
the daughter of Zeus. Forgive me for what I said.

HELEN But who are you? Where did you come here from?

TEUCER A Greek soldier, woman, and a poor wretch...

HELEN Ah, then it's no wonder you hate Helen.

TEUCER ...driven into exile, banished from home.

HELEN Wretched indeed! But who drove you away?

TEUCER The man who's closest to me: my father, Telamon.

HELEN But why? Something must have gone badly wrong.   90

TEUCER Ajax, my brother, destroyed me when he died at Troy.

HELEN Surely it wasn't your sword that killed him?

TEUCER Throwing himself on his own sword killed him.

HELEN Did he go mad? Only a madman would do that.

TEUCER Have you heard of Achilles, Peleus' son?

HELEN Yes. Wasn't he once a suitor for Helen's hand?

TEUCER His death started a squabble over his armor.

HELEN But how could that have done Ajax any harm?

TEUCER Someone else got the armor, so he killed himself.

HELEN And it was his death that undid you, too?   100

TEUCER My fault was that I did not die with him.

HELEN So you went with him to the famous town of Troy?

TEUCER I helped in its destruction, and it in mine.

HELEN So, Troy has been sacked and put to the torch?

TEUCER You couldn't find even the outline of its walls.

HELEN Helen! The Trojans died because of you.

TEUCER Greeks, too. Yes, there was suffering to spare.

HELEN And how long now has the city lain in ruins?

TEUCER Seven harvests, seven long years have passed.

HELEN And before that, how long did you fight at Troy?   110

TEUCER Month after month, for ten endless years.

HELEN And that Spartan woman—did you capture her?

TEUCER Menelaus grabbed her and dragged her off by the hair.

HELEN Is this hearsay, or did you see the wretch yourself?

TEUCER With my own eyes, just as I see you now.

HELEN Could it have been an illusion sent by the gods?

TEUCER Forget about Helen. Let's not talk about her.

HELEN And Menelaus? He's safe at home with her?

TEUCER No, not in Argos, nor in Sparta either.

HELEN Oh no! bad news—for those who care, I mean.   120

TEUCER They say he disappeared, and she with him.

HELEN But didn't all the Greeks set sail together?

TEUCER They did, but then a fierce storm scattered them.

HELEN Where was the fleet when the storm struck?

TEUCER Just at the mid-point of the Aegean crossing.

HELEN And since then no one has seen Menelaus?

TEUCER No one. In Greece they say that he is dead.

HELEN *(aside)* I'm done for! *(to Teucer)* And Helen's mother?
    She's alive?

TEUCER You mean Leda? No, she's dead and gone.

HELEN It wasn't Helen's shame that killed her, was it?   130

TEUCER They say so. She slipped a noose around her neck.

HELEN And Castor and his brother—are they alive?

TEUCER They died and they didn't; there are two stories.

HELEN Which one is true? *(aside)* O, I am truly wretched!

TEUCER Some say they're gods in heaven, in the shape of stars.

HELEN Thank you for that; but what is the other story?

TEUCER That shame for their sister Helen drove them to kill
themselves. But enough of these stories! Why should I
mourn a second time? I've come to this palace
to see the prophetess Theonoe.   140
Please, will you introduce me to her? I want
to ask how best to set my sail for the island
of Cyprus. That's where Apollo has decreed
that I must settle and give my new city
the name "Salamis," in honor of my old home.

HELEN The right course will show itself to you, my friend.
Leave now, get away before Theoclymenus,
the king here, sees you. He is out with his hounds
in pursuit of game, but he'll kill any Greek
he catches, too. Do not ask why, for I'll say   150
no more. What help would it give you if I did?

TEUCER Thanks for your advice, woman. May the gods
reward you in return. Even though
your body is like Helen's, your minds are not
alike, but very different. May *she* die
a wretched death and never return to Sparta;
but may good fortune always be with *you*.   *(Teucer exits)*

HELEN *(chanting)* Such great griefs cry out for great laments,
   but what cries
could ever match my misery? To what spirit of song
shall I turn with these tears, this pain, this mourning? Ah!

(*singing*) Wingèd maidens,   160
virgin daughters of Earth, you Sirens,   *strophe 1*
    come to answer
my cries with Libyan pipes, or lyres.
    Send tears to fit
my troubles, sorrows matching my sorrows,
    songs to answer
mine, a gathering of song in tune
    with my laments,
and let Persephone, goddess of the dead,   170
    receive as my
offering for the dead and departed, down
    in her chambers
of night, a song of healing grief.

CHORUS (*enters as Helen's song ends, responding in song*)

Beside the dark   *antistrophe 1*
blue currents of the river, midst
    the curling grasses,
we were spreading robes
    of royal purple
over shoots of bullrush in   180
    the sun's gold rays,
when we heard a cry, shrill
    with terror, a lament
unlike those sung to the lyre, as if
    some mountain Naiad
were hurling a cry of anguish through
    the rocky hollows
as she fled Pan's eager clutches.

HELEN   Dear friends, daughters of Greece   *strophe 2*
enslaved and abducted on foreign ships,   190
    a sailor has come from Athens,
come bringing new tears to add to my old tears.
    All-consuming fire
has razed Troy to the ground, and it is I
    who am the cause of all
that killing, my name the cause of so much grief!

Leda chose to die
by hanging for my shame; my husband, wandering
    far and wide, has died
at sea and is no more; and the twin-born glory   200
    of our homeland, Castor
and his brother, have vanished, no longer ride
    the hoof-clattered plain
or wrestle beside the reeds of the Eurotas,
    where the young men train.

CHORUS   Aiiiii! What a fate this is,   *antistrophe 2*
woman. Your sorrows bring us to tears.
    A life that's no life at all
was your lot from the moment Zeus flashed
    through the air on a swan's   210
snow-white wings and made Leda your mother.
    What wrongs have you been spared?
What blows have you not endured? Your mother
    is gone, the dear twin sons
of Zeus have seen luck turn away,
    and you're trapped far from home,
while a rumor travels from town to town,
    that calls you, my lady, a traitor
reveling in a foreign bed. And now
    your husband's drowned at sea,   220
never to gladden his hearth or kneel
    to Athena in her House of Bronze.

HELEN Aiiiii! Who was it, Trojan or Greek,   *epode*
    who felled the pine
that dripped with tears for Troy? When Priam's
    son had hewn it
to shape that cursed ship, he sped
    to my hearth, driven
by foreign oars toward the disastrous
    loveliness of marriage   230
with me, and alongside him sailed cunning
    Aphrodite, cause of
the killing, bringing death to Danaus' sons,

               death to the children
of Priam. What misery my life has been!
          Then Hera, who sits
enthroned in gold, resting in Zeus'
               solemn embrace,
sent Hermes, Maia's swift-footed son,
               to find me as I   240
gathered roses into the folds of my cloak,
               to take to Athena
in her House of Bronze. He snatched me up
               and carried me away
through thin air to this hapless, hopeless
               land, and made me
the cause of the wretched war Greece waged
               on Priam's children.
At Troy, along Simois' stream,
               my name is stained,   250
defiled with false and ugly fame.

CHORUS LEADER *(resuming spoken dialogue)*
               You have sorrows enough, I know, yet what is left
               to you but to bear them as lightly as you can?

HELEN Dear women, what is this fate to which I'm bound?
       It seems my mother bore me as a monstrous
       sign of some kind. No other woman,
       Greek or foreigner, ever birthed her child
       in a white shell, as they say Leda did
       when she bore me to Zeus. My life has turned out
       monstrous, and everything about me, partly   260
       through Hera's envy, but partly because of my beauty.
       If only I could be erased, like a picture,
       and redrawn in a plainer form, the Greeks might forget
       the bad about me and recall the good, and then
       they wouldn't hate me as they do. If a man
       pins his hopes on just one throw of the dice,
       then sees the gods desert him, it's a heavy
       blow, but he can bear it. Look at me:
       I'm hemmed in by disasters on all sides! First,

although I'm innocent, my reputation   270
is ruined, and it is worse than real guilt
if you bear blame for what you never did.
Next, the gods have torn me from my home,
set me down among foreigners, and cut me off
from everyone I love, and I, who was
born free, am now a slave—since all
except the Greeks call one man master, the rest
his slaves. My only anchor in this sea
of troubles was the hope my husband would come
and rescue me—when he died, that died, too.   280
There's more: my mother is gone, and I am her slayer,
guiltless though the guilt's still mine. And my daughter,
the delight of all our house, my own darling,
grows gray without a husband, a virgin still.
My brothers, the twin sons of Zeus, have vanished.
No, I have nothing but misery, and all my misfortunes
have killed me, even though I am still alive.
And here's what's last and worst: suppose I did
get home, they'd bar me at the gates, thinking
that I was the Helen who went to Troy, returning   290
without Menelaus. Of course, if he were still
alive, he'd find out who I really am
(we have our secret tokens), but he's not,
he's dead, poor man. So why do I go on living?
What's left for me? Should I choose marriage to
a foreign husband instead of the woes I've got
and take my place at his rich table? No—
for when a wife finds her husband hateful,
she comes to hate her very body. You see
the depths of my despair: other women   300
owe their happy fortune to their beauty,
but beauty is the thing that has brought me down.

CHORUS LEADER   Helen, don't be so sure that everything
that stranger who came here told you is the truth.

HELEN   But he said clearly enough my husband's dead.

CHORUS LEADER Much that is spoken clearly turns out false.

HELEN And just as often, what we hear is true.

CHORUS LEADER You're drawn toward disaster, not what's good.

HELEN Yes—fear surrounds me and drives me to more dread.

CHORUS LEADER How well disposed are the people in the palace? 310

HELEN All friends, except the one who's hunting a marriage.

CHORUS LEADER Do you know what you should do? Leave this tomb.

HELEN Leave my refuge? What sort of advice is this?

CHORUS LEADER Go to the palace and ask the sea nymph's child,
the maiden who knows all things, Theonoe,
whether your husband is still alive or has left
the light. And when you have learned for sure, rejoice
or weep at the turn of fortune. What good is it
to lament before you know exactly how
things stand? Take my advice. I'll gladly 320
go with you to ask for the virgin's prophecies.
After all, women should help one another.

HELEN *(chanting)*
Dear friends, I welcome your advice.
Hurry to the palace, go inside
and ask what struggles face me.

CHORUS *(responding in chant)*
Gladly, you need not tell me twice.

HELEN I fear this day, I fear the words
I'm about to hear, words steeped in tears,
to my unending misery.

CHORUS   Don't play the prophet. It's no use   330
         to weep in advance or mourn too soon.

HELEN   My poor husband, how has he fared?
        Does he watch the Sun race across the sky
        in his fiery chariot? Can he still
        trace the stars' glittering flight,
        or does fate's everlasting night
        hold him in earth among the dead?

CHORUS   Whatever face the future may show,
         my dear, believe it will be for the best.

HELEN   Eurotas, river of home, green   340
        with reeds that love the water,
        witness this oath: if it is true
        what they say, that my husband is dead ...

CHORUS   What are you saying? What do you mean?

HELEN   ... I'll wrap my neck in a strangling noose,
        or thrust a sword deep inside
        my flesh and, spewing blood, make steel
        my test of strength, and let my death
        be a sacrifice to that triple yoke
        of goddesses, and to Priam's son,   350
        who lolled in Ida's hollows, tending
        his herd, until desire won.

CHORUS   Bad luck turn elsewhere, strike others,
         and let yours change at last for the good!

HELEN   Aiiiii! Troy, what utter wretchedness,
        undone by deeds that were never done,
        made to suffer for nothing! The gift
        Queen Aphrodite made of me
        bore a monstrous brood of blood,
        of tears, of sorrows piled on sorrows.   360
        Who could tell the agony of Troy?
        Mothers lost sons, and virgin sisters

sheared off their hair for brothers slain
beside Scamander's swirling flood.
Greece, too, screamed, burst out in groans;
women beat their heads, their sharp
fingernails scraped furrows in soft
skin, and drenched their cheeks with blood.

(Chorus begins to exit, crossing to the doors of the palace)

Callisto, happy virgin in Arcadia long ago,
you left the bed of mighty Zeus on four paws,
    shaggy-limbed.   370
A fierce-eyed bear, you cast off every care when you lost
your human form. How much better your fate than mine!
Luckier, too, was the maiden, Merops' child, whose beauty
    angered
Artemis. She paid the price when, banished from the dance,
she vanished into the body of a hind with horns of gold,
and her sorrows ended. But *my* body destroyed the towers
of Troy, and *my* beauty fell like a curse on Greeks and killed
    them.

(Helen exits into the palace)

MENELAUS *(enters in rags, looks about, and sighs)*
Pelops, my grandfather, you who bested old
King Oenomaeus in that famous chariot
race and won yourself a wife, if only   380
you had never lived that long! You should
have died the day they served you up as supper
for the gods, but you survived to sire
my father, Atreus, who took Aerope
to his bed; and they produced a famous
pair of sons, Agamemnon and myself,
Menelaus. I believe—and I don't say this
to boast—that I took the largest fighting force
to Troy on my ships, not as a tyrant, not
by force, but as the commander of brave young   390
Greeks who went to war with willing hearts.
The ones who died there, and those lucky enough
to survive the treacherous sea and get home safe
to name the dead—*they're* all accounted for.

But *I've* been wandering ever since I sacked
the towers of Troy, an outcast on the bleak,
salt, rolling sea, longing for home,
and the gods so far have found me undeserving.
I've sailed to every empty, friendless harbor
on the Libyan coast. Whenever I get near home,   400
a sudden headwind pushes me back, never
the favoring breeze I need to fill my sails.
So here I am, shipwrecked and a wreck myself.
I've lost my comrades and been cast ashore here,
my ship smashed to a thousand bits of wreckage
on the cliffs. Of all its intricate parts,
only the keel survived intact, and on that
I managed to escape by the merest luck,
along with Helen, whom I dragged with me
from Troy. I do not know what land I'm in   410
or what the people here are called, for I was
too embarrassed to fall in with the crowd
and ask. I felt shame at showing my wretchedness.
When a man in my position falls on hard
times, it hits him harder than someone who's known
misfortune all his life. But now my need
has got the better of me: I have no food,
no proper clothes to wear. You've guessed *that*
already from these rags, all I could salvage
from my ship. The clothes I had before,   420
my splendid cloaks, all my fine garments?
The sea stole them! So I hid my wife,
the one who started it all, deep inside
a cave and made the few companions I have
left keep careful watch, and here I am.

(approaching the door of the palace)

I have come alone, to search out and bring back
everything my comrades need. I saw this house
with its fine stone cornice and majestic gate, clearly
a rich man's mansion, and made straight for it.   430
Sailors may hope for help from a wealthy house.
Those who have nothing, even if they wanted to, could
give us nothing.

(knocking at the door)

Hello! Who's there? Come out
and take news of my troubles back inside.

OLD WOMAN *(appearing at the door and making threatening gestures)*
Who's at the gate? You'd better go away!
And don't hang about near the courtyard wall.
You're trouble for my master, and he'll kill you.
You're a Greek, and Greeks have no business here.

MENELAUS *(backing away)*
All right, old woman, it's good advice, I'm sure.
I'll do just as you say. Only don't be angry.   440

OLD WOMAN *(pursuing him and pushing)*
Away, I said! Stranger, I've got orders
not to let any Greeks get near this house.

MENELAUS Ha! Don't shake your fist at me! Stop pushing!

OLD WOMAN You're not listening, so it's your own fault.

MENELAUS And I'm telling you to let your master know . . .

OLD WOMAN I'd only get somebody into trouble if I did.

MENELAUS I'm a shipwrecked stranger; that should protect me.

OLD WOMAN Off to some other house with you. Right now!

MENELAUS *(trying to force his way in)*
No, I'm coming in, and you'll do as I say.

OLD WOMAN *(blocking him)*
You're a nuisance, you know, and you'll be thrown out   450

MENELAUS Ah! Where are my famous armies now?

OLD WOMAN You may have been great elsewhere. Here, you are not.

MENELAUS My luck is gone! I don't deserve this treatment.

OLD WOMAN Why the tears? Who's going to pity you?

MENELAUS Only the fortune that used to smile at me.

OLD WOMAN Go on, then, take your tears to your old friends.

MENELAUS Tell me: what land is this, whose royal palace?

OLD WOMAN This is Proteus' house; the country's Egypt.

MENELAUS Egypt? Of all the places to have sailed!

OLD WOMAN Oh? You have something against this Nile of ours?   460

MENELAUS Not really. It's my luck that I can't bear.

OLD WOMAN Many fare poorly, not just you, you know.

MENELAUS Is he at home, this king, whatever he's called?

OLD WOMAN This is his tomb. His son's the ruler now.

MENELAUS And where might *he* be? Away or in the palace?

OLD WOMAN He's not inside. But listen, he hates Greeks.

MENELAUS What did we do to earn such cordial disdain?

OLD WOMAN Helen is here in the palace, the daughter of Zeus.

MENELAUS How's that? What did you just say? Tell me again.

OLD WOMAN Tyndareus' daughter, who used to live in Sparta.   470

MENELAUS How did she get here? *(aside)* What can this possibly mean?

OLD WOMAN From Sparta of course. You know, Lacedaemon.

MENELAUS When? *(aside)* Surely they can't have brought her from the
cave?

OLD WOMAN Just before the Greeks went off to Troy,
stranger. *(in a confidential tone)* Listen, you must get
away from the palace!
Things here have taken a bad turn, and set
the household reeling. You've come at the wrong moment.
If my master catches you, death will be
the only guest-gift you'll get. I like you Greeks,
believe me I do, despite what I said before.   480
I only spoke so harshly for fear of my master.

(exits into the palace)

MENELAUS What am I to make of this? I'm absolutely
at a loss. A nasty turn of events, after
everything I've already been through! Can it be
that I captured my wife from the Trojans, brought her all
this way, hid her safely in a cave, only
to find that another woman, with the same name
as hers, is living in this very palace? *And*
the old woman called her the daughter of Zeus! Is there
really someone named Zeus living on the banks   490
of the Nile? No! there's only one Zeus, and he's
in heaven. And where will you find a second Sparta,
apart from the one built beside Eurotas'
reedy shores? Can Tyndareus' name belong
to someone else, and can there be another
land called Lacedaemon? Or another Troy?
I can't think what to say. *(pauses briefly)* Well, after all,
is it so strange, on this wide earth, for many
men to share one name, or many cities,
or women, for that matter? It's really nothing   500
to marvel at. And I'm not going to let
a serving woman's bluster run me off!
Surely no man is so uncouth that he'd
deny me food once he heard my name.
The fires of Troy are famous, and the man who lit them
is not entirely unknown.

HELEN

(moving to the far side of Proteus' tomb)

I'll wait here
for the king's return. That way, I'll have two
safe choices: if he's some sort of savage
I'll keep hidden, then make for the wreck; but if
he shows a gentle side, I'll ask him to give me   510
everything my wretched circumstances require.
Of all my miseries, this is the very worst:
that I, a king myself, should have to ask
another king for even a crust of bread.
Still, ask I must. It was a wise man,
and not myself, who said it best: nothing
is more powerful than harsh necessity.

CHORUS *(reenters from palace, without seeing Menelaus)*
(chanting) We heard inside what we desired.
The prophet-maiden said that earth
has not yet covered Menelaus.   520
He hasn't gone to the darkly shining
realm of gloom, but wastes his strength
in endless voyaging from Troy
across the storm-tossed swollen sea.
His homeland's harbor still eludes him,
and sore of heart, bereft of friends,
starvation always near, he grounds
his ship on every alien shore.

HELEN *(following the Chorus from the palace)*
I return to my refuge at the tomb after hearing
Theonoe's welcome words. She knows the truth,   530
and she says he's alive. My husband lives,
sees daylight still! He's wandered back and forth,
crossed and recrossed the sea, wrestled with every
kind of trouble, but when all the roving's done,
he'll be coming here at last. There's only one
thing she didn't say: will he be safe
when he gets here? I was so overjoyed
at the news that he survived, I didn't want
to ask. She did say that he's somewhere near,

shipwrecked and cast ashore with a few comrades.   540
Oh, please come soon, come and still my longing!

> (*moves toward the tomb and catches a glimpse of
> Menelaus*)

Wait! Who's that? Can this be some plot, some trap
set by Proteus' scapegrace, impious son?
I must run like a racing filly to reach the tomb,
or like a bacchant in the throes of the god's frenzy.
He looks like a wild man, and he wants to hunt me down!

MENELAUS *(coming between Helen and the tomb)*
Stop! Why struggle so to reach the steps
of the tomb? Why this desperate race? Wait!
Don't run away! Now that I've seen your face,
you fill me with amazement and leave me speechless.   550

HELEN *(turning to the Chorus)*
Women, I am being wronged! This man is barring
my path to the tomb. He wants to seize me and hand me
over to the tyrant whose bed I've been avoiding.

MENELAUS *(withdrawing from Helen's path)*
I'm not a bandit, and I don't work for one, either.

HELEN And yet that cloak of yours is shabby enough.

> (*dashes toward the tomb*)

MENELAUS There's no need to run, nothing to be afraid of.

HELEN *(reaching the tomb)*
I'm not running—now that I'm safe at the tomb.

MENELAUS Who are you? Whose face do I look upon, lady?

HELEN *(observing Menelaus more closely)*
And you? Who are you? The same question troubles us both.

MENELAUS *(aside)* I have never seen anything like her resemblance to
Helen!   560

HELEN *(aside)* Dear gods! For it is godly to recognize one's own!

MENELAUS Are you a Greek or a native of this place?

HELEN A Greek; and you? I want to know more about you.

MENELAUS You look so very much like Helen, lady.

HELEN And you like Menelaus. What can I say?

MENELAUS You have recognized the most wretched of men.

HELEN *(taking hold of Menelaus' cloak)*
Then welcome at long last to your own wife's arms!

MENELAUS *(drawing back anxiously)*
Don't touch my robes! Wife? What wife do you mean?

HELEN The one my father, Tyndareus, gave you in marriage.

MENELAUS Hecate, torchbearing goddess, send kindly phantoms!   570

HELEN I'm no nighttime accomplice of the queen of crossroads.

MENELAUS Nor am I, believe me, a husband with two wives.

HELEN Who is this other woman you call your wife?

MENELAUS The one I brought from Troy and hid in a cave.

HELEN I am your only wife; you have no other.

MENELAUS Maybe my mind's all right, and my eyes are wrong.

HELEN Look at me. Don't you think you see your wife?

MENELAUS You look like her, but how can I be sure?

HELEN Look again! What better proof could you want?

MENELAUS You do seem to be Helen. I can't deny it. 580

HELEN What better teacher than your own two eyes?

MENELAUS My eyes are the problem! I have another wife.

HELEN I didn't go to Troy; that was a phantom.

MENELAUS And who makes living, breathing bodies like hers?

HELEN A god molded and shaped her from thin air.

MENELAUS Which god was that? This is beyond belief.

HELEN Hera. She made a changeling to fool Paris.

MENELAUS Then you were here and in Troy at the same time?

HELEN A name can do what a body never could.

MENELAUS Let me go; I came here with troubles enough. 590

HELEN What? leave me and run off with a shadow-bride?

MENELAUS Yes, and fare well, for you look so much like Helen.

HELEN I'm dead! I got my husband back—and lost him.

MENELAUS The suffering at Troy carries more weight than your words.

(moves to leave)

HELEN Aiiiii! Was ever a woman more wretched? My dearest

love deserts me, and now I shall never reach Greece,

never see my homeland again, no, never.

OLD MAN *(entering just as Menelaus is about to exit)*
Menelaus, I've been scouring every foot

of this strange land, and here you are at last!
The comrades you left behind sent me to find you. 600

MENELAUS What is it? The natives haven't robbed you, have they?

OLD MAN Something amazing. There are no words to describe it.

MENELAUS Tell me. Strange news, to judge by your excitement.

OLD MAN I'll tell you this: all your struggles were in vain.

MENELAUS You're mired in old sorrows; what is your news?

OLD MAN Your wife has vanished, swept from the depths of her cave
into thin air. The heavens hide her now.
But as she left, she said : "You poor, long-suffering
Trojans, and all you Greeks, it was because
of *me* you kept dying on Scamander's shore, 610
just as Hera planned. You thought Paris
had Helen in his bed, but he never had her.
Now that I've stayed just long enough to bring
to pass what fate decreed, I'm going back
to the sky that gave me life. Tyndareus'
poor daughter has had to hear her name befouled
with baseless slanders; but she is innocent."
(seeing Helen) Oh, daughter of Leda, have you been here
all along? I was just reporting the news
that you had disappeared, or so it seemed, 620
into the starry sky. I didn't know
that you had really sprouted wings! I won't
let you make fools of us again this way.
You already gave grief enough to your husband
and his allies when we were camped at Troy.

MENELAUS There's the proof! Her story fits this new one,
and now I know it's true. (to Helen) How I have longed
for this day that brings you back to my embrace!

HELEN (who has now joined Menelaus in an embrace)

Menelaus, dearest of men, time
has grown old, but joy comes to us fresh and new.   630
(to Chorus) I have my husband back, dear friends, and it is bliss;
after so many flights
of the sun, after so many nights
I clasp him again in my loving arms.

MENELAUS   *(speaking)* And I hold you, but with so many stories
to tell between us, I don't know where to begin.

HELEN   I am full of joy: the hairs
of my head stand up straight with excitement;
I shiver, and tears of sheer delight roll down my cheeks.
I throw my arms around you,   640
husband, hold your body close
to my own, and at last I am happy.

MENELAUS   A happy sight, this faultless face: this is
my wife I hold, the daughter of Zeus and Leda . . .

HELEN   whom by torchlight those lads on white horses,
my brothers, called blessèd, your blessèd bride . . .

MENELAUS   long ago, but the god who stole you from my house . . .

HELEN   now leads us to a better end. Good
that came from bad brought you to me, and now you are mine,
at last, after so long a time.   650
I pray I may enjoy this fortune!

MENELAUS   May you enjoy it. I join your prayer, for where
there are two, one can't be happy if the other isn't.

HELEN   *(to Chorus)*
Friends, dear friends, I no longer lament
what came before. All pain is past.
I have my husband back, I hold the one I waited for
these many years, yearning
for my man to come from Troy.

MENELAUS   You hold me, and I hold you. I've struggled
            through countless circlings of the sun, and only now   660
            begin to understand what the goddess was up to.
            I am weeping for joy. My tears
            fall more for pleasure than for pain.

HELEN   What can I say? Who could have hoped for *this*?
            I clasp you all unhoped for,
            I clasp you to my breast.

MENELAUS   And I hold you close, who we all thought had gone
            to the city beneath Mount Ida,
            the ill-fated towers of Troy.

                    (suddenly withdraws from Helen's embrace, speaking
                                                              again)

            By the gods, how did you steal away from home?   670

HELEN   Aiiiii! A bitter beginning
            you drive me back to. Aiiiii!
            Bitter the telling you ask for.

MENELAUS   Tell me. What the gods gave, I must hear.

HELEN   I spit away the words
            that you would have me say.

MENELAUS   Still, tell me. There's a pleasure in hearing sorrows.

HELEN   I didn't flee to a foreign bed,
            oars flying, aflutter
            with lust for a shameful marriage.   680

MENELAUS   What god, then, or what power seized you as spoils?

HELEN   The son of Zeus, dear husband,
            the son of Zeus and Maia,
            brought me to the banks of Nile.

MENELAUS Hermes? Who sent him? This story is strange and troubling!

HELEN I wept for it then, and now, as I tell it
again, I burst into tears: the wife
of Zeus destroyed my life.

MENELAUS Hera? Why should she wish to do *us* wrong?

HELEN Ah, what began for me at those springs   690
where the goddesses bathed to make
their beauty bright for the contest!

MENELAUS But why did Hera hurt you on account of this contest?

HELEN So she could rob Paris...

MENELAUS What do you mean?

HELEN ...of me, Cypris' prize...

MENELAUS My dearest, how cruel!

HELEN ... she brought me to Egypt, cruelly indeed.

MENELAUS And then, I take it, gave Paris the phantom instead.

HELEN And you, Mother—the sorrows, the suffering
under your roof!

MENELAUS What are you saying?

HELEN My mother is dead; she knotted a noose   700
around her neck for shame
at my supposed disgrace.

MENELAUS Poor woman! And is there word of our daughter,
Hermione?

HELEN She's unwed and childless, my husband.

All she can do is bewail my shameful
marriage that is no marriage at all.

MENELAUS O Paris, you sacked my house from top to bottom!

HELEN All these things have destroyed you, and hurled
countless bronze-armed Greeks to their deaths;
but a god stole me from home, cursed to a bitter life   710
far from my city, far from you,
I left those halls and your bed—
but not for a marriage of shame.

CHORUS LEADER But if the future brings good fortune, that blessing
will make amends for all these sorrows past.

OLD MAN Menelaus, tell me what gives you both
such joy, which I see, but don't really understand.

MENELAUS By all means, old man, share in our happy news.

OLD MAN This woman did not oversee our agony at Troy?

MENELAUS No. The gods played us for fools, and instead   720
sent a sorry image made of clouds.

OLD MAN So, we struggled for nothing over a cloud?

MENELAUS Hera's handiwork, because of the goddesses' contest.

OLD MAN Then this woman here really is your wife?

MENELAUS The very same. You can take my word for it.

OLD MAN *(to Helen)*
Daughter, the path of the god is devious and hard
to trace. He twists all our affairs this way
and that, and back again, for a purpose all
his own. One man has to struggle hard,
another doesn't, but then ends in misery,   730

since his fortune won't hold steady. You and your husband
had your share of struggles, *you* beset
with slanders, *he* with spears. All his battles
won him nothing, but now the greatest good
has come his way of its own accord. And you
did not disgrace your father in his old age,
or your divine twin brothers, and do what people
say you did. I'll raise your wedding song
again, remembering the torches I held high
as I ran beside the yoke of four, when you   740
were leaving home at this man's side, in his chariot,
a bride.
          It's a bad sort, you know, who doesn't
take his masters' affairs to heart, rejoice
with them and share their griefs. Even though
I was born to serve, I want to be numbered among
the noble slaves who have a free man's mind,
if not the name. Better that by far
than to have the double misfortune of obeying others
while nursing a slavish spirit of one's own.

MENELAUS Come, old fellow, you have tasted the hardships of battle, 750
struggling at my side; now you share my luck.
Take news of what you found here back to the comrades
I left behind and tell them how our fortunes
stand. Have them wait at the shore for the struggle
I'm sure will come when I try to steal back
my wife. Tell them to watch for the one chance
we'll have to regroup and escape from the native horde.

OLD MAN Consider it done, my lord. But I see now
what a paltry thing, how full of lies this whole
business of prophecy is. Was there ever anything 760
sensible in the flames of burnt offerings or the cries
of birds? It's stupid even to think that birds
can help us. After all, Calchas, that great seer,
never said a word or gave a sign to the army
that he saw his companions dying because of a cloud,
nor Helenus either. Instead, Troy was stormed

and plundered in vain. You might say: "That was because
the gods didn't wish them to." Then why resort
to prophecy at all? We should sacrifice to the gods,
pray for blessings, and leave divination alone. 770
It was invented to tempt the gullible. No one
gets rich by being lazy and relying on seers.
Common sense and caution are the best prophets. *(exits)*

CHORUS LEADER My view of prophets agrees with his. Make friends
with the gods, and you've found the best oracle of all.

HELEN *(to Menelaus)*
All right, so far, so good. But, my poor dear,
how did you survive after Troy? There's no advantage
in knowing, but there is a sort of desire loved ones
have to learn about their loved ones' sorrows.

MENELAUS One question that needs many, many answers. 780
Must I rehearse our shipwrecks in the Aegean,
the false beacons Nauplius lit on Euboea,
the ports of Crete and Libya where I was forced
to land, or Perseus' fabled cliff? I could never
satisfy your longing for my tales, but in telling you
I'd have to endure the pain all over again.

HELEN You've already answered better than I asked; let
the rest go, and tell me this: How long
were you battered and tossed across the broad sea?

MENELAUS After ten years spent at Troy, seven 790
more years came and went aboard my ship.

HELEN How dreadful! Such a long time, poor man, and to think
you escaped from all that only to come here and be killed.

MENELAUS What do you mean? You'll be the death of me, woman.

HELEN You will die at the hands of the man who rules here.

MENELAUS What have I done to deserve such a wretched fate?

HELEN Your unexpected appearance will stop my wedding.

MENELAUS You mean that someone wants to marry my wife?

HELEN Yes, trying to force me. What I've had to endure!

MENELAUS Some powerful private man, or the ruler here?   800

HELEN The lord of the land himself, old Proteus' son.

MENELAUS That answers the riddle I heard from a serving woman.

HELEN What foreigner's door have you been standing at?

MENELAUS This very door, from which I was shooed like some beggar.

HELEN Surely you weren't begging? I feel such shame!

MENELAUS That's what it was, although without the name.

HELEN Then you know all about my marriage, it seems.

MENELAUS One thing, I don't know: Did you escape his bed?

HELEN You can be sure I preserved myself untouched.

MENELAUS What proof can you offer? I'd like to believe it's true.   810

HELEN Do you see my wretched place beside the tomb?

MENELAUS I see a bed of straw—yours, poor dear?

HELEN It has been my refuge from his bed.

MENELAUS Was there no altar, or is this some foreign custom?

HELEN This tomb protected me like a god's own temple.

MENELAUS And now I can't just sail you safely home?

HELEN You'll find your grave before you find my bed.

MENELAUS If that's how it is, I am the sorriest of men.

HELEN Don't be ashamed—escape now, while you can!

MENELAUS And leave you? I sacked Troy because of you! 820

HELEN Better that than let our marriage kill you.

MENELAUS Cowardly advice, unworthy of the conqueror of Troy.

HELEN You can't kill the king, if that is what you have in mind.

MENELAUS What, does he have a body steel can't pierce?

HELEN You'll see. It's an unwise man who dares the impossible.

MENELAUS So, shall I just stretch out my hands for binding?

HELEN You've reached a dead end. We need to think of something.

MENELAUS Better to die in action than through inaction.

HELEN One hope, and only one, might save us yet.

MENELAUS Bribery, you mean, or boldness, or smooth talk? 830

HELEN We must keep the king from knowing you've arrived.

MENELAUS He won't know who I am. And who will tell him?

HELEN He has an ally, a woman like a god.

MENELAUS Some oracle hidden inside the palace?

HELEN No, his sister; they call her Theonoe.

MENELAUS The name's oracular; what powers does she have?

HELEN She knows everything, and she'll tell her brother you're here.

MENELAUS I'm a dead man; there's nowhere for me to hide.

HELEN If we both fall at her knees, we might persuade her...

MENELAUS To do what? At last a ray of hope! 840

HELEN ... not to tell her brother that you are here.

MENELAUS And if we persuade her, we might be able to escape?

HELEN With her help, easily; on our own, never.

MENELAUS This is a job for you, woman to woman.

HELEN She'll find my arms around her knees, I promise.

MENELAUS But if she's deaf to our appeals, what then?

HELEN Then you will die and I'll be forced to marry.

MENELAUS You betrayer! That "force" is just an excuse.

HELEN I swear a solemn oath, by all that's holy!

MENELAUS Swear you'll never remarry? You'll die instead? 850

HELEN Yes, by the same sword as you, and I'll lie at your side.

MENELAUS Well, then, take my right hand to seal the oath.

HELEN *(linking hands with Menelaus)*
I swear that if you die, I die, too.

MENELAUS And I will kill myself, if I lose you.

HELEN But how to die in a way that brings repute?

MENELAUS We'll climb atop the tomb. I'll kill you first,
and then myself. Before that, though, I'll fight
an all-out war to defend your married honor.
Let anyone who dares come at me; I'll not
put the fame I won at Troy to shame,   860
reap ridicule by sneaking off to Greece.
You're looking at the man who left the goddess
Thetis bereft of her Achilles, who witnessed
Ajax, Telamon's mighty son, crash
on his sword, old Nestor, too, weep for his child.
Shall I not think my wife worth dying for?
Of course I shall, for if the gods are wise,
they'll cover the brave heart who died at his enemy's
hand lightly with earth, but cowards they'll cast
away unburied on some barren reef.   870

CHORUS LEADER Dear gods, turn the fortunes of Tantalus' tribe
around at last. Let them stand free of their troubles!

(sounds from within the palace)

HELEN *(startled)*
Aiiiii! My luck never changes. We're done for
now, Menelaus: The prophetess is coming out,
I hear the servants unbarring the doors. Run!
But what is the point of running? Whether Theonoe
is here or far away, she knows you've come.
I am undone—my ruin is at hand!
You come from Troy, survived a foreign war
only to meet once more with foreign swords.   880

*(As Helen speaks, the palace doors swing open and Theonoe
appears, preceded by two attendants, one carrying
a vessel in which sulphur is burning, the other a torch.)*

THEONOE *(to one of her attendants)*
Lead the way with torch held high, purge

the air to its outer limit, as sacred custom
demands, so I may draw pure breath from heaven.
(to her other attendant) And you, in case some unhallowed
    foot has sullied
my path, cleanse the ground with your holy flame
so I may pass. When both of you have rendered
my customary service to the gods, take the fire
back to the palace hearth.

(turning to Helen)

Helen, what

do you say to my prophecy? Menelaus is here,
Your husband stands before you, after losing his ships   890
and the counterfeit Helen.

(to Menelaus)

And you, unhappy man—

to escape so many perils, come this far,
and still not know whether you will ever reach
your home, or if this is the end of your road. You see,
this very day the gods will argue your case,
debate your fate before the throne of Zeus.
Hera, your enemy of old, now wishes you well
and wants to see you safely home, with Helen,
so Greece will know the bride that Aphrodite
gave to Paris was a lie, no gift at all.   900
But Aphrodite wants to wreck your homeward
journey to keep the world from knowing how
she bought her beauty-prize with the false coin
of Helen's marriage. The decision rests with me.
I can destroy you, as Aphrodite wishes,
by telling my brother that you are here, or
I can take my stand with Hera and save your life
by keeping him in the dark, even though
he ordered me to report if you arrived.

HELEN   Maiden, I fall at your knees in supplication   910
and beg you humbly, for my own sake and for his,
for the man I just got back and am on the point

of seeing killed: Please don't tell your brother
that my husband, my best beloved, has come to my arms
again. No, rescue him. I am begging you.
Never betray your holy nature to buy
your brother's favor, tainted with injustice and shame.
The god who hates violence orders us all to get
whatever we possess without plunder. After all,
the sky and the earth are common to all of us,   920
and when we fill our houses, we must not keep
what belongs to others, or take it from them by force.
Though it made me wretched at the time, Hermes helped me
when he entrusted me to your father, to keep me safe
for my husband. Now Menelaus is here, has come
to reclaim me. How can he do that if he dies?
How could Proteus give the living to the dead?
Ask yourself this: Would Hermes, would your dead father,
wish to give back what belongs to another, or not?
I think they would, and so you would do wrong   930
to put a foolish brother before your worthy
father. You are a seer and you respect
the divine; if you defile your father's justice
to do a favor to your unjust brother, how shameful
for you to know all that the gods intend,
now and for the future, but not know what is just!
You see how miserable I am. Rescue me
and strike a blow for justice in the bargain.
There's no one alive who doesn't despise Helen.
The Greeks all think that I betrayed my husband   940
and ran off to a pampered life in the golden mansions
of Troy. But if I once reach Greece, set foot
again in Sparta, and they hear and see that the gods
played a ruinous trick, and that I never
betrayed my loved ones, they'll give back my good name,
and I'll see my daughter married, whom no one now
will wed, and leave the bitter beggary of exile
far behind to enjoy wealth stored at home.
If Menelaus had died and been given a soldier's rites,
I'd have honored him in his absence with my tears;   950
but now that he's here, safe and sound, am I

to have him snatched from me? No, maiden, no!
I implore you as your suppliant: Do this favor
for me, and you will be imitating your father's ways,
the ways of justice. Nothing is nobler for children
born of worthy fathers than to match their example.

CHORUS LEADER The plea you have put before us stirs our pity,
and so do you. Now I long to hear
how Menelaus will argue for his life.

MENELAUS *I'm* not going to fall at your feet in tears. I couldn't   960
bear to show such cowardice. It would disgrace
the memory of Troy. And yet, they say it suits
a man of noble birth to shed a tear
amidst disaster. Still, I will not choose
that good, if good it is, over courage.
But if you think it right to save a stranger—
myself, in fact, rightly seeking to reclaim
my wife—then give her back, and save us both
into the bargain. And if you don't, well,
it won't be the first time I have tasted grief,   970
but *you* will stand revealed as a craven woman.

(moving toward Proteus' tomb)

What I consider right, and worthy of myself,
and likeliest to touch you, I will say
on my knees at your father's grave. Old man
dwelling in this tomb of stone, give her back!
I'm asking for my own wife, whom Zeus left here
for me, in your safekeeping. I know that you
will never give her back, since you are dead;
but surely this woman won't let her father, whose fame
once stood so high, be summoned from below to hear   980
his name maligned. It's all in her hands now.
Hades, lord of the world below, I call you
as my ally. You have received so many
corpses on my wife's account, men fallen
to my sword—you have had payment in full.

Now return them to life, or else compel
this woman to show even greater piety than
her father by giving back my wife, my Helen.

(turning to Theonoe)

But if you and your brother steal my wife, let me
tell you what she neglected to say. You should know,   990
maiden, that I swore an oath to fight your brother
to the death—

(draws his sword)

              his or mine, it's that simple.
If he refuses to fight me man to man,
and tries to trap us in our refuge and starve us,
I'm prepared to kill Helen, and then
to thrust this two-edged sword straight to my heart,
standing atop the tomb so streams of blood
will gush down and defile it. And there we'll lie,
two corpses side by side on the polished stone
an undying torment for you, and a reproach to your father. 1000
Your brother will not marry Helen. No one will.
I'll take her, home if I can, and if not, down
to the dead below. But why do I keep on talking?
I'd have won more pity with womanly tears than the words
of a man of action. Kill me, if you like,
I have my claim to glory. Better, though,
to let my words persuade you; you will honor
justice and I shall have my wife once more.

CHORUS LEADER Maiden, it is for you to judge these pleas.
              Decide in a way that will please all who are here!   1010

THEONOE I was born to act with reverence, and that is what
            I want to do. I must be true to myself.
            I will not defile my father's fame or do
            my brother a favor that holds me up to dishonor.
            A temple of Justice lodges deep in my nature,

an inheritance from my mother's father, Nereus,
and I will make every effort to keep it safe.
Since Hera wants to help you, Menelaus,
I gladly cast my vote as she casts hers;
may Aphrodite be gracious, though she and I   1020
were never close, and I trust we never shall be.
The reproach you addressed to my father's tomb applies
to me as well: I would do a great wrong,
if I did not give Helen back. Suppose my father
were still alive, he would surely return her to you,
and you to her, because there are rewards
and punishments not only for everyone here above,
but also for those below. The minds of the dead
do not live on, but neither does consciousness die
after it blends with the deathless air above.   1030
Enough! To make a long story short, I will not
betray the secret you beg me to keep and will never
be counsellor to my brother's folly. It may not seem so,
but I do him a true service if I can steer him
from impiety to reverence. You yourselves must find
some means of escape; I shall go away
and keep my silence. *(to Helen)* Start with the gods; implore
Aphrodite to let you return home,
and pray that Hera's willingness to help you
and your husband reach safety remain unchanged.   1040

(turning to the tomb)

My dear, dead father, as long as I have strength
no one will have cause to doubt your reverence.

(exits into the palace)

CHORUS LEADER The unjust person's happiness won't last;
what hope we have of safety rests with justice.

HELEN Theonoe has assured our safety, but now,
Menelaus, it is up to us to put our heads
together and make a plan for our escape.

MENELAUS Then listen. You have been living under this roof
long enough to know the servants well.

HELEN Yes, but why mention that? You seem to think   1050
it offers some hope. What do you have in mind?

MENELAUS Could you persuade one of the men who run
the king's stables to let us have a chariot?

HELEN I could, but how will we escape, since neither
of us knows our way in this strange land?

MENELAUS Impossible, you're right. Well, what if I hide in the palace
and kill the king with this double-edged sword of mine?

HELEN His sister would never let you do that; she'll
break her silence if you try to kill her brother.

MENELAUS But we don't even have a ship to make   1060
our escape in; the sea took the only one we had.

HELEN Listen, maybe a woman can say something clever.
Let me report you dead, even though you're not.

MENELAUS A bad omen, but if it brings me gain,
go ahead and say I'm dead, even though I'm not.

HELEN And then, as women do, I'll shave my head
and sing a dirge to fool that impious man.

MENELAUS How will all this help us escape? There's some
old-fashioned trick lurking behind your plan.

HELEN I'll ask the king to bury you in an empty tomb,   1070
just as if you had really died at sea

MENELAUS Say he agrees, how do we save ourselves
with this empty burial, if we don't have a ship?

HELEN I'll insist that he give us one, so we can lower
burial goods into the sea's embrace.

MENELAUS A fine plan, except for one thing. If he orders you
to perform the burial on land, you've accomplished nothing.

HELEN But I will tell him that it's not the Greek custom
to bury on land those who are lost at sea.

MENELAUS You've thought of everything. And I'll sail out on the same 1080
ship to help you with the burial offerings.

HELEN Of course, you above all; and you must bring
with you all the sailors who survived your shipwreck.

MENELAUS Yes, once I get hold of a ship at anchor,
my men will embark fully armed and in fighting order.

HELEN That is for you to decide. Only let our sails
catch a favoring breeze, and our course run smooth!

MENELAUS So it shall, for the gods are ending my troubles.
But how will you say you heard that I was dead?

HELEN From you. And you'll confirm you were the sole 1090
survivor of the wreck and saw Menelaus die.

MENELAUS Why yes, and the tattered sail I'm wearing will add
its own testimony to my story of disaster at sea.

HELEN Those rags will come in handy, though losing your clothes
was a blow at the time. Bad luck can work in our favor.

MENELAUS Should I go inside with you, or would it be better
to sit here quietly by the tomb and wait?

HELEN Stay here. Even if he makes some outrageous move,
the tomb will protect you—that and your sword. I'll go

inside to cut my hair, change into black   1100
for mourning, and drag these nails across my cheeks
until they bloody the skin. The struggle is starting,
the balance could tip either way. If I'm caught at my plotting,
I die; if not, I'll make it home and save
your life as well.
Hera, mighty queen,
you who share the bed of Zeus, grant
an end to the troubles of two mortals worthy
of your pity. This I pray, lifting my arms
to heaven, where you dwell amidst the spangled beauty
of the stars. But you, Dionë's mighty daughter,   1110
Aphrodite, who won your beauty-prize
at the price of my false marriage, do not destroy me
completely. You covered me with filth enough before
when you lent my name, though not my body, to
those foreigners! If you want to kill me, let me die
in the land of my fathers. Why do you never tire
of making trouble, and always deal in trysts,
intrigues, deceptions, and philters that bring only death?
If you could just learn moderation, you'd be
the sweetest, the dearest of gods. I don't deny it.   1120

> (Helen enters the palace and Menelaus retires to the
> tomb.)

CHORUS Tuneful, tearful nightingale, perched
in a bower of leaves   *strophe 1*

to trill your descant, spill your melody,
saddest, sweetest nightingale, I would share your song.
Draw mournful notes from your golden throat
to match my lament for the sorrow of Helen, and the wretched
tears
that Greek spears brought to the women of Troy
when that man skimmed the waves in triumph, bringing you
back,

>   dear Helen, from Sparta to be his bride
> and a bane for the sons of Priam; the fatal bridegroom, Paris,
>   sped on his way by cruel Aphrodite.   1130
> So many Greeks breathed their last at the cast of a spear

Or a stone. Now they roam the gloom
  of Hades' realm   *antistrophe 1*

>   and their wives have shorn their hair in mourning.
> The bridal chambers lie deserted. One Greek, a man
>   who rowed alone, lured many more to death

with beacon-fires, false stars, blazing on sea-girt
          Euboean cliffs, to send men crashing headlong
against the rocks. But Menelaus was swept by storms
          ، to dismal lands, regions far from home
whose strange coasts hold no harbor and offer no welcome,
carrying   1140
          a prize that was no prize, that won him only
war, the holy phantom, the Helen Hera made.

What is god? Or what is not?   *strophe 2*

          What lies in between?
Who can say, even searching
          long and hard? We reach
our limit when we see the gods'
          power leap here and there,
and back again in unexpected
          twists and turns of luck.   1150
Helen, you're the child of Zeus,
          who swooped down to Leda's lap
on wings to conceive you—and yet all Greece
          calls you a traitor, faithless,
lawless, godless. Nothing's sure
          in what men say. Only
the word of the gods turns out true.

They're all mad, those who try   *antistrophe 2*
      to prove their courage with spears
and settle their quarrels in war, dealing   1160
      death for an answer. If blood
is to decide, fighting will never
      be driven from among our cities.
Many sleep in the soil of Troy
      who might have laid their battle
over you, my Helen, to rest,
      set right with peaceful words.
Instead, Death has them in his grip,
      and flames as fierce as lightning
from Zeus have blasted the city walls,   1170
      and your life, Helen, is all
an agony piled on yet more grief.

THEOCLYMENUS *(enters dressed for the hunt, with attendants, stops at the tomb, but does not notice Helen's absence or the presence of Menelaus)*

Tomb of my father, I salute you. I buried you
here at the gate so I, your son Theoclymenus,
could greet you, dear father Proteus, every time
I leave or come home again.

      (to his attendants)

      Now then, servants,
take the hounds and hunting nets into the palace.

      (Servants exit)

I've said it before and I'll say it again: my one
mistake is that I don't execute all evildoers.
I just found out that a Greek has entered our land   1180
quite openly, and yet he slipped past all my lookouts.
No doubt he's here as a spy, or to hunt for Helen

and kidnap her. He'll die—if only I catch him.

(suddenly noticing that Helen is missing)

Ah! Am I too late? It looks like the job's
been done: Helen left her refuge and someone
smuggled her out of the country. Ho! Unbar
the doors! Open the stables, men, and bring out
the chariots! I won't let them rob me of the woman
I want to marry—not if I can help it.

*(The doors open, revealing Helen in mourning clothes
and with hair cut short)*

Stop! She's here in the palace after all,   1190
she didn't escape. Woman, why are you dressed
all in black? Why did you take shears
to that noble head of yours and attack your hair
this way? You are weeping, wetting your tender cheek
with tears fresh as dew. Why? Are you mourning
because of some dream that came in the night, or is there
news from home that has wracked your mind with grief?

HELEN My lord—now I may call you by that name—
I'm ruined. My hopes have died, and so have I.

THEOCLYMENUS What's the matter? What has upset you so?   1200

HELEN Menelaus—how can I say it?—is dead.

THEOCLYMENUS How do you know? Did Theonoe tell you this?

HELEN She said so, as did a man who was there when he died.

THEOCLYMENUS So he gave an exact report. Is he still here?

HELEN He is here—may he go where he deserves!

THEOCLYMENUS Who is he? Where is he? I want to know everything.

HELEN He is sitting right there, huddled at the tomb.

THEOCLYMENUS Apollo! What disgusting rags he's wearing!

HELEN Aiiiii! I suppose my husband looked like that.

THEOCLYMENUS Where is this man's home, and where did he sail
here from? 1210

HELEN He is a Greek who was sailing from Troy with my husband.

THEOCLYMENUS What sort of death does he say Menelaus died?

HELEN The saddest and most pitiful. He drowned at sea.

THEOCLYMENUS Where was he sailing, in these waters so far from home?

HELEN His ship smashed on Libya's harborless cliffs.

THEOCLYMENUS And how did this man survive, if he was aboard?

HELEN Common people can be luckier than their betters.

THEOCLYMENUS Where did he leave the wreckage of his ship?

HELEN Where I wish he died—not my Menelaus!

THEOCLYMENUS But he *is* dead. And how did this man get here? 1220

HELEN Some sailors happened by and rescued him.

THEOCLYMENUS What about the accursèd phantom that went to Troy?

HELEN You mean my cloud-image? It vanished into air.

THEOCLYMENUS Poor Priam, wretched Troy! Destroyed for nothing!

HELEN I, too, shared the disasters of Priam's people.

THEOCLYMENUS Did this sailor leave your husband unburied?

HELEN Yes, unburied. Such a misery for me!

THEOCLYMENUS And is that why you have cut your lovely curls?

HELEN He is as dear to me as if he were standing here.

THEOCLYMENUS You are understandably upset at this turn of events.   1230

HELEN This man has brought me news that breaks my heart.

THEOCLYMENUS But how do I know that he is telling the truth?

HELEN Oh, so you think it's easy to fool your sister?

THEOCLYMENUS Of course not. Will you still be staying at the tomb?

HELEN By avoiding you, I am keeping faith with my husband.

THEOCLYMENUS Why tease me? Why don't you let the dead man go?

HELEN All right, then. Begin the arrangements for my wedding.

THEOCLYMENUS This has been long in coming, but I am glad.

HELEN Now you and I must both forget the past.

THEOCLYMENUS On what terms? I'm willing to be gracious if you are.   1240

HELEN Let's make a truce and reconcile our differences.

THEOCLYMENUS I give up my quarrel with you; it's already gone.

HELEN *(falling at Theoclymenus' feet)*

Then I kneel and beg you, since you are dear to me . . .

309

THEOCLYMENUS Why grasp my knees? What are you hunting for?

HELEN Only this: I want to bury my husband.

THEOCLYMENUS How so? A grave with no body? Will you bury his shade?

HELEN We Greeks have a custom that whoever dies at sea...

THEOCLYMENUS What do you do? Greeks are wise in such matters.

HELEN We hold a burial with empty winding-sheets.

THEOCLYMENUS Give him full honors. Set up a tomb where you will.   1250

HELEN That's not how we bury sailors lost at sea.

THEOCLYMENUS What do you do, then? I can't keep up with you Greeks.

HELEN We sail out to sea with all that the dead require.

THEOCLYMENUS In that case, what can I give to your former husband?

HELEN This man knows. I've never done it before.

THEOCLYMENUS *(addressing Menelaus)*
Stranger, you have brought me welcome news.

MENELAUS Not to me, and not to the dead man either.

THEOCLYMENUS How do you Greeks bury those who died at sea?

MENELAUS That depends on how wealthy they are, or how poor.

THEOCLYMENUS Wealth? Just say what you want, for her sake.   1260

MENELAUS First, we offer blood to the spirits below.

THEOCLYMENUS What animal do you need for the sacrifice? I'll see that
you get it.

MENELAUS Decide yourself. Whatever you give will do.

THEOCLYMENUS Here in Egypt, a horse or a bull is customary.

MENELAUS Only make sure that your gift has no defect.

THEOCLYMENUS I have splendid herds. That will be easy.

MENELAUS Next, we bring a bed for the missing body, with covers.

THEOCLYMENUS It will be done. What else do you usually offer?

MENELAUS Weapons of bronze; after all, he loved the spear.

THEOCLYMENUS What I give will be worthy of the line of Pelops.   1270

MENELAUS And fruits, the best of everything that grows here.

THEOCLYMENUS How will you sink all that into the waves?

MENELAUS Well, we'll need to have a ship and rowers.

THEOCLYMENUS How far out from shore does the ship have to go?

MENELAUS Until the foam of her oars can hardly be seen.

THEOCLYMENUS And what is your purpose in observing this strange rite?

MENELAUS To keep the waves from washing impurities ashore.

THEOCLYMENUS You'll have use of a swift Phoenician galley.

MENELAUS That will be fine, and a kindness to Menelaus.

THEOCLYMENUS Surely you don't need Helen's help for this?   1280

MENELAUS It's a job for the mother, or wife, or children to do.

THEOCLYMENUS So it's her duty as wife to bury her husband?

MENELAUS Piety forbids us to cheat the dead of their rites.

THEOCLYMENUS She may go. After all, it is in my interest
to foster my new wife's piety. Look inside
and take all the finery the dead man needs. If you do
what pleases Helen, you won't leave here empty-handed.
You have brought excellent news, and I intend
to reward you. I see you're in a pretty sorry way,
so I'll give you some proper clothes to replace those rags,   1290
and enough food to see you home. *(to Helen)* And you,
poor dear, don't wear yourself out in useless mourning.
You are alive and Menelaus has met his fate.
Tears won't bring a dead man back to life.

MENELAUS You know your duty, woman: You must love
the husband you have here, and free yourself
from the one who is no longer. That will be best
in light of all that's happened. If I reach Greece
and safety, I'll put an end to all the lies
they tell about you. Just be the wife you should   1300
to the man who loves you and shares your marriage bed.

HELEN My husband will have no cause for complaint, and you
will be close enough to know the truth of it.
Now, poor fellow, go inside to take a bath
and change your clothes. I'll tend to all your needs
without delay, since I know that the sooner I give you
what you deserve, the more eager you'll be
to do what my belovèd Menelaus would want.

*(exit into the palace Theoclymenus, Menelaus,
and Helen)*

CHORUS   Once, time out of mind, Demeter,   *strophe 1*

Mother of gods who roams the mountains,   1310
ran frantic through thicket and wooded glen,
across streams in flood, alongside the seas' thundering surf,
searching, searching, wild with worry,
crazy with longing for the lost maiden,
her daughter whose name must not be spoken.
Clappers crashed with piercing clamor as the goddess yoked
her lions
to a cart and set out to find her daughter,
snatched from the circle of the maiden-dance.
And storm-swift to the search came Artemis,
armed with arrows, and Athena, too, brandishing her mighty
spear,   1320
the Gorgon grinning from her shield.
But Zeus looked down from his heavenly throne,
almighty, and decreed a different fate to follow.

When the Great Mother gave
up her search,   *antistrophe 1*

her weary wandering over the world
to find the maiden so cunningly captured,
she crossed the snow-capped peak where the nymphs of Ida
hold their watch,
and threw herself down among thickets and rocks
deep in winter's white. Grieving,
she willed a blight over all the earth.   1330
The fields turned barren, and the work of plowing no longer
brought forth fruit.
She would not send up curling shoots,
tender fodder for the flocks.
She was destroying the human race,
life was deserting the cities, no offerings were being burnt on
the altars,
She stopped the springs from pouring out
the bright, dewy coolness of their waters,
all for grief that her child was gone.

But when she had put an end to the feasts
of gods and men,   *strophe 2*

            Zeus spoke to soothe her bitter rage: 1340
"Go, holy Graces, charm Demeter, wild with anger
            for the child she lost, her darling.
Shout your happy *alalai* to turn her heart
            from grieving. And you Muses, too,
bring her the sweet forgetfulness of songs and dances."
            Then Aphrodite, loveliest
of all the gods, beat the taut hide of the drum
            and made the bronze-voiced cymbal roar.
The Mother smiled at last. She took a flute in hand.
            The deep, wild sound beguiled her mind.   1350

You lit unhallowed fire in the inner
chambers, child,   *antistrophe 2*

            but failed to honor the Great Mother.
You made her angry. Yet there is power in her rites,
            in the dappled fawn-skin robe,
in ivy tendrils wound around the sacred wand;
            in the ceaseless, frenzied shaking
of tambourines held high to whirl in airy circles,
            hair flying like a devotee's
set free for mighty Bromius; in the ecstatic vigils,
            the all-night revels of the goddess   1360
whose glory outshines the moon. But you, Helen, gloried
            in nothing but your own beauty.

HELEN   *(entering from the palace)*

Friends, it all went well for us inside.
Proteus' daughter kept our secret; when
her brother asked point blank if Menelaus
had arrived, she denied it, and as a favor
to me she even said that he is dead.

My husband saw his chance and made the most
of it. The armor he was meant to throw
into the sea—he's wearing it himself,   1370
his powerful left arm slung through the shield-strap
and a spear in his right hand, as if to help
pay honor to the dead. So now he's dressed
for battle, because he plans to celebrate
the victory he'll win over the Egyptian horde
once we get aboard the galley. I myself
gave him proper clothing in place of the rags
he salvaged from his shipwreck, and washed his body
in sweet water at long last, and dressed him.

(the palace doors open)

      But here's
the man who thinks my marriage is in his grasp.   1380
I must be quiet, and I ask you for the favor of your silence,
too. Keep your lips sealed now, and if
we escape, we may be able to save you one day.

*(Theoclymenus enters from the palace, followed by
Menelaus and a number of slaves, some of
whom bear offerings)*

THEOCLYMENUS Men, go in good order, as the stranger told you,
to take our gifts for the burial at sea. But first,
Helen, unless you have some objection, please
let me persuade you to stay behind. You'll do
your husband the same service, whether you're here
or there. I fear that passion will overcome you
and you'll throw your own body into the sea,   1390
in thrall to thoughts of the joys you shared with your husband
in years gone by. You mourn the man too much—
after all, he's no longer here among us.

HELEN My dear new husband, I am bound to honor
my first marriage and the intimacies of a bride.

And yes, I could even die for the love I bear
that man, but what favor would it be, now
that he's dead, to join him in death? Just let me go
in person to give him burial honors. And may
the gods grant what I wish for you, and also   1400
for this Greek who shares my burden. You shall have
the wife you deserve, since you show such kindness to me—
and to Menelaus. Something good will come
of all this. Now, tell one of these men
to show us the ship in which we'll carry out
our rites, and your generosity will be complete.

THEOCLYMENUS *(to one of his servants)*
            You, go and give them a fifty-oared
            Sidonian galley, and put rowers aboard.

HELEN   And won't you let the man in charge of the funeral
            rites also command the ship and its crew?   1410

THEOCLYMENUS   Of course I will; my sailors must obey him.

HELEN   Repeat that order, so everyone hears it clearly.

THEOCLYMENUS   I do, and I'll say it a third time, if you like.

HELEN   Blessings upon you—and on my undertakings.

THEOCLYMENUS   The dead are nothing, and all your work is wasted.

HELEN   Something will come of it, in our world as well as theirs.
            (breaks into sobs)

THEOCLYMENUS   There, don't spoil your complexion with too much weeping.

HELEN   This day will show you just how grateful I am.

THEOCLYMENUS   You shall have a husband no worse than Menelaus.

HELEN   You have been kind. Now all I need is luck.   1420

THEOCLYMENUS It's yours to have—if you are kind to me.

HELEN I need no lessons on how to love my loved ones.

THEOCLYMENUS Would you like me to help by seeing you on your way?

HELEN But of course not. You must not slave for your slaves,
my lord.

THEOCLYMENUS Very well, then. I'll forego your Greek
customs. After all, my house is clean.
It wasn't here that poor Menelaus breathed
his last.
>   *(to the servants)*
One of you go tell my nobles to bring
their wedding gifts to the palace. The whole land
must resound with joyful song to make sure   1430
my marriage to Helen is enviably happy.
>   *(to Menelaus)*
>   And you,
stranger, give these offerings to the sea's embrace
for the man who was Helen's husband long ago,
and hurry back to the palace with my wife,
to join me in giving the wedding feast. Then
set out for home, or stay and enjoy life here.

>   *(Theoclymenus exits into the palace)*

MENELAUS Zeus, we call you father and a wise god.
Look upon us and free us from the troubles
that have dogged our steps. Now, as we drag our misfortunes
up the rocky slope, reach out your hand.   1440
If you but touch us with a fingertip,
we'll reach our aim. Surely we have suffered
enough already! Gods, how often have I called you
in fruitless and painful prayer. I don't deserve
to stumble through my life in misery. I want
to walk upright. Grant me this one favor,
and I'll be happy for all the rest of my days.

(Helen and Menelaus follow the retinue of slaves that
has already begun to exit)

CHORUS   Swift Phoenician galley, whose beating
oars make music   *strophe 1*

for Nereus, leader of the dance—
      sail home, sail home—   1450
leader of the lovely dance of dolphins when the sea is quiet
  and the winds are lying low—
      sail home, sail home—
and Galaneia, grey-green goddess of calm seas,
  cries: "Spread the sails—
      sail home, sail home—
leave them to the breezes, sailors; take up your oars and bring
  Helen to harbor at home"—
      sail home, sail home!

Beside the river, at Athena's temple,
she'll meet Leucippus' daughters   *antistrophe 1* 1460
      and join the dance again—
        at home, at home—
after so long away, share the nighttime joy of the revels
      for Hyacinthus, the boy—
        at home, at home—
Apollo loved and killed with a careless throw of the discus,
    and made a festival—
      at home, at home—
to honor him. And she will meet her daughter, whose wedding
    torches have not yet blazed   1470
    at home, at home.

O, for wings to fly with the flocks   *strophe 2*
of cranes that flee the rains of winter,
led by their eldest, trumpeting his orders
as he flies above the African plains,
      rainless but fruitful.

Now is the time to return, you wingèd
long-necked partners of the racing clouds.
Fly through the night, beneath Orion
and the Sisters at their zenith.   1480
            Bring Sparta the news.
Alight on the banks of Eurotas and tell
his people that Menelaus, the hero
of Troy, is coming home.
And you, Tyndareus' sons, now gods

in heaven, living amidst the brightness   *antistrophe 2*
of the whirling stars, speed your horses
down paths of air, come back to us now
            as saviors of Helen.
Comb the foamy breakers, skim   1490
the dark-skinned sea swell, bring fresh breezes
from Zeus to speed the sailors' work.
Free your sister from the slander of a shameful
            foreign marriage,
punishment meted out unjustly
for the contest on Mount Ida, since
she never went to Troy.

MESSENGER *(entering on the run)*
        Women, can you tell me where to find the king?

CHORUS LEADER *(as the palace doors open)*
        Why, I think he's just coming out now.

MESSENGER My lord, I know you'll find it hard to believe   1500
        the strange and terrible news I'm about to tell you.

THEOCLYMENUS Out with it!

MESSENGER You're going to have to find yourself
        another woman to marry. Helen's escaped.

THEOCLYMENUS   Escaped? Are you telling me she flew away,
                       or did she manage to cross the desert on foot?

MESSENGER   Menelaus carried her off by ship; the man
                       who reported his death—that *was* Menelaus.

THEOCLYMENUS   This is awful! What ship did he carry her off in?
                       Just dreadful! I can hardly believe my ears.

MESSENGER   The ship you gave him yourself. He took your sailors   1510
                       and he's gone, to make a long story short.

THEOCLYMENUS   How? I have to know. It never entered
                       my mind that one man by himself could manage
                       to overcome the whole crew of you.

MESSENGER   We escorted Helen from the palace down to the sea.
                       When we got there, all her wiles were on display.
                       As she walked along in that ladylike way of hers,
                       she started weeping and wailing for her husband,
                       who was right there next to her, not dead at all.
                       We reached your shipyards and hauled out a Phoenician
                            galley   1520
                       for her maiden voyage, with fifty rowing benches.
                       We set about our work. One man put up
                       the mast and another set the oars in their locks.
                       The sail was stowed on board and the double rudders
                       lowered along the stern by their guide ropes.
                            In the midst all this, watching for the right moment,
                       as we realized only later, Greek sailors
                       from Menelaus' crew trooped down the shore
                       decked out in shipwreck rags, fine-looking men
                       but much the worse for wear. When Menelaus   1530
                       saw them, he called out in a show of pity meant
                       for us: "Poor lads! What Greek ship did you sail on,
                       and how did it crack up? But come, help bury
                       the son of Atreus, who died at sea. Helen
                       is giving him rites of burial in his absence."
                       They wept feigned tears and rushed aboard, carrying

the sea-gifts meant for Menelaus. By now
we were suspicious and whispered to each other
what a crowd of extra passengers had come aboard.
Still, we held our tongues. We didn't want   1540
to disobey your orders, but when you put
that stranger in command of the ship, you ruined everything.
    We stowed the cargo on board without any trouble,
since it was light—all except the bull,
who wouldn't set foot on the gangplank, but arched his back,
bellowed, rolled his eyes, and squinted over
his lowered horns to keep from being touched.
But Helen's husband called out: "You men who sacked
the city of Troy, come hoist this bull Greek-style
onto your young shoulders and throw him on deck."   1550
They had their orders, hoisted the bull, and carried
him to the rowing deck. Then Menelaus,
stroking the neck and forehead of the horse,
coaxed it on board. When the ship was fully loaded
at last, Helen climbed up every rung
of the ladder with her dainty steps and sat down
on the quarter-deck with Menelaus, the man
we all thought was dead. The rest of the Greeks sat
man by man in close formation, half
on the left side, half on the right. Their swords were still   1560
hidden under their cloaks.
                              Now the waves
echoed our shouts as we took up the bosun's cry.
When we reached a point no longer near the shore,
but still not too far out, our helmsman asked:
"Stranger, shall we still sail further or will this do?
You're in command of the ship." Menelaus answered:
"It's far enough for me." Then he walked to the prow,
sword in hand, and got ready to sacrifice the bull.
But he wasn't thinking of any dead man; instead,
as he cut the bull's throat, he prayed: "Poseidon   1570
lord of the sea, you who dwell in the depths,
and you, holy daughters of Nereus, rescue me
and my wife, too. Take us away from here
and bring us safe to Nauplia." The bull's blood

spurted into the sea, a good omen
for the stranger.
                    Then someone said: "This is treachery!
We've got to sail back. Bosun, give the command!
Helmsman, turn about!" But from where he stood Eurotas
over the slaughtered bull, the son of Atreus
called to his allies: "What are you waiting for?   1580
You're the pride of Greece! Kill these natives,
cut them down, throw them off the ship
into the sea." Now the bosun was shouting
to your sailors: "Come on, one of you pick up a spar,
you, break a bench, and you, take an oar from its lock,
and bloody the heads of our enemies." Everyone sprung
to their feet, some holding scraps of wood, others
with swords in their hands. The ship was flowing with blood.
Then from the stern came Helen's rallying cry:
"Where is your Trojan glory? Show it off   1590
to these natives!" Men were falling in the fight;
some got up, others you saw lying dead.
Menelaus was wearing armor, and wherever
he saw his allies in trouble, there he was,
brandishing his sword, until your sailors started
diving off the ship, and he emptied the benches.
Then he told the helmsman to steer straight
for Greece. They hoisted sail, and a favoring wind
sent them on their way. They're gone now.
                    As for me, I managed to escape death   1600
by sliding down the anchor into the sea.
A fisherman picked me up when I was already
near exhaustion, and put me out on land
so I could bring you the news. I've learned one thing:
There is nothing more useful than healthy skepticism.

                                                            (*exits*)

CHORUS LEADER Who could have imagined, my lord, that Menelaus
was here, and you didn't know it—nor did we.

THEOCLYMENUS I'm a wretched fool, snared by women's wiles.
My bride has escaped. If I could overtake
that ship, I'd do it and soon catch those Greeks.   1610
As things stand, I'll punish the sister who betrayed me.
Theonoe knew Menelaus was here in the palace
and never told me. Well, she's not going to fool
anyone else with that kind of prophesying.

                    (begins to exit into the palace, but is stopped by a
                    servant, who takes hold of his robe; in the course of the
                    following dialogue, Theoclymenus gets the upper hand)

SERVANT Where are you going, master? To commit murder?

THEOCLYMENUS Where justice commands. Now get out of my way.

SERVANT I won't let go. You are rushing to a great wrong.

THEOCLYMENUS A slave would rule his master?

SERVANT   Yes, since it's for the best.

THEOCLYMENUS Not for me, if you won't let me . . .

SERVANT   No, I won't!

THEOCLYMENUS kill a most wicked sister . . .

SERVANT   Most god-fearing, you mean.   1620

THEOCLYMENUS who betrayed me . . .

SERVANT   A noble betrayal, to do what is just.

THEOCLYMENUS by giving my wife to . . .

SERVANT   . . . the man who has the greater right.

THEOCLYMENUS Over what belongs to me?

SERVANT   Her father gave her to *him.*

THEOCLYMENUS But fortune gave her to me.

SERVANT   And necessity took her away.

THEOCLYMENUS What right have you to judge me?

SERVANT   Because I know what's right.

THEOCLYMENUS And I've lost my right to rule.

SERVANT   Only to rule unjustly.

THEOCLYMENUS You seem to be in love with dying.

SERVANT *(now caught in a wrestling hold)*
                                        Kill! But you won't
            kill your sister, not if I can help it.
            Kill me instead. The way for a noble slave
            to win glory is to die for the sake of his master.   1630

            (The action is halted by the sudden appearance of the
                    Dioscuri, suspended above the stage building on
                            the theatrical crane [Greek: *mêchanê*])

CASTOR Restrain the rage that is driving you astray,
            Theoclymenus, king of Egypt. We, the twin
            sons of Zeus, have come to set you straight.
            Leda gave us birth together with Helen,
            who has fled your palace. The lost marriage that made you
            blaze with anger was never part of destiny.
            Your sister, the maiden Theonoe, child of the divine
            daughter of Nereus, did you no wrong by honoring
            the ways of the gods and her father's just commands.
            It was Helen's fate to live in your palace until   1640
            the walls of Troy were uprooted from their foundations,

and her name had done its service to the gods.
That time is long gone, and her stay was bound to end.
Now she must go home to her old marriage
and her husband's bed. So keep your sword from your sister's
throat, knowing that she acted with good judgment.
As for our sister, we would have rescued her
long ago, as soon as Zeus made us gods,
but we didn't have the strength to change what fate
and the gods had already decided. That is all   1650
I have to say to you, but to our sister I say:
Sail on with your husband, and you shall have favoring winds.
We, your brothers, the rescuers, will ride
beside you over the sea, till we've seen you home.
And when you reach the end of your life, you will have
the name of goddess and a share in the gifts and feasts
men offer us; for that is how Zeus wants it.
The place where Hermes first brought you to rest
when he stole you from Sparta, so Paris couldn't have you—
I mean the island that stretches out to guard   1660
the coast of Attica—will be known for the rest of time
as "Helen" since it held you after you were kidnapped.
Menelaus the wanderer will live on the Island of the Blessed
forever. The gods grant him this fate, for they
don't hate the well-born, though they make them endure
more troubles than the common mass of men.

THEOCLYMENUS Sons of Leda and Zeus, I give up my old
quarrel over your sister; let her go home,
if the gods will. And I'll no longer kill
my own sister. You are the blood brothers   1670
of the best and purest sister in the world,
and may the noble mind of Helen bring you
joy. There aren't many women like her.

CHORUS The gods appear to us in many shapes,
bring many things to unexpected ends.
What we supposed would happen, did not happen;
for what we never even dreamed, god found
a way. And that is what you saw today.

NOTES

1–157 / 1–163 *Prologue* A monologue sets the scene and explains the situation, followed by a dialogue scene with which the action begins; this is Euripides' favored procedure, but unusually it will be followed by a "second prologue" of closely corresponding form; see note on 378–517.

1–68 / 1–67 *Helen's prologue speech* This is one of a number of plays that begin with a suppliant tableau. If the Greek theater had a curtain, it would rise to show Helen already seated at Proteus' tomb; since there is none, the audience sees her enter and take her place. This arrangement is often described as a "cancelled entrance," with the play only beginning when the first words are spoken. However, since almost one-fourth of the surviving fifth-century dramas begin with some sort of tableau, the convention likely had a more positive function. In this case, for example, we can imagine that Helen begins the drama by miming her initial act of supplication, which the prologue then gradually explains and motivates. Alternatively, as my stage directions suggest, she might only take up her suppliant posture as her speech ends, the actor transforming himself fully into the character "Helen" in the course of narrating of her story.

1 / 1 *Lovely virgin streams* May refer to a special purity that some Greek writers attributed to the Nile as being fed only by melted snow (**2–3 / 3**), but the likelier meaning here is "streams with fair maidens," i.e., inhabited by river nymphs. In any case, the phrase introduces in the first line of the play the thematics of virginity (see Introduction, p. 249).

3 / 4 *Proteus* In Homer (*Odyssey* 4.351–582), he is an "old man of the sea," a shape-shifting deity who can only be made to reveal his knowledge of the future by being held fast and forced to resume his true shape. Euripides follows Herodotus 2.112ff. in making the virtuous king of Egypt who kept Helen safe in his palace (see Introduction, pp. 232–34).

5 / 7 *Psamathë* "Sandy," one of the Nereids, the fifty daughters of Nereus, another "old man of the sea" (see note on **12**). Hesiod, *Theogony* 1004–5 mentions Psamathë's marriage with Aeacus, but the second marriage to Proteus seems to be Euripides' invention. The fact that she "broke off" her first marriage gives her situation a suggestive similarity to what is believed about Helen, that she left one husband and took another.

8–9 / 11–13 *Eido...Theonoe* The childhood name, short for Eidothea ("image of divinity"), the name of Proteus' daughter in Homer (*Odyssey* 4.366), emphasizes appearance, the adult name ("she whose mind is a god's" i.e., wise/clairvoyant), knowledge. The shortened version of the Homeric name used by Euripides evokes, in the context of this play, *eidolon*, "image," the word repeatedly used to denote Helen's phantom. Theonoe leaves image behind when she receives the prophetic knowledge implied by her new name. Etymology is used here in a manner reminiscent of Aeschylus a generation before or Plato's *Cratylus* a generation later, as a way of revealing the nature of a character who will play a decisive role in the drama. Homer's Eidothea took pity on Odysseus, but Theonoe's intervention will be predicated on knowledge and moral judgment as well as pity. The change of name in effect gives the prophetess a clear position on the side of reality in the play's dichotomy of appearance and reality (see Introduction, pp. 247–49).

12 / 15 *Nereus* In Homer, Proteus has prophetic powers; Euripides has transferred these to his daughter by making them her inheritance from her maternal grandfather Nereus, a sea deity who could be expected to have such powers. Hesiod (*Theogony* 233–36) mentions Nereus' truthfulness and knowledge, and at 1003 Theonoe says that her devotion to justice comes from him.

13 / 16 *you will have heard of* Literally, "not nameless," famous. Name as fame is fundamental to the play's thematics, particularly as regards Helen's bad (false) fame as faithless wife and cause of the Trojan War. See Introduction, p. 248.

15–16 / 17–18 *Tyndareus...Zeus* Double paternity is a regular feature of heroic legend (e.g., Theseus and Heracles) and, in Helen's case at least, apparently reflects her original status as a Spartan deity.

16 / 20–21 *pretending to flee from an eagle's attack* A curious doubling of Zeus' role, since the eagle is a common symbol of Zeus.

17–18 / 21 *and it may / be true* A characteristic form of Euripidean irony, and characteristically difficult to interpret. The extreme case is Heracles' notorious rejection of stories that impute illicit love affairs and other failings to the gods as "the foolish tales of poets" (*Herakles* 1346), which appears to undermine the whole basis of the play by denying Zeus' paternity and Hera's subsequent jealousy. Skepticism and criticism of the mythical tradition are by no means the only possible explanations. Critics have suggested, e.g., that Helen may merely be drawing attention to the very oddity of the story: "incredible as it may seem"; or that the irony is directed at the cleft between what a child of Zeus might expect and Helen's present misery. The story of Helen's birth will be referred to directly three more times: once more by Helen in a playful and even parodic manner (**255–59 / 256–59**) and twice by the Chorus, in contexts that do not appear to allow an ironic reading (**208–11 / 213–16, 1151–56 / 1145–48**).

25 / 27 *if you can call this curse of mine beauty* This paradoxical expression (beauty being Helen's traditional identifying characteristic and her glory) introduces the idea, which she will often repeat in the first scenes of the play (e.g., **300–302 / 304–5, 358–60 / 364–65, 376–77 / 383–85**), that her exceptional beauty leads to exceptional suffering.

30 / 32 *blew … to the winds* The Greek verb here, *exanemoô*, can mean "inflate," "puff up," suggesting the essential falsity of Paris' marriage, and is almost punningly appropriate, since the image that falsified it was "conjured out of thin air" (**32 / 34**).

34–39 / 36–41 *Zeus devised a plan …* Zeus' plan to relieve the earth's overcrowding is reported in a fragment of the *Cypria*, part of a lost cycle of epic poems about the matter of Troy; his plan to *show the Greeks who their mightiest warrior is* (i.e., Achilles) is of course central to the plot of the *Iliad*. Euripides' allusion to these strands of epic tradition completes a picture in which Helen is both helpless victim and unwilling accomplice of apparently unrelated, but closely intertwined, acts of divine will.

42 / 42–43 *not me at all … just my name* The first of a long series of explicit antitheses between the (corporeal and moral) reality of Helen and her appearance (name, reputation); cf. note on **67–69**.

43 / 44 *Hermes* His role here combines his well-attested functions as divine messenger, guide of travelers, and god of deception.

44 / 44 *the folds of air* Greek *aithêr* (aether), the thin upper air of the heavens, in this play both the medium of Helen's flight and the material from which the phantom Helen was molded, and to which it will return (**606–7 / 605**).

51 / 50–51 *to hunt me down, his kidnapped wife* Literally, "he hunts my seizings." The phrase reminds us that Menelaus has been pursuing the wrong prey and taking vengeance for the wrong "seizings." It also suggests the idea of erotic pursuit. Sexual chase and capture are indicated with hunting words at **64 / 63, 311 / 314, 546 / 545, 1182 / 1175**, all with Helen as object.

53 / 51 *because of me* The first expression of Helen's complex feelings of guilt. Helen knows that she is loathed only because she appeared to betray her husband and kindle a great war, but she is unable to separate herself entirely from the phantom that shares her name and her beauty and has done so much harm.

65–66 / 64 *I sit / as a suppliant at this tomb* Formal supplication involves physical attachment to the place of refuge, for this in effect makes a suppliant the property of the protecting divinity and therefore inviolable, on pain of arousing divine wrath. Proteus' tomb is not strictly the shrine of a divinity; the very act of supplication, however, confers upon the man thus honored something akin to the status of sacred hero, and upon his tomb the numinous power of a hero's grave.

67–69 / 66–67 *name/. . ./body* This antithesis, which Helen will repeat twice (**589 / 588, 1114 / 1100**), expresses concisely the contrast between appearance and reality that underlies her role (see Introduction, pp. 247–49). The disjunction of name and body is an obvious trope for a disjunction of elements ordinarily felt to constitute a unitary self. "Name" can also refer to reputation, but since Helen's reputation is quite literally a phantom, that "body" in her case must here stand for the person, as can be seen by the fact that its place is taken in the similar antithesis at **42 / 42–43** by the pronoun "I." This, in turn, is deeply problematic, especially in terms of heroic culture, where reputation is so essential to identity. There is also an irony implicit in the use of "body" to represent Helen's real nature, since her bad reputation depends upon her extraordinary, seductive beauty.

70–157 / 68–163 *Helen-Teucer scene* Having explained her painful past and the new threat of forced marriage, Helen now hears of disasters still unknown to her: the death of her mother, the disappearance of her brothers, the destruction of Troy, and above all the apparent death of Menelaus. Her informant is Teucer, a veteran of the Trojan War, which cost the life of his brother and led to his banishment from home. His initial revulsion and hostility provide Helen with a reminder, and the audience vivid evidence, of the hatred the Greeks feel for her. He recognizes, by separating the woman he sees from her appearance, that she is not what he believes Helen to be, but, like Menelaus later, he cannot believe that she *is* Helen. He is the first of many in the play who find it difficult or impossible to overcome the power of appearances.

This scene not only adds to Helen's sufferings, it connects her to the sufferings of those who fought and died at Troy. She never went there, but must pay for all that her phantom has wrought. Teucer, who did go but returned more a victim of this senseless war than a conqueror (**103** / 106), is thus ideally suited to the role he plays here.

71 / 69 *the god of wealth* There may be an additional meaning to this invocation of Plutus (Greek: Ploutos) was also associated with Pluto (Greek: Ploutôn), king of the underworld, and the scene will be filled with thoughts of death.

73–78 / 72–76 These lines typify the fusion of comic technique and tragic content that characterizes this scene and much of the play. Teucer imagines the real Helen to be a "deadly image" of the woman he hates, whereas (as we know) it is really a phantom that has caused his sorrows.

75 / 74–75 *My curse on you* Literally, "May the gods spit you out." Spitting is a simple form of purification, and this common apotropaic gesture evidently lies behind the metaphorical sense "abominate."

77 / 75–76 *on foreign soil* The relation of a foreigner (*xenos*, a word that also means "guest-friend") to his host is reciprocal. Those who expect protection and aid from their hosts must themselves refrain from doing them any harm. Teucer is not yet in fact a *xenos* in the full sense of the word, and one might expect him to explain his unwillingness to kill the woman who so resembles Helen by mentioning her sanctuary at the tomb instead. *Xenia* is, however, fundamental to the Troy story: Paris' abduction of Helen in particular was understood primarily as a breach of the code of guest-friendship.

84–136 / 83–141 This passage illustrates the surprising effectiveness of *stichomythia* (line-for-line exchange) in presenting narrative. Teucer unfolds his own painful story haltingly, whereas Helen, while hiding her identity, keeps turning the conversation back to herself and tries, however allusively, to suggest the truth about herself to this (fellow) victim of the war of which she is ostensibly the cause. Teucer is trying to put his past behind him, but his very reticence betrays his wounds. Helen's life will make sense again only if she can reclaim her past, and her emotions are particularly evident when the subject turns to Menelaus. We hear her despair as she elicits, step by step, the evidence that her husband is dead, along with her mother and brothers.

91 / 94 *Ajax, my brother* The story of Ajax's death, known from Homer and dramatized in Sophocles' *Ajax*. The treatment is allusive, as the wide currency of the story permits and his own distaste for retelling it makes appropriate; see Ajax in Glossary.

96 / 99 *a suitor for Helen's hand* This appears to be a Euripidean invention; at any rate we do not have any earlier mention of Achilles as one of Helen's suitors. In the traditional chronology of the Trojan War, Achilles would have been too young to woo her. However, a connection between the most beautiful of women and the greatest of warriors seems somehow inevitable, and the two are often explicitly connected in our sources in various ways, including the legend that they lived together after their deaths on the island of Leuke in the Black Sea.

99 / 102 *someone else* Odysseus. The missing name may reflect Teucer's scorn for his brother's enemy. Cf. Homer, *Odyssey* 11.543ff., where the shade of Ajax turns away without answering Odysseus.

104–7 / 107–10 The universality of the suffering caused by the Trojan War will be emphasized repeatedly (**355–68** / 362–74, **376–77** / 383–85, **608–12** / 608–11, **1126–42** / 1112–37). In Helen's anguish there is also a bitter lament for her implication in the disaster, even though the phantom truly bears the responsibility that everyone attributes to her.

119 / 124 *In Argos* Euripides follows the tradition (Homer, *Odyssey* 3.306–12) that Menelaus, upon his return to Greece, went to Argos (or Mycenae) before going home to Sparta.

120 / 125 *for those who care* Helen disguises the emotions that provoked her initial response.

123 / 128 *a storm* Homer, *Odyssey* 3.130–83, offers a version of the Greeks' return from Troy in which Menelaus left Troy before Agamemnon and so avoided the great storm that destroyed much of the Achaean fleet; Euripides follows the version found in Aeschylus, *Agamemnon* 617–33, in which it was the storm that separated the brothers. For the dangers of the voyage, see **780–91** / 765–76 with **1134–42** / 1126–36.

129 / 134 *dead and gone* The story that Leda committed suicide is, as far as we can tell, Euripides' invention. It serves, like the supposed suicide of her brothers, (**137–38** / 142), to increase Helen's burden of sorrow and guilt.

141 / 146 *will you introduce me* The Greek term *proxenos*, used in general of a person who represents foreigners or foreign interests, specifically designates one who provides hospitality and an introduction to those seeking to consult an oracle.

143 / 148 *Cyprus* The story of Teucer's foundation of a new Salamis on Cyprus can be traced back only as far as Pindar, *Nemean* 4, 46, generally dated to the mid-470s. Teucer's question for Theonoe would presumably have been not only the route he should take, but where on Cyprus he should head for.

146 / 151 *The right course will show itself* Helen may mean that Teucer will find the answer by experience, or that the place for his city will be where he comes ashore, i.e., that Apollo will see to the fulfillment of the oracle. Perhaps, however, Euripides alludes here to the ancient tradition that the Nile flowed directly to Cyprus.

150 / 156 *Do not ask why* Helen cannot explain without revealing who she is, and Teucer goes on to make clear again how unwise that would be by damning Helen once more while wishing this woman well. Ironically, though his distinction is false, he predicts the right outcome: the phantom Helen will be destroyed, and the real Helen's luck will change.

158- 251 / 164–252 *"Parodos" (entrance song of Chorus) in the form of a lyric exchange with Helen* Strictly speaking, the *parodos* begins only at **175 /** 179, but the Chorus presumably begins to enter before the end of Helen's song, and the entrance of these sympathetic Greek slave women is precipitated by her lament, which forms the first member of a *kommos* (lyric exchange). Although the kommatic *parodos* is quite common, this one is the only one that is begun by a single actor. A second structural peculiarity is that, instead of the usual succession of Chorus and actor within each single strophe and antistrophe, here Helen sings the entire first strophe and the Chorus responds with an antistrophe, followed by a second strophic pair similarly divided. The effect of the metrical and musical repetition of the protagonist by the Chorus is to suggest how deeply it shares her sorrows.

As regards its contents, the *parodos* is primarily an emotional response to the situation set out in the prologue, repeating with highly formalized lyric intensity the elements of the initial exposition. The style of the *parodos* combines poetic elaboration and rhythmic urgency. Euripidean lyrics of this kind are often referred to as "ornamented" or "decorated" because they are marked by fullness of description, elaborate development of pictorial detail, and a tendency to emphasize mood rather than narrative continuity. It should not be forgotten, however, that these qualities usually serve to stir the emotions, and not merely for decoration.

162 / 169 *Sirens* Euripides' picture combines the daemonic musicians of *Odyssey* 12, whose songs lure sailors to their death, with the bird-women connected with the cult of the dead, familiar from archaic vase-painting and depicted on fifth-century Attic grave-steles and vases with the kinds of musical instruments mentioned in **164 /** 170–71. That they are called "daughters of Earth" presumably emphasizes this connection with the underworld, rather than making a strictly genealogical claim (elsewhere they are said to be daughters of a river god or Achelous or the Muse Melpomene); their virginity brings them explicitly into the orbit of Helen's "virginal chastity (see Introduction, p. 249).

164 / 170–71 The Greek mentions (apparently; the text is problematic) two types of wind instruments, the "Libyan lotus," to be identified with the *aulos*, an ancient oboe-like instrument used in the Greek theater, and the "syrinx," the shepherd's pipe associated with Pan, along with the lyre, the oldest and most widely used Greek stringed instrument.

170 / 175 *Persephone* The story of her abduction by the lord of the underworld and her grief-stricken mother's search for her will be sung by the Chorus at 1309–62 / 1301–68.

174 / 176–77 *a song of healing grief* In Greek, this is "a paean accompanied by tears," a paradoxical phrase, since the paean is a hymn of celebration and thanksgiving, originally to Apollo, and as such is out of place in the world below. The paradox is, however, widely employed in tragedy.

175–88 / 179–90 Choruses occasionally motivate their entrance by announcing that something they heard aroused their concern. The closest parallel to this stanza is the beginning of the parodos of Euripides' *Hippolytus* (121–30), also a description of a laundry-scene interrupted by ominous words. In both cases, a contrast is created between a scene of women's work described in idyllic terms and a moment of crisis for the female protagonist. The literary antecedent for such scenes is Homer, *Odyssey* 6.85ff., where Nausicaä and her companions are washing their clothes in a river on the coast of Phaeacia. Rather than hear cries of others, however, the maidens' shouts while playing ball awaken Odysseus, who then appears before them.

184 / 185–6 *unlike those sung to the lyre* A Euripidean epithet for songs of mourning, which would normally be accompanied by the *aulos*.

188 / 190 *Pan's eager clutches* Pan is the goat-god of Arcadia, whose legends emphasize abundant sexual energy and the ardent pursuit of nymphs and boys. Implicit in this comparison is the suggestion of sexual violence awaiting Helen at the hands of Theoclymenus.

189–90 / 191–92 These lines constitute an informal introduction of the Chorus and indicate its affinity to Helen as "daughters of Greece enslaved / and abducted" in foreign parts. The phrase translated "daughters of Greece" has overtones not only of youth but of virginal status. This is emphasized by verbal as well as metrical response with 162 / 168, where the Sirens are called "virgin daughters of Earth." The point is not to equate the two groups, but rather to draw both into the thematics of virginity surrounding Helen (see Introduction, p. 249).

195–96 / 198–99 *all / that killing . . . so much grief* In Greek, these are two similar, highly assonantal compounds (*poluktonon, polyponon*) at the ends of adjoining lines. In conjunction with the double self-accusation "I who am the cause . . . my name the cause," this device emphasizes the ironic identity-in-difference of Helen's true self and false reputation. Furthermore, *onoma polyponon* (literally, "name of much woe") plays with the etymology of Helen's name from the root *hel-* ("seize," "destroy"); see Aeschylus, *Agamemnon* 687–90.

201–2 / 205 *Castor / and his brother* Polydeuces (Latin Pollux). Euripides regularly treats Castor as the more prominent of the two, and in the final scene of this play—as in Euripides' *Electra*, where the speaker identifies himself as Castor, 1240)—Castor evidently speaks for both brothers.

203–5 / 207–10 *the hoof-clattered plain/ . . . /where the young men train* The Dioscuri are closely associated with horse-riding (see note on **1487–88**), and in the epic tradition Castor in particular was known as a horseman, Polydeuces as a boxer. Sparta itself was famous throughout the Greek world for the physical training of its youth.

209–11 / 214–16 *Zeus flashed / through the air . . . / and made Leda your mother* For the theme of Helen's paternity in this play, see note on **17–18**.

222 / 228 *Athena in her House of Bronze* A famous Spartan Athena whose cult was celebrated in a temple covered in bronze plate. Mentioned again at **243 / 245** and **1460 / 1466–67**.

223–251 / 229–52 *Epode* A single stanza concludes the lyric sequence: Helen summarizes her disastrous connection with Troy, beginning with the arrival of Paris and ending with the slanderous reputation that has defiled her name. Helen is the victim of pursuit by the "foreign oars" (**229 / 234**) that brought Paris to Sparta, led by Aphrodite, not the traitor "reveling in a foreign bed" (**219 / 224–25**) that everyone believes her to be. She was snatched up (like all the innocent maidens seized by the gods) while gathering flowers for Athena—and by Hermes, not Paris. And yet Troy has suffered ruin and Helen is everywhere reviled.

223–24 / 229–31 *Who was it . . . / who felled the pine* Helen makes the felling of the tree from which Paris' ship was built into the symbolic starting point for all subsequent disasters; the idea that "ships began the evils" goes back to Homer (*Iliad* 5.62–63). Whether a Greek or Trojan felled the pine is not in itself a serious alternative, but is simply a form of "polar expression," the equivalent of "who in the world?" It does, however, suggest that the final responsibility is hard to pin down.

232–33 / 238 *cause of / the killing* The epithet that Helen applied to herself in **195 / 198**.

233 / 239 *Danaus' sons* The Argives, after the mythical king Danaus, and hence the Greeks in general.

240–41 / 244 *as I / gathered roses* Like Persephone and other victims of divine abduction; see Introduction, p. 237.

246–47 / 248 *made me / the cause of the wretched war* A phrase that betrays the complex relationship of Helen's true self and false reputation.

252–322 / 253–329 *Dialogue (Chorus Leader, Helen)* What in the usual tragic structure would be the first episode is here a short spoken scene between lyric exchanges (163–252 and 330–85), involving no new characters and largely given over to a speech in which Helen reacts to Teucer's news. The reprise in spoken dialogue of material already developed in lyric form permits a fuller rhetorical elaboration and is found frequently in tragedy.

254–302 / 255–305 Helen's speech rehearses her history from birth to the apparently desperate situation in which she now finds herself, as a kind of brief for the singularity of her misery and the futility of continuing to live. The bulk of the speech (**265–99 / 267–97**) is devoted to a demonstration of the number and variety of her sorrows in the methodical manner of a practiced orator. First is the destruction of her reputation, second her exile to Egypt, then the deaths of her husband and her mother, her daughter unmarried, her brothers gone. All that is left is an unwelcome marriage to a foreigner. This exposition leads inexorably to the conclusion, why go on living when one is as good as dead? Contemporary readers or spectators may find the further rehearsal of Helen's sorrows excessive, but what this speech emphasizes in its rhetorical clarity and completeness is her lucid (though mistaken) understanding that she has no escape but death. The speech thus both deepens the pathos and prepares for the next stages in the drama.

256–57 / 258 *birthed her child / in a white shell* Literally, "brought forth a white vessel for her chicks." The description of Helen's birth has been regarded by many editors as an interpolation, but the clever extravagance of the periphrasis and the wit and technical accomplishment of the lines point to Euripidean authorship. The lightly grotesque and mocking

tone must be understood as ironic, but coming from Helen the irony
need not express skepticism about the story so much as frustration and
bewilderment at the strangeness of her life from its very outset.

261 / 261 *Hera's envy . . . my beauty* A compact statement of the complex relation of the
two Helens. Hera, as the maker of the phantom Helen, bears blame for
all that followed, but the phantom's power stems from Helen's own
beauty.

276 / 275 *a slave* This is hyperbole, and Helen immediately goes on to explain that
she is referring to the subjugation of all to the will of a single ruler,
a standard contrast between Greeks and barbarians in the political
rhetoric of contemporary Athens. At this point, however, Helen is
entirely dependent for her safety on Theoclymenus' respect of her
supplication.

281–82 / 280–81 *I am her slayer / guiltless though the guilt's still mine* A strong statement
of Helen's complex feelings of responsibility for what her appearance—
both her own beauty and the image that went to Troy—has caused.

282 / 282 *my daughter* Hermione, whom Helen has not mentioned until now and of
whom she has had no news. What she has learned, however, permits
her to deduce her daughter's fate and adds one more element to her
sorrows. With father and mother absent, uncles gone, grandmother
dead, Hermione has no one to see to her marriage, and her mother's
shame must also weigh against her (see further **704–6 / 688–90**).

286–87 / 285–86 *my misfortunes / have killed me, even though I am still alive* This is a
surprising version of the appearance/reality antithesis (see Introduction,
pp. 247–49) whose full implication resists translation. It employs the
synonyms *pragma* and *ergon* antithetically, although both can be translated "deed" and are regularly used to describe what is real as opposed to
what is said or seems to be real (in this play, see **602 / 601** [*pragma*], **806 /
792** [*ergon*] with their respective notes). However, since the former often
denotes "troubles" or "adverse circumstances" and the latter something
like "in fact," the obvious sense is that Helen is all but dead because of
her troubles. Euripides' antithetical phrasing nevertheless leaves open
another possible meaning, or at least an undertone: Helen has been
destroyed by actions beyond her control (*pragmasin*), not by anything
she did herself (*ergoisin*)—yet both constitute the reality with which she
must come to terms (cf. **270–72 / 269–72**).

288–93a / 287–92 These lines contain a number of linguistic anomalies and may
be a later interpolation, but I retain them with an emendation (*dikha*

"without" for *meta* "with" in **291** / 289) that gives them, a any rate, a plausible sense. As the following lines show, Helen's problem will be precisely that Menelaus is not there to confirm her *bona fides*. The motif of identifying tokens occurs nowhere else in the play or indeed the Helen tradition. There is, however, a parallel in Homer (*Odyssey* 23.107–10), and if the lines are authentic it provides the only overt allusion to the play's underlying parallels of Helen and Penelope, Menelaus and Odysseus; see Introduction, pp. 234–36.

293b / 293 *So why do I go on living?* Repeats **55–56** / 56. There, the question led to Helen's affirmation of Hermes' promise that Menelaus will come and take her home; here, the question is essentially rhetorical, since she now believes that Menelaus is dead: a striking index of Helen's changed mood.

303–23 / 306–29 The Chorus Leader enters the action directly, first by responding to Helen's speech not with a more or less conventional exhortation, as at 252–53, but with the specific advice not to assume that Teucer has told her the truth, and then by suggesting that Helen consult Theonoe. Apart from the few tragedies in which choruses are major actors, it is rare for a chorus (or its leader) to affect the course of the action, except by their silence. Here, the Chorus Leader successfully persuades Helen to a new course of action, although the effect is primarily a matter of staging: Helen and the Chorus will exit, leaving the stage empty for Menelaus' entrance (see note on **377** / 385).

311 / 314 *hunting for marriage* I.e., King Theoclymenus; for the image, see note on **51**.

315 / 317 *the maiden who knows all things* Reminds the audience of what Helen herself said at **10–11** / 14 and at the same time helps prepare for Theonoe's decisive role in the drama (cf. **837** / 823, **934–36** / 922–23).

320–22 / 327–29 *I'll gladly / go* Although the Chorus Leader is speaking (in 1st person sing.), she represents the entire Chorus, who has only a group identity. The idea that *women should help one another* motivates the choral exit necessary to clear the stage for Menelaus' entry. It is noteworthy, however, that despite the sympathy between Helen and the Chorus the hint of reciprocal benefit to these Greek slave women will be left unfulfilled (see further the note on **1382**).

323–77 / 330–85 *Kommos (lyric exchange between Helen and the Chorus)* This lyric exchange, whose dramatic function is to prepare the exit into the palace of Helen and the Chorus, replaces the more usual *stasimon* (choral song) at the close of the first episode. The first *stasimon* comes only at

1121 / 1107. Apart from facilitating the exit (it would be impossibly clumsy to have the Chorus leave in silence after performing a *stasimon*, and absurd for Helen to wait and then leave with Chorus members), this arrangement allows a contrast between the distraught extremity of Helen's outbursts and the more hopeful moderation of the Chorus.

340 / 350 *Eurotas, river of home* A famous Spartan landmark, used by metonymy for Sparta here and elsewhere in the play.

345–52 / 353–59 These lines provide the climax of Helen's long series of laments: if Theonoe confirms that Menelaus is dead, Helen will take her own life, either by the noose or the sword. The noose is the preferred form of female suicide in tragedy, but Helen's language suggests a preference for a "masculine" death by stabbing, which provides a *test of strength* that ensures the heroic character of her death in question. At the same time, suicide by the sword will mark Helen's death out as a "sacrifice" (349 / 357: *thuma*, properly of animals slaughtered at the altar) to those who have made her suffer, "that triple yoke / of goddesses" (349–50 / 357: Hera, Athena, and Aphrodite) and "Priam's son" (Paris 350 / 358)—a bitter final twist that singles out the judgment on Mount Ida as the source of all her sorrows (cf. 19–29 / 22–30).

353–54 / 360–61 The Chorus, having failed to moderate Helen's laments tries to deflect Helen's ill-omened words about her own death.

355–68 / 362–74 On the heels of her invocation of the judgment of Paris, Helen opens out her lament to include the destruction of Troy and the agony of Greece, all for nothing: "deeds that were never done" (356 / 363: Helen's supposed betrayal) and "the gift / Queen Aphrodite made of me" (357–58 / 364: literally, "my gifts of Cypris," which might also mean "the gift she gave me," i.e., Helen's beauty). Either way, Troy was destroyed by an illusion.

363 / 368 *sheared off their hair* A rite of mourning that is presumably related to the custom of placing an offering of shorn locks on the body or grave of the deceased.

366–68 / 372–74 Traditional gestures of mourning, associated primarily with women. Descriptions of such ritual disfigurement are frequent in tragedy. In the Greek text they are metaphorically given to the land of Greece herself.

369–77 / 375–85 This final stanza of the *kommos*, in a different meter, offers the fresh perspective of two mythological parallels to Helen's fate. Both have to do with beautiful maidens transformed into beasts. Their beauty destroyed them, but metamorphosis robbed them of human understanding, and with it of suffering. Thus, paradoxically, Helen can call them blessed by comparison to herself, whose beauty not only causes her pain still, but has destroyed Troy and Greece as well.

369 / 376 *Callisto* The name itself denotes beauty. Zeus found her among Artemis' maiden band, made love to her, and fathered a son, Arcas. In the best known version of the story (Ovid, *Metamorphoses* 2.401–95), Artemis, discovering the pregnancy, drives Callisto from her maiden band. Callisto is then turned into a bear by the jealous Hera (elsewhere by Artemis or Zeus himself; Euripides is not committed to a specific account). Zeus eventually immortalizes her and her son as the Great Bear and Small Bear constellations.

373 / 382 *the maiden, Merop's child* Nothing else is known about her except the name Cos, supplied by a late antique lexicographer. The association with the eponymous island may be reinforced by the fact that it bore the alternative name Meropis. What matters here, however, is what we are told: her beauty caused divine anger and led to her transformation, and thus her story offers a particularly meaningful parallel to Helen's.

So concludes the first large poetic and dramatic unit that encompasses the kommatic parodos, an iambic scene (253–329) and a second, astrophic *kommos* (330–385) between Helen and the Chorus, ending most unconventionally with an *exeunt omnes*. The unifying theme of this unparalleled structure is Helen's seemingly unending misfortune, the subject of sustained and variegated lament in word, music, movement, and gesture.

377 / 385 *Note on staging:* Helen now exits into the palace. The Chorus has preceded her, presumably beginning to leave when the meter changes at 369 / 375, but in any case early enough to complete its passage across the stage and through the main door of the stage building before Helen begins hers. Clearing the scene in this fashion is a rare procedure; extant tragedies show only five cases, of which four (including this one) prepare for the arrival of new characters to enact scenes that could not be played in the presence of a chorus. In this case, the presence of the Chorus would allow them to explain Helen's presence in Egypt to Menelaus, thus spoiling the recognition scene that Euripides is so carefully arranging (and postponing). Euripides makes the most of necessity by staging a whole new beginning in the form of Menelaus' "second prologue." Helen's exit presents a different kind of peculiarity by its non tragic treatment of supplication. The tragic suppliant, facing an immediate and usually deadly threat, would be expected to remain at the altar until

the threat is lifted. Helen's breach of this convention is one of a number of ironies that characterize her situation, one that Euripides again turns to dramatic advantage by letting Helen cast Menelaus briefly in the role of attacker (**541–55** / 541–56).

378–517 / 386–514 *"Second prologue"* A striking structural feature of *Helen* is its careful doubling of prologue-scenes: both Helen and Menelaus enter an empty scene and deliver monologues that provide necessary background; both then engage in dialogue (largely in the form of *stichomythia*, line-for-line exchange) with a minor character who appears only once and serves chiefly to complicate their situations: Helen with Teucer, who gives her the idea that Menelaus is dead, Menelaus with the Old Woman, who tells him of Theoclymenus' hostility to Greeks and the presence in at the palace of a Helen, daughter of Zeus, from Sparta. Helen's distress is expressed in lyrics that lead directly into the *parodos*; Menelaus considers his situation and masters his initial confusion in a second monologue, in which he concludes that the Old Woman must be speaking of a different woman of the same name. This parallel arrangement of scenes vividly links the stories of Helen and Menelaus as they are about to be reunited, while at the same time it also clearly differentiates them through self-presentation. Helen understands herself primarily as a victim of divine manipulation, condemned to suffer for wrongs she never committed but for which she must nevertheless bear responsibility, and comes to feel increasingly trapped and desperate. Menelaus, on the other hand, turns the pathos of his situation into quasi-comic bathos by wavering between boastful bravado and undignified self-abasement, and his resilience seems to be based in part on incapacity for hard thought. Although there has been much debate about the extent and significance of comic elements in the presentation of Menelaus, it is hard to deny that technique and tone in this scene are closely allied to those of comedy. The treatment of Menelaus in this play seems largely amused and mocking. His pathos is not so much in the fall from greatness that he invokes as in the revelation that he is the rather ludicrous victim of a meaningless war.

378–433 / 386–434 *Menelaus' monologue* Menelaus enters in rags; he himself makes this a symbol of his loss of status (**418–22** / 421–24), and, as if in confirmation, Helen will at first see only his mean appearance (**546** / 544–55, **555** / 554). Later, the rags will become part of the escape plan (**1092–93** / 1079–80, cf. **1208** / 1204), and finally they will be exchanged for the new garments that symbolize the restoration of Menelaus' fortunes (**1286–91** / 1281–84, **1304–8** /

1296–1300, **1369–79** / 1375–84). We do not know how realistic the cos-
tuming was, but to judge from Aristophanes' repeated jokes on the subject
of Euripidean "kings in rags," costumes that conveyed the pathos of a
character's situation were regarded as peculiarly Euripidean. In the extant
plays, Menelaus is the only male in rags; Electra, however, also appears in
rags in her name play, and she too laments her unsuitable clothing.

As in Helen's prologue speech, this monologue conveys basic information (the identity of the speaker, how he came to be here, and his present
circumstances), but since the scene has been set and the context fully
established, exposition can be more fully subordinated to self-character-
ization by the speaker. The essential information is simply that this is
indeed Menelaus, that he has lost his ship and most of his crew, and
that the phantom Helen is with the others who survived the shipwreck.
The rest is divided between boasting of past glory and lamenting present
misfortune. The unmistakable movement of the speech is encapsulated
by the contrast between the evocation of high birth and great deeds
with which it begins and the hope of a handout with which it ends.

378–87 / 386–96 Menelaus identifies himself by giving his pedigree, in the form of a
slightly comic variation on the proverbial wish never to have been born,
articulated as a counterfactual desire that Menelaus' grandfather,
Pelops, had died before begetting his father, Atreus. The text as transmitted specifies that Pelops should have died on the day that he was
served up to the gods by his own father, Tantalus, who killed him, cut
him up, and served him to the gods at a feast. Although one of the gods
(in some accounts Demeter, in others Ares or Thetis) ate his shoulder,
the others recognized the human flesh, reconstructed Pelops' body,
replacing his shoulder with one made of ivory, and brought him back
to life. The story seems out of place here because it spoils the point of
mentioning the chariot race that led to Pelops' marriage and hence to
the birth of Menelaus' father. It may be due to corruption of the original
text or an interpolation by someone (an actor?) who wished to add
pathos or mythological completeness by alluding to a famous story
about Pelops. It is at least possible, however, that the opening apostrophe
is merely Menelaus' attempt at embellishing his self-presentation with a
decorative bit of family history, and that the serving up of Pelops to the
gods is indicated as the logical moment for a premature end to his life.
The focus of Menelaus' apostrophe, at any rate, is his grandfather's best
known exploit, "that famous chariot / race" (**380–81** / 386–87; Euripides
could count on his audience to know that Pelops, by defeating Oenomaus, king of Pisa in the Peloponnese, won the hand of his daughter

Hippodameia. They would also be aware that Pelops bribed Oenomaus' charioteer, Myrtilus, to remove the linchpins from the king's chariot, thus causing him to be thrown and killed, and that Pelops subsequently killed Myrtilus. The earlier crimes that led to the family curse do not, it seems, obtrude upon Menelaus' pride in his noble ancestry.

390–91 / 395 *not as a tyrant, not by force* A claim whose mythological context is the oath sworn by all who sought Helen's hand to come to her aid should she ever be abducted. Elsewhere, it is always Agamemnon who is depicted as supreme commander of the Greek forces, but Agamemnon has no part in this story, and in any case both Menelaus' claim of sole leadership and his insistence that the Greeks fought of their own free will are meant to emphasize that his subsequent troubles are undeserved. That need not, however, exclude an impression of undeserved self-satisfaction in his tone.

395 / 400 *But I've been wandering ever since* At the end of the greatest military expedition known to the Greek world, only Menelaus remains unaccounted for and has not reached home. The model here comes from the famous opening of the *Odyssey*, where we are told that all those who survived war and sea have returned except for Odysseus (1.11–15). Altogether, lines 392–422 / 397–424 have a noteworthy concentration of verbal and thematic reminiscences of the *Odyssey*. Apart from possible specific allusions, such as that of lines 400–402 / 405–7 (Menelaus' repeated repulsion by storms just as he nears home) to *Odyssey* 9.79–81, and 403–10 / 408–13 (his reaching shore after shipwreck by clinging to the keel) to *Odyssey* 12.420–5, there is a marked resemblance between Menelaus' situation here and that of Odysseus in Book 6, when he arrives at the island of the Phaeacians after surviving shipwreck, covers his nakedness as best he can, and asks for help. The woman he encounters, however, is no Nausicaä, nor does he get what he seeks. Menelaus assumes the role of beggar out of need and with shame; Odysseus does so willingly and with a plan (Books 13–21). Thus, although Menelaus' initial appearance evokes more insistently than elsewhere the play's Odyssean subtext (see Introduction, p. 235), the comparison with Odysseus is not to his advantage, and if anything heightens the comic coloring of the scene.

394 / 399 *to name the dead* The Greek phrase "bearing the names of dead men" might equally well mean that those who escaped returned only after having been given up for lost. The thought would then resemble that of the Herald in Aeschylus, *Agamemnon* 671–75, who depicts each group of Achaeans dispersed by the great storm as speaking of the rest as lost. The use here of *onomata* ("names") in implicit contrast to the bodies that

perished reinforces an important element of the play's thematics of appearance and reality (see Introduction, p. 248).

395 / 400 *But I* Note that the death and sorrows of all the other Greeks are but a prelude to Menelaus' unique suffering.

400 / 404 *Libyan coast* Part of the tradition of Menelaus' wanderings already in Homer, *Odyssey* 4.85.

404 / 408 *my companions lost* Another Homeric detail (cf. *Odyssey* 12.417–19), but not strictly true here, since we learn at **425–26 / 426–27** that others reached shore with Menelaus. These companions, indeed, will play a decisive role in the escape from Egypt (see esp. **1578–99 / 1591–1613**). The evocation of the Homeric lone survivor is part of Menelaus' emphasis on his own misfortunes.

418–22 / 421–44 For Menelaus' costume and its significance, see note on **378–433**.

423 / 425–56 *the one who started it all* Like everyone else, Menelaus sees his wife above all as the cause of the war and thus of his own sufferings. The casual remark is telling; Helen's reputation is simply taken for granted.

432–81 / 435–82 *Menelaus–Old Woman scene* This exchange is, from Menelaus' point of view, unexpectedly disturbing, from that of the audience, surprisingly comic. It is a typically playful Euripidean variant of the sort of "door-opening scene" more frequent in comedy than in tragedy. It provides information, but also plentiful confusion. Beyond simply informing Menelaus that he is in Egypt, it underlines the extremity of his situation by warning him of Theoclymenus' intention to kill any Greek he finds. The Old Woman's revelation that there is a Spartan Helen in Egypt complicates his position considerably, both preparing for the coming recognition scene and providing the basis for prolonging it. Euripides develops Menelaus' reaction to all this with a brilliant balance of pathos and humor. In contrast to Menelaus' initial bravado, the scene juxtaposes his claim to Trojan glory with a verbal and physical defeat at the hands of an old Egyptian woman, and a slave at that, a situation unparalleled in extant Greek tragedy. The closest parallel in the tragic corpus is the scene between the drunken Heracles and a servant of Admetus in Euripides' *Alcestis*, known to have been presented in lieu of a satyr play, and the fierceness of the Old Woman would be quite at home in comedy. Here, it provides the sight, both amusing and pathetic, of an old slave woman rebuffing the hero of Troy verbally and even physically (**443 / 445**), reducing him to tears (**454 / 456**), and leaving him in utter confusion.

438 / 440 *You are a Greek* How does the Old Woman know? Menelaus has just spoken Greek but of course so do all the Egyptian characters. His "rags" are not likely to betray his origin. Perhaps the masking convention offered a way of distinguishing Greeks and foreigners, but in any case the audience, knowing who he is, would hardly have stopped to wonder.

443 / 445 *Stop pushing* The Greek here (*biâi*, literally, "with violence") signals the most extraordinary feature of the exchange: the use of force by a barbarian slave woman against a Greek man. Violence in tragedy is often threatened, but rarely carried out on stage, and then only to mark outrageous or extreme situations. Here, it is part of the play with appearance and reality (see Introduction, pp. 247–49): Menelaus may be a hero to the Greeks, but to the Old Woman he is nothing but a forbidden intruder (cf. 451–56 / 453–58).

447 / 449 *that should protect me* Literally, "an inviolable clan," expressing the stranger's claim to protection in a civilized land that was a fundamental element of Greek religious sensibility. The principle is well explained by Nausicaä for the archetypal castaway, Odysseus (Homer, *Odyssey* 6.206–8): "But this one comes here an unfortunate castaway, and we must take care of him; for all strangers and beggars are under the protection of Zeus."

449 / 451 *you'll do what I say* After an initial attempt at appeasement (440 / 442, "I'll do what you say"), Menelaus has got his back up and decides to resist, but by 456 / 458—despite his plea for pity and his tears—it is clear that the Old Woman has bested him.

456 / 458 *your old friends* Greek *philois*, "friends and family"; ironic, of course, since the one closest to Menelaus is here.

461 / 463 *It's my luck* The problem is not Egypt *per se*; but the fact that Menelaus, at the southern edge of the known world, is imaginatively as far from home as he can be. Ironically, of course, this is just where he needs to be.

467 / 469 *to earn such cordial disdain* Menelaus' question enfolds a series of ironies: he is himself the cause of the Hellenophobia, and despite the immediate disappointment of his hopes he will earn more than just disdain—the unexpected retrieval of the real Helen, who is named in the very next line.

468–74 / 470–76 This exchange lays the foundation for the comedy of errors that surrounds Menelaus' delayed recognition of Helen Ironically, the Old Woman's increasingly precise identification—"the daughter of Zeus" but also "Tyndareus' daughter" (for the dual parentage see note on 15–16), from Sparta in the land of Lacedaemon—only makes Menelaus more and more confused, as his asides indicate. Menelaus, given the information he needs to recognize the real Helen, will twice reject her in favor of the "apparent" Helen whom he has brought from Troy (**497–501 / 497–99, 568–94 / 567–93**); only the phantom's disappearance finally realigns appearance and reality (**626–27 / 622–23**).

475 / 477 The Old Woman abruptly breaks off the conversation (as did Teucer at **139 / 143**) and returns to her task of turning away Greeks. The cryptic remarks concluding with "You've come at the wrong time" will remain a "riddle" (**802 / 788**) to Menelaus until Helen explains.

479 / 480 *guest-gift* A guest (*xenos*) would ordinarily expect guest-gifts (*xénia*); for such gifts as part of proper hospitality (*xenía*), see, e.g., Homer, *Odyssey* 4.589ff., 13.7ff. The ironic suggestion of death as guest-gift has a specific Odyssean precedent: at 9.369–70, Polyphemus says that eating Odysseus after the rest of his companions "will be my guest-gift to you."

482–517 / 483–514 *Menelaus' monologue* Menelaus attempts to make sense of the news of a "second" Helen, eventually deciding that she must be an entirely different person, despite the extraordinary series of coincidences. His situation is parallel to that of Helen herself responding, after Teucer's departure, to what she takes to be news of Menelaus' death; the tone of this speech, however, is utterly different from that of Helen's lyric lament. Menelaus' difficulties are to be expected, but not his distinctly comic manner. Lines 483–496 enumerate all the coincidences and emphasize Menelaus' perplexity by ring composition ("What am I to make of this?" **482 / 483**; "I can't think what to say," **497 / 496**). Then the perplexity simply vanishes: Menelaus dismisses what he can't explain on the grounds that the world is a big place after all. And yet, immediately after accepting the idea of such multiplicity he reaffirms his trust in his own uniqueness and vast reputation (**503–6 / 501–4**). All this suggests a rather comic lack of mental clarity. Although some commentators are reluctant to allow any hint of humor or irony, it appears that Euripides has chosen here, as he will later when Menelaus devises a series of useless escape plans (**1047–61 / 1035–48**), to emphasize the contrast between his self-presentation as the hero of Troy and his obvious limitations.

503 / 501 *so uncouth* Literally, "with so barbarian a mind." The notion of savagery is taken up again at **508 / 506** in similar terms: the Greek word translated "savage" literally means "raw-minded." The note of Greek superiority continues in Menelaus' assumption that his name is universally known, but there is perhaps a touch of bathetic humor in the fact that the sentence ends not with something like "will render me appropriate honor," but with the food Menelaus hopes to get.

518–28 / 515–27 *Epiparodos* This term (known from Pollux, a rhetorician of the second century A.D.) denotes the re-entry song of a chorus that has left the stage. The length and form of our few surviving examples vary. Here, the Chorus performs a single brief stanza, reporting the happy news they have learned from Theonoe.

520–21 / 519–20 *the darkly shining / realm of gloom* "Realm of gloom" (*Erebos*) is a synonym for Hades already in Homer and Hesiod; "darkly shining" a type of compound color term favored by Euripides, here has special appropriateness as a willful oxymoron describing the lurid light of the underworld (cf. Milton's "darkness visible").

529–1120 / 528–1106 *First episode* Having staged two "prologues" that occupy fully 500 lines of the play, Euripides now gives us an unusually large and varied episode (as defined by Aristotle, *Poetics* 12.1452b20–1, "the whole part of tragedy that comes between whole choral songs"). The almost 600 lines that separate the brief *epiparodos* from the first *stasimon* or choral ode (**1121–72 / 1107–64**) are divided into a continuous series of scenes organized symmetrically and articulated by significant entrances and exits, with all but first and last concluded by a choral tag: 1) **529–597 / 528–96**, Helen and Menelaus; 2) **598–775 / 597–760**, Helen, Menelaus, Menelaus' servant (within this scene, Helen and Menelaus sing a "reunion duet," **629–713 / 625–97**); 3) **776–872 / 761–856**, Helen and Menelaus; 4) **873–1044 / 857–1031**, Helen, Menelaus, Theonoe; 5) **1045–1120 / 1032–1106**, Helen and Menelaus.

Section 1 leads to a crisis—Menelaus' refusal to recognize Helen as his wife—that is resolved in section 2 by news of the phantom Helen's disappearance brought by the servant. Reunion is followed in section 3 by the realization of the precarious situation. This crisis is alleviated in section 4 by Theonoe's decision not to betray Helen and Menelaus to her brother Theoclymenus. Section 5 brings the forging of a plan for escape. This elaborate structure, the heart of both the dramatic action and its thematic development, organizes the action into large, through-composed blocks and renders the traditional division into episodes of very limited use.

529–41 / 528–40 *Helen's return* The first part of Helen's speech largely repeats what the Chorus has just said, and this has led to sometimes extreme deletions by editors; the point of these lines is not to provide new information, but to see and hear Helen's reaction to the news we have just heard—her delight in hearing that Menelaus is alive and on his way and her remaining uncertainty about what the future holds once he has arrived. The shock of finding (as she believes) her path to the tomb blocked by an enemy gains effect from the emotional state revealed in these lines. Note that Helen's mention of returning to her "refuge" in the opening line of the speech already prepares for her perception of an attack, and that the obvious but effective irony of Helen's pathetic plea to the "absent" Menelaus, which comes (**541** / 540) just before she sees him—and mistakes him in his shabbiness for an attacker.

542–96 / 541–96 *Encounter of Helen and Menelaus* The reunion of husband and wife begins as a tragicomedy of errors, in which first Helen and then Menelaus literally run away from recognition of their spouses. The initial encounter is staged as a brief pursuit scene, like those found in conventional suppliant dramas when an enemy tries to seize the suppliant, but turned farcical because Menelaus is instead the long-awaited champion made momentarily to play the wrong role. (The closest parallel, however, is not from a suppliant play but from Euripides' *Electra* 215–27, where Orestes and Pylades appear from hiding and Electra, like Helen, believes that she has been ambushed and tries fruitlessly to escape.) Throughout the scene, stage action builds tension. Helen, moving towards Proteus' tomb, catches a glimpse of Menelaus and recoils in terror, thinking that she is being ambushed; this is one way in which Euripides makes dramatic use of Helen's absence from sanctuary. Helen tries to dart around Menelaus, finally reaching the tomb after he stands back, indignantly denying her charges. When she does recognize her husband, the audience may imagine that the long-delayed recognition is at hand, but it is now his turn to retreat from her, whom he imagines to be an apparition of some kind, and her turn to attempt to persuade him. Helen fails, and Menelaus' rejection appears to be final when he starts to depart, only to be stopped by the arrival of his servant with news of the other Helen.

The theme of appearance and reality (see Introduction, pp. 247–49) is given several new twists in this encounter. Helen is at first deceived by Menelaus' appearance; note her insistence on his ragged squalor, 544–45, 554. He recognizes and marvels at her appearance, but cannot believe that she is truly his wife, for he is sure that he has fought for and won the real Helen, and has her now safe in his cave. Ironically, Helen's insistence that he trust his eyes—trust to appearances—makes him more wary (580–51). Only the disappearance of the phantom, recounted by Menelaus' servant, will permit the realignment of appearance and reality that makes reunion possible at last.

544–45 / 543–44 *I must run...to reach the tomb* Actual physical contact with the place of refuge is the guarantor of the suppliant's safety; see note on **65–66**.

like a bacchant in the throes of the god's frenzy The god is Dionysus, whose ecstatic female devotees are known as "bacchants" after his cult-name Bacchos, and also as "maenads," precisely for their frenzy (cf. the Greek verb *mainomai*, "rage"). Horses and bacchants are also linked again at Euripides, *Bacchae* 165–66.

546 / 545 *to hunt me down* Ironic, since Menelaus is indeed "hunting" his wife, although he doesn't yet know it. For the metaphor of hunting Helen, see note on **51**.

555 / 554 *And yet that cloak* Helen focuses on Menelaus' dress rather than himself, a way of prolonging the moment of recognition, but also an extension of the ironic play of appearance and reality that his rags evoke.

561 / 560 *godly* Literally, "a god." The deification of abstractions is common in Euripides; the oddity here is that the deity is not a conventional personification. The usage underlines Helen's passionate agitation at the sight of her long-lost husband, a sense of awe at the fulfillment at last of her prayers.

562 / 561 A line dropped out here at some point in the transmission of the text. Fortunately, **562–67 / 561–66** are parodied in Aristophanes, *Thesmophoriazusae* 907–12 (see Introduction, p. 227), and **562 / 561** can thus be supplied by 907. The wording is probably, but not necessarily, identical; the sense is guaranteed by context. The loss of the line from our manuscripts is an apparent example of damage caused by repetition in successive lines of initial words. Unfortunately, it has proved impossible to render the witty way that 561–63, beginning *Hellenis, Hellenis, Helenê* ("Greek, Greek, Helen") suggest the recognition that doesn't happen.

566–67 / 565–66 *the most wretched of men* Because Greek *anêr* regularly means "husband" as well as "man," Helen hears "your most wretched husband" and responds openly as his wife.

568 / 567 *my robes* The Greek word *peplos* can be extended to any sort of covering, as in the phrase *nauphthorois...peploisin* below ("shipwreck rags," i.e., attire salvaged from shipwreck, **1529 / 1539–40**). Used unmodified by Menelaus, however, and after considerable attention has been drawn to his rags, it would be hard to hear without a touch of comic irony. And although Menelaus' reaction might be understood as that of a self-consciously dignified man to uninvited physical contact, there is something comic in the fact that it is now Menelaus who feels threatened.

570 / 569 *torchbearing Hecate* This goddess is depicted as a maiden, like Artemis, with whom she comes to be identified, but carries torches rather than the bow. Her pathways are those of night and magic, and her attendants are of the spirit world.

  kindly phantoms Menelaus imagines that he is seeing a vision of the kind associated with Hecate, and utters an apotropaic prayer. The irony here, of course, is in what we know but Menelaus does not: that the wife he fought for and won is the phantom, and that the Helen whom he supposes to be a phantom is his real wife.

571 / 570 *queen of crossroads* Where Hecate's shrines were characteristically located.

576–82 / 575–81 These lines continue to ring the changes on the appearance/reality antithesis (see Introduction, pp. 247–49). Menelaus first wonders whether his eyes rather than his mind are deceiving him; the implicit contrast is between the hallucinations just pondered, which would be a sign of god-sent madness, and the possibility of simple mistaken identity. The latter is figured, however, as a different form of ill health: "my eyes are wrong" (literally, "my eye is diseased"). Helen responds with the language of appearance ("you look ... don't you think you see"), and when Menelaus admits that she *seems* to be Helen, she presses the point, urging to accept the evidence of his own eyes. Menelaus' response shows that he has decided that it is precisely his eyes (i.e., her appearance) that he cannot trust: "My eyes are the problem" (literally, "it is there that we are diseased"). Ironically, what should prove the truth of Helen's claim—her singular, unmistakable appearance—causes bewilderment and doubt.

585 / 584 *thin air* aether; see note on **44**.

589 / 588 *name ... body* A characteristic expression of the reality/appearance dichotomy; see note on **67–69**.

594 / 593 *The suffering at Troy* This line reveals the full pathos of Menelaus' situation: if the woman he confronts is Helen, then his sufferings (and all the sorrows of Troy) were endured for nothing—as the phantom Helen will herself imply (**608–12 / 608–11**), his servant will remark (**722 / 707**), and even the rather dense Theoclymenus will also see (**1224 / 1220**). With this bitter turn, the recognition scene appears to end, against expectation, in failure.

598–775 / 597–760 *Messenger scene and "reunion duet"* The second scene in the series that makes up the first episode (see note on **529–1120**) brings the reunion of husband and wife at last. The entrance of Menelaus' old retainer begins a messenger scene divided in two by the lyrics that constitute the actual reunion. The messenger speech itself is a very brief account of the phantom Helen's disappearance, followed by the servant's surprise at finding her again, as he supposes. Comparison with the more typical messenger scene at 1512–618 shows both how much less elaborate the "message" itself is here, and how much more emphasis is given to the reaction of the messenger. For Menelaus, the servant's account is the missing piece of the puzzle that makes recognition possible at last. Thus, it is only after the extended reunion that the messenger scene is resumed, with a closing dialogue devoted largely to the servant's response to his newly won understanding about Helen. This extended exchange is and its long separation from the messenger speech is unparalleled.

598–600 / 597–99 Euripides connects Menelaus' (aborted) exit with his servant's entrance in search of him; the resulting staging presumably made it more natural for the servant to give his report before seeing Helen at Proteus' tomb.

602 / 601 *There are no words to describe it* Literally, "having less the name [i.e. "amazing"] than the deed," another ringing of the changes on appearance and reality.

605 / 604 *old sorrows* Menelaus takes his servant to be making something like the same complaint about the futility of all his efforts that he himself made at **395–402 / 400–407**.

606–25 / 605–21 *Messenger speech* The news of the phantom's disappearance, which makes clear that the Helen Menelaus has just rejected is the real one, is presented in a manner that has both tragic and comic overtones: on the one hand, the servant's failure to understand the meaning of his own message, embodied in his "discovery" that Helen's escape was mere trickery, is amusing; on the other, his account of the phantom's last words evokes again the meaninglessness of the sufferings at Troy. Crucial as the servant's report is, his reaction to Helen carries the emotional weight here, and it is through him that we see how a simple man—a slave who fought at Troy (see **750–51 / 734–35**)—feels about Helen and the war. The servant's rather comic bluster when he sees Helen is followed in the final words of the speech by an explicit reference to the suffering she has caused. The servant cannot yet separate the Helen he sees from her phantom, but the words of the phantom's farewell that he reports links the two more closely than ever, her own words picking up closely what Helen herself has said (e.g., **34–35 / 35–36, 51–52 / 52–53, 196 / 198, 270–72 / 270–72**).

606 / 605 *thin air* aether again, from which the phantom was made and to which she now returns. At **615 / 613** the phantom calls sky (equivalent here to aether) her father; paternity here is not to be understood but metaphorically for the living substance out of which the phantom was made.

618 / 616 *Oh, daughter of Leda* The servant has moved far enough towards center stage to see Helen, whom he has no way of distinguishing from the Helen who has just escaped from the cave. (Alternatively, Helen may come towards him in excitement at what she has overheard.)

626 / 622 *There's the proof* Literally, "this is that," a colloquial recognition formula.

628 / 624 *back to my embrace* Menelaus moves towards the embrace that he rejected at 567; this line provides a transition to a duet that stages and celebrates it.

629–713 / 625–97 *Reunion duet* Recognition is now capped by a sequence, partly sung and partly spoken, in which the long-separated couple first celebrate their happiness (625–59) and Menelaus then questions Helen about her disappearance and learns the cause and nature of her sufferings (660–97). The duet thus moves from present joy to the array of past sorrows associated with Troy. Eleven Euripidean duets survive analogous to this one in their astrophic form and combination of sung and spoken verse. The closest parallels are the roughly contemporary reunion duets of mother and son in *Ion* 1437–1509 and of brother and sister in *Iphigenia in Tauris* 827–99. This duet, however, remains unique in some important respects; the fact that it is the only reunion duet of husband and wife affects both tone and content.

Precisely how such musical scenes were performed is impossible to reconstruct with any certainty, but the lyric meters used seem to allow passage among song, recitative, and spoken, and thus among differing degrees of emotional intensity, delivery without abrupt rupture of continuity. It is worth noting that the two main sections of the duet are musically distinct: in **629–70 / 625–60** both Helen and Menelaus have a mixture of sung and spoken verses, whereas **671–713 / 661–97** are cast in what has been called "punctuated monody": Helen's part is entirely in lyric meters, to which Menelaus responds in single iambic trimeters, with the exception of three brief outbursts.

634 / 628 *I clasp him again in my loving arms* Physical embrace is part of all surviving reunion scenes, but nowhere else is it as prolonged or as emphatically present in the text. Notice in particular the repetition of the exchange I hold you . . . And *I* hold *you* (**634–35** / 628–30, **640–44** / 634–37, **656–596** / 650–52, **665–67** / 657–58), a strong indicator of the mutuality of Helen's and Menelaus' emotions.

635–36 / 630 *so many stories / to tell between us* Menelaus has discovered that there is a whole new tale of Helen that "fits" (**626 / 623**) but must still be reconciled with his own stories, the past as he experienced it.

646 / 640 *called blessèd, your blessèd bride* The Dioscuri are pictured as pronouncing a blessing, the repetition here conveying both the high emotions connected with the situation and, perhaps, a ritual repetition of the blessing.

648–49 / 644 *Good / that came from bad* Literally, "the evil good," an oxymoron that expresses the fortune in what has until now seemed only misfortune.

654–69 / 648–59 The celebratory half of the duo comes to a conclusion with reflections on the unexpectedness of the reunion, and this line of thought leads naturally to Menelaus' question about Helen's disappearance (670 / 660), with which the second part of the duo begins, and the focus shifts to the pain of the past.

661 / 653 *the goddess* Hera, whose responsibility for the fashioning of the phantom Menelaus has just learned about (587 / 586) and is now beginning to assimilate. The reunion not only has confirmed the truth of the strange story of the phantom but also begins to give shape to a divine purpose behind the events that has been hidden until now.

670–713 / 660–97 In the second main division of the duet, Helen evokes her sorrows by lyrical rather than narrative procedures, with Menelaus' role limited to questioning and prompting.

675 / 664 *I spit away* Spitting, a simple from of self-purifications, becomes a common apotropaic gesture, and this evidently lies behind a metaphorical use in the sense of "spurn" or "loathe."

677 / 665 *there is pleasure in hearing sorrows* A version abbreviated to the point of paradox of the well-attested notion that there is pleasure in recalling one's sufferings after they are safely over. In this truncated variant, concerned with the sufferings of others, Euripides comes close to expressing the perennial paradox of tragic pleasure. Cf. 778–79.

690–93 / 676–78 The judgment of Paris appears here allusively as a lament; the background is being laid for the answer that actually begins in 680.

697 / 683 *I take it* This is Menelaus' deduction from 587 / 586.

700–706 / 684–90 Helen evokes Leda's suicide, of which Teucer had informed her at 128–31 / 133–36 and which she had then repeatedly lamented; here as before she emphasizes that it was caused by "my supposed disgrace" (literally, "my ill-wed shame"), i.e., the belief that she had left Menelaus for Paris. Then, in answer to Menelaus' question about their daughter, Helen repeats in lyrical form the unhappy surmise she made earlier to the Chorus; see note on 282.

707 / 691 *you sacked my house* An ironic reversal, since it was Menelaus who sacked the house of Paris.

712–13 / 696 *I left… / but not for a marriage of shame* Literally, "I left, yet did not leave" using a verb associated with Helen's adultery from Homer (*Iliad* 3.174–75) and the lyric poets onward to construct a paradoxical defense of her departure. The phrasing negates a false appearance, but the idea is complex, since one can understand both as translated here, "I left, but not for a marriage of shame" (cf. 678–80 / 666–68) and "I left and did not leave for a shameful marriage," both of which in different ways accurately express Helen's situation.

714–15 / 698–99 The Chorus Leader's distich marks the end of the duet and refocuses attention from the sorrows of the past to the future of the reunited pair.

716–75 / 700–758 The old servant, who has witnessed the reunion but does not yet understand what he has seen, is given assurances about its meaning, reflects on what he now knows, and is then sent back to report to the other Greeks. The scene has little bearing on the plot; its function is rather to emphasize, through the reactions of a sympathetic third party, that knowledge of the truth does in fact restore Helen's reputation, and at the same time to restate the futility of the war fought over her phantom.

723 / 708 *Hera's handiwork, because of the goddesses' contest* An elliptical phrase, but sufficient to connect the "beauty contest" (about which the servant can be expected to know) with the new element of Hera's vengeful reaction; Menelaus in effect summarizes what Helen told him at 690–97 / 676–82.

726–73 / 711–57 The servant's speeches are undeniably wordy. He is a minor figure, and his moralizing has often been criticized for irrelevance. Many lines have been excised by editors as superfluous. Inevitably, subjective judgments about the purpose of the scene must be made before a decision can be reached about what should or should not be cut. It is not at all clear that we should expect the servant to say just what is necessary; he is struggling with a realization that has robbed years of toil and loss of their meaning. Some of what he says may well reflect a penchant for sententious utterance that is a trait of Euripdean servants elsewhere. Certain reflections relate to important themes of our play. On the other hand, sententious passages are particularly liable to interpolation, and some lines might easily have slipped into our text from a parallel passage written in the margin of an early exemplar. For the rest, much depends on how much sententiousness and irrelevance one thinks appropriate to the speaker or possible for Euripides. This translation gives the passage in its entirety.

726–34 / 711–19 The servant begins with a general reflection about the unpredictability of the divine and the uncertainty of fortune, then applies it to the cases of Menelaus and Helen, who struggled so long and accomplished nothing, until now good fortune has found them of its own accord.

726 / 711 *the path of the god is devious and hard to trace* Literally, "what an intricate and inscrutable thing god is"; "god" (singular) does not imply a monotheistic conception, but rather, as the neuter predicate in the Greek suggests, an abstract notion of divinity or divine power operating in the world; see further note on 918. Similar language is also applied to fortune, which may or may not be considered a deity.

733 / 717 *with slanders* Literally, "in words," as opposed to deeds, i.e., in the cost to your reputation; once more, and from another character, an affirmation of the disjunction between Helen's reputation and her true nature.

735–41 / 720–25 The servant draws the conclusion that Helen is innocent both of the deeds for which she is known and of the shame that they have brought to her parents and brothers; note that he puts the shame in first place. Now, at the appropriate moment, we learn of an old tie to Helen: the servant recalls his joy as a torchbearer in her wedding procession.

742–49 / 726–33 Reflecting that only a "bad" (*kakos* can also mean "base-born") slave would not share in his master's joys and sorrows, the servant expands on his wish to be a "noble" slave, with "a free man's mind, if not the name." This is yet another version of the appearance/reality disjunction (see Introduction, pp. 247–49); the wish to preserve his integrity despite the powerlessness of slavery aligns this old slave with Helen.

750–57 / 734–43 Menelaus dismisses his servant with orders to return to the other survivors of the shipwreck and inform them of how things stand, thus preparing the role that they will play in the escape from Egypt. These lines thus present a shift of theme from reunion to rescue.

758–73 / 744–57 The servant, before he disappears, reflects on what the recognition scene has taught him: the complete futility of prophecy. Note, however, that this does not entail irreligiosity, but rather a lack of trust in the authenticity of divination and diviners (769–73 / 753–57). The Chorus Leader expresses agreement 774–77 / 758–60, but of course they know that Theonoe, at least, is a prophet who can be trusted (314–18 / 317–21), and at no point in the play are her powers in doubt.

763–66 / 749–51 *Calchas . . . Helenus* The most important seers on the opposing sides at Troy, neither of whom divined the gods' deceit.

776–872 / 761–856 Next in the series of scenes that compose the first episode (see note on 529–1117), a spoken dialogue shifts our attention from reunion to the problem of escape. Helen informs Menelaus of the threat that now faces him at the hands of Theoclymenus and then brings him to recognize that their best hope of safety lies in convincing Theonoe not to share her prophetic knowledge of Menelaus' presence in Egypt with her brother. The scene moves to its conclusion with a mutual decision on suicide before surrender; Menelaus imagines a battle to the death that will make his death a glorious one. As yet, no realistic plan for escape is possible; everything now depends on Theonoe.

778 / 762 *survive after Troy* Helen's inquiries about the perils from which Menelaus has been saved serve primarily as an ironic foil to the danger from which rescue is far from certain. The passive voice of the verb *sôizein* (save), translated "survive" here but variously elsewhere, is used repeatedly in this segment of the play to emphasize the rescue theme: 757 / 743, 793 / 778, 809 / 795, 829 / 815, 879 / 863.

778–79 / 763–64 For the sentiment, cf. 677 / 665.

780–86 / 766–71 Menelaus' answer avoids a detailed account of his travels, which at this point would only delay the action, by enunciating his unwillingness to dwell on past sufferings. He alludes first to the storm that destroyed part of the fleet and separated him and his men from the other survivors (for the "shipwrecks in the Aegean" see note on 123), then to the subsequent destruction of another part of the fleet by the false beacons Nauplius set up on Euboea (for the story, see note on 1132–35); and to fruitless landings in Crete, Libya (mentioned already at 400 / 404), and at "Perseus' fabled cliff." The name evidently refers to the place where Perseus rescued Andromeda from the sea-monster, but its location is uncertain. Herodotus, *Histories* 2. 15 places it at the western edge of the Nile delta, which we would expect to be the location assumed here; but fragment 145 of Euripides' own *Andromeda*, performed with *Helen* (see Introduction, note 1), suggests a setting in the far west. "I see the monster speeding to his maiden-banquet from the Atlantic sea."

794–807 / 779–94 Even at a moment of high emotion, Euripides permits notes of ironic humor to surface, as in the scene with the Old Woman (see note on 432–81), to which this passage alludes at 802–7 / 788–93. Much of the wit is lodged in playful allusion to the tradition surrounding Helen herself. Menelaus, hearing that he faces death, tells Helen, "You'll be the death of me" (794 / 779), the very charge that has falsely blighted her reputation (cf., e.g., what Teucer says at 73–75 / 72–74). When Helen informs him that he stands in the way of a new marriage for her, he replies to the woman desired by all men and, in the tradition, married both to Paris and Deiphobus after leaving him, "You mean that someone wants to marry my wife?" (**798** / 784). Menelaus' evocation of his humiliation as a beggar at Proteus' door strikes a chord with Helen, who seems as susceptible to social disgrace as Menelaus, and prompts her outburst, "I feel such shame!" (**805** / 791). Menelaus excuses himself with a version of the appearance/reality antinomy that had earlier caused him such confusion: he did indeed beg, "although without the name" (see note on 806). The dialogue as a whole suggests a Menelaus who, as the archetypal cuckold, can hardly believe that Helen has indeed been faithful.

799 / 785 *trying to force me* In classical Greek, *hubris*, refers primarily to violence, extreme insolence, or outrage; it is thus often used of rape or attempted rape. The phrase translated here by the verb "force" (*hubrin hubrizôn*) is a doubling of the concept, "forcing force," favored by Euripides. It does not, however, state unequivocally whether Helen did in fact succumb, an element of ambiguity that Menelaus will pursue at 808 / 794.

806 / 792 *what it was, although without the name* An amusing use of the appearance/reality antinomy so characteristic of this play to assert that the *appearance* of propriety (*onoma*, "name") was upheld despite the *reality* of the situation (*ergon*, "deed")—for which see **427-33** / 428-34).

810 / 796 *what proof* Literally, "persuasion" or "means of persuasion." Menelaus is not yet ready to accept the "new" Helen at face value.

814 / 800 *is this some foreign custom?* For Greeks, not even the tombs of heroes would customarily have the same status as altars of the gods, or be used for refuge by suppliants. Menelaus' question is therefore natural enough and may allude to the Egyptian cult of the dead. What Helen is doing is, however, entirely comprehensible in Greek terms. She replies that the tomb has protected her like a temple, and tragedy elsewhere offers examples of this kind of connection between tomb and altar: in Aeschylus, *Libations Bearers* 106, Agamemnon's tomb is revered like an altar; in Sophocles, *Ajax* 1171-81, Ajax's son is made a suppliant at his father's body; in Euripides, *Alcestis* 995-99, Alcestis' tomb is given honors like those given the gods. All these instances emphasize the sacred status of the deceased, and Proteus, too, is treated throughout the play as a figure of exemplary wisdom and piety (see also note on **47**).

820 / 806 *I sacked Troy because of you!* Another example of the ironies of the Troy theme in this play. Menelaus sacked Troy for Helen, but not for *this* Helen.

825 / 811 *You'll see* At **837 / 823**, Helen explains that Theonoe can reveal Menelaus' presence to Theoclymenus; when at **1058–59 / 1043–44**, Menelaus once again proposes killing the king, Helen reminds him that Theonoe will not be silent if he tries.

830 / 816 *Bribery, . . . or boldness, or smooth talk?* Literally, "bought, ventured, or by speech?"—a somewhat ill-assorted list from the mouth of a hero, more reminiscent of fifth-century Realpolitik than the Homeric warrior ethos. (Thucydides, *History of the Peloponnesian War* 3.40 has the demagogue Cleon speak with scorn of "hope that trusts in speech or is bought by bribes," and "boldness" covers acts both daring and foolhardy.

834 / 820 *Some oracle* Greek *phêmê* refers to inspired or prophetic utterance, here by metonymy for a prophetess who, Menelaus assumes, dwells in the palace. A parallel of sorts is offered by mention in Aeschylus of "household prophets," (*Agamemnon* 409) perhaps official domestic seers; and of dream interpreters in the palaces of Clytemnestra (*Libation Bearers* 37) and Atossa (*Persians* 226).

836 / 822 *The name's oracular* For its meaning, see note on 8–9.

844 / 830 *This is a job for you* Helen will take the initiative with Theonoe, as indeed throughout the plotting of escape, but the primary function of Menelaus' deferral here is to set up the sequence of appeals that the two will make to Theonoe; see note on **873–1044 / 857–1031**. This phrase recurs, in a context saturated with comic irony, at **1295 / 1288**.

    woman to woman Literally, "woman is a fitting thing for woman," a version of the Greek commonplace that like attracts like, as old as Homer, *Odyssey* 17.218 ("a god leads like to like always") and repeated in a series of proverbs preserved by Aristotle, Plutarch, and others.

845 / 831 *my arms around her knees* The gesture regularly used in supplicating a person. Knees and chin are the parts of the body characteristically touched, the contact forming a ritual bond that requires response.

848 / 834 *You betrayer!* Helen's coupling of Menelaus' death with her forced marriage to Theoclymenus provokes an outburst of jealousy (the lingering effect of the "old" Helen on her much-tried husband), but the new Helen prefers death to betrayal, and swears an oath to die with her husband (**849–51 / 836–37**).

849–70 / 835–54 The suicide pact is open to very different interpretations, but such elements as Menelaus' deep mistrust of Helen's fidelity and veracity and his characteristically overblown evocation of a renewed Trojan War (see note on **856–70**) suggest that some degree of amused detachment is not an entirely inappropriate response. (Contrast the properly pathetic suicide threat of 348–59.)

855 / 841 *repute* Having decided on death, Helen wishes to achieve it heroically; and indeed a suitably noble death now seems to be her only way to restore her reputation, to bring it in line with her true story. She chooses, however, the word *doxa* ("seeming," "opinion," "reputation"), which ironically evokes the world of appearances from which she is attempting to escape.

856–70 / 842–54 Menelaus grandly imagines the resistance he will offer at Proteus' tomb as "an all-out war to defend your married honor" (858 / 843–44) thus subsuming the coming struggle to the Trojan War itself, ostensibly fought to win Helen back. He then elaborates the theme, insisting that since he caused so much pain at Troy he should be ready to die himself. This neatly, perhaps too neatly, reverses the usual blame of Helen herself for all the suffering at Troy. Menelaus' combination of rhetorical exaggeration and self-aggrandizement is reminiscent of his initial appearance.

859–60 / 845 *I'll not / put the fame I won at Troy to shame* Menelaus is as intent on retaining his honor as the conqueror of Troy as Helen is in reclaiming hers as a faithful wife. Cf. 822 / 808.

862–66 / 847–50 Menelaus cites three parents as exemplary sufferers of loss in the Trojan War: a mother, Thetis, whose coming grief for her son is foreshadowed in her every appearance in the *Iliad*, and two fathers, Telamon (for his reaction to the suicide of Ajax, see 87–101 / 90–104) and Nestor, the aged king of Pylos, whose favorite son, Antilochus, also a prominent warrior in the *Iliad*, was killed at Troy. From the surviving summary, we know that in the *Aethiopis*, one of the poems of the Trojan epic cycle, Antilochus sacrificed his own life to save his father's. The group of fallen heroes seems to be traditional, but Euripides adds to its pathos by emphasizing the parents, who might especially resent the survival of the man who sent their sons to their deaths. That the enduring sorrow of the parents contrasts with the illusory cause of their children's death is unstated, but there is a reminder implicit in the concluding question "Shall I not think my wife worth dying for?" that the heroes died—as they believed—for someone else's wife.

867 / 851 *if the gods are wise* Need not express skepticism about divine wisdom; Menelaus explains his decision to die if necessary on the basis of a view of the differential treatment in death of heroes and cowards that

wise gods would enforce, and he implicitly claims that they do. The contrast between the brave man's and the coward's fate is expressed in terms that would have strong emotional associations for Euripides' audience. The image of the brave man's burial takes up a commonplace of funerary epigram, "may the earth lay light upon you." The fate Menelaus recommends for cowards, on the other hand, suggests the treatment reserved for traitors and those convicted of serious sacrilege under the Athenian law in force during Euripides' day.

871–72 / 855–56 *the fortunes of Tantalus' tribe* For the story of Tantalus, here as often taken as the beginning of the curse on the house of Atreus, see note on 378–87 / 386–96. The Chorus's prayer for release from troubles is answered dramatically by the next round of trouble, part of an elaborate effort to heighten the sense of danger in the encounter with Theonoe.

873–1044 / 857–1031 *Theonoe scene* Next in the series of scenes that compose the first episode (see note on 529–1120) is the "Theonoe scene," whose function in and larger meaning for the play as a whole have been much discussed (see Introduction, p. 256). It begins almost precisely at the mid-point of the play and divides the recognition and reunion plot from the intrigue and escape plot to come. Thus, on any reading, it provides a crucial turning point. Both the figure of Theonoe and her role in the drama show Euripides at his most innovative. Dramatically, the scene is constructed like a formal debate (*agôn*) in which an arbiter listens to opposing pleas and judges between them; here, however, both Helen and Menelaus are pleading for the same thing—that Theonoe not betray Menelaus' arrival to her brother, Theoclymenus. Helen appeals as a suppliant; Menelaus vehemently refuses that model. Theonoe announces her decision not as a judgment between opposing arguments, but as a decision motivated by her sense of justice and of her own honor. Theonoe's knowledge "of all / that is and is to come" (10–11 / 14) permits her to connect her decision to a debate among the gods themselves about Menelaus' fate. Her intimate knowledge of the workings of the divine and what we may call her personal spirituality give this scene a different tone from everything that comes before and after.

878–80 / 862–64 Helen's anxiety heightens the tension surrounding Theonoe's response to Menelaus' presence; the mention of "foreign swords" emphasizes an irony of his predicament: victory at Troy seems only to have won him a further, doomed battle in Egypt.

881–88 / 865–72 Theonoe's entrance will have struck the Athenian audience as exotic. She is preceded by at least two female attendants. One carries burning sulfur to purify the upper reaches of the air. The second attendant uses the flames of a torch to purify the ground. Greek use of sulfur for cleansing and purification appears already in Homeric epic (*Iliad* 16.228, *Odyssey* 22.480–81), but the rite here has no close Greek parallel. Euripides has Ethiopians purifying their doorways with scented fumes in a fragment of *Phaethon*, but he may also have known of an Egyptian ritual described by Plutarch in which priests burn incense resin and myrrh to disperse the heaviness and turbidity of the air.

895–96 / 878–79 *the gods will. . . / debate your fate* Theonoe offers the startling revelation that she is privy to a divine debate "before the throne of Zeus," implying that Zeus will preside over and judge an *agôn*, thus suggesting a parallel between the proceedings on Olympus and the scene about to be enacted before our eyes, as well as (since the contestants are Hera and Aphrodite) a kind of reprise of the judgment of Paris.

897 / 880 *Hera, your enemy of old* Not a personal hatred of Menelaus, but the result of Hera's anger at Aphrodite over the loss of the earlier *agôn*, the beauty contest on Mount Ida.

902–3 / 885–86 *to keep the world from knowing how she bought her beauty-prize* Ironically, although Hera is responsible for making a mockery of the marriage of Helen and Paris, it is Aphrodite who fears exposure of the phantom, because it would convict her of weakness in failing to carry out the bargain she made with Paris. She reacts, in short, with the fear of ridicule so characteristic of the mentality of traditional heroic culture.

904 / 887 *The decision rests with me* Theonoe has told us that the final decision as to whether Menelaus will survive and return home lies with the gods, but if she betrays Menelaus' presence to Theoclymenus, she will foreclose any hope of rescue. Thus, the importance of her decision remains paramount. Still, she can only make his homecoming possible, not certain, and she will conclude by urging Helen and Menelaus to pray both to Hera and Aphrodite for their favor (1037–40 / 1024–27).

910–56 / 894–943 Helen's plea has a clear formal structure. After an introduction which emphasizes her position as suppliant (reinforced by the gestural language implied in her words), she pleads on behalf of Menelaus, then for herself, and closes with an appeal to the noble tradition of Theonoe's father Proteus, whose tomb is nearby. There is an element of ring-composition in Helen's reminder of her status as suppliant (910–11 / 895–96; 953 / 939). Within this framework, Helen deftly varies the emotional tone, blending increasingly personal pleas with appeals to moral principle and to Theonoe's innate sense of justice.

918 / 903 *the god* Can refer, depending on context, to a particular deity or to a more general conception of "divinity" or "divine power" operating in the world (see the notes on **726** and **1143–50**), though of course it is never equivalent in classical texts to God with a capital G.

923 / 909 *Though it made me wretched...helped me* Literally, "advantageously, although miserably." The contrast expresses a fundamental duality of Helen saved on the one hand from betraying her marriage-bed, but subject on the other to all the shame and suffering her phantom caused.

928–36 / 915–23 Helen develops an argument she had already touched on at **916–17 / 900–902**, equating justice with Theonoe's father and injustice with her brother (note the prominence "just" and "unjust" in **933–36 / 920–23**). Helen appeals to Theonoe's honor as well as her moral rectitude by pointing out that if her prophetic gift cannot recognize the demands of justice, it is something base and shameful. See further the note on **1011–17**.

938 / 925 *strike a blow for justice in the bargain* Literally, "giving a work of justice as an appendage." With appealing modesty, Helen asks for her own rescue as an act of justice incidental to Theonoe's sparing of her husband.

945 / 932 *they'll give back my good name* Literally, "they will lead me back again once more to virtue," emphasizing the desired rehabilitation with double pleonasm. Helen's reputation is clearly what is at stake here, but the fact that she says "virtue" suggests once more that the phantom has implicated her in guilt despite her objective innocence. *To sôphron*, "virtue," "temperance", "sanity," etc., can refer specifically to sexual self-control, and given the nature of Helen's reputation, its use in her regard would almost necessarily raise the issue of her chastity.

947–95 Menelaus' plea, like Helen's, has a clear formal structure: an introduction in which he rejects the posture of suppliant in favor of one befitting the conqueror of Troy, and challenges Theonoe to make her decision accordingly; pleas to Proteus and Hades to return Helen to her rightful husband; a threat, directed to Theonoe, of polluting Proteus' tomb by killing Helen and himself upon it; and a concluding appeal to Theonoe's sense of nobility and justice.

960 / 947 *I'm not going to fall at your feet in tears* Menelaus refuses to play the role of suppliant, affecting instead a more heroic pose. The emphatic "I" with which his speech begins already distances him from Helen's more submissive behavior. Menelaus refuses to shed tears, although he recognizes that it is not unbefitting for the highborn to weep when they are in trouble, as indeed Homeric heroes tend to do. Implicit in this choice is

the notion that tears and pity show feminine weakness (cf. "womanly tears," 1004 / 991), but there is a contrast between Menelaus' attitude here and his apparently copious shedding of tears in his comic exchange with the Old Woman (454–56 / 456–58). It is not clear whether we are to smile as we remember the earlier scene or to regard Menelaus' attitude here as a sign that he is regaining his self-confidence and self-control as he warms to the struggle for his wife and his life—probably a bit of both.

971 / 958 *you will stand revealed as a craven woman* The Greek adjective *kakê* implies that Theonoe would prove to be both a coward and a woman of low birth, unable to carry out justice and thus lacking her father's nobility.

973 / 960 *likeliest to touch you* Menelaus, moving away self-consciously from his direct challenge of Theonoe to an attempt to win her over, kneels at last, but before Proteus' tomb. Invocation of the heroic dead is not new or unusual, but Menelaus' plea is surely for Theonoe's ears, and it is hard not to feel some amusement at his elaborate appeal to the father for what he himself says only the daughter can give. On the other hand, Theonoe herself clearly takes Menelaus' "reproaches" at the tomb to heart (1022–23 / 1009–10).

977 / 964 *in your safekeeping* Picks up Helen's argument at 923–25 / 910 that she was entrusted to Proteus "to keep me safe / for my husband," raising the stakes, as it were, by attributing the intention directly to Zeus, not merely to his servant Hermes.

982 / 969 *Hades, lord of the world below* Although the dead and the gods who dwell below are often addressed in prayer, the only other certain example of a prayer addressed to Hades occurs in a fragment of Euripides' lost *Cresphontes*.

984 / 970 *on my wife's account* Despite Menelaus' knowledge of Helen's innocence, he continues to think of the war, just as she does, as fought for her sake. This would hardly seem odd to the Athenian audience, so deeply is the theme embedded in the tradition, from Homer (e.g., *Iliad* 9.339) onwards and often reflected in Euripides' other Trojan plays. It speaks once again, however, to the complex interlocking of the real Helen with her disastrous phantom.

991 / 977 *I swore an oath* See 849–58 / 835–44.

993–1000 / 981–87 Greek understandings of both supplication and pollution are at play in these lines. Suppliants are safe only if they remain in their sanctuary (see note on 65–66), but an enemy might force them to leave by starving them out without actually violating their immunity.

If the suppliants were to die, however, their corpses would pollute the shrine in which they were taking refuge. This gives suppliants a potential weapon—the threat of suicide in the sacred precinct. Menelaus makes the most of this by threatening to stain the tomb of Theoclymenus' and Theonoe's father with his and Helen's blood, thus also depriving the king of his chosen bride. Cf. Aeschylus, *Suppliant Women* 455–67, where the daughters of Danaus threaten King Pelasgus with terrible pollution by hanging themselves on the statues of the gods at the altar where they are supplicating.

994 / 981 *trap us* Literally, "hunt," a verb closely associated with Theoclymenus and his pursuit of Helen (see note on 51).

1003–8 / 991–95 These lines create a kind of ring composition by returning to Menelaus' decision not to resort to tears and the choice he has set out for Theonoe, and they provide a suitable conclusion by urging her to heed his words and do what is just. There are elements of ring composition in the conclusion to Helen's plea (see note on 910–56), and again more prominently in Theonoe's final distich (see 1041–42 / 1028–29).

1011–41 / 998–1029 Theonoe's reply, calm and direct, makes clear that she has already reached her decision. The first part of the speech gives the grounds for that decision: her own nature prompts her to place reverence, honor, and justice above all and thus to vote with Hera rather than Aphrodite; and she sees the fact that her father would have given Helen back to Menelaus as a moral obligation that outlasts his individual life. These lines strike a note of almost mystical solemnity in their evocation of a continuing collective consciousness after death. The second part of the speech sets out the terms of the decision—Theonoe will keep silent about Menelaus' arrival and do nothing to abet her brother's schemes (1017–21)—and encourages Helen and Menelaus to work their own rescue, thus turning attention to the next stage of the drama. As with the speeches of Helen (953 / 939) and Menelaus (1003–8 / 991–95) the closing lines provide ring composition: addressing Proteus, Theonoe reaffirms her resolve to protect his reputation for reverence.

1011–17 / 998–1004 Theonoe begins with a statement of what she regards as her essential nature. In so doing, she confirms Helen's association of her with her father's justice in opposition to her brother's injustice (see note on 928–36). As in Helen's speech, justice, piety, and personal honor are inextricably linked.

1015 / 1002 *a temple of Justice* A daring metaphor in that it makes a shrine (cf., e.g., "the great altar of Justice" in Aeschylus, *Agamemnon* 383–84) immanent in a person, although without entirely losing the personification of the divinity. Euripides, in a fragment from his lost *Antigone*, expresses a similar idea more expansively: "There is no altar of Persuasion other than discourse [*logos*], and her altar is in human nature."

1016 / 1003 *from . . . Nereus* See note on 10.

1018 / 1005 *since Hera wants to do you good service* In 897–900 / 880–83, Theonoe made clear that Hera's good will was based on her own interest; she adds her vote to Hera's, however, because it does serve justice.

1026–30 / 1013–16 The problematic character of these lines can be measured by the critical response to them. The passage was regularly excised in the nineteenth and although its authenticity is accepted by almost all recent critics, opinions about its significance range (to cite the polar views of two mid-twentieth-century editors) from "the essential passage of the tragedy" to "a piece of high-toned but vague mysticism appropriate to Theonoe." One may conclude that the lines add a certain solemnity and grandeur to Theonoe's explanation of her decision without treating them as a piece of systematic eschatology. The traditional use of "those below" to indicate the dead in the underworld, combined with the notion of a consciousness that "blends with the deathless air [*aithêr*] above," suggests the notion that at death the body returns to earth, but the soul departs for the aether can be found in a number of epigraphical and literary sources, including Euripides, *Suppliant Women* 533–4. What is new here is the notion that "there are rewards / and punishments" not only for the living but also for the disembodied conscience of the dead person. The punishment of the dead here is obviously nothing like the traditional tortures of famous sinners in Hades (e.g., Tityus, Tantalus, and Sisyphus in Homer, *Odyssey* 11.576–600), or even the Furies' threatened pursuit of Orestes in the world below after his death (Aeschylus, *Eumenides* 174–78 etc.). How an entity imagined as pure mind or spirit could experience punishment or reward remains entirely unexplained.

1033 / 1020 *It may not seem so* Another variation on the theme of appearance and reality (see Introduction, pp. 247–49). Theonoe, whose knowledge of hidden truths puts her clearly on the side of reality, will appear to be harming her brother when she is in fact helping him.

1037 / 1024 *Start with the gods* Theonoe, who has done all she can for Helen and Menelaus, suggests that they begin their escape by trying to propitiate the goddesses who have taken sides for and against them. Helen will do so at 1105–20 / 1094–1106.

1040 / 1027 *safety* In the Greek text, repetition and positioning gives heavy emphasis, which unfortunately cannot be reproduced in the translation, to *sôs*-words denoting safety and escape: *sôtêrias* ends this line and recurs in the same position at 1031 (= **1044**) and 1034 (= **1047**), with *sesômetha* ("we are safe") at the end of 1032 (= **1045**). There is a similar burst of these words at 1047, 1055, 1060 in the Greek text (= **1061, 1068, 1072**). Cf. note on **778**. The rescue plot is beginning in earnest.

1041–42 / 1028–29 Theonoe concludes by addressing the spirit of Proteus directly (as do Menelaus at **974–81** / 961–68 and Theoclymenus at **1173–36** / 1165–68). Theonoe's use of ring composition reaffirms her initial resolve not to damage her father's (or, by implication, her own) reputation for reverence.

1045–1120 / 1032–1106 The final scene in the long sequence that makes up the first episode (see note on **529–1120**) is given over to Menelaus and Helen's attempts to plan the escape that Theonoe's promise of silence has made possible. The planning proceeds in two distinct stages: a series of un-workable proposals by Menelaus is followed by a far more plausible plan developed and explained by Helen. The scene concludes with a prayer to Hera and Aphrodite (as Theonoe had recommended, 1024–27). Eu-ripides gives this lively dialogue a rigorous shape: after three lines that focus attention on the need to find a means of reaching safety, the dialogue continues in an unbroken exchange of couplets (*disticho-mythia*) through **1097** / 1084. The scene concludes with Helen's instruc-tions to Menelaus and prayer to Hera and Aphrodite.

1048–61 / 1035–48 Menelaus makes two proposals—flight or assassination of the king—that Helen shows to be entirely unworkable. The dead end reached here replicates the result of the prior discussion of escape (**819–27** / 805–13: there, Helen proposes that Menelaus flee alone, which he rejects, and Helen informs him that his notion of killing the king has no chance of success. The duplication, by reminding us of the difficulty of finding a way out, emphasizes the novelty and brilliance of the plan Helen will offer next. In the process, however, the dialogue shows that Menelaus can only think in terms of physical daring and force of arms, which are entirely insufficient in the present circum-stance, and this makes the contrast with Helen even more blatant. It is hard to avoid the feeling that Menelaus is once again being treated with a certain ironic condescension, perhaps to suggest that he is not yet ready to play the part of rescuer; Helen must still provide the means for him to become the hero of Troy once more. See further the note to **1062–1105**.

1060 / 1047 *But we don't have a ship, either* Menelaus recognizes the futility of trying to kill the king, but counters, rather, with the impossibility of escape without a ship. The effect is to underscore the apparent hopelessness of the situation, which Helen will now reverse.

1062–1105 / 1049–92 Helen takes charge and sets out her own carefully elaborated plan. She proposes to convince the king to give her a ship by pretending that Menelaus has died at sea, and that in such cases Greek custom requires funeral offerings to be made at sea. Menelaus and his comrades (apparently forgotten until now) are to take part in the rite, then overpower the crew and sail home to Greece. Helen manages to win her husband's assent by answering his skeptical questions and then gradually prepares him to take command of the operation, as he must do if it is to succeed. Menelaus' own ineptness makes Helen's intervention necessary: she offers "something clever" (**1062 / 1049**) that, it seems, can come only from the woman, since the man has failed to provide it. Helen's cleverness will be a recurrent theme in the remainder of the play (e.g., **1516 / 1528, 1608 / 1621**), and will involve above all deception, the canny substitution of appearance for reality, effectively reversing the negative effects of their confusion that have caused them so much suffering (see further note on **1173–1308**). This cleverness, however, also aligns her with the womanly "wiles" of which the phantom Helen has been the symbol and she herself so long the victim.

1062 / 1049 *Listen, maybe a woman can say something clever* In appearance a gesture of appropriate female modesty (the sentiment is paralleled in other Euripidean passages where women take over: *Medea* 1081–89, *Suppliant Women* 294), here it strikes an ironic, almost mocking, note after the utter lack of cleverness in Menelaus' proposals.

1062 / 1050 *report you dead, even though you're not* Literally, "say, although you did not die, that you have died in word"; the Greek sounds even more pleonastic ("say in word" is *legesthai . . . logôi*) than the English, but it softens as much as possible the ill-omened verb "to have died." The ominous quality of using such a word derives from a residual sense of "word magic": saying something may make it happen, whether one wishes it or not. Menelaus' careful repetition of Helen's exact phrase in **1064 / 1052** confirms the point of her scrupulous formulation.

1065 / 1054 *shave my head* See note on 363.

1068–69 / 1056 *some / old-fashioned trick* The point of this puzzling remark is likely to reside in a metatheatrical joke. Orestes' revenge, as dramatized in Aeschylus' *Libation Bearers* and Sophocles' *Electra*, is by far the best-known Greek tale of feigned death. In the Sophoclean play, which may have been performed shortly before *Helen*, Orestes, like Menelaus, uses the language of "dying in word" (59) and asserts that it is worth doing if it brings "gain" (61, cf. *Helen* 1064 / 1051). Furthermore, Orestes mentions how many false reports of deaths he has heard before (62–64). The passages, then, are so closely related that it is hard to imagine that they are entirely independent. Euripides' mischief, if that is what it is, has a point. What Menelaus doesn't know is that his wife is about to become the "author" of an elaborate play-within-the-play of staged lament and funeral rites that will challenge any previous scenes of feigned death and provide the impetus and excitement of the last third of the play.

1076–79 / 1063–66 This exchange anticipates and prepares for 1245–53 / 1239–47, and Helen's assertion that "it's not the Greek custom / to bury on land those who are lost at sea" begins an emphasis on the contrast between Greek and "barbarian" that will be developed as a central theme of the escape sequence. In fact, Greeks did provide tombs and funerary monuments for those whose bodies could not be recovered; see further note on 1246.

1098 / 1085 *Stay here* Helen's and Menelaus' positions are now in effect reversed. She had been sitting at the tomb for protection while she hoped against hope that he would come; now Menelaus must wait at the tomb while she prepares to set their escape in motion.

Some outrageous move Literally, something "discordant" or "out of tune," then "unfitting," "unpleasant." The word itself might simply indicate something that does not harmonize with Helen's plan, but her reference to tomb and sword makes it clear that she is concerned about a violent attack.

1100–1102 / 1087–89 These lines prepare the audience for Helen's appearance in the next episode with a new costume and a mask with cropped hair. See further note on 1190–97. Does the mask go so far as to disfigure her legendary beauty with bloodied cheeks? Presumably not, since when Theoclymenus sees her, he calls attention to her black robes and shorn locks, but mentions only that her cheeks are wet with tears. Bloodying the cheeks is, however, a standard image of tragic lament, and the audience would expect it here.

1105–20 / 1093–1106 The scene, and with it the enormous first episode as a whole, comes to a fitting close with the prayer Theonoe prescribed as the starting point of the quest to return home (1037–40 / 1024–27), which in effect becomes a prayer for the success of Helen's plan. The preceding lines have reminded us that success is by no means assured, and the prayer underscores that the action of the play has reached a decisive moment. Fittingly, Hera—who favors Helen and Menelaus' return—is addressed first and briefly, Aphrodite—the source of so much woe—at more than twice the length and argumentatively, even reproachfully.

1106 / 1093 *you who share the bed of Zeus* Hera is asked as the goddess of marriage and mistress of the great household of the heavens to honor Helen's marriage and to help her return with her husband to their own home.

1114 / 1100 *my name, though not my body* For this antithesis, see note on **67–69**.

1116–20 / 1102–6 *you never tire of making trouble . . . the sweetest, the dearest of gods* Similarly contrasting ideas about Aphrodite's power are frequently expressed in Euripides (*Medea* 630–31, *Hippolytus* 443–46 and 525–34, *Iphigenia in Aulis* 552–57). Helen or course has reason both to denounce the excessive power of sexual attraction and to rejoice in her reunion with Menelaus, but there is the additional irony that she is about to escape from Theoclymenus' advances by means of the very "intrigues and deceptions" with which she upbraids the goddess.

1121–72 / 1107–64 *First stasimon* The first regular "episode dividing" song comes late in the play, at the end of the long series of scenes that constitute formally a single episode (see note on **529–1120**). Two more *stasima* will follow at far closer intervals (**1309–62 / 1301–68, 1448–97 / 1451–511**). This song returns to the sufferings of the past one more time before the final sequence of intrigue and escape gets under way. It takes no account whatever of the new turn in Helen's fortunes, providing a somber backdrop to the fast-moving climax to come. The *stasimon* is divided into two distinct parts, corresponding to its two strophic pairs. In the first, the Chorus recalls (in the allusive and pictorial "decorated" style: see note on **158–251**) the abduction of Helen that led to so much sorrow (strophe), and the Greek who suffered in the war or on the journey home, concluding with Menelaus' wanderings with the phantom Helen (antistrophe). In the second pair, Chorus members attempt to draw some meaning from these miseries, asking what the role the gods in all this might mean (strophe) and condemning the foolishness of resolving conflict with violence rather than reason (antistrophe).

1121–24 / 1107–12 The Chorus members invoke the nightingale to aid them in their lament. The song of the nightingale was connected in myth (already in Homer, *Odyssey* 19.518–23) to her unending sorrow for the death of her son Itys, whom she killed before her transformation into a bird.

Invocations of this lament are frequent in Greek poetry because it was held to be exemplary for the transformation of grief into beautiful song.

1125–26 / 1113–16 *Helen... the women of Troy* Their very different sufferings are, as Helen herself recognized (see especially **355–68 / 362–74**) inextricably linked, and both appropriate, as sufferings of women, for the nightingale to match in lamentation. Neither here nor in the mention at **1127–30 / 1117–21** of Helen's abduction is any distinction is made between Helen and her phantom.

1129–30 / 1120–21 *Paris... Aphrodite* Withholding the names until the final clause of the sentence, and making the goddess's name the final word of the entire strophe, give particular emphasis to the association of human agent and divine patron. Something similar happens with the names of Menelaus and Hera at the end of the antistrophe, which likewise closes with the goddess's name. By reminding us of Aphrodite's role in Paris' abduction of Helen and Hera's substitution of the phantom for Helen, Euripides evokes the destructive consequences of the rivalry of the two goddesses to whom Helen has just prayed.

1133 / 1123–24 *have shorn their hair in mourning* See note on **363**.

1132–35 / 1126–31 *One Greek, a man who rowed alone* Nauplius, already mentioned at **782 / 767**. He was the father of Palamedes, a warrior who died at the hands of his fellow Greeks at Troy, by most accounts stoned to death on charges of treachery trumped up by Odysseus. Thereafter Nauplius devoted himself to taking revenge on the Greeks. He is said to have persuaded the wives of several absent heroes to take lovers. But his most famous act of vengeance is alluded to in these lines: on a stormy night, as the main Greek fleet was sailing homewards from Troy past Euboea, the large island that lies off the eastern coast of Attica, Nauplius lit a beacon, luring the ships to crash against the rocks. The story was dramatized in lost plays by Sophocles and Philocles (a nephew of Aeschylus) that probably preceded *Helen*. It appears to have been foretold in Euripides' *Palamedes*, performed as part of a group of Trojan War plays of 415, of which only *Trojan Women* survives intact.

1143–50 / 1137–43 The Chorus, like the servant at **726–29 / 711–13**, attributes the inscrutability of human fortunes to our inability to perceive any pattern of divine ordering beyond sudden and unexpected change. The formulation of the initial question, however, "What is god? Or what is not? / What lies in between?" is not simply a general question about the nature of the divine, with the final clause tacked on for completeness or to express the uncertainty of any statement about what "god" is or means.

Rather, it points in a particular way to a paradox of Helen's situation referred to in 1151–55 / 1144–48. In parallel expressions—e.g., Euripides, *Iphigenia in Tauris* 895, "what god, or mortal, or what unexpected thing"—the third element clearly refers to a third kind, of which off-spring of gods and mortals are perhaps the most obvious example. Here, the disjunction leads to a consideration of the case of Helen as a special test of divine ordering. As Zeus' own daughter, she should be able to expect special protection from the gods and yet she is wrongly hated by all. For the use of "god" (singular) to denote the notion of "divinity" or "divine power" operating in the world, see the note on **726**.

1151 / 1144 *the child of Zeus* For the theme of Helen's paternity, see note on **17–18**.

1156–57 / 1149–50 The text is highly uncertain, but the meaning of the original must have been something like "I cannot find anything certain, any true word of [or about?] the gods among mortals."

1158–72 / 1151–64 The "pacifism" of this antistrophe cannot not be assumed to be a pointed political comment on the (still ongoing) Athenian disaster in Sicily, since Euripides gives very similar sentiments to Adrastus in his *Suppliant Women* 747–49 and 949–54, written before the reverses in Athens' fortunes. It certainly cannot be taken as the "moral" of this many-layered drama, in which, after all, the saving deed of violence is still to come. It is, however, part of the play's rethinking of the meaning of the Trojan War. See Introduction, p. 254.

1173–1308 / 1165–1300 *Second episode* Theoclymenus, whose advances Helen has long and successfully resisted, appears at last, and Helen's plan quickly gets under way. Dressed in mourning and with her long hair cropped, she pretends to have received news of Menelaus' death and persuades the king that she will be his once she has given Menelaus the last rites Greeks prescribe for those who die at sea. Helen and then Menelaus trick Theoclymenus into providing a well-provisioned ship under Mene-laus' command. The wily Greeks completely outwit their self-assured but rather slow-witted barbarian opponent.

The confusion of appearance and reality have thus far worked only to Helen's disadvantage; now, she and Menelaus in effect take charge of the confusion by staging a play-within-the-play (see note on **1190–97**), in which Helen takes on the appearance of a mourning widow, Menelaus that of the messenger of his own death, and together they direct an action that will accomplish its ends triumphantly, but by deception and at some danger and cost to others (see Introduction, p.). An untragic mood is set by the almost continuous undertone of comic irony in the dialogue; examples at note on **1205**.

1173 / 1165 *Tomb of my father, I salute you* The emphasis on Theoclymenus' piety towards his dead father is surprising, given the earlier character-izations of him as "impious" (**543 / 542**), "foolish" (**931 / 918**), "unjust (**934 / 921**), etc. On the other hand, it is a basic premise of the plot that Theoclymenus respects Helen's supplication at Proteus' tomb, and in this scene it is precisely his respect for ritual propriety that will prove his undoing. Theoclymenus' explanation that he has placed his father's tomb "here at the gate" of the palace in order to greet him as he leaves and returns also serves to explain its location to a Greek audience used to strict separation of the dwellings of the dead from those of the living.

1177 / 1169 *hounds* The presence of animals on the tragic stage is unusual, but cf. the entrances of the chariot-borne Agamemnon and Cassandra at Aeschylus, *Agamemnon* 782, and of Andromache with her child Astyanax on a cart presumably drawn by animals at Euripides, *Trojan Women* 568. It is possible that the audience is meant merely to imagine the hounds, but why refer to them at all unless they are to be seen?

1178–89 / 1171–83 Theoclymenus' increasing anxiety ensures the maximum dramatic effect for Helen's entrance. He has heard that a Greek has arrived and, assuming that he has come in search of Helen, is determined to find and kill him. The abrupt discovery that Helen has left the tomb leads Theoclymenus to imagine that she has gone off with the Greek, and he gives a series of frantic orders to his men to prepare for pursuit.

1182 / 1175 *to hunt for Helen* Theoclymenus, returning from a literal hunting exped-ition, is figuratively the "hunter" of Helen (e.g., **64 / 63, 311 / 314**), but turns the tables with ironic accuracy by accusing "a Greek" of the same thing. He will later ask Helen what she is "hunting for" when she supplicates him (**1244 / 1238**).

1190–97 / 1186–92 The "play-within-the-play" begins with Helen's entrance in the guise of mourning widow, dressed in black and with cropped hair. Self-conscious role-playing within dramatic roles here becomes sufficiently complex to take on the characteristics of a dramatic action in its own right. Helen (who "scripted" and rehearsed the scene, **1062–1105 / 1049–92**) plays herself as a widow and Menelaus, a comrade of Menelaus who witnessed his death. This kind of device is very much at home in comedy, but there are several examples in Greek tragedy, including the feigned death of Orestes in Aeschylus and Sophocles (see note on **1068–69**) and, in Euripides, Pentheus' assumption, under the direction of Dionysus, of the role of bacchic devotee in *Bacchae* 810–61, the action that will lead to his death.

1203 / 1199 *She said so* A convenient lie, which Helen cleverly turns into an opportunity to introduce Menelaus in a way that deflects suspicion. We will later learn that Theonoe, when asked about Menelaus' whereabouts, repeated the lie as a favor to Helen (**1364–67 / 1370–73**).

1205 / 1201 *may he go where he deserves* Literally, "where I would have him go," a good example of an expression meant to be understood one way by Theoclymenus but heard in another by the audience. Much of the comic irony of this scene is in this vein (e.g., **1209 / 1205, 1219 / 1215, 1254–57 / 124–51, 1269–70 / 1263–64, 1279 / 1273**), and it comes to a head in the final exchange of the scene (see note on **1295–1308**).

1207–8 / 1203–4 That the great hero of Troy should be discovered by his enemy crouching in rags—and thus not be recognized—is of course richly comic, and this moment has been called "the nadir of Menelaus' fortunes as a tragic hero," but it is also a triumph of his and Helen's strategy. Both observations reflect the primacy of appearance in this part of the play. Just as Helen's black robes and cropped hair help convince Theoclymenus of Menelaus' death, so the rags make it easy for him to believe that this is no Greek hero to be viewed with suspicion, but merely a lucky survivor. Menelaus' loss of heroic status is connected from the beginning with his lack of proper clothing (e.g., **420–22 / 421–24** and **554–55 / 553–54**), and the exchange of his rags for garments that befit his reputation (e.g., **1369–79 / 1375–84**) will signal its restoration.

1208 / 1204 *Apollo* Invoked in his role as averter of evil.

1213 / 1209 *the saddest and most pitiful* Above all because it involves the loss of burial rites, a genuine Greek view that underlies the fictional custom of "burial at sea" upon which the escape plan is built.

1214 / 1210 *so far from home* Literally, "in barbarian seas," but (as is suggested by hearing it from the mouth of the "barbarian" Theoclymenus) Greek *barbaros* does not necessarily have the associations of the English word. At **1264 / 1258**, Theoclymenus will describe a sacrificial custom Greeks would find entirely inoffensive as "barbarian," implying nothing more than the Greek division of the world into Greek and non-Greek— however odd it may seem to us that he adopts it to describe his own world. To avoid misunderstandings, *barbaros* is generally rendered by "foreign" in this translation.

1219 / 1215 *Where I wish he died* Literally, "may he [it] perish wretchedly," with no stated subject. The Greek phrase amounts to a curse, and could be applied to the wreck ("damn the wreck—but not my Menelaus," exempting Menelaus as a kind of precaution, since her words might somehow yet implicate him in disaster); but there is a delicious irony if the subject is understood to be the man who survived the wreck to report Menelaus' death, and whom Helen now curses for that. The exemption of Menelaus from the curse is now essential, since he *is* the survivor, and without it she would be cursing him. Strict grammar might demand "would that he had died," but with this formulaic expression, the distinction does not carry great weight.

1224 / 1220 *Destroyed for nothing!* Theoclymenus, who had no stake in the fate of Troy, exclaims, like Menelaus' old servant (**721 / 707**), who did, that all the death and destruction was in vain.

1231–32 These lines are a makeshift to fill what seems inescapably a lacuna in the transmitted text, since nothing in **1230 / 1226** prepares for the shift to Helen's question about Theonoe.

1240 / 1234 *I'm willing to be gracious if you are* Literally, "let favor come in exchange for favor." Theoclymenus properly offers *charis* (favor given or reciprocated, "gratitude," "goodwill") in return for Helen's *charis*. In so doing, however, he opens the way for Helen to put her plan into action.

1243 / 1237 *I kneel and beg* Helen, who had been a suppliant at Proteus' tomb for protection from his son, now supplicates the son as the next step in her plan to win freedom from him; to this end, she cleverly now calls him "dear to me [*philos*], the term she used of Menelaus twelve lines earlier (**1229 / 1225**).

1244 / 1238 *What are you hunting for* With unwitting irony, Theoclymenus applies to Helen the hunting metaphor used repeatedly to describe his pursuit of her. The tables have turned. See note on **51**.

1246 / 1240 *A grave with no body? Will you bury his shade?* Although presented disjunctively, these phrases both seem to refer to the same idea, that of the "empty tomb" (cenotaph) for one whose body cannot be recovered for burial. This is the suggestion anticipated by Menelaus and Helen at **1067–69 / 1063–66**. The notion would be familiar to a Greek audience. It was customary in cases where bodies could not be recovered to erect monuments over empty graves and to bring to them the usual tomb offerings. Already in Homer, *Odyssey* 1.289–92, Athena advises Telemachus, if he learns that his father is dead, to raise a mound and give him full funeral honors; and we have many grave epigrams written for (or as if for) such cenotaphs. However, the denial of normal Greek custom for strategic purposes is itself part and parcel of the Greek cleverness here.

1248 / 1242 *Greeks are wise in such matters* Literally, "the descendents of Pelops." The choice of wording underlines a number of ironies. Theoclymenus speaks better than he knows in the sense that the burial rite about to be described is in fact part of a clever "Pelopid" plot. "Pelopidai" denotes in the first instance the descendants of Pelops (including Menelaus), and at 1270 /1264 "of the line of Pelops" ("Pelopidôn") clearly does refer to Menelaus' royal descent. Here (and again at 1425–26 / 1429), however, the word is used in the broader sense to denote the people of Pelops' land, i.e., Greeks in general. Theoclymenus' respect for Greek ritual, which he seems to regard as a superior form of wisdom, is what gives Helen and Menelaus their chance to prove the superiority of Greeks over "barbarians." Finally, those in the audience who were familiar with the elaborate Egyptian science of embalming described by Herodotus, *Histories* 2.86–90, and in general with the great pains taken concerning the dead in Egypt, would be amused at an Egyptian who "can't keep up with you Greeks" in matters of funerary custom (1252 / 1246)—though indeed, as regards what is really going on, Theoclymenus is certainly being left in the dust.

1249 / 1243 *with empty winding-sheets* See note on 1267.

1255 / 1249 *I've never done it before* Literally, "I have no experience, having had good fortune before," an ironic comment on a number of levels. There is of course an obvious comic irony, since *we* know that Helen's earlier luck has been bad and has only now begun to turn good. In addition, the disclaimer might remind the Greek audience that even if Helen only thought she had lost her husband, her phantom was unlucky enough to lose two—Paris, and after his death, Deiphobus. The story of this second marriage, though not in Homer, was certainly current in Euripides' day.

1261 / 1255 *we offer blood to the spirits below* That is, an animal is sacrificed and its blood poured out as an offering to the dead. There is of course irony in Menelaus' mention of blood-sacrifice, given his plans.

1264 / 1258 *Here in Egypt* Literally, "among barbarians." See note on 1214.

1265 / 1259 *no defect* Literally, "nothing low-born" or "ill-bred." Greek sacrificial practice demanded animals that were whole, healthy, and unblemished;

as regards Egypt, Herodotus, *Histories* 2.38 mentions a series of tests that a bull had to pass before it could be sacrificed.

1267 / 1261 *a bed for the missing body, with covers* This would be familiar to the Athenian audience; Thucydides, *History of the Peloponnesian War* 2.34.3 describes the custom of carrying, along with the bones of fallen soldiers brought back to Athens for burial, an empty bed strewn with covers for those whose remains could not be found.

1269 / 1263 *he loved the spear* Indeed, he loves it still and is tricking Theoclymenus into putting it into his hands!

1284 / 1278 *She may go* Literally, "Let her go," but since *itô* is a regular formula of resignation, a kind of verbal shrug of the shoulders, it might equally well be rendered "Let it go," i.e., "So be it."

1290 / 1282–83 *I'll give you some proper clothes to replace those rags* Menelaus' assumption of new clothing (and armor) will mark the restoration of his fortunes and the resumption of his heroic role (cf. **1369–79 / 1375–84**). Helen will arrange for his bath and change of clothes (**1304–8 / 1296–1300**), an act whose appropriateness escapes Theoclymenus, but underlines for the audience Helen's careful management of the intrigue.

1295–1308 / 1288–1300 The final exchange of the episode is spoken in the presence of Theoclymenus with a combination of playful daring and emotional urgency. In a series of emphatic ambiguities (the most obvious being the repeated references. to Helen's "husband," which might refer either to Menelaus or Theoclymenus) Menelaus appeals for Helen's loyalty and she assures him of it, while at the same time both are playing their parts in the intrigue. The unambiguous ambiguity of this exchange is what one expects to find in comedy, not tragedy. Unlike any other victim of tragic intrigue, Theoclymenus' blindness is that of a lover, and the equivocal references to Helen's "husband" lend to the intrigue a touch of comic cuckolding.

1295 / 1288 *You know your duty* The same phrase as at **844 / 830** (where it appears as "This is a job for you"), but with a different emphasis. Practically every word in this sentence, including "duty," carries a double meaning.

1309–62 / 1301–68 *Second stasimon* The song is devoted to Demeter (here identified with the Phrygian Mother Goddess) and her search for her lost daughter, Persephone. This is one of Euripides' "dithyrambic *stasima*," so called because they provide a mythical narrative told in a highly decorated style (i.e., highly pictorial, allusive, and expressively charged, with an emphasis on mood rather than narrative continuity). The story sweeps on briskly and colorfully, in a series of vivid vignettes rather than a straightforward continuous narrative. The emphasis is thus on the emotional burden of each of each successive moment presentĕd. Of all such stasima, this one has seemed to many commentators the least closely connected to the action of the drama, the clearest example of a tendency to turn choral odes into interludes that will characterize fourth-century tragedy. Unfortunately, the corruption of just those two portions of the final antistrophe that appear to make a direct connection between Helen's story and that told in the ode (**1351–52** / 1353–54, **1361–62** / 1366–68) makes any definitive judgment impossible. Nevertheless, significant connections can be shown on a number of levels. The abduction of Persephone is, in more than one way, like Helen's own story: she makes a connection herself at **170–174** / 173–78, and cf. the implicit allusion to Persephone's abduction in the language of **240–46** / 243–48 (see Introduction, p. 237). Helen is also like Demeter in having, in effect, lost her daughter Hermione (**283–85** / 282–83, **703–6** / 688–90), but with the hope of regaining her in the end (**946–47** / 933, **1469–70** / 1476–77). Like both Demeter and Persephone, her story is finally one of return to life and to the world. Other connections include: the grieving Mother's retreat to Mount Ida, the place where Helen's troubles began (see note on **1327**). Aphrodite, who caused Helen so much sorrow, brings the Mother comfort (**1346–48** / 1346–49). Zeus' hand guides both stories (see note on **1322–23**).

Perhaps the most noteworthy feature of this ode is its thoroughgoing syncretism. Eleusinian Demeter, Asiatic Cybele ("Great Mother" or just "the Mother"), and even Dionysus ("Bromius" **1359** / 1364) are assimilated to each other and share each other's attributes. The cult of Cybele was first introduced to Greece in the sixth or fifth century, and her identification with Greek deities seems to have proceeded very rapidly as part of a larger syncretistic integration of cults that promised release through ecstatic experience and rites of initiation. Some further aspects of syncretism are discussed in the notes that follow.

1310 / **1301–2** *Mother of gods who roams the mountains* "Mountain Mother" was one of the cult names of the Phrygian Mother Goddess. The Mother's frantic search for her lost daughter puts syncretism in evidence from the first words of the song. She is identified with Demeter simply by inhabiting her story; Demeter is not named at this point in the Greek text.

1312 / **1305** *thundering* Greek *barubromon* ("deep-roaring"), the first of several words associated with Dionysus in this song to describe sounds; the rest are specifically descriptive of the raucous music of this song, which stands in contrast to the music of lament that dominates the first *stasimon*. The Dionysiac association is attested by the god's most prominent cult-name,

Bromius (**1359** / 1364), which apparently derives from *bromos*, used to describe any loud roar or crash, but in his case perhaps refers specifically to Zeus' thunder and lightning, by which his mother was inseminated.

1315 / 1307 *whose name is not spoken* An apparent allusion to the Eleusinian habit of using substitute names for the deities of the cult (in the case of Persephone, Korê or Kora, "Maiden"). The prohibition was by no means absolute, and Helen has already spoken the goddess's name at **170** / 175.

1316 / 1308 *clappers* A castanet-like instrument made of two short lengths of wood, reed, or bronze, specifically associated with the rites of both Dionysus and the Mother Goddess. (In the Greek, the clappers are given the Dionysiac epithet *bromia*, "thundering.")

1316 / 1310 *lions* Literally, "team of beasts," but Cybele is regularly portrayed as accompanied by, or riding in a chariot drawn by, lions.

1322–23 / 1317–18 The text of these lines is incomplete, but it has been brilliantly restored with support from later sources to give us a version in which Demeter is aided in the attempt to halt her daughter's abduction by the armed goddesses Artemis and Athena, but stopped by the greater might of Zeus, who has another plan for Persephone. That he presides also over a reconciliation becomes clear in **1340–44** / 1339–45.

1327 / 1324 *Ida* One of the important cult sites of the "Mountain Mother" was on Mount Ida, whence her cult-name "Idean Mother" (e.g., Euripides, *Orestes* 1453). In the earlier Homeric *Hymn to Demeter* 296–304, the goddess sits mourning in the temple built for her at Eleusis. Here she retreats to her mountain fastness, in keeping with the syncretic identification of Demeter with the Mother of the gods. Mount Ida also brings her story into association with Helen's, since it is repeatedly mentioned both as site of the judgment of Paris (**20** / 24, **350–52** / 357–59, **1495–96** / 1508–9).

1339–50 / 1337–52 The second strophe diverges from the story told in the *Hymn to Demeter* 314–56, where Zeus first sends Iris to ask the goddess to return to Olympus and then, when she refuses, other gods promise honors and gifts. When she still refuses to return before she has seen her daughter, Zeus sends Hermes to fetch Persephone. Here, Zeus simply heals the Mother's anger by sending the Graces and the Muses, who, together with Aphrodite, are able to make her smile and feel pleasure once more. The power of music and poetry to console and restore one's spirits is a recurrent theme of Greek verse.

1340 / 1339 *Zeus* Zeus' role in the reconciliation takes on a particular—though entirely unexplained—significance in this version of the story, in which Zeus allowed the Maiden to be seized in the first place (see note on **1322–23**).

1341–44 / 1341–45 *Graces...Muses* daughters of Zeus, often associated as figures of beauty and inspiration in Greek lyric and elegiac poetry.

1341 / 1343 *Demeter* The goddess is named at last (in the Greek the short form "Dêô").

1343 / 1344 *Shout your happy "alalai"* The uses of this exclamation range from war cry to shout of joy (e.g. Aristophanes, *Lysistrata* 1291); here it is clearly the latter, since it produces divine laughter (**1349 / 1349**). Its use in cult is particularly associated with orgiastic rites like those of the Mother Goddess and Dionysus. Neither the Graces nor the Muses are usually associated with such rites, and their presence is further evidence for the easy pervasiveness of syncretism in this *stasimon*.

1346 / 1349 *Aphrodite* Not explicitly sent by Zeus, but her appearance in the company of the Graces is made easy by the fact that they are so frequently depicted as her companions and so closely associated with her from Homer, where they make a robe for her (*Iliad* 5.338) and bathe and dress her after she is caught in Hephaestus' net (*Odyssey* 8.364–66), onwards. Aphrodite's presence, like the mention of Mount Ida (see note on **1327**), provides a link to Helen, whose misfortunes began when she became the goddess's unwitting prize in the beauty contest; and Cypris' enmity has persisted. Here, however, she brings comfort and consolation.

1349 / 1349 *the Mother smiled at last* The smile (or laugh) is a sign of the softening of the goddess's anger, as is her participation in the music-making. In *Hymn to Demeter* 195–210, it is Iambe, the eponym of iambic (satiric) verse, who makes Demeter smile and laugh at her jests, and the assuaging of Demeter's spirits is sealed when she drinks *kykeon*, water mixed with barley and mint; in a fragmentary "Orphic" version of the story (*Orphica* fragment 52 Kern), the woman who brings Demeter to laugh and drink is named Baubo, and she does so by exposing herself. Euripides has taken a tradition in which jokes and indecent behavior distract Demeter from her sorrow and recast it as an example of the healing power of music.

1351–62 / 1353–68 The final antistrophe apparently contained the key for connecting this *stasimon* to the play as a whole, but since both beginning and end are damaged beyond any certainty about their meaning, few definite conclusions are possible. It seems clear that Helen is charged with committing offenses involving some form of impiety and neglect of the Mother's rites. There follows further praise of the cults of Dionysus and the Mother Goddess, which are once again fully assimilated. The closing lines again refer to Helen, but again remain enigmatic.

1351–53 / 1353–57 No other account of Helen's story sheds light on this accusation, which apparently involved burnt sacrifice of unlawful items, or conducted in an unlawful way that constituted dishonor of the Great Mother's rites. The first word of the Greek text has no construction and the phrase "in the inner chambers" has no convincing explanation or emendation.

1353–60 / 1358–65 Although the context of these lines is the worship of the Mother Goddess, the attributes are taken from the cult of Dionysus as much as that of Cybele, underlining the syncretism that characterizes the entire song: the "fawn-skin robe" is the characteristic garb of maenads; "ivy tendrils wound round the sacred wand" denotes the "thyrsus," an attribute of Dionysus and his followers; ancient "tambourines" consisted of circular discs whirled about on the end of a thong and were associated with the festivities of both gods. Implicit in "hair flying like a devotee's" (*bakxeuousa*, literally, "celebrating with Bacchic frenzy") implies the metaphorical possession of the worshipper's very locks by the god's power. "All-night revels" would be as much at home in the cult of Dionysus as they are in that of the Great Mother.

1359 / 1364 *Bromius* Dionysus "the Roarer"; see note on **1312**.

1361–62 / 1368 *gloried in nothing but your own beauty* The significance of this line cannot be firmly established. There may be a contrast between Helen's reliance on her own beauty and her neglect of the power of the Great Mother's rites, but in the absence of any known incident, there is no way to flesh this out. It certainly contrasts with what Helen says in the play about how much she despises and despairs of her beauty (see note on **25**). The remark fits better the "traditional" Helen: cf., e.g., Euripides, *Trojan Women* 1022–28, where Hecuba rebukes her for being dressed in all her finery when she should be trembling in rags.

1363–1447 / 1369–1450 *Third episode* Helen completes the outwitting of Theoclymenus; at her prompting he orders a ship to be made ready and appoints "the man in charge of the funeral / rites" (**1409–19 / 1414**), i.e., Menelaus himself, as its commander. The comic irony continues, with Helen promising to be the wife Theoclymenus deserves and with him making plans for the wedding. After the king exits, Menelaus concludes the episode with a prayer to Zeus and the other gods for success.

1380 / 1386 *thinks my marriage is in his grasp* The Greek here is nearly identical to that describing Paris' apparent but unreal marriage to Helen ("thinks it's me he's embracing," 33 / 35). The second threat to Helen's true marriage will be as fictitious as the first, but through human rather than divine agency.

1382 / 1388 *Keep your lips sealed now* Seeking the Chorus's silence is a standard feature of deception plots, but here, as at Euripides' *Iphigenia in Tauris* 1056–77, the request is combined with the prospect of eventual freedom and homecoming for the Chorus. In comparison with the elaborate development of these motifs in *Iphigenia*, however, the treatment in *Helen* is perfunctory. Iphigenia makes an extended and touching appeal to the Chorus and elicits its explicit agreement; Helen makes the briefest of requests and receives no answer. Iphigenia's promise of freedom for her temple maidens is fulfilled at 1467–79 by Athena's command to send them home; Helen's vague suggestion is never mentioned again. In *Helen*, of course, the dramatically crucial request for silence is not made to the Chorus, but to Theonoe, whose acquiescence is made to seem far less inevitable than that of Iphigenia's fellow temple servants.

1384 / 1390 *go in good order* In Greek tragedy, as a general rule, orders given and not countermanded are executed without delay. In this case, however, unless there is a separate group of servants carrying the burial goods and an additional group of Egyptians assigned to be Menelaus' crew, it appears that those who are to serve Menelaus (presumably those carrying the offerings) remain on stage and hear the order that puts Menelaus in command. They depart for the shore with him only when Theoclymenus exits into the palace. This staging is confirmed when, towards the end of the scene, Theoclymenus tells Menelaus to give "these offerings to the sea's embrace" (1432 / 1437), implying that they are still on stage.

1393 / 1398 *after all, he's no longer here among us* Inadvertent irony, since Menelaus *is* very much "here." For the culmination of this sort of thing, see note on 1435–36.

1394–95 / 1400–1401 *I am bound to honor my first marriage* A typical example of the ironic equivocation that characterizes Helen's dialogue here. Whereas the king's irony stems from ignorance of the real situation, Helen's is self-conscious, drawing on what she knows—and we do, too. Note the continuing stream of such ironies in 1399–1404 / 1405–9 and 1414–22 / 1418–26.

1407–8 / 1412–13 *a fifty-oared / Sidonian galley* A type of ship that for the original audience would have chosen represented a large warship of an earlier age. Ships with fifty rowers appear already in Homer (*Iliad* 2.719–20, 16.169–70, *Odyssey* 8.34–36), but by the fifth century had largely been replaced by the trireme.

1415–16 / 1421–22 For the purposes of this translation, I accept a proposed transposition of these lines to follow **1414 / 1418**, where they certainly fit more comfortably than after **1418 / 1420**, as transmitted.

1418 / 1420 *just how grateful I am* For the motif of *charis*, introduced by Theoclymenus, see note on **1240**; Helen's false (or at least equivocal) promise brings it to a suitably ironic close.

1423–36 / 1427–40 Theoclymenus' departure gives us the comic culmination of his discomfiture. Helen parries his solicitous offer of seeing her to the ship with an inspired retort that ends the discussion simply by invoking Theoclymenus' royal dignity. Theoclymenus' exit speech then underlines with its inadvertent ironies how fully he has been outwitted. He is already planning the celebration of his marriage, and goes so far as to invite Menelaus to the wedding feast!

1426 / 1430 *my house is clean* The presence of a corpse would have polluted a house, so that those who entered required purification. We are reminded that if Theoclymenus had caught him there, he would have killed him.

1434 / 1438 *hurry back to the palace with my wife* Theoclymenus himself contributes (though of course without knowing it) just the sort of ironic ambiguity that marks Helen's words: "hurry back to the palace" refers to his own palace, but the words can also mean "hurry back home"—which is precisely what Helen and Menelaus will do.

1437–47 / 1441–50 Menelaus' prayer corresponds to Helen's prayer to Hera and Aphrodite at **1105–20 / 1093–1106**. Like hers it is divided into two parts, the first addressed to Zeus, the second a more anguished appeal to the gods in general; like hers it is a reproach as well as an exhortation and ends an episode.

1448–97 / 1451–1511 *Third stasimon* Where the first *stasimon* looked back at Helen's sorrows, the third looks forward to her homecoming; where the second *stasimon* had only a loose connection to the plot of the play, the third is entirely devoted to imagining its continuation. The ode is cast in the form of a *propemptikon*, a poetic wish for a safe journey. The first strophe is pervaded by images that augur a smooth voyage; the antistrophe, addressed to Helen, pictures her arrival at Sparta in the midst of festivities, finding friends, joining in the dance, and meeting her daughter at last. The second strophe bids migrating cranes to land at the Eurotas and announce that Menelaus will soon return from the conquest of Troy; the antistrophe invokes Helen's immortalized brothers, the Dioscuri, to bring favoring breezes to guide the ship home and restore Helen's reputation. This *stasimon* shows the salient traits of the decorated style (in such elements as the fantasy of the sea-scene with its dancing dolphins and tutelary seanymph, the evocation of the nighttime rites of the Spartan Hyacinthia, and the picture of the Dioscuri speeding to aid their sister) in the service of an almost rapturous propitiation of safety and future happiness.

1449 / 1452 *Nereus* Presumably appropriate as the leader of the "chorus" of dolphins as father of the Nereids, who are often depicted as dancing. In this play, of course, he is the source of Theonoe's prophetic powers (see 1016 / 1004) and thus on the side of piety and justice.

1451 / 1458 *Galaneia* An apparently Euripidean form of the name Galene, the personification of a still sea.

1458 / 1464 *bring Helen to harbor at home* Literally, "sending Helen to the well-harbored shore of Perseus' home," i.e., Mycenae, of which Perseus was the mythical founder. Mycenae is not on the coast, but the harbor at Nauplia, where Menelaus will pray to land (1574 / 1586), provided easy access. For Menelaus' return to Sparta via Mycenae (or Argos), see note on 119.

1460 / 1464–66 *beside the river, at Athena's temple* The Eurotas, named at 1482 / 1492 and which stands for Sparta here and elsewhere (see note on 340), and Athena's famous Bronze House, another great Spartan landmark (see note on 222).

1460/ 1466 *Leucippus' daughters* Leucippus was a brother of Tyndareus, Helen's mortal father, and his two daughters were married to her brothers, the Dioscuri. They were thus both cousins and sisters-in-law. In the bestknown version of the story, the Dioscuri abducted the sisters from the men to whom they were engaged, Idas and Lynceus, sons of Aphareus, another brother of Tyndareus. Their story thus connects with Helen's in a number of ways. It appears that they were originally divinities; the sisters, under the names Hilaera and Phoebe, had a cult at Sparta, as did Helen herself.

1463–67 / 1469–75 *the revels for Hyacinthus* The Hyacinthia, one of Sparta's most important festivals, was held in late spring at nearby Amyclae to commemorate the death of Hyacinthus, a beautiful boy whom Apollo loved but accidentally killed with a discus that swerved, or hit a rock and rebounded. Hyacinthus apparently began as a vegetation deity, and it is perhaps significant for the tone of the *stasimon* that the Hyacinthia, like other festivals connected with the death and rebirth of such gods, featured laments on its first day and exuberant, cheerful celebration on the second. Mention of "revels" and of joyful rites performed at night clearly indicates that Helen is imagined as joining in celebration rather than lament.

1469 / 1476 *her daughter* Hermione; in Greek, simply her "young one" (*moskhon*), literally, "heifer" or "calf," a word generally applied to an unmarried girl or boy.

Hermione's unwed state has weighed heavily on Helen (see note on **282**), and implicit in the mention of wedding torches is the wish, now that Helen has returned, that she will see her daughter married at last. For the torches as metonymy for marriage itself, cf. **738–42 / 722–25**.

1472–84 / 1478–94 The Chorus members wish they could fly to join the cranes that winter in North Africa; they urge the birds to fly north so they can tell the Spartans of Menelaus' approach. The wish to fly away, either to escape a terrible situation or to get quickly to where one wishes to be, is a commonplace of tragic lyrics, and Euripides has a particular fondness for it. The dream of flight here expresses the Chorus members' joy at Helen's and Menelaus' escape; they do not imagine returning to Greece themselves, wishing instead simply to make contact with the cranes and give them the good news to take to Greece. The picture of cranes migrating south from Greece to escape the rains is a traditional one (see Homer, *Iliad* 3.3–7, Hesiod, *Works and Days* 448–49), and the imagined season of this flight, "beneath Orion and the Sisters at their zenith" (**1479–80 / 1489–90**) appears to be the fall, when the cranes fly south from Greece. This presents a problem if one imagines the cranes carrying the message of Menelaus' homecoming on their return to Greece in the spring. It is of course possible that Euripides simply provided the temporal coordinates for migration from north to south rather than from south to north because that is the one celebrated in Greek lore. It seems likelier, however, that we are to understand the Chorus as intercepting the cranes on their arrival in Africa and asking them to return to Sparta with the great news—the last impossible link in a chain of fantastic wishes.

1475 / 1479 *African plains* The Greek text refers to Libya, but this name is used in antiquity to indicate a far wider swathe of the North African desert, including much of what is now Egypt.

1485–97 / 1495–1511 This stanza provides an answer (later confirmed by Castor himself, **1648 / 1659**) to the question raised in **132–138 / 137–42** about what has become of the brothers, thus preparing the way for their appearance at the end of the play.

1486–87 / 1499–1500 *living amidst the brightness of the whirling stars* The bothers, who were regularly invoked, with the title "savior" (as here, as "saviors of Helen" **1489 / 1500**), for the protection of sailors from storm and shipwreck, appear to get their association with stars initially through the phenomenon of St. Elmo's fire, luminous discharges of electricity sometimes seen extending from the tip of a ship's mast. The sparks of St. Elmo's fire were likened to stars, and at some point the Dioscuri became identified with the constellation still known as Gemini ("the Twins"). According to Teucer, one story told about the Dioscuri was that they had become gods "in the shape of stars" (**135 / 140**); whether that means they have become stars or appear as points of light like stars (i.e., St. Elmo's fire) is uncertain.

1487–88 / 1495–96 *speed your horses / down paths of air* The Dioscuri were imagined as riding their horses through the sky; in art, they appear on or with their horses, as they do in the two Homeric *Hymns to the Dioscuri.* **1487–88.**

1493–97 / 1506–11 The final clauses of the Chorus's prayer recall the great theme of Helen's disastrous and undeserved reputation ("slander of a shameful / foreign marriage") with a paraphrase of the famous beginning of Stesichorus' "Palinode:" "...nor did you go to the citadel of Troy" (see Introduction, pp. 231–32). The Greek text of the *stasimon* concludes with an elaborate periphrasis for Troy, "the towers of Ilium built by Phoebus." This alludes to the story, told in Homer *Iliad* 21.441–57, that Apollo and Poseidon were required to work for a year for King Laomedon of Troy, who had them build walls for the city and then refused the promised payment, leading to the city's first destruction.

1498–1678 / 1512–1692 *Final scenes (exodos)* Aristotle uses the term *exodos* to refer to "a whole part of the tragedy, after which there is no song of the chorus" (*Poetics* 12.1452b21–2); thus, it is usually not a single scene, but a series of scenes that bring the action to its conclusion. In *Helen*, the *exodos* is clearly divided into three main sections: a long messenger scene in which the story of Helen and Menelaus' escape is told in detail and with great dramatic flair; a brief and agitated scene in which Theoclymenus decides to kill his sister Theonoe for what he now understands was her betrayal, but is opposed by a servant; and a scene in which the Dioscuri suddenly appear to put a stop to Theoclymenus' planned revenge, win his acquiescence in all that has happened, and foretell the future fortunes of Helen and Menelaus.

1498–1607 / 1512–1620 *Messenger scene* After a corrupt and almost certainly truncated beginning (see note on **1498–1500**), the scene proceeds in the usual way: a short dialogue reveals the gist of the matter—Helen is gone, spirited away by Menelaus, who had faked his own death, and has hijacked the ship and its crew to Greece—and leads into the detailed narrative of the messenger speech itself, followed by a choral "tag." The Messenger narrates the denouement of Helen and Menelaus' plot in a final contest, a bloody battle in which Greeks show their "Trojan glory" (1603) by fighting barbarians again—this time the unarmed and thoroughly outwitted Egyptians. Appearance and reality are finally reunited, but only by the success of the most elaborate deception. Responses to all this have varied widely; see Introduction, pp. 252–54.

The Messenger identifies himself as a participant, explaining at the end in proper sequence that he jumped ship and was rescued to return and tell his tale. He gives a chronologically continuous exposition of events that is also an interpretation drawn in hindsight from the experience of having been caught up in them himself (see note on **1516–19**). The speech as a whole shows how exciting messenger scenes can be, particularly in bringing to life events that would make gripping cinema but could not be shown to anything like the same effect on the fifth-century stage.

1498–1500 These lines are the translator's rudimentary restoration of what appears to be a lost beginning of the scene that was patched up with a line for the Messenger, which at least as transmitted is defective in meter and sense. Typically, a messenger enters and the ruler (or other intended interlocutor) is summoned from within; occasionally, a messenger arrives midscene and finds his interlocutor already on stage. Here, neither situation obtains, and the perfunctory stage management makes it likely that an initial dialogue between the Messenger and Chorus Leader has dropped out.

1502–14 / 1514–25 Theoclymenus learns that Helen has escaped. One might expect an immediate display of anger, but the exchange with the Messenger is managed so as to elicit the king's incredulity and curiosity, motivating the lengthy messenger speech but postponing the king's fury. When the outburst comes at last (**1611–14 / 1624–26**), it will be directed against the sister who betrayed him, thus producing the final crisis of the play.

1504–5 / 1516 *flew away, or…on foot* It is striking that Theoclymenus misses the obvious way to escape, by ship. He has proved an easy mark!

1516–19 / 1528–29 *her wiles... that ladylike way* As usual, attention is drawn to Helen's appearance, but its meaning is recorded here with hindsight, the Messenger now recognizing her acting for what it was, and he makes clear (with emphatic alliteration: *posin pelas paronta*) that Helen lamented a "husband who was right next to her, not dead at all." In addition to naming Menelaus from the outset, the Messenger continues to narrate in terms of what he could only have realized later, e.g., "a show of pity meant for us" (**1531–32 / 1542**), "feigned tears" (**1536 / 1547**), "their swords were still / hidden under their cloaks" **1560–61 / 1574–75**.

1524–25 / 1536 *the double rudders / lowered... by their guide ropes* Two "steering oars" were attached to ropes on either side of the ship that permitted them to be turned in tandem. These rudders were raised on the ropes when the ship was at anchor, lowered for sailing.

1542 / 1553 *you ruined everything* The triumph of Helen's Greek cleverness, since it was she who insisted that the king announce publicly and repeatedly that the Egyptian sailors were to obey only Menelaus (**1409–13 / 1414–17**). The slave's daring rebuking of his master for doing so underlines the folly of the deed.

1545 / 1555–56 *who wouldn't set foot on the gangplank* Literally, "but the bull's foot did not wish to advance straight along the gangplank." The bull's resisting foot is the momentary center of attention, because animals were supposed to go to sacrifice willingly, so this was a bad sign.

1548–49 / 1560 *You men who sacked / the city of Troy* See note on **1548–49**.

1549 / 1561 *hoist this bull Greek-style* Commentators have doubted whether lifting a bull onto the shoulders for sacrifice, as opposed to raising its neck or forequarters at the moment of sacrifice, is a Greek custom, or indeed whether it is possible. There is, however, considerable body of evidence (including an Athenian inscription of the fifth century) that such rituals did take place, not as the usual practice but on special festive occasions.

1553 / 1567 *the horse* Evidently Theoclymenus, having been told that a bull or a horse would make an appropriate offering (1258), has provided both.

1556 / 1570 *with her dainty steps* Literally, "with lovely-ankled feet." This is another detail suggesting both the attention that Helen's appearance drew to her and her self-consciousness in playing her role, a "close-up" that keeps before us the impression that Helen makes and has always made, of which she was earlier the victim but now puts to such effective use.

1557–58 / 1572 *the man / we all thought was dead* Literally, "the one no longer existing in words" (*logoisi*). This is the role that Helen proposed and he agreed to (**1062–65** /1050–52).

1571–72 / 1586 *and my wife, too* Only with these words does Menelaus make it unequivocally clear that *he* is Menelaus.

1574 / 1586 *Nauplia* see note on **1458**.

1590–91 / 1603–4 *Where is your Trojan glory?* Helen raises a cry that descends from the exhortations of epic heroes (e.g., Homer. *Iliad* 4.234, "Argives, do not let go of your furious valor"). Like Menelaus at **1548–49 / 1560**, she reminds the Greeks of their earlier triumph to strengthen them for the struggle that lies ahead. "Show it off to these natives!" in effect casts the battle as a reprise of the Trojan War.

1602–3 / 1615–16 The story of the Greek survivor's rescue confected for Menelaus by Helen (cf. **1221 / 1217**) becomes the true story of the messenger who alone has returned to tell the tale.

1604–5 / 1617–18 The Messenger ends his account in the usual way, with a reflection meant to draw a lesson from it: it is easy to be fooled by words that are persuasive but false, and therefore best to practice "moderate disbelief" until one has achieved a degree of certainty. Implicit of course is criticism of the king, and once more, also implicitly, appearance and reality have been shown to be at odds.

1606–7 / 1619–20 Amusingly, the Chorus Leader practices her own bit of deception by feigning surprise that Menelaus was ever here. Helen's request for the Chorus's silence (**1381–82 / 1387–89**) was designed to protect her and Menelaus; the Chorus Leader's obfuscation is designed to protect herself and her fellows from the king's anger.

1608–30 / 1621–41 *Dialogue scene* Theoclymenus recognizes, like any love-blinded victim of duplicity in comedy (see note on **1295–1308**), that he has been "snared by women's wiles" (**1608 / 1621**) and understands that Helen has escaped his grasp forever, and this recognition immediately motivates a shift of focus to exacting revenge from Theonoe, whose failure to tell him of the arrival of Menelaus he still has power to punish. This short scene stages the final crisis of the play as an unexpected physical and verbal confrontation between the king and someone who bravely opposes the threatened killing of Theonoe. Our manuscript tradition makes the Chorus (i.e., the Chorus Leader) the king's interlocutor, but such speaker attributions do not carry much weight, and many editors attribute the lines to a male slave, either the Messenger or an otherwise

NOTES

unidentified servant. No solution is free of difficulty. There can be no certainty here, but on the whole the most satisfying staging of this scene appears to be the barring of Theoclymenus' path back into the palace by a servant, who either accompanied him on stage before 1512 or appears at the door of the palace as the king approaches.

This dialogue is cast in trochaic tetrameters, said by Aristotle (*Poetics* 1449a21–4) to be the original meter of tragic dialogue, and which reappears in the later plays of Euripides (and, perhaps following his lead, of Sophocles) for moments of great agitation and high emotion. Here, it underlines the violent onset of the king's anger and the unexpected and spirited resistance of his Servant. One of the advantages of tetrameter is that its length and ease of division into two roughly equal parts provides an excellent medium for *antilabê*, the division of lines between speakers to produce a rapid-fire exchange (here at 1618–27 / 1630–39).

1618–19 / 1630–31 The translation cannot capture a subtlety of the exchange here, the difference in idiom between *eu phronein* ("be in one's right mind") and *eu phronein tini* ("be well disposed to someone"). "Yes," says the Servant, "[I overrule you] because I am in my right mind," but the king's answer, "Not to me, at any rate," converts the phrase to its second meaning.

1626 / 1638 *Only to rule unjustly* Literally, "to do things allowed by divine law, not unjust things." Showing proper respect for the gods, the Servant implies, is tantamount to avoiding injustice.

1629–30 / 1640–41 For the notion of the noble slave, see 745–49 / 728–33.

1631–73 / 1642–87 *"Deus ex machina" scene* As do fully eight other surviving plays of Euripides, *Helen* ends, with a divine epiphany. The Dioscuri are gods for whom epiphany is, as it were, a daily occurrence as they go about their work as saviors or rescuers (*sôtêre*, 1489 / 1500 and 1653 / 1664) of those at sea. It is particularly appropriate for them to make an appearance here, since they are Helen's brothers, mentioned several times during the play and specifically asked at the end of the third *stasimon* to give Helen a safe journey home. The normal duties of divinities in such epiphanies all have a place here: preventing misguided human actions (Theoclymenus is stopped from murdering his sister), providing an Olympian view that corrects the limited perspective of the human actors and helps reconcile them to what must be (Theonoe did her brother no wrong by obeying the gods' will that Helen and Menelaus be reunited and go home), and foretelling the future that destiny has in store (Helen will be made a goddess and give her name to an island off the coast of Attica; Menelaus will be rewarded by ending his wanderings on the Island of the Blessed). On the other hand, there is undoubtedly a feeling of artificiality induced by the appearance of the gods in response to a crisis precipitated by a threat to Theonoe, a relatively minor figure, after the rescue of Helen and Menelaus has already been accomplished, and the explanation of the name of the island of Helen seems unusually inorganic (see on 1658–62).

Although the text provides no explicit evidence for the staging of this scene, there is no reason to doubt that the gods appeared on the theatrical crane (*mêchanê*). Given their role, it is probable that they were swung above the palace on the crane riding on dummy horses. Both Dioscuri appear, but the speech is evidently spoken by one actor, presumably understood to be Castor (see note on 201–2).

1649 / 1660 *we didn't have the strength* Castor explains the brothers' failure to rescue their own sister by invoking the superior power of destiny combined with the wishes of other gods. Gods often offer such explanations to make clear the inevitability of what has happened or is about to happen without giving it their consent or support.

1650–51 / 1662 *That is all / I have to say to you, but to our sister I say* A characteristic transition in *deus ex machina* speeches persons is addressed separately, made slightly odd here (and in *Iphigenia in Tauris*) by the fact that the addressee is not actually there to hear the god's words, having escaped by sea.

1655–57 / 1666–99 The prophecy of Helen's apotheosis to join her brothers corresponds to a joint cult of Helen and the Dioscuri first attested by Pindar, *Olympian* 3.1–2 (dated to 476). Mention of "a share in the gifts and feasts / men offer us" alludes to Helen's part in the *theoxenia*, a traditional and widespread "feast of the gods" whose primary guests were the Dioscuri.

1658–62 / 1670–75 The island that "will be known for the rest of time as 'Helen'" stretches north along the eastern coast of Attica from the promontory of Sounion. Later sources preserve alternative traditions about the origin of the name: that it was the place where Paris and Helen first made love when he carried her off from Sparta, or the place where Helen landed when she returned from Troy. Euripides makes the naming part of the tale of Helen in Egypt by connecting it to Hermes' flight there with her, despite the fact that it would not ordinarily be on the route from Sparta to Egypt. Aetiologies of institutions, customs, and names are regular features of Euripidean endings, but comparison with the others makes this one see unusually perfunctory and inorganic.

1663 / 1677 *the Island of the Blessed* Echoes Homer, *Odyssey* 4.563–9, where Menelaus is promised an afterlife of ease in the Elysian fields with Helen. The
Island of the Blessed, like Elysium, is imagined as a bounteous land
where those favored by the gods enjoy a life full of pleasure after death.

1688–92 All surviving plays of Euripides conclude with choral tailpieces, mostly in
marching anapests and presumably chanted as actors exit and choruses
leave the orchestra. A large number of these "last words," however, are
suspected of being interpolations. The tailpiece of *Helen* also concludes
Alcestis, *Medea* (with a different first line), *Andromache*, and *Bacchae*.
Views on authenticity range from the assertion that the lines are a kind
of Euripidean "signature" to skepticism that they stem from Euripides
at all. On the other hand, if such closing "tags" are merely exit lines
not meant to provide a key to understanding what has come before,
arguments about authenticity based on appropriateness of content or
originality of thought may be mistaken from the start.

CYCLOPS

Translated by

HEATHER McHUGH

With Introduction and Notes by

DAVID KONSTAN

INTRODUCTION

When tragedy was performed in classical Athens (we are speaking here of the fifth century B.C.), each of three competing playwrights staged, on successive days, a set of four plays, called a tetralogy, at the major dramatic festival of the year. The first three were proper tragedies: they might make up a continuous story, as in Aeschylus' *Oresteia*, or else be unrelated in plot, like the *Bacchae*, the *Iphigenia in Aulis*, and the (lost) *Alcmaeon* of Euripides, mounted together in a single (posthumous) performance. The fourth play in the series, however, was something different: This was the satyr play, a burlesque version of a traditional myth, named for the chorus of satyrs or half-human figures—they are goats or horses from the waist down—that was specific to the genre (it is possible that some satyr plays lacked satyrs, but if so, these exceptions were few). One supposes that by this device the grim mood of tragedy was lifted before the audience went home for lunch. One ancient critic (Demetrius, in his essay "On Style," 169) neatly characterized satyr drama as "tragedy at play." But perhaps the element of parody in the satyr play had a deeper significance, offering not so much farce or escapism as a kind of joyful triumph, in which man rescues god instead of abjectly enduring what the gods send.[1]

The only satyr play to survive entire is Euripides' *Cyclops*. There are substantial fragments of some others: Sophocles' *Trackers*, for example (the recent adaptation of this play by Tony Harrison, under the title *The Trackers of Oxyrhynchus*, was a remarkable success), and Aeschylus' *Net-Fishers*, both recovered from papyrus dumps, but Euripides' is the only

---

1. On the satyr play in general, see Dana F. Sutton, *The Greek Satyr Play* (Meisenheim, 1980).

one to be transmitted by way of continuously copied manuscripts. Why it was selected for transcription by Byzantine scholars and teachers is unknown.

To judge from the *Cyclops*, satyr plays were short: At just over seven hundred verses, this one is about half the length of a typical Greek tragedy, and barely counts as a one-act play on the modern stage. It appears that the scene was usually set in some remote place—an island or a deserted seashore—where one might expect to encounter these Pan-like creatures; in the *Cyclops*, the action is located on the island of Sicily, near Mount Aetna, the great volcano that erupted violently early in the fifth century B.C. It is not the real Sicily of Euripides' own time, however, but a mythical place, populated by the giant Cyclopes (three syllables) who were imagined, in some accounts, as forging Zeus' thunderbolts in the furnace of the volcano. This faraway, semiprimitive location is quite different from the setting of Greek tragedy, which was characteristically in front of a royal palace or other populated site, though there are exceptions to this rule: Think of the isolated crag to which Prometheus is tied in the play *Prometheus Bound* (attributed to Aeschylus, but likely a posthumous adaptation by Aeschylus' son of one of his father's unfinished works).

Satyrs painted on vases are often shown wearing short, furry pants with an arc of a horsetail at their rears and, sometimes, an erect penis sticking out in front. They were supposed to be sons of Silenus, who, like them, had equine or caprine accoutrements.[2] Silenus was the boon and boozy companion of Dionysus (Bacchus), the god associated with wine, revelry, masks, and mystery; sometimes, he was represented as Dionysus' foster-parent. The satyrs' connection with the festive wine god contributed to the air of lasciviousness and celebration that attaches to them in the satyr dramas. The trajectory of the satyr plays in general seems to have been from captivity to liberation, as they overcome their separation from the source of joyous frivolity and are reunited with their convivial deity. At all events, this is the pattern of the *Cyclops*. Dionysus was also the patron god of the theater—his priests sat front and center at each dramatic performance—and the theatrical entertainment was part of a festival in his honor. It would appear that the plots of the satyr plays, more than those of either tragedy or comedy, best corresponded to the ritual occasion.

---

2. For representations of satyrs in art, see François Lissarrague, "Why Satyrs Are Good to Represent," in John J. Winkler and Froma Zeitlin, eds., *Nothing to Do with Dionysus?* (Princeton, 1990), 228–36.

II. PRODUCTION

The Athenian theater was part of a holiday ceremony, sponsored by the state, and it differed in important ways from modern dramatic productions. To begin with, a playwright presented his work, perhaps in summary form, to a state official, whose responsibility it was to select the submissions of three dramatists for performance at one of the two citywide festivals: the Great Dionysia, held in early spring, which was the only one to feature satyr plays, and the Lenaea, which took place at the onset of winter (December-January), and again related to Dionysus, as indicated by his cult title, Lenaeus. In the case of comedies, the archon, as the official was called, chose one play from each playwright; the tragedians, as we have seen, submitted sets of four for the Great Dionysia, concluding with the satyr play (playwrights wrote either comedies or tragedies, not both). Once the selection was made, the official assigned to each playwright a troupe of actors—early on, just two, but in Euripides' time a company of three—and a chorus, made up of Athenian citizens. The expenses of training and outfitting the chorus for the citywide performances were undertaken by individual rich citizens and were treated as a kind of tax, like the responsibility of providing the rigging for a naval ship. A trainer was assigned to each chorus, and rehearsals could be time-consuming and intense.

The actual performances at the Great Dionysia were preceded and followed by ritual events in honor of Dionysus. On the day before the shows, there was a procession to and from a nearby village called Eleutherae (related to the Greek word for "freedom"). There was also a public preview of the subjects of the plays, in which the dramatists and actors took a bow. Finally, there was a grand parade in town culminating in a sacrifice of bulls. In Euripides' time, if not earlier, there were also ceremonies in the theater before the performances proper. These included a libation by the ten elected Athenian generals, an announcement of public awards for especially deserving citizens, and a display of the tribute that had been paid by the subject states in Athens' empire; in addition, war orphans who had reached military age, and who had been raised at state expense, were presented in full armor. Theater was a political event as much as a religious expression and a form of entertainment.[3]

At a typical festival, the performances began early in the morning and were over by midday. Tragic competitors had a day to themselves, for the

---

3. For the festival context of the dramatic performances, see Simon Goldhill, "The Great Dionysia and Civic Ideology," in John J. Winkler and Froma Zeitlin, eds., *Nothing to Do with Dionysus?* (Princeton, 1990), 97–129.

exhibition of their four plays (three tragedies plus a satyr play); the comic playwrights, who mounted only one comedy each, all competed on a single day. In addition to the dramatic performances, however, there were contests involving a kind of choral song called a dithyramb. The Athenians were divided into ten broad associations, called tribes, and each tribe mounted both a men's and a boys' chorus. Since these choruses were made up of fifty people each, a quick calculation indicates that one thousand Athenians participated in the dithyrambic competitions alone. To these we must add the choruses in the tragedies and comedies (if we assume that they numbered fifteen each, we get ninety more) and the actors, not to mention a supporting cast of silent supernumeraries, flute players and other musicians, scenery artists, stagehands, judges to choose a winner among the competitors, and who knows how many others. It begins to look as though a good percentage of the Athenian male population was involved simply in putting on the show.[4]

The theater of Dionysus, where the festival of the Great Dionysia was celebrated, was at the foot of the acropolis and probably held as many as twenty-five thousand people. This number represents, on a reasonable estimate, something approaching the total adult male citizen body of Athens. It is unknown whether women attended the theater in Euripides' time (what evidence there is points both ways). But whether they did or did not, the Athenian theater was a huge spectacle, comparable not so much to modern Broadway as to the Super Bowl in the United States or the World Cup in soccer everywhere else. Practically everyone was there to watch.[5]

Physically, the theater was in the shape of a semicircle, slightly prolonged in front and tapering inward. The backdrop, behind the acting area (which was probably on a low, elongated platform in Euripides' time), cut the circle like a cord at the stage end. The seats rose up in tiers, separated by aisles that divided the audience space into wedges. We do not know in what order the general public was seated; it may have been randomly, first come first served (there was a small fee for attendance). I have already mentioned that the priests of Dionysus sat in the front row along with other civic dignitaries; this row curved around

4. General information on the dramatic festivals may be found in A. W. Pickard-Cambridge, *The Dramatic Festivals of Athens*, 2nd ed', rev' by J. Gould and D. M. Lewis (Oxford, 1988); for translations of the texts cited in Pickard-Cambridge and further commentary, see also Eric Csapo and William J. Slater, *The Context of Ancient Greek Drama* (Ann Arbor, 1995).

5. See further Simon Goldhill, "The Audience of Athenian Tragedy," in P. E. Easterling, ed., *The Cambridge Companion to Greek Tragedy* (Cambridge, 1997), 54–68.

what was probably a flat, roughly circular area in front of the actors' platform. It was in this space, called the orchestra and symbolically detached from the stage proper, that the chorus performed. The back wall, behind the stage, contained doors through which actors might pass; very rarely did the chorus leave or enter by this means, which would have meant crossing the stage. On each side, where the seating area terminated, there was an open passage by which the chorus or actors might enter and exit. One direction conventionally led toward a harbor or the sea—Athens' own port, Piraeus, was at some distance from the city—while the other was imagined as heading inland. In the *Cyclops*, for example, Odysseus would have entered and exited on the harbor side, while the Cyclops, who arrives from the wilds where he has been hunting, would have used the other ramp or gangway. When he attempts, later in the play, to visit his brothers, he probably sets out in this same direction.[6]

The differentiation between the space of the chorus and that of the actors bears a relationship to the structure of Greek drama. Typically, the chorus did not intervene directly in the action, and its role, insofar as the plot was concerned, was largely limited to commentary. Hence, they often seem, to the modern viewer, hesitant or passive, as when the chorus of old men in Aeschylus' *Agamemnon* debates whether to rush into the palace when it hears the outcry of the king. In the *Cyclops*, Euripides turns this characteristic of the chorus to advantage, when he has the chorus of satyrs dither and make excuses for not entering the Cyclops' cave—represented by the central door at the back of the stage—and helping Odysseus blind the monster. Euripides wants the satyrs to appear cowardly; in this way, too, perhaps, he sends up the protocol as it functions in tragedy, where playwrights—Euripides included—had to work to preserve the dignity of a do-nothing company of onlookers.

The chorus's chief function in drama, whether tragedy, comedy, or satyr play, was to sing and dance (the word *orchestra* literally means dancing place) in the interludes between the dramatic episodes involving the actors proper. When they had to speak as an individual, in conversation with a regular character in the play, they were normally represented by one of their number, who was the leader. Spoken dialogue was in verse, but of a kind that was, like the Shakespearean iambic pentameter, relatively compatible with ordinary speech. Choral song, however, was metrically more complex and always accompanied by dance steps that were probably executed in unison. On occasion, an

---

6. On the Greek theater, see J. R. Green, *Theatre in Ancient Society* (London, 1994).

actor might sing antiphonally with the chorus (as the drunken Cyclops does at one point in our play) or even interrupt their song at the end of a stanza with a line of dialogue. If the action of the play had reached a delicate point at which silence was required, a playwright might exploit the occasion by having the actor try to hush the chorus, always in vain, of course. For a chorus had no alternative but to sing. In the *Cyclops*, Odysseus comes out of the giant's cave, where the besotted monster is sleeping, to scold the satyrs for their noisy chanting, which threatens to wake Polyphemus. What else were they to do, with the stage momentarily empty, if not perform a choral interlude? Once again, we have a spoof on tragic convention, which is perfectly at home in the parodic atmosphere of the satyr play. In the same way Papageno, in Mozart's opera *The Magic Flute*, lends a comic touch by being obliged to sing with a padlock on his mouth.

We have said that there were three actors who played all the speaking parts. Hence, there could be a maximum of three speaking characters on stage at any one time. In the more complex tragedies, which had several speaking roles, the actors had to change costume between scenes in order to play different characters, or sometimes make a quick change within a scene by exiting and entering through one of the stage doors. The *Cyclops* has only three characters apart from the Chorus (the Chorus Leader, as we have said, functions as a fourth speaker)—Odysseus, Cyclops himself, and Silenus, the satyrs' father and fellow slave. Thus, each actor would have had a single role: the lead actor, called the protagonist, no doubt played Odysseus, while the deuteragonist and tritagonist took the parts of Cyclops and Silenus. These same actors, of course, had played tragic characters in the three tragedies by Euripides—whatever they were—that preceded his satyr play on this occasion.

The actors in the Greek theater could change parts so easily because— in addition to their costumes, which could be very lavish, depending on the generosity of the producer—they wore masks: tragic masks in tragedy, comic masks in comedy, and satyr-play masks in this kind of drama. The masks were largely stereotyped, and indicated at a glance the kind of role that was being played. The masks of the satyrs, for example, were probably more or less similar from one satyr play to another, though no doubt the mask makers could introduce variations and nuances of their own. Vase paintings from a later period give some idea of what these grotesque masks would have looked like. Silenus' mask would have resembled that of the Chorus, only it would have been suitable to an older and more decrepit individual. The mask of the Cyclops was monstrous and had only one eye. Odysseus' mask, and those of his men, who were played by silent extras, will have been human in appearance, like tragic masks, though perhaps with some exaggeration in the features appropriate to the farcical nature of the genre.

Little is known about the acting style of ancient drama. The plays do not come accompanied by stage directions, save for a very few marginal notes (there is one such direction in the *Cyclops*). Thus one is obliged to infer from sparse external evidence and the plays themselves how lines were delivered and what kinds of gestures accompanied them. It is likely, but not absolutely certain, that the action was far more stylized than in the modern theater—more akin to operatic performances, for example. The actors, who were invariably male, presumably adapted their voices to the parts assigned them, rendering them more high-pitched when they played women, for example, although this, too, is conjectural. They were performing in an open-air theater that was the size of a small athletic stadium, and would have had to project their voices to the bleachers. Correspondingly, all the action on stage was imagined as taking place out of doors. That is in part why the Cyclops' gory meal, which occurs inside the cave, cannot be directly represented; it is instead reported at length by Odysseus to the chorus, who have been waiting outside in the orchestra. Odysseus here assumes the role of the messenger in tragedy, a stock figure created to narrate offstage events. Because he has to recount to the audience what has happened indoors, Odysseus must himself be outside the cave, at least temporarily. This puts a strain on his status as captive, and Euripides again makes the best of it by having Odysseus remark openly on his escape, and then, in a gesture of loyalty to his comrades still within, deliberately return in order to rescue them. Thus, dramatic necessity is exploited in the service of characterization. Another reason why the Cyclops' act of cannibalism occurs offstage is that brutal slayings of this sort were not usually represented directly in the Athenian theater, but were reserved by preference for a thrilling messenger speech.

Once all three tetralogies were over, judges (who were appointed by lot) voted prizes for the best set of plays and the best actor. The competitive ethos penetrated almost every activity in ancient Greece, from war to oratory to poetry (compare the contest between Aeschylus and Euripides staged in Aristophanes' comedy *The Frogs*). Within the plays, too, there were often paired speeches in which two characters squared off against one another like opponents in a courtroom (Odysseus and the Cyclops debate the ethics of hospitality versus cannibalism in this formal manner), or else a line-for-line alternation between speakers. And then, when the awards were announced and the festival was ended, the season was over until the next dramatic festival with its entries for that new competition. In the fifth century B.C., that is, from the time of Aeschylus' earliest productions to the deaths of Euripides and Sophocles, a given tetralogy would normally be mounted just once on state occasions in Athens, without the possibility of a repeat performance. True, there were dramatic shows at local village fiestas in the countryside, where plays might be presented a second time, maybe in a reduced or modified form. Perhaps with such rural exhibitions in mind, the dramatists preserved their scripts, even though there was no prospect of a revival at the Great Dionysia or the Lenaean festival. In the fourth century, the works of the great tragedians were put on again, posthumously, and in time acquired sufficient prestige to be copied out officially for the state archive. From there, authorized editions made it to the library of Alexandria and elsewhere, whence a selection, including the *Cyclops* of Euripides, survived in Byzantine copies and, after the fall of Byzantium, in Italian libraries and elsewhere until the coming of print rescued them from the constant threat of disappearance.

III. THE STORY

Euripides based the plot of his *Cyclops* on the famous version of the story recounted in Book 9 of Homer's *Odyssey*, in which Odysseus, having arrived, ten years after the end of the Trojan War, at the land of a civilized people called Phaeacians, relates to his princely hosts the narrative of his wanderings (the full tale of his woes continues until Book 12). Odysseus begins his story with a brief account of a raid on a shore-dwelling population called the Cicones, where he and his men slay the natives and carry off their cattle. Here, Odysseus acquires a special vintage of wine from a priest of Apollo named Maron, whose life he spares (this wine will become important in the episode involving the Cyclopes). As they dawdle over their plunder, Odysseus and his sailors are attacked by local reinforcements (who arrive from the interior) and barely escape on their ships after suffering heavy losses. Odysseus' ships are blown off course in a storm, and their next stop is in a more fantastic place, the so-called land of the lotus-eaters, a people who feed on a narcotic plant that rids them of all thought for the future or the past. After this, they put in at an uninhabited island that lies opposite the territory of the Cyclopes.

Curiosity drives Odysseus to explore the facing shore, where he discovers, just as he does in Euripides' satyr play, the empty cave of a giant, stocked with cheeses and animals too young to pasture; the major difference is that, at this point in the account in the *Odyssey*, there are no satyrs. Odysseus' men urge him to carry off what he can to the ships and make a break for it. Odysseus, in retrospect, recognizes that this would indeed have been sensible, but he determines to await the return of the monster in order to see whether he can extract still greater gifts from him. Odysseus' motives are hardly altogether benign; he is as much a plunderer as the Cyclops will prove to be (Polyphemus himself suspects as much), although he is less savage in that he abstains from eating the carcasses of his victims and contents himself with pillaging their cattle and other provisions. Euripides, we may remark, has sanitized the hero; his Odysseus offers to pay for his provender from the beginning, without thought of theft.

Once Homer's Cyclops returns home, he proceeds directly to the business of his dinner, having imprisoned Odysseus and his men within the cave by means of a great slab of stone placed over the entrance. Odysseus, far from helpless against the giant, is on the point of stabbing him with his sword when he realizes that if he does so, he will be trapped inside. Odysseus then conceives the plan of getting the Cyclops drunk on Maron's wine and grinding out his eye with a stake, expertly hewn as a carpenter would trim a ship's mast. For good measure, Odysseus conceals his identity under the phony name of No-man, a ruse that immediately serves him well when, after the blinding, Polyphemus' brother Cyclopes come running in response to his cries of pain. It is they, rather than the satyrs as in Euripides' play, who answer in all seriousness that if no man is harming him, then Polyphemus must pray to his father Poseidon for relief from his god-sent agony. As his last trick, Odysseus fastens his men and himself beneath the Cyclops' rams, and they escape from the den as the monster lets his animals out to pasture. From there, he and his men return to their ship.

The contest between Odysseus and Polyphemus, then, is not really one of righteousness versus savagery, though the Cyclops' violation of the conventions of hospitality, not to mention his barbarous appetite, convict him of more than human viciousness. Basically, Odysseus is smart, and the Cyclops is big, mean, and dumb, though in his pastoral manner of life and his confidence in the earth's spontaneous bounty he breathes a kind of primitive simplicity: half caveman and half throwback to a bountiful Golden Age. Odysseus triumphs by his wits over the raw brawn of the giant, and this contrast is given point through Odysseus' ruse in dubbing himself No-man. Briefly, the Greek for *no* or *not* is *ou*, which appears in English as *u* in *u*-topia (no-place); the pronoun *one* or *someone*, in turn, is *tis*. Hence Odysseus christens himself *Outis* (No-one). There is, however, a second form of the word *not*, used mainly in hypothetical clauses: this is *mê*. When Polyphemus says that Outis has wounded him, the other Cyclopes, misunderstanding the name, naturally reply that if—note the hypothetical conjunction—*mê tis* (no one) is at fault, then they cannot be of help. However, *mêtis*, read as one word rather than two, is the standard Greek term for *cunning*, and, in the form *polumêtis* (very wily) is one of Odysseus' standard epithets. So it is cunning, the Cyclopes affirm in an unwitting pun, that has brought their brother low.

Once safely on his ship, Odysseus reasserts his true identity: he is not a nobody after all, though he might have seemed such in the Cyclops' cave; rather, he is Odysseus of Ithaca, son of Laertes. But this boast will cost him heavily, not just because of the huge boulders that Polyphemus, guided by the sound of Odysseus' voice, tosses at the ship, nearly sinking it, but also because of the curse that the Cyclops utters in prayer to his father, Poseidon, that Odysseus (for now he knows his name and can aim his imprecation) should reach home after long years and the loss of all his men, only to find his house beset with tribulations. Poseidon gives his assent. This grim prophecy and its consequences are condensed, in the conclusion to Euripides' satyr play, into two and a half brief verses, and thus haven't the resonance that they do in Homer's *Odyssey*. To a Greek audience, Homeric epic was as familiar as a nursery tale, and they would have filled in the denouement unconsciously. Heather McHugh has chosen to flesh out the Cyclops' curtain-closing taunt in Euripides' version in order to restore to the monster something of the fearsome dignity that is his even in defeat.

For the story of Dionysus' capture by pirates (mentioned in the opening verses of the play), Euripides drew upon one of the so-called *Homeric Hymns*, that is, poems in honor of various of the gods composed in a hexameter verse that closely resembles that of the epics—though most of the hymns originated (in all likelihood) a century or more afterwards. The seventh hymn, dedicated to Dionysus, recounts how the god, disguised as a handsome young man, was abducted by Etruscan pirates who planned to hold him for ransom. The silver shackles drop spontaneously from his hands and feet, but the brigands (apart from their pilot) are not discouraged by this sign and force the god on board. Once at sea, vines sprout from the mast, a lion and a bear materialize fore and midships, and the sailors in a panic leap overboard and are transformed into dolphins—save for the pious pilot, whom the god pities and makes prosperous.

Euripides takes advantage of this episode to explain why the satyrs, who are normally in the company of Dionysus, find themselves separated from him and in captivity on this occasion: They had set out in pursuit of their kidnapped god but were shipwrecked on the Aetna side of Sicily, where the Cyclopes dwell. For the duration of the play, they are helpless—estranged from the magical power that Dionysus displays so terrifyingly on the pirate ship—and they depend for their rescue entirely on Odysseus and his men. But the god is, nevertheless, on the scene and active in the form of the wine with which he is identified—to the Cyclops' amused surprise since he finds it absurd that a divinity should choose to reside in a wineskin. In a sense, then, Dionysus does deliver his goatish slaves—by rendering the Cyclops blind drunk—but only when his brew (that is, the god himself) is administered by a human being who is not totally addicted to it.

IV.   INTERPRETATION

Commentators have, in general, described Euripides' version of the Cyclops story as a minimal adaptation of the Homeric narrative, adjusted for performance on stage—Odysseus must be able to get out of the cave, for example, since the classical Greek theater did not enact indoor scenes—and adjusted as well to allow a role for Silenus and the satyrs, who had to be spliced into the tale, however implausibly, in conformity with the conventions of the satyr play. The basic armature of the episode, however, was presumed to have survived these changes intact.

A closer examination reveals, however, that the shift from the essentially two-person story of the *Odyssey,* in which Odysseus outwits the burly but bird-brained monster who has cornered him, to a three-way narrative structure that incorporates the satyrs has a deep effect on the tale and transforms the roles or functions of all the players. In place of Homer's polar opposition between Odysseus and the Cyclops, Euripides offers a ternary pattern: two extremes mediated by a middle term. Let us begin with Euripides' Cyclops: He is brutal and violent, but he is hardly a savage. On the contrary, he speaks and thinks like a sophisticated egoist, in the manner of those self-centered freethinkers whom Plato's Socrates liked to stump with his dialectic—Thrasymachus in the first book of Plato's *Republic,* for example, or the cynical Callicles in the *Gorgias.* In Euripides' time, some of the itinerant teachers known nowadays as sophists as well as other subversive intellectuals drew a sharp distinction between human convention and the laws of nature: Nature, they held, tolerated aggression of any kind in the service of one's appetites, provided one was strong and smart enough to get away with it. Human law was just a ruse on the part of the weak to tame the powerful. So Polyphemus ridicules human legislation as needlessly complicating our lives, rejects the gods' authority with flippant braggadocio, strips nature of all intentionality and responsiveness to justice, and reveres nothing apart from his own belly. This Cyclops is not so much primitive as decadent.

The satyrs, by contrast, are peaceful types, given to partying, and desolate in captivity. Whereas the Cyclopes are in general loners, each dwelling in his own cave with little use for one another, the satyrs are just the reverse: They are sociable creatures, and their role as a chorus neatly symbolizes their primitive solidarity as they speak with a single voice and express themselves indifferently as "I" or "we" (this is standard practice for Greek choruses in any genre). Theirs is the community of booze, egos merged in drunken ecstasy. They are likable enough, but wholly unreliable and irresponsible. Fun-loving cowards like these are of no use when it comes to fighting, even in their own interest. They prefer to stand by while Odysseus takes the risks, without the foresight to realize that their own freedom is at stake.

In their collective devotion to festivity, the satyrs seem to be the diametric opposite of the dour and doughty Cyclops, who lives for himself alone; but extremes have a way of meeting, and the Cyclops shares some fundamental traits with the goat-men. Once he is inebriated, for example, he becomes gregarious enough and seeks out the company of his brother Cyclopes, eager to share his wine and dance for joy with them. Odysseus' problem at this stage of the action is precisely how to keep the beast at home and contain his sudden enthusiasm for good fellowship. Meantime, just as Odysseus is on the point of blinding the monster, the satyrs seem to lose their common identity as chorus and speak severally, each coming up with a different excuse for why he can't participate in the action. Despite their propensity to merrymaking and pack life, the satyrs are as selfish as they come, out for themselves first and last. In particular, Silenus, their father, is a nasty old coot, ready to sell the Cyclops' wares for a sip of wine and to lie through his teeth when the giant returns to his cave; he is even prepared, one surmises from a reckless oath he swears, to sell his own children down the river if it will save his skin.

The chief differences between the satyrs and the Cyclopes seem to reside in their dissimilar diets and the disparity in their physical strength. Polyphemus has the confidence of his toughness and will eat humans when he has the chance. It is noteworthy, however, that he does not consume satyr meat. That is, I think, another connection between the two species: They do not cannibalize each other. The satyrs, by contrast, are timid, though by no means humble. What they eat is a mystery, though they clearly find the Cyclopes' anthropophagy horrible and disgusting. They are, however, deeply dedicated to drink.

Set off against this codependent dyad of bully and crybaby is Odysseus, who is, one may recall, the only human actor on the stage (along with the silent extras who play his mates). Whereas the beast-men, both the Cyclopes and the satyrs, are supremely selfish and materialistic, thinking of nothing beyond their immediate carnal urges, Odysseus is quite civilized and humane—more so, to our lights at least, than his Homeric avatar. Right from his first entrance, he announces his intention of purchasing provisions honestly, without a hint that he might plunder others' goods (this is a comic turn as buying and selling have no place in tragedy). Then, in his exchange with Silenus, he asks whether the Cyclopes have cities and government and whether they respect strangers—as he himself presumably does or would. The absence of civic life leads Odysseus to inquire whether human beings or wild animals inhabit the land, to which Silenus replies ambiguously: "Cyclopes," insinuating that they are neither the one nor the other. Nor are they—any more than the satyrs themselves are. The uncertain species status of the Cyclopes raises, indeed, an interesting puzzle: If they are not human, then neither are they cannibals for eating men, any more than lions are or humans who consume cattle. After all, the Cyclopes do not feast on one another, nor, as we have seen, do they include satyrs in their cuisine. To the extent that they are other, then, they are no worse than carnivores. The Cyclopes are a strange hybrid: They speak and think and this is enough to qualify them as human (especially to a Greek) and to make their culinary habits abominable; yet they, like the satyrs, are of a different race. This conundrum is a reminder that the monstrous is precisely that which defies classification rather than that which is violent or hideous by nature.

To return to Odysseus, not only does he reveal himself as law abiding with respect to trade or exchange of goods, he is also a model of loyalty to his men. When he finds himself outside the Cyclops' cave—as he must, since the constraints of Greek theatrical conventions (we have said) did not permit interiors to be shown—he declares aloud that he could save himself, if he chose, but that would be an injustice to his friends. Odysseus lives by a code of reciprocity and fairness, whether in regard to commerce or allegiance to his subordinates—and in his relations, we may suppose, with guests as well. In this he differs from the Cyclops and the satyrs alike. Where they are self-centered and given only to consuming, not to conferring in return, Odysseus both gives and takes: The satisfaction of his needs is matched by his generosity. Thus, Odysseus—or humanity in general—is the necessary third term between the egoistic isolationism of the Cyclops and the collapse of self represented by the satyrs: He stands for interconnectedness, which mediates between extreme individualism and the sameness of the horde.

If the extremes represented by the satyrs and the Cyclops tend to meet, however, in a common voracity and narrow devotion to pleasure, how can Odysseus' sense of mutuality mediate between them? What comes first, it seems, is the human idea of relatedness, which presupposes termini that are distinct yet united. One can destroy a relationship between two things either by cutting the cord that joins them, as it were—thus converting the endpoints into independent monads like the Cyclopes—or collapsing the extremes together into a single mass: This is the undifferentiated unity of the mob. This is a very abstract way of talking about Euripides' *Cyclops*, of course; it is offered merely as a diagram or simplification of the complex social behaviors that operate within the play.

To take another set of differences among the personalities in the *Cyclops*, Odysseus is the only character who does not drink wine in the course of the action. Not that he is a teetotaler, of course; he has no objection to drinking wine when it is appropriate to do so. But he knows how to do so in moderation and is capable of exercising self-control, in particular in the difficult circumstances in which he finds himself in the Cyclopes' territory. Neither Silenus nor Polyphemus exhibits a comparable restraint. Further, both the Cyclops and the satyrs have an inordinate interest in sex. Polyphemus threatens to rape old Silenus; the chorus of satyrs draws a lubricious inference from the Greeks' recovery of Helen, imagining that her liberators must have taken turns screwing her. Odysseus, in this play, has no time for such monkey business. He is in perfect control of his appetites.

I do not want to convert Euripides' Odysseus into a Boy Scout, although his impassioned defense of the Trojan War as a fight to preserve the gods' shrines and keep the Greek world safe and free rings of juvenile patriotism. It is not as though the Trojans had attacked Greece, after all. (Granted, Odysseus is striking a pose in his attempt to sway Polyphemus.) What is more, Odysseus himself had a seamy family history, according to an account that is alluded to by Silenus, which made him the son or grandson of the thieving Sisyphus rather than of Laertes, as in the *Odyssey*. Human beings undoubtedly come off as superior to Cyclopes and satyrs in this play, but Euripides, with the impartial calumny of satire, also undercuts their pretensions to transcendent virtue.

While the date of the *Cyclops* is unknown (metrical and stylistic features suggest a time late in Euripides' career, but this method of dating is insecure, particularly for a satyr play, since this is the only complete one we have), it certainly coincided with the period of Athens' imperial hegemony, and very likely with the Peloponnesian War, the great conflict between the Athenian and Spartan confederacies that dragged on over the last third of the fifth century B.C. In the year 415, the Athenians launched a huge armada with the intention of reducing Syracuse, the chief city on the island of Sicily, and bringing the western sea under its control, thereby choking off Sparta and its allies. It is tempting to see an allusion to this expedition or its aftermath in Odysseus' encounter with the monster who resides beneath Mount Aetna, but there is little in the play that suggests political allegory. It is safer to suppose that Odysseus' participation in the campaign at Troy, and the justifications he offers for it, smack of Athenian imperialism in a general way, and that the Cyclops may not be wholly fatuous or out of character when he derides the war as a hideous waste of life for the sake of one faithless woman. Again, Polyphemus' dark prophecy at the end, muted though it is in the original, may have resonated, however subtly, with fears or memories of Athenian naval disasters in distant parts.

Finally, what of the gods? The Cyclops believes he himself is one, and descended from another, Poseidon; the satyrs and their father Silenus are the constant companions of Dionysus. Odysseus is only a mortal, but he claims to have protected the gods' rites and temples, the means, that is, by which humans render unto the gods what is their due and receive from them in turn aid and sustenance. In his two prayers for the gods' favor, Odysseus makes clear their obligation to deal justly with mankind in return for the worship that is given them; if they fail their part of the bargain, then there remains no reason for human reverence or faith. Here again, we see the code of reciprocity that governs and defines human conduct in all domains. For all its spirit of caricature and travesty, Euripides' *Cyclops*, and perhaps the satyr play in general, offers an optimistic vision of human ties—as opposed to raw nature—that can hold its own against the somber universe of tragedy.[7]

V.   STYLE AND TRANSLATION

The *Cyclops*, like all classical Greek drama, is written in verse. It is thus poetry, albeit in a less elevated register than the great choruses of Aeschylean tragedy and similarly sublime lyrics. Most of the lines are in the verse characteristic of dialogue, which contains six iambic beats in three pairs of two beats each; marked breaks in the line (caesuras) tend to fall within a foot, rather than between feet, to prevent the line from collapsing into its parts. The iambs are not constituted of unstressed and

7. For interpretations of the *Cyclops*, see William Arrowsmith, 'introduction' to his translation of the *Cyclops*, in David Grene and Richmond Lattimore, eds., *The Complete Greek Tragedies* (Chicago, 1956); Robert G. Ussher, "The *Cyclops* of Euripides," *Greece and Rome*, n.s., 18 (1971), 166–79; David Konstan, "The Anthropology of Euripides' *Kyklōps*," in John J. Winkler and Froma Zeitlin, eds., *Nothing to Do with Dionysus?* (Princeton, 1990), 207–27.

stressed syllables, as in the English iambic pentameter, but rather of short and long syllables, an effect unfamiliar in English verse but which we are attuned to hear in songs. Besides straight dialogue, there are also choral odes, but in the *Cyclops* these are few and brief. The odes, which were accompanied by an oboe-like instrument and sung rather than recited, had complex metrical patterns based on rather free combinations of longs and shorts, something like the lines of varying length and rhythm that make up Wordsworth's *Ode on Intimations of Immortality*. Vocabulary and, in one detail, pronunciation, too (a broad, Doric *a* in place of *e* in certain word forms), distinguished the choruses from spoken verse.

The diction of the *Cyclops* is in general less grandiose than that of tragedy, admitting more colloquialisms and witty turns of speech, but it never loses a stateliness in language and syntax that it shares with the higher genres of Greek poetry. Anyone who reads ancient Greek can tell in a moment that this is not prose, even apart from the fact of meter; the comic effects in the play, in turn, do not rely mainly on violations of linguistic decorum. Euripides does vary the tone and style for humor's sake, but it is done subtly rather than in a spirit of verbal slapstick.

For this translation, Heather McHugh relied in the first instance (as she explains in her foreword) on David Kovacs's version (1994) in the Loeb Classical Library series (which the reader may confidently consult for a literal prose rendition of the original) in combination with other translations; but the result resembles only accidentally, when at all, any of the versions with which she worked. I contributed clarifications of some particular points of exegesis (we do not always follow Kovacs's text, for example), and a few suggestions on phrasing. I was thrilled when Heather elected to adopt a couple of them.

I can assure the reader that the present translation is faithful to the original. I mean faithful first of all in the literal sense, that is, the translator honestly reproduces the meaning of the Greek text, passage for passage, rather than bending it to an interpretation of her own. Here and there, especially in the choral songs, which cannot withstand word-for-word conversion, Heather has permitted herself slightly greater liberties. A few times, for example in the wordplay on numbers in the prologue and in the Cyclops' final prophecy, she has expanded on hints or possibilities in the original in order to give more bite to the English version. None of this obscures the significance of the Greek, and it will not mislead the reader as to the import of Euripides' text. Such changes as Heather made are, in my view, in the service of a second and higher kind of fidelity, which is to the poetry of the Greek. One can be faithful to this only by rendering it into English poetry, and what is more, poetry that can be read aloud, and on the stage. The present translation is for the ear as much as for the eye. It is Euripides in English, and I hope that those who hold the book in their hands may also have the pleasure one day of seeing the play performed in the theater.

DAVID KONSTAN

ON THE TRANSLATION

It would be hard to miss one fundamental metaphor in any story involving disreputable giants: The one giving rise to the question what, in any sense that matters, makes a mortal being big. For it is the Cyclops' own sense of engorged self that Odysseus must topple in the course of the action. And this giant's dimensions are constantly materialized in the play by reference to the size of the meals or drinking vessels he requires or how many men would be needed to drive the sharpened tree into his eye. Like any great poet's details, these narrative particulars are not without significance in the moral field of the story. Polyphemus is the son of the geosphere and his self-centered universe has a single moon-eye. Insofar as Number One is all he's looking out for, he's the perfect figure of the global consumer, mere amounting's profanation of the very *art* of numbers, the very essence of magnanimity. And when, in that moment of doubt every great figure experiences at its nadir, Odysseus fears that the greatest One might not come to his aid, his dread is of an emptiness at the heart of the most transcendent numbers: Zeus may be nothing but a zero.

I've emphasized the numbers-play throughout the dramatic play because numbers afford us such a fertile field for cultivating questions of value. Luckily for the comic registers of the play, there's something not only vile but also preposterous about the value systems of Silenus and his sons: Silenus is introduced melodramatically enumerating the sufferings he's endured in the service of Dionysus. (The satyr's mimicry of the epic sufferings of Odysseus, whose traveler's travails are the very stuff of epic figures, is only one of the play's many mirrorings.) I've emphasized this satyr-element by stylizing the ludicrousness in Silenus' self-pity-as-self-promotion: He contradicts himself, even as he counts off his agonistic accomplishments—for with each enumeration of his sufferings, he claims that they're innumerable. By foregrounding this tallying of countlessness, I hoped comically to activate the rhetorical equivalent of a moral motif, one that might help prepare the audience for what will later crop up not only in Silenus' own effusions (see 264–73 / 232–40), in which Silenus so overplays his betraying hand, and also 293–99 / 262–69, where he swears by too much to be true) but also in the prolix language of the Chorus (Silenus' sons), whose long-winded hyperspecifications about how precisely to be of service turn out to be precisely self-serving. The Chorus gives us to understand how a word like *consideration* might have come to mean mere *compensation*. All its big words are to little ends, as a sufficient dilation on action amounts to an evasion of it.

This is just one trail of emphases I've highlit for figurative contrast, a contrast between the circles of the richest human relation and the zeros of mere accumulation, of social and spiritual indifference. Silenus claims that he loves his sons "more than anything on earth"—but offers *their* lives as collateral, not his own. And when the sons hear of that, they damn their father. By contrast, the circle of faith to which Odysseus pays homage very much comprehends the circle of family loyalty (which he defends when Silenus insults Odysseus' father, Sisyphus; and which he invokes in alluding to the Cyclops' filial relation to Poseidon). And insofar as Odysseus is *not* merely self-interested, his concerns extend beyond those of his own family. Indeed the largest interests to which he alludes include the interests of civility, a principle that would admit to its realm and benefits even the Cyclops, were the creature to honor family (see 321–33 /290–98), or honor the community of mortal moral code (334–38 / 299–303). Odysseus finally appeals to the Cyclops on the Cyclops' own grounds: All these social sympathies may ultimately benefit the individual, whereas self-interest unrefreshed by communal empathy ends up incurring its own demise.

But the Cyclops' circles of authority are empty, involving as they do the evacuable rounds of the belly, the wheel of seasons without will, and gaping holes in human law. (The zeros of the legal nooses and loopholes to which he alludes will seem familiar to contemporary audiences.) The Cyclops (who himself is named for circularities of vision) thus becomes the foil for the more transcendent circles of Zeus. In the lineage of storytellers, Odysseus is kin to the playwright himself, a "no one" who knows much, and who is in fact the grounding figure. Unlike the Chorus, Odysseus weaves a story not for sensational or voyeuristic ends, but to elicit human sympathy, greatening human action beyond the spheres of merely local identity. Some time after Euripides, medieval theologians will propose for divinity the circle whose center is everywhere and whose circumference is nowhere, its boundaries beyond all mortal ken. This construction of divinity's circle is close kin to Odysseus' ringing, concentrifying senses of relation.

Silenus and his sons are, by comparison, the moral relativists. Expedient, they are the sneakiest things afoot. Their idea of poetic license is opportunistic, and when the balance of power swings from one figure to another, they change their footwork to save their skins. They want to be part of the big triumph, they dream of fame—but when the mortally dangerous, morally decisive act looms, they bog down in questions of critical one-upmanship: Whose hand should be first on the weapon, whose hand number two? So they evade the act itself. At times they seem to represent the decline of servile nature into mere aestheticism: Given the chance, they set themselves up as the music critics of the singing Cyclops, so that ultimately even their consternation seems trivial, in view of the brutalities the Cyclops has committed. Where Silenus and his sons could be said to be doubletalkers, forked of tongue, Polyphemus speaks in only one tongue, and the one tongue says there's no god bigger than himself. When Odysseus tries to address Polyphemus' sense of honor and human community, Silenus tells the Cyclops to ignore him: The only fat you should chew with him, he says, is his own. Have his tongue for dessert, and then in how many voices you'll speak!

But Odysseus is a world traveler. If he speaks in many tongues, it is as often for establishing a mutuality as it is for selfish guile or guise. So the question of numbers is the question of language as well: How can one represent oneself without duplicity? La Rochefoucauld's acid aperçu (that the function of language is to conceal our thoughts) smacks of Silenian intercourse. Self-service is intimate with duplicity. A self-serving nature is by nature a slave (and when circumstances release the Chorus from one slavery, it looks forward to another, as the play's last line suggests). The Chorus toadies up to whatever power seems likeliest at the moment to afford a reprieve. Odysseus is, by contrast, the figure of nobility, and nobility (it needs repeating, in the context of America's distaste for even its own aristocratic histories) does not impose the hierarchies of order—it *incurs* them. The great man knows there is always something greater than himself.

The selfish man, however well fed, is the small man: He thinks of nothing beyond his own circle of interests. The Cyclops with his overfed emptiness, his diminished firsts, his fattened fists, his infinite regress of an eye trained only on itself, has something in common with Silenus. But Silenus stands on slipperier ground. The Cyclops stands, at least, on a single solid mortifying philosophical ground; by comparison the members of the Chorus seem all the more detestable as they hold no premises undesertable.

Of course, all these figures seem reprehensible in comparison with the figure of Odysseus as he appears in this play, where he makes, even to the Cyclops, civilized appeals on moral and ethical grounds, and promises to save even the traitorous Silenus and his sons. But Euripides does not oversimplify Odysseus' virtues. The Greek audience would come to the play knowing the *Odyssey*'s history of plunderings and subterfuge; and with good reason Homer refers to Odysseus as Polytropos, man of many turns, man of many tropes. When Polytropos meets Polyphemus, we have a metamyth: a meeting of the figures of figures.[1]

And in this play the field of character *resemblances* is exploited as fruitfully as is the field of *distinctions*. For example, the argument—at 316–92 / 285–345—between Odysseus' version of a life of traditional honor and the Cyclops' version of a life of self-satisfaction finds its mirror-image in the later responsorial between Odysseus-as-entrapper and a rather endearingly drunken Cyclops. Here the positions of honor are reversed: Odysseus has to deceive the Cyclops in order to avenge his companions. (Honorable necessity, like honorable men, is submitted to hierarchical patterns.) And when the Cyclops proposes in his sentimental wallowing a sort of love, that is, puts forth the virtues of sharing some wine with his brother Cyclopes down the road, he has to be dissuaded of this virtuous impulse by Odysseus, who steers him back toward more selfish grounds (594–97 / 531–34):

CYCLOPS: I'd like to give my brothers some of this stuff.
ODYSSEUS: You keep it to yourself, and they'll admire you more.
CYCLOPS: But giving it, I'd be a better brother.
ODYSSEUS: The best of revelers wind up in fisticuffs.

Here Odysseus becomes the legalistic hairsplitter and noose-looper: In order to serve the larger justice, he has to commit an injustice. In consequence, a civilized reader finds himself sometimes sympathizing with the monster, whose cries of pain and betrayal will soon be derided by both Chorus and Odysseus, commoner and nobleman alike.

The world's worth cannot be weighed according to numerical incidence—numbers of people per usual unit or type—whether the type is of

---

1. Interesting to consider, in this connection, the early seventeenth-century grammar play the *Heteroclitanomalonomia*, based on Andrea Guarna's *Bellum Grammaticale*, in which parts of speech are personified, and engage in warfare. Indeed, another play from the same period, the *Gigantomachia*, equips its giants with the weapons of whole hills—which they heave at foes, as does Euripides' Cyclops—and then calls those hills a grammarian's "heteroclites" (the Indo-European root, in its suffixed form, is *klei-tor*, "incline, hill"). I do the ancient dramatist the homage of assuming that (since his audience would have come to the performance equipped with a rich foreknowledge of the stories) he might well enjoy not only the play *of* the fable, but the play *with* it.

nation or decade or color or faith. American democracy pays lip service to this largest principle, but there's another principle we find our natures less well equipped to sponsor. The majority will not always be just. And if one has to be *like* to be liked, sooner or later one has (like Silenus) to lie: One cannot always resemble without dissembling. Odysseus' strength of character shines out most forcefully when he finds he stands alone.

As I say, I've emphasized a number of numbers in my rendition of the play, in an effort to counterpose the footwork of fancy (poetry and pleasure, the Bacchic virtues) against its mimicry in the fancy footwork of evasion and unreliability; the number one of the logos against the number one of self-interest; the sphere of moral nourishment versus the zero of empty self-satisfaction or godlessness; and so on. The gist of the numbers-play, it seems to me, remains of use today, to those of us who live in latter-day versions of the very democracy to which Odysseus first alludes when he arrives in Cyclopsland. Its gist is this: The man who carries within himself a sense of the cumulative value (not additive progress) of human history; the man aware of the depth of his relation-ship to other living beings (including beasts); the man aware that family relations and the relations of myth are similarly "telling"; the man aware of his subordination before the orders of nature and god; and, finally, the man aware of the ultimate insufficiency of any one group-interest or self-interest—that man achieves greatness. His richest holding is insight. No other material greatness will matter, no other carnal accounting can count.

Thus can poetry count. I've replicated no accentual or syllabic fea-tures of the Greek original, but I have tried to recognize affinities within word-strings, echo-effects, and emanations (sound-trails, image-con-trails) that are the very stuff of poetic configuration. Some of my early efforts to raise to the surface the "round eye" etymologically present in the word *Cyclops*, or more conspicuously to apply inside the poetry the many-storied etymology of Polyphemus, were ultimately relinquished in the course of making this translation. Where I have kept some stubborn fidelity to the linguistic freight of the original is where song-shapes were called for or where words repeated themselves for poetic purposes. The Chorus abuses its brutes in brutish language (48–68 / 41–62); and the beasts and their keepers alike are subordinate to an *Über*-brute. Insofar as the Cyclops is the god of his underworld, his hierarchy is the mirror image of Odysseus' godly one. And if at the end I'm tempted to empha-size the inverse orders of Polyphemus' mephitic domain, his stubborn conviction that by digging deeper in, he can come out on top, perhaps that spiritual topography will concatenate with the end of the *Inferno*, where it's hard to know which way is up until the reader emerges again out of the world of fable and into that of his own life's story.

At the play's outset, the Cyclops was said to be out "tramping the wilds," but the audience soon discovers to what extent Polyphemus harbors the wilderness inside himself: Civility is carried in the single soul. It's not achieved by the superaddition of mere numbers of people. A city can be a wilderness, as in our day we know too well. In the mock-civilization of which the Cyclops is the emperor, he becomes also the very figure of spoiled refinement. To the extent that Polyphemus is a delectator and gourmand who might be recognizable to American audiences, I felt entitled to update some of the references (availing myself, for example, of certain polycultural culinary registers; it never hurts when a hint at the eater lurks within the eaten, like a Gorgon in the Gorgonzola). The figure of corrupt or self-absorbed wealth is satirically registered in the passages in which Polyphemus mulls over his meals—at 245–46 / 218, for example, where he might as well be the orderer of adjectives in a Seattle cappuccino-line (is it no accident Seattle's best anagram is "let's eat"?)—or later, at 277–81 / 244–49, where he savors the competing claims on his prandial imagination: how much to have of roasted man, how much of braised.

It's clear from very early on that Silenus and his kin are of a different herd than is Odysseus: Indeed, there's a closer kinship among the sheep, the Chorus, Silenus, and the Cyclops than there is between any of them and Odysseus. (Odysseus' ruses in other stories of his travels, his thefts of provision, his infidelities to family, are not featured in the Euripidean Cyclops.) Here Odysseus is, among all the characters, the one most prepared to sacrifice himself for something bigger than himself. Even the uppermost figure in any human order (and perhaps especially that figure) must acknowledge an order greater than its own; and until the spheres of relationships are seen to radiate toward and comprehend the uncontainable, no man's figure is of value, and Zeus' zero threatens to be one more empty Cyclops eye: means without meaning.

The eye that matters, of course, is the mind's eye, eye of empathetic imagination. Even when Odysseus is free from the cave, he can't stop seeing the plight of his friends and so is driven by imagination (the mind's eye) to return to their aid. By contrast, the Chorus solicits prurient details about the rape of Helen and all the sensational particulars of the torments of Odysseus' friends (as something sufficiently bestial in contemporary folk is drawn to highway carnage or the most predatory particulars of the dirty-movie channel). The Chorus does not possess the solitary eye of the Cyclops: it has the compound eye of the voyeur. Moral blindness has everything to do with the action of this play.

The Cyclops, if Silenus' own testimonies are to be believed, has never before been known to revel. Yet when the intoxicated creature bursts into song, Silenus mocks the rural oaf who never took singing lessons. Silenus savages the Cyclops not for his savagery, but for his want of singing skill—his lack of taste—and so manages less to distinguish himself from, than to resemble, the Cyclops (who fancies himself a sort of culinary connoisseur, as cannibalistic characters go). Silenus would enlighten the Cyclops only to lord it *over* him: wants first for the lout to "see the lyric light," and then wants both his lights put out—of sight and song alike.

At the dramatically crucial moment, when the Chorus members give their last-minute (lame!) excuses for not helping Odysseus (I think I'm suffering from leg cramps, I think I've got a sprain), America's colloquial application of "I think" seemed to me to be opportune: far from securing, it makes insecure. For despite the human presumption to distinguish itself from all lower orders by virtue of its intellect, and despite the elaborate word-works of the Chorus members' excuses, these guys aren't so much turning things over in mind as they are turning tail. To the enlightenment that really counts, a 20/20 vision can be blind. What matters most is visible by insight.

I shouldn't leave David Konstan with the sole burden of explaining the liberties I've taken at the end of the play. The abruptness of Euripides' ending was the most dramatically frustrating element of the play for me, as a literary artist. In Kovacs's literal version, the Cyclops ends by saying: "Oh no you won't: I shall break off a piece of this crag, hurl it, and crush you, companions and all, to bits. I'm going up to the hilltop, blind though I am, by climbing through my tunnel." Then the Chorus ends the play by proclaiming, as if it had not heard the Cyclops' threat: "As for us, we shall be shipmates with Odysseus and ever after serve in Dionysus' train." And that's that. An entire drama has been predicated on the suspense of our wish to know whether or not the Cyclops would prevail over his guests, and we wind up with only these three last turns in the dialogue: Odysseus saying "Now we'll escape"; the Cyclops saying "No you won't"; and the Chorus saying "Now we are saved." By way of culminating dramatic sequence, that one (in and of itself) strikes me as fatally inconsequential.

Euripides is no fool. He could count on something we can't count on now. A contemporary audience may not know the Cyclops episode takes place early in Odysseus' journey home; indeed, it's likely to know nothing of the story of Odysseus at all. The Greek audience, acquainted with the myths revisited in this play's performance, knew the Cyclops wouldn't kill Odysseus, yet also knew Odysseus was wrong to think his sufferings were all behind him. That's why I felt I had to compensate for the dramatic incommensurability of my audience with the Greek one—somehow, for the drama's sake, fill in some of the story's once-implicit play of mutualities, to serve Euripides' ends today.

Odysseus has just revealed himself to have a flaw, after all: He dismisses the blinded Cyclops just at the moment the creature acknowledges that "There was a story to the effect that you would cause me this suffering—but in that story you went on to suffer." This is a crucial point, it seems to me. The telling of stories has all along been coded into Polytropos' name (man of many turns and tropes) and into Polyphemus' name (the many-storied, often-spoken-of, much-famed). These names are earnable only after notable deeds take place: So there's a delicious anachronism (and metanarration) at work in the Greek drama. And it is Polyphemus, not the polytropic Odysseus, who recalls to the audience that fact—the fact of foretelling's force, and memory's. But this reminder of the power of the story is dismissed by Odysseus. He thinks he has already put behind him the narrative of his suffering. That's the pride preceding a fall. Odysseus may mock the Cyclops, but in fact the Cyclops is seeing clearly for once in his life, and at this moment Odysseus seems the blinder one. In a sense, he wants to preempt history all by himself, turn into mere *fait accompli* the everunwinding fable of past and forecast. Such a disposition is of moment for dysmemoried America. Here is my version of the concluding lines of the play (696–709 in the Greek expanded to **798–828**):

CYCLOPS   There was an ancient prophecy that said
                  I would be blinded by you, in this way.
                  It also prophesied a punishment for you:
                  to roam around the sea for what
                  would seem an endless age.

ODYSSEUS   So now you are a sage. I say the future you predict
                  is history already. Take all your time warps and
                  your prophesies,
                  and go to blazes. I, for one, am going to the beach.
                  A boat awaits, to take us home
                  from this infernal Sicily.

CYCLOPS   Oh no, you don't. I'll break this rock apart
                  and throw down boulders, till your boat and you
                  and all your friends are smithereens.
                  I may be blind, but you are all at sea—
                  I may be single-minded: you are all adrift.
                  You think a son of earth was what you dropped—
                  but I'm Poseidon's son as well, and I can lift.
                  You twisted time to your own ends—

> but I can still negotiate a twisted space:
> I'll feel my way to Nomen's land. My blindness
> knows its place: it has no boundaries, it doesn't stop.

And only then did I return to what literally occurs as the Cyclops' last line in Euripides' text:

> I'll take an under-tunnel to the mountaintop.

Not only the Cyclops' darkness, but the Chorus's self-absorption won't be stopping, either. Unlike the Cyclops, the Chorus has suffered no rebuke, and no enlightening. It continues with characteristic sweeping statement and unreliability, blind faith in itself and its day:

> CHORUS LEADER   Forget his malices and miseries. What future
> could so big a blindness tell? His selfishness
> is ancient history. Whereas, now, we—
> we are the model of modernity—that's why
>
> we're saved: to multiply, at last, in luxury!
> By change's wind and by the future's wave,
> let's sail, O brave Odysseus!
> Just forward us to Bacchus, and
> we'll be the best of slaves.

That snap into fast-forward, to escape ambiguous questions (such as those the Cyclops has raised about time's telling and retellings) is a familiar chronic mechanism. There's a blindly buoyant cheerfulness about the Chorus's evasions, a turning away from all but the moment's most convenient histories and ends; it may ring a bell for Americans who chance to see this play. As I write at the end of the twentieth century, most of my fellow citizens (for all their investment in education) have at best a dim familiarity with the venerable stories of human history. Even a great civilization may wind up deepening its moat: Its security in its own premises becomes a form of provinciality. The insular condition isn't only rural Sicily's. I hope my modest embellishments at the end of the play supply for such an audience some of the links and bridging that Euripides' audience would have assumed from the popular legacy of fable.

To those who would admonish my audacity, I submit by way of exculpatory evidence the literary quality of the result in English. The second life of poetry, says Eugenio Montale, is memory. And if ancient poetry is to be taken to heart by new worlds of English-speaking consumers, the first obligation of the translator is to its memorability as English poetry. It was in the first place only with trepidation that I accepted Oxford's challenge to create yet another version of Euripides' *Cyclops*—a poet's version abetted (and not restricted) by the scholar's understandings. The very thought of identifying—and then hashing out—questions of poetic interpretation, negotiating the resources and limitations of two languages at once, is enough to daunt any sensible soul. On my own, I had done translations from the French (a language I knew well); and I had collaborated with my husband in translations from the Bulgarian and German (languages as Greek to me as Greek is). Comparing the products of my solitary enterprises with those of the collaborations made it apparent how much is possible if you are conversant with, and confident of, your consultant's gifts. Most important is the capacity richly to read poetic turns of mind wherever they occur, in source and target languages alike—for the greatest of all translatorial paradoxes is this: So few native speakers of *any* language speak Poetese.

Just as rural islanders off Maine and Norway and Chile may have more in common with each other than with inland citizens of their own nations' capitals, poets everywhere may be more perversely versatile, more diction-addicted, more word-working, and more language-loving than even the most knowledgeable other readers and writers. Artists everywhere may be uncannily alert to perceptual patterns, image-grids, sound-systems, frames and flows of relation: and indeed there were times in collaborative translation when I could intuit (from patterns in the raw material of the literal versions I was supplied) image-thoughts or figural ideas my collaborator may at first not even have noticed—despite his being the native speaker or scholar in the source language—but later confirmed. It's a translatorial truism that one cannot hope to duplicate in another language the precise music or senseshades of the original; but it's less often observed, and no less important, how rarely native speakers of the target language imagine the ranges of musics and means, spare or sumptuous, the spirit of a poem might require. Of my competence in the sensual and syntactical resources of the English language I am as confident as I am of the scholarly skills, literary instincts, and collaborative understanding of David Konstan, to whose remedying astuteness my first drafts were submitted. To be consigned to such auspices proved most reassuring: For fine scholarship requires more than one kind of vision, and Konstan's insights were compounded at once of authority and of grace.

There were two other overwhelming inducements to accept the project. One was the sudden appearance just then, by chance, in my readerly purview, of an inspiring translation from the ancient Greek— Seamus Heaney's version of *Philoctetes* (a book Heaney calls *The Cure at Troy*).[2] To read it was to be reminded (with that rush of thrill one feels at

2. *The Cure at Troy: A Version of Sophocles' "Philoctetes"* (London, 1990; New York, 1991).

an old knowledge reinvigorated) how livening an act of interpretation can be. Heaney's *Philoctetes*—with its glimpses of human being in the act of being (and even not being!) itself, feeling (and even not feeling!) itself—amounts to a lovely rereading of the old drama: a resuscitation of identity's ancient social senses, inside a contemporary reader's ever-perishing self-senses. The poetic intelligence with which Heaney approached the already long-known *Philoctetes* gave me heart: for great literature is new again and again, in each reader's acts of best attention. And a translation is not a review, nor is it the same view from a different angle: It is, in fact, a new view.

The *Cyclops* itself I'd known through translations (including the most literal prose versions) already available: First and foremost, the authoritative groundwork of David Kovacs's *Cyclops* in the Loeb Classical Library series (published by Harvard University Press). On this version (considered by most scholars to be the most dependable literal rendering in English) I relied most heavily—with gratitude for the Greek *en face* and critical notes throughout. I was also notably served, as the work proceeded, by an extraordinary resource: the on-line Perseus Project. Accessible on internet instruments not even dreamt of a few years ago, it seems, for classical studies, already a hermeneutic indispensability. It's hard to overstate the delight one feels (literally! at one's fingertips!) on double-clicking any word in the Greek play, and finding oneself zoomed straight to the comprehensive reference, a collation of some of the best classics authorities in the world. Not only the scholars but also the universities that collaborate to administer the Perseus Project deserve high praises for their service to the students and standards of Greek and Roman literary studies.

But it is first and finally Euripides—with all the life still in him—who most irresistibly tempted me to venture forth, despite my remove from the grounding Greek, on a careful rendition of his satyr play (the only complete extant satyr play!)—and to do so with all the fierce affections of my own inheritance and readership, the American momentum of my love of language in general, and of poetry in particular. The *Cyclops* you see here was written with an English-speaking audience—perhaps especially an American audience—in mind. I've adjusted the colloquial tones and comic registers to provoke that audience in ways I hope are consonant with the satyr-play's own raucous origins. The Cyclops who, on his island of *ipse*, appears as a connoisseur of carnal indulgence, an apologist for modern self-gratification, broken off from the old-world chain of faith and family, is a timeless figure (and so can seem American to an American): He's a skeptic about "piety and empty sentiment"; he sees the rule of law as no more than a noosework of loopholes. More reflexive than reflective, oriented more to logistics than to the logos, he can be found in contemporary life making his solitary rounds in a cell-phoned Lexus. . . .

One of the ancient masters is said to have said: "Let other men praise ancient times. I am glad I was born in these." It is just as blind to think of Greek and Roman cultures as originary as it is to think of our own as ultimate. Perhaps we're too fond of the human narrative we've made so emphatically our own, the one we imagine will end in our own time: Perhaps we have not imagined some of the eternities in which human souls might yet survive. But what a contemporary Polyphemus has in his head to love, he has in his life to lose: for we lose our selves, having each but one. The grossness of the single Cyclops, and the meanness of the collective Chorus, mustn't make contemporary audiences shrug "We're not like those old cannibals and cowards." The people we are blindest to, inevitably, anatomically, are we. It is ourselves, therefore, the greatest poets stage.

We're no less villains at our worst than are Silenus with his tribe or Cyclops in his greedy solitude; and no more heroes at our best than is Odysseus, always accompanied, and always alone, in his own ways. He wasn't always just, and wasn't always true, but kept the two ambitions simultaneously alive, in the circuit of a single human gaze. Imagination's greatest contract is with the universal moral insight: "one's all" must be doubly understood. As of yet—this writing, this millennium—the mind's eye isn't guttered out.

HEATHER MCHUGH

CYCLOPS

Translated by

HEATHER MCHUGH

With Introduction and Notes by

DAVID KONSTAN

CHARACTERS

SILENUS companion of Dionysus

CHORUS satyrs, sons of Silenus

ODYSSEUS king of Ithaca

POLYPHEMUS a Cyclops

ODYSSEUS' SHIPMATES (silent parts)

Line numbers in the right-hand margin of the text refer to
the English translation only, and the Notes beginning at p. 459 are
keyed to these lines. The bracketed line numbers in the running
heads refer to the Greek text.

SILENUS O Dionysus, do you know
how many times—not only now
but since I was a youth—I put myself
through agonies for you? So many times
they're numberless. Number one: that time
the jealous goddess Hera made you crazy,
and you strayed away from home, away from all
your mountain nymphs and nannies—and I
went after you. Innumerable labors! Labor number two:

when you were battling to protect   10
Olympus from the geosphere's gigantic sons,
and I was there beside you, shield in one hand,
spear in the other, goring that enormous Enceladus
dead, right through his armor! (Wait a minute,
am I spinning fables as I speak? By Jove,
I'm not! I swear I shared
the war-spoils with you later.)

And Dionysus, here I am today, suffering more than ever.
The torments can't be counted. Torment number three:
when Hera riled those pirates out of Tuscany: they
        seized you   20
for their slave trade overseas, and I got wind of it.
        We took to sail,
my own sons manning oars on either side, while I
        stood tiller. Lord,
how high and low we looked for you! We whipped the
        gray sea white!

But rounding Cape Malea we were cast
by a bad east wind upon this Aetna headland.

Living in the nearby caverns—last not least—
were Cyclopes: Numberless Horror Number Four,
Poseidon's lawless sons. One-eyed, but with a thousand
stories to his name, Polyphemus is known abroad
for his uncommon fondnesses for men: 30
he eats them raw.

And he's the one who keeps us here as slaves, my sons
        and me,
who meant to save *your* skin from slavery. So I, Silenus,
and my family, instead of being wined and dined,
must tend this faithless creature's flocks. My young
must raise the young of sheep, there on the hillsides;
here my labors take a more domestic form:
to swill and sweep, make ready for his meals.
And now if you'll excuse me—work is work—
I have to rake this floor before   40
the one-eyed one gets home.

        Enter at Ramp A the CHORUS OF SATYRS, *driving sheep.*

But wait—those are my sons approaching with their
        flocks.
Hello, my boys! How lively is your step!—one *two*, one
        two—
the same, it seems to me, as back in our old salad days,
when you and Bacchus partied all the way
to sweet Althaea's house, in lyric
choreography, instead of lack-lust chores.

CHORUS   (*to a recalcitrant ram*)

Where do you think you're going,
you son of a high-class dam? What path
do you think you are taking there?—it goes   50
to the crags. Have you eyes in your head?
Can't you see how much better this breezy way is,
to the green? There's a meal and a river-wave
there at the cave-mouth, all of your little ones
bleating in bed—

come on, now, git! Over here to the slaphappy slopes
of home sweet home! Git on now! Git this minute! or
be got by me, with the help of a stone. You, there!
You horny old head of the household—get a move on!
You're supposed to be guardian of guardians,   60
top dog in the Cyclops sheepfold, for as long
as he's out trekking in the wild.

                                                    (*to a ewe*)

That goes for you, too, sweetie—get
those mammaries on home! it's time you were nursing
your young in that cave. The little bleaters
slept like lambs all day but now they're missing you.
Come on! Get in! Give up your Aetna meadows
and enjoy this nice big pen.

Alas for me, this barnyard's
far from Dionysian—not a wine-god to be found,   70
no dancing, no amazing wands or holy ecstasies,
no drums or fountainheads of youth, no wineskin's savor.
Not a single mountain Nymph with whom
to strike up drinking songs
for the goddess Aphrodite. Ah,

how fast we chased the god of love in the good old days,
I and my lady-friends, so fleet on their white-hot feet! . . .
Dear Dionysus, where are you without us?
Tossing your golden hair for nobody? while I,
who was your happy servant, serve the worse for exile,   80
wearing nothing but these awful skins,
and missing your fine company,
a man-slave at the mercy of

some giant one-eyed misbegotten thing . . .

SILENUS Be quiet, my sons! Get inside quickly, with the animals!

CHORUS LEADER   (*to the attendants*)

You heard him! Move it!

They and the animals enter the cave.

But, father, what's the hurry?

SILENUS I see a ship on the beach down there! It's Greek!
Yes, those are sailors coming toward our cave
with someone who appears to be their captain.   90
They've got some empty sacks about their necks,
presumably for food; and pails for water.
O unlucky visitors! Who could they be?
They can't imagine what Polyphemus is like, or just
how inhospitable this ground is, where they disembark;
they haven't got a clue what bad luck brought their trip
to Cyclops territory, where a man is made a meal—
but not the way he wants. Now you be quiet, and we'll
    learn
exactly where these men are from, who land at Aetna's
    very lip . . .

Enter at Ramp B ODYSSEUS *with his men.*

ODYSSEUS Strangers, can you show us to a drinking stream?   100
Our thirst is killing us. Or tell us who might sell
provisions to my starving crew?
                                By God, it seems
we've happened on a Bacchanalia! I see
a festival of Satyrs near the cave. I'll greet
the eldest first. Hello, there, venerable one!

SILENUS I greet you, stranger, in return. But tell me
what's your name, and nation.

ODYSSEUS I am the lord of Cephallene, from Ithaca. My name's
    Odysseus.

SILENUS   (*aside*)

I've heard of this guy—he's a sponger if I ever saw one!
Son of Sisyphus, the famous pusher.   110

ODYSSEUS I am the son of Sisyphus—but spare us the aspersions.

SILENUS Where did you sail from, to end up in Sicily?

ODYSSEUS From Ilium, and from the war in Troy.

SILENUS What happened, couldn't find your way home?

ODYSSEUS I am here because a windstorm overpowered me.

SILENUS Ill winds! The very devils that did me in!

ODYSSEUS So you were forced ashore as well?

SILENUS I was chasing pirates who had kidnapped Dionysus.

ODYSSEUS What's this country? Tell me who its people are.

SILENUS This place is Aetna, highest mountaintop in Sicily.   120

ODYSSEUS But where are all the city walls and fortresses?

SILENUS There is no city. This is not a place of men.

ODYSSEUS What then? Wild animals?

SILENUS In a manner of speaking. They are Cyclopes,
          and take to caves, not houses.

ODYSSEUS Who's their king? Or is it a democracy?

SILENUS It's each man by and for himself. There is no
          government.

ODYSSEUS Is Demeter respected here? I mean,
          do they plant grain? What do they live on?

SILENUS Curds and whey and sheepflesh, sir.   130

ODYSSEUS And are they friends of Dionysus? lovers of a good
          retsina?

SILENUS Not a chance. No dancing goes on here.

ODYSSEUS   Do they at least love gods, and welcome strangers?

SILENUS   Strangers are their favorite appetizer.

ODYSSEUS   Surely you aren't saying that they *eat* them?

SILENUS   Every man who's set foot here since us.

ODYSSEUS   This local Cyclops, at the moment,
            just where is he? Over there in his abode?

SILENUS   He's off on Aetna with his hounds, to hunt for game.

ODYSSEUS   You've got to help us get away. You know what you can
            do?   140

SILENUS   Not yet. I bet you'll tell me.
            What I can, I will.

ODYSSEUS   Just sell us bread—we haven't got a single crust.

SILENUS   I told you, we have nothing here but lamb.

ODYSSEUS   A lamb chop wouldn't hurt a human hunger.

SILENUS   There's also milk, and cheese.

ODYSSEUS   Well, daytime is the right time for a business deal.
            Give us a look at the inventory.

SILENUS   Tell me, first, just how much gold you said you had?

ODYSSEUS   It isn't gold we carry, but the wealth of Dionysus: we
            have wine.   150

SILENUS   You've got some wine with you? That's just
            what we've missed most! Best news in a blue moon!

ODYSSEUS   It was Maron, son of the wine-god himself, who gave it to
            me.

432

SILENUS   You're telling me you got your wine from the child I
                cradled in my arms?

ODYSSEUS   I mean from Bacchus' own child, if saying so will mean
                my meaning's any plainer.

SILENUS   Now, about this wine, is it still on the ship out there,
                or here with you?

                                            ODYSSEUS *takes out the wineskin.*

ODYSSEUS: Right here, old man! A wineskin full of it, before your
                eyes.

SILENUS   That's barely a gulp, by my standards.   160

ODYSSEUS   I dare you to drink this wineskin dry, you and your whole
                entourage.

SILENUS   Is there some magic way to make
                more wine flow in?

ODYSSEUS   I'll say—and twice the volume that flows out.

SILENUS   Now that sounds like the fountain of *my* youth!

ODYSSEUS   Perhaps you'd like to taste a bit before . . .

SILENUS   I would indeed! A touch is halfway to a handshake.

                                            ODYSSEUS *brings out a drinking bowl.*

ODYSSEUS   Look, I've even brought the stemware.

SILENUS   Holy Dionysus, give me some—I can hardly remember
                what it's like to wet my lips.   170

ODYSSEUS   Your wish is my command.

SILENUS   (*sniffing*)

            O my! O my! A fine bouquet!

ODYSSEUS So there's a wedding in the works?

SILENUS Not yet—but I can smell
some serious deflowering to come.

ODYSSEUS *hands him the cup.*

ODYSSEUS Indulge, then—take a taste. A praise
should never smack of empty words.

SILENUS Oo whee! Oo whee! I think the god of wine has just
invited me to dance! O lay! O lay!

ODYSSEUS It goes down nicely, doesn't it? 180

SILENUS Right to the toenail-tips!

ODYSSEUS We'll pay you, too, of course.

SILENUS Just keep the red stuff flowing, we'll forget the gold.

ODYSSEUS Then you bring out the lamb and gorgonzola.

SILENUS Yes, indeed I will, my master can be damned.
I'd give his many flocks for just one cupful
of this wine—I'm dying for a topflight lowbrow
tippler's kind of time, a little jump off lovers' leap
in old Leucadia, a good long bob there in the brine.
The man who doesn't love a drink has got a few 190

screws loose: one swig and look! your stick stands up,
your hand gets deep in cleavage and you start
the breaststroke toward her burning bush,
you're dancing with the Nereids, nary a care
in the world. I could *kiss* a drink like this!
To hell with the Cyclops! Tell him where to put it—

head up his bumhole, and mud in his eye!

Exit SILENUS *into the cave.*

CHORUS LEADER Listen here, Odysseus. We've got to have a little talk.

ODYSSEUS Of course, since we are such fast friends.

CHORUS LEADER Did you really take Troy, and then take Helen, too?   200

ODYSSEUS We laid waste to the whole of Priam's house.

CHORUS LEADER And tell us, once you had the girl, did you take turns
        with her?—
    the traitoress, craving such multitudes beyond her mate!
    One look at all those fancy breeches, foreign colors,
    gold around his neck, and she was in a fever,
    sure as sin, and hapless Menelaus left behind,
    poor man. Ah, womankind! I say
    let *all* of them go down—
    and preferably on *me*!

Enter SILENUS *from the cave.*

    And here you go, my lord Odysseus—   210
    the tenderest of lambs, a flock of them;
    plus cheeses in abundance, made of finest milk.
    They're yours. But now you've got
    to leave, and quickly—only first
    I need a little more to drink.
        Uh-oh! Somebody's coming!
            It's the Cyclops! God, what should we do?

ODYSSEUS If what you say is true, there'll be a big to-do,
    and then we're done for. Where's a place to hide?

SILENUS Inside the cave, and quick—in there you can't be seen.   220

ODYSSEUS A dangerous idea, I think, to fly into a cage.

SILENUS Don't worry—there are many nooks and crannies in
    there.

ODYSSEUS I won't do it. All of Troy would turn in its grave if I ran
    from just one man, after standing up with shield in hand
    against so many. If I must die, I'll do it nobly;
    and if I live, I'll have my reputation.

Enter at Ramp A, the CYCLOPS.

CYCLOPS   Make room! Get out of my way! What's happening here?
          Or maybe I should say, what *isn't* happening? You, boy,
          standing around so underemployed, is this your idea
          of a Dionysian holiday? Can't say I notice   230
          any evidence of your beloved Bacchus in the area,
          don't hear his drums and castinets. How are my lambs?
          Are all the newborns nursing? Is the milk put up
          in curdling buckets yet? Somebody answer me!
          I have a club that soon enough will raise
          a hue and cry, if you do not.
          Look up, not down,

          when I am speaking to you!

CHORUS LEADER   (*looking up at Polyphemus*)

          I'm looking up! My head is turned toward God himself
          and all his starry retinue—by God, I think I see Orion!   240

CYCLOPS   But have you got my dinner ready yet?

CHORUS LEADER   There's something very to your taste, in fact.

CYCLOPS   And milk in mugs?

CHORUS LEADER   Milk by the barrelful, if you desire.

CYCLOPS   Cows' milk or sheep? Or maybe for today
          some exquisite blend of the two?

CHORUS LEADER   Anything you say—just don't take any slugs of me.

CYCLOPS   Don't flatter yourself. All that fancy
          footwork in my belly? It would be my death.
          Now, wait a minute!—who are all those people near my
              cave?   250
          Did pirates come ashore? And why are my lambs outside,
              tied up
          with willow-ropes—my cheese-bins strewn about—

436

what's going on? Who's that old baldie there,
the swelled-up one, so red in the face you'd think
he came here straight from battle?

SILENUS Ooo! Ooo! the pain! the pain!
I'm feverish from taking all those punches.

CYCLOPS What punches? Who would beat you up, old man?
You certainly look the worse for wear.

SILENUS These men, my lord—attacked me when I tried   260
to stop them robbing your own lordship blind.

CYCLOPS But don't they know I am a god,
from gods descended? How could they dare?

SILENUS I said the same thing, but it didn't stop their
        plundering—
they even pinched your best cheese, though I fought
        them
valiantly, in vain. And then they started carrying
off your sheep. They said they'd leash you, too,
like any ugly dog, and under your own eye

they'd cut your guts out, lash your back with whips,
and then tie you up completely, hand and foot, and
        throw you   270
into the darkest dungeon of their ship, and then . . . and
        then
they'd sell you for somebody's heavy labor, or maybe it
        was
make you do their millwork somewhere . . .

CYCLOPS You don't say. (To SILENUS) You there! On the double!
        Sharpen up
my carving knives and get a good blaze going on the
        hearth.
(SILENUS makes a movement toward the cave) I'll slaughter
        these offenders
in a flash, and have my fill of them. I think I'll serve one
        up
as barbecue, straight off the coals; the others should be

delicately braised—for tenderness's sake. I've had
too many mountain meals—enough of lions,   280
deer and such. It's far too long since I enjoyed a man.

SILENUS After so much ordinary venison, my lord, variety is
             pleasant.
         Indeed, it's quite a while since we had guests for dinner.

ODYSSEUS Polyphemus, hear out your visitors. We left our ship
             only to ask where we could buy some food. This man of
                 yours,
         after a drop of wine, decided he would sell us all these
             sheep
         for just one cup. He was a willing businessman—
         we didn't twist his arm. You can't believe a word he says;
         he's covering his *own* malfeasances, now that he's caught
         red-handed, selling goods of yours without authority.   290

SILENUS Are you accusing me? Then I say go to hell.

ODYSSEUS I'll go to hell if I am lying.

SILENUS O Cyclops, I will swear by your own father, great
                 Poseidon,
         by the venerable Nereus and Triton, by Calypso, by
                 Nereus'
         good daughters, by the holy oceanful and all the fishes in it,
         dearest master, sweetest master, o most handsome
                 Cyclops, I would never
         sell your private property to men. If I am lying, let my
                 sons
         (whom more than anything on earth I love)
         themselves be damned to hell.

CHORUS LEADER Be damned *yourself!* I saw you selling food to them!   300
         If I am lying, let my father rot! Don't blame the strangers.

CYCLOPS   (*to the* CHORUS LEADER):

         And why should I take *your* low word for it? I've trusted
             this Silenus more

than any judge on Judgment Day. I won't believe he's
    lying now.
But still, I'd like some answers from you foreigners:
Where are you from? Where is your homeland?
What's your native town?

ODYSSEUS We're Ithacan by birth. We sailed here after sacking Troy,
    when we were blown off course by storms.

CYCLOPS So you're the ones who went to punish Ilium
    for kidnapping that good-for-nothing, Helen?   310

ODYSSEUS We are the very ones who did
    endure those awful wars.

CYCLOPS What a disgraceful mission!
    Sailing all that way to Phrygia
    for just one worthless whore!

ODYSSEUS It was a god's design: don't blame us mortals for it.
    You, who are yourself a noble sea-god's son,
    we beg you: do not kill in mere cold blood
    such men of innocent goodwill, who merely chanced
    upon your house. Don't make a godless meal of us.   320
    All over Greece we kept your father's temples
    sacred: there at Taenarum his harbor's
    perfectly secure; safe are his caves
    at Cape Malea, sound is Sunium,
    Athena's holy ground, and rocks
    still glitter with the silver there.
    Wherever we have gone
    Poseidon rules.

    The real disgrace would be
    if we'd surrendered to the Trojans   330
    all these Greek possessions. In a sense,
    we fought for you—who (living here at Aetna,
    where a rock can flow like fire) are living in the farthest
        reach of Greece.

    But if these points don't move you, take to heart
    the universal law of men: a shipwrecked stranger must

be treated kindly, given gifts of hospitality and clothes,
instead of being turned like beef on spits, to bloat
a rude host's belly. Priam's land has treated us already
to an orgy of bereavement, too many men were speared,
and too much blood drunk up by battlefields. Too many
    wives   340
made widows, too many gray-haired parents sent on
childless to their graves. If you wolf down today what's
    left of us,
to whom can anybody turn for help? I beg you, Cyclops,
put aside mere gluttony, and call upon your godlier re-
    serves:
unholy self-indulgence will, in the long run, hurt you
    most of all.

SILENUS Here's my advice, Polyphemus: don't chew the fat
with the likes of him, that is, unless the fat you chew
is his. I wouldn't let a bit of him be wasted, sir, if I were
    you.
And after every delicacy's done, and finally you put his
    tongue
into your mouth, just think how many tongues you'll
    speak in, then,   350
preeminent Polyphemus, and all of them as eloquent as
    his.

CYCLOPS I'm quite fed up, but not quite fed,
my puny little visitors. You ought to keep
a fact or two in mind: the wise man worships
no god more than wealth, and its self-satisfactions:
all the rest is so much piety and empty sentiment.
As for the headlands of my father's seaside temples,
I live well enough without them. Why throw them
into your argument? Of Zeus' flaming anger, I don't fear
a lick: I don't believe he's any more a god   360
than I am. He won't worry my hereafters.
Let me tell you why.

Whenever he sends down his storms, I find my shelter
in a well-sealed cave, I dine on roasted calf,
I lie there belly-up and satisfied, I drink
a whole damn milk-vat dry, and then

I drum on the resounding tub until
the sound drowns out his thunder.

As for fierce north winds and snow, I wrap myself
in warmest suede and fur, I bank the blazing fire,   370
no cold can bother me. My animals are fed all season
on the grass the summer lavishes on us
whether it wishes to or not. I dedicate
my profits all to me—and not to any far-off god.
I sacrifice the best of everything to this: my belly.
Show me a bigger divinity! Simply to eat and drink,
day in day out, to give oneself no pain—
in the eyes of any sensible man

that's all the Zeus that matters.
As for senators and lawyers, turning the world   380
into a noose of cleverness and net
of complications, I say let them
hang themselves in their own loopholes! I will not
deny my heart's delight. And at the moment,
it would be my heart's delight
to eat you up. You'll get
some presents from me, sure enough—
a nice big fire to warm you, and a lot of sea-salt
sent with father's compliments, a good bronze pot
to keep you toasty warm. Now I suggest   390
you go inside my cave, and pay your homage
to the god who dwells within—

and soon we'll add your ego to his altar.

ODYSSEUS   God, have I escaped the tribulations of the Trojan War,
and all the gales at sea, only to wash up here at last,
where nothing holy can be harbored in a heart?
Athena, Zeus' daughter, help me now! My danger
is too great for words. O Zeus above, the guardian of guests,
whose home appears so bright up there among the stars,
look kindly on our low condition! If you don't watch over
            us,   400
who worshiped you so many years,
you're more a Zero than a Zeus.

The CYCLOPS *herds* ODYSSEUS *and his men*
into the cave. SILENUS *follows.*

CHORUS O Cyclops, you may open up
the gaping gateworks of your throat,
and baste and braise and broil and roast
the devil from your guests—
and then recline in fleeces, the better
to rip and rend and tear and taste
the morsels of their flesh—

but leave me out of it. I want no share.   410
You fill your vessels as you will. I say
someone should do away with this unholy house!
Away with all its self-indulgence, greed and godlessness!
Away with any cruelty that treats
itself to other creatures' torture, or
a refugee to nothing more
than the rotisserie....

Enter ODYSSEUS *from the cave, distraught.*

ODYSSEUS My God, what can a human being say
in the face of a horror story come to life—
I'd never have imagined I would see,   420
in mortal form or time, such searing
inhumanity....

CHORUS LEADER Odysseus, what are you saying?
Surely he hasn't already consumed
one of your beloved shipmates?

ODYSSEUS He has indeed—he looked to find,
and hefted in his hands,
the plumpest two
of all our company.

CHORUS LEADER Poor souls! But tell me every last detail.   430

ODYSSEUS We got into his cavern where he heaped the fire with
              hardwood,
logs enough to load three wagons easily, and then

442

he set the kettle on the fire to boil. Near by the fire
he spread the ground with fir boughs, for a bed;
then milked the cows till he'd filled to the brim
a ninety-gallon tank, and next to that he set
a cup of ivywood—it must have measured
more than four feet, rim to rim,
and six feet to the bottom.

Next he set to whittling spits   440
of buckthorn, burnt the ends
and scraped them with a blade.
When all was done to the satisfaction of
the cook from hell, he grabbed my friends.
He cut the first man's throat with one
quick swipe, and drained his blood
into the cauldron; then he seized
the second by the foot, and dashed
his brains out on a rock. He cut them up
with an atrocious knife, and roasted   450
all the fleshy parts upon the fire;
the arms and legs he threw into the stewpot.

I stood there in my utter wretchedness, the tears
were streaming from my eyes as I was forced
to watch him work. The others cowered farther off
like swallows in the crannies of the cave, their faces
drawn and pale. And when the glutton finally fell back,
all sated with his meal and belching something foul—

I had a sudden thought, as if from heaven.

Filling a cup with Maron's wine I offered it to him: 460
I said, "O Cyclops, son of sea-gods, you should try
this drink the Greeks think so divine. A ruby cupful,
worthy of a god." His belly filled to bursting with
his execrable meal, he still took up the cup, and drank it
     down,
then raised a hand in sudden admiration. "Dearest
     friend,"
he said, "this drink is very good, on top of my good
     meal."

I saw that he took pleasure in it, so I filled the cup
    again—
I knew the wine would be his own undoing: wine
would make him pay.
                             Eventually he felt
inspired to sing. I went on plying him, cup after cup,   470
amounts of wine that couldn't fail to make a stone heart
    feel
a little overwarm. And even as we speak, my crew
is sitting there in tears, while he belts forth
the discord of his songs; the cavern echoes
with the awful sound. I've managed to escape,
and wish to save us, you and me, if you should so desire.

But are you really ready now to leave the clutches of this
    brute—
to live in the Naiads' halls? Your father wants to go,
but he's so weak he's stuck to the winecup there,
a bird in lime, his flapping all in vain. But you—   480
you still are young. You could have Dionysus
for your lord—he's not the Cyclops kind.

CHORUS LEADER Dear friend, I long to see the day
    when we are free from this unholy creature!
    Not to mention that I've had too long
    a widowed wine-spout of my own—
    it needs a lick or two.

ODYSSEUS Then listen to my plan, and we can still escape.

CHORUS LEADER Believe me, I'm all ears.
    There is no dulcimer I'd rather hear   490
    than news of dead Polyphemus.

ODYSSEUS The Cyclops wants to take this Dionysian drink
    over to the other Cyclopes, for partying.

CHORUS LEADER I get it. You want to catch him in the woods
    and cut his throat, or push him off a cliff.

ODYSSEUS Not quite. I tend to work more cunningly.

CHORUS LEADER So tell us then. We've heard
               that you are clever.

ODYSSEUS First of all, I want to keep him here. I'll tell him wine is
               such a pleasure
          he should keep it for himself, and never share. But when
               he falls asleep   500
          (as he will do, for Bacchus packs a wallop) then I'll take
          that olive stake I noticed in his house: it has a point
          I'll sharpen with my sword, and darken in the fire. And
               then
          when it is good and burning, I'll remove it from the
               flame
          and tiptoe to his very face and drive the paling
          deep into his eye. I'll melt that eye with fire,
          I swear, I'll make his mountain weep.
          The way a master carpenter applies
          a turning drill, I'll whirl
          the firebrand down   510

          into his sphere: I'll burn
          his only eyeball out.

CHORUS LEADER Hear hear! The thought of such inventions makes me
               giddy with delight!

ODYSSEUS And after that we'll go, together with my friends, and
               your old father
          all aboard my ship of ebony, away from this forsaken
               land.

CHORUS LEADER Is there some way that I could help you do this
               brilliant blinding of the Cyclops, just as men will share
               in tributes to the gods? I want to play a part
               in this remarkable revenge.   520

ODYSSEUS Indeed, I'll need your help: the branding-tree
          is far too big for just one man to heft.

CHORUS LEADER I'd lift a hundred wagons'-worth of torch
               to smoke the wings and stingers from
               that wasp nest of his eye.

ODYSSEUS Now that you know my plan, just keep it quiet.
Once I give the word, do everything
your master carpenter commands.

Just being free this moment from that awful cave—
imagine how I long to flee! But saving myself   530
is nothing short of evil if it means
I leave my friends in there to die.

CHORUS LEADER Now tell us, when we have our hands there
on the firebrand, who should be first to grip it,
who the second? Under the Cyclops' eyebrow,
actually to grind his lights to dust, just
how shall this huge instrument be handled?

Singing from inside.

Sh! He's coming from the cavern,
he's completely drunk—and badly out of tune, to boot.
He ought to pay for this offense to sense, the sheer   540
inharmony of it. Let's sing him one better,
my boys! The lout's in need
of lyrical enlightenment—
without our best
aesthetic help
he'll soon be *doubly* blind.

Enter the CYCLOPS *from the cave, leaning on* SILENUS.

CHORUS The man who revels raises high
a lusty Bacchic air,
a vineyard breeze with which to ply
his trades to anywhere.   550

He dances out and round the bend
to seek a layman's sport:
his arm around his trusty friend
for immoral support.

The girl who lies upon the bed
voluptuous and young

can make men speechless, it is said
with just a touch of tongue.

With that, and wine, he has to shine.
He'll sing—and then he'll score.   560
His rod is red, his staff divine—
just open up the door!

CYCLOPS   Oh lah, oh lay, her hold is deep—
we'll drink it to the lovely lees.
My heart is skipping steps to keep
abreast of her festivities.

I'm loaded to the topdecks—sing!
Spring's in the bed, spring's in the year.
To brother Cyclopes let's bring
the cheapest gal—a gallon's cheer.   570

Come on, now, friend, give back that wineskin.

CHORUS   Handsomely disposed to come
and show a wench your family jewels,
don't wait for candlelight and gloom—
a maiden's made for you to rule

in daybreak's shift, and daylight's gown.
She's dewy there, inside her nook.
But more than that will bait your hook.
(And more than that will be your crown!)

ODYSSEUS   Now listen, Cyclops, as it happens   580
I know very well
this Dionysus you've been drinking.

CYCLOPS   Now wait a minute—you don't mean the god's the *drink*
itself?

ODYSSEUS   The very wellspring of our *joie de vivre*.

CYCLOPS   Well, I belch his airs with pleasure, I'll say that.

447

ODYSSEUS And that's the way he likes it. He won't hurt a hair on
          anyone.

CYCLOPS   But why would a god want to live in that hole?

ODYSSEUS Wherever he goes, he feels at home.

CYCLOPS   No god should wear just one bare skin.

ODYSSEUS Why not, if it creates delight? You mean   590
          you don't enjoy it?

CYCLOPS   Hate the skin, but love the wine.

ODYSSEUS Then drink your fill, Polyphemus. Here's to your health.

CYCLOPS   I'd like to give my brothers some of this stuff.

ODYSSEUS You keep it to yourself, and they'll admire you more.

CYCLOPS   But giving it, I'd be a better brother.

ODYSSEUS The best of revelers wind up in fisticuffs.

CYCLOPS   They wouldn't dare. I may be drunken, but I won't be
          smashed.

ODYSSEUS My friend, a drunk should stay at home.

CYCLOPS   The man who drinks without a lively crew is crazy.   600

ODYSSEUS The man who drinks within a living room is wise.

CYCLOPS   What should we do, Silenus? Stay at home?

SILENUS   I say we stay. Why bring more banqueters to bear?

ODYSSEUS What's more, the ground right here is flowery and soft.

SILENUS   What's more, the sun right here is perfect for a draft.
          Why not lie down, and rest your bones?

The CYCLOPS *reclines.* SILENUS *puts the bowl behind him.*

CYCLOPS Hey, why put that bowl back there?

SILENUS So no one knocks it over.

CYCLOPS I know how you work—you'll drink it dry
　　　　 behind my back. I say   610
　　　　 you put it here between us.
　　　　 Stranger, tell me now
　　　　 what name you go by.

ODYSSEUS Call me No-man. In return,
　　　　 to win my thanks, what favor will you do?

CYCLOPS Of all the number of your men,
　　　　 I promise I will eat you last.

SILENUS That's a good gift, for a guest!

　　　　　　　　　SILENUS *surreptitiously helps himself to drink.*

CYCLOPS What are you doing there? Wetting your lips with the
　　　　 wine?

SILENUS Not quite. The wine has wet its lips with me: 620
　　　　 it seems to find me irresistible.

CYCLOPS You'll soon be sorry. That wine doesn't love you.

SILENUS On the contrary, I swear, it's falling for me:
　　　　 I believe it loves my inner beauty.

CYCLOPS Slave, you're here to pour, and hand the cup to me when
　　　　 it is full.

SILENUS I need to keep an eye on how the wine is doing. Just a
　　　　 little look.

CYCLOPS You're driving me entirely mad. Now hand the tankard
　　　　 over!

SILENUS Not until I've given you a crown

(*He puts a garland on the* CYCLOPS)

and given myself a little tip as well.

CYCLOPS This wine-pourer is nothing but a cheat.   630

SILENUS This wine-pouring is nothing less than sweet.
Now wipe your mouth: here comes a swig.

CYCLOPS (*wiping his lips and beard*) All right, I'm ready.

SILENUS Tilt back on your elbow as you drink—like this.
See how I tip it up and up, so far you cannot see.

He drinks with head back, hidden by the cup.

CYCLOPS Hey, what are you doing there?

SILENUS You see? Elegantly down the gullet.

CYCLOPS Stranger, I want you for my pourer.

ODYSSEUS I'm not entirely unacquainted with the stuff.

CYCLOPS So pour, already.

ODYSSEUS I am pouring. You just quiet down.   640

CYCLOPS That's not so easy when you're all tanked up.

ODYSSEUS (*handing him the bowl*) There you go:
now drink it dry! Here's looking at you! Bottoms up!
A whiner and his wine should end together.

CYCLOPS God, this grapevine is a clever sort of plant.

ODYSSEUS Drink deeply after eating well, and you'll
sleep like a baby. But leave even a single drop,
and the wine-god makes you parched.

The CYCLOPS *takes a long drink.*

CYCLOPS   Ahoy, ahoy! I nearly drowned in there. What pleasure I am
          feeling—I see earth and heaven whirlpooling together.
          There's the throne of Zeus and all his wheeling retinues!
          I think I'll give them each a kiss. I'm feeling quite seduced. 650
          But I'll be damned if any of those Graces gets me—not a
          chance! Instead, I'll take this charmer of a Ganymede to
          bed. He suits me better. Boys are always more appealing.

SILENUS   Who are you talking about? Not me, I hope?

CYCLOPS   Oh yes, by Zeus, from whom I'm now about
          to spirit you away!

SILENUS   My sons, I'm done for! This is a fate worse than death.

CYCLOPS   You do not like your lovers drunk?

SILENUS   By god, the taste of wine   660
          is turning sour on me.

          Exit the CYCLOPS, *dragging* SILENUS *into the cave.*

ODYSSEUS   Come on, now, noble sons of Dionysus,
          soon he'll be asleep in there, still belching from his meal.
          The firebrand's waiting for us, sending smoke-signals—
          there's nothing but the deed to do: burn out his bloody
              eye.
          Just pull yourselves together now, with all your might and
              bravery.

CHORUS LEADER   Our hearts are strong as iron and our will is strong as
              stone.
          Go quickly, or my father will end up the shafted one. We
              stand prepared.

ODYSSEUS   Hephaestus, rid us of this pestilence. With Aetna's
              metalwork and sparks
          (of which you are the god) now to your neighbor's awful
              eye, apply your arts.   670
          And Morpheus, o god of sleep and child of darkness, pray

come over him, don't leave a glimmer: blind his gaze.
Don't let Odysseus—for all his Trojan glories—
die ingloriously here, at the hands of a man-eater,

cheater of heaven. Help us, or else chance itself
will seem to be the greatest god, and heaven
just a happenstance.

Exit ODYSSEUS *into the cave.*

CHORUS   Now soon the host who swallows up his guests
will feel the touch of fire-tongs at his neck,
and tongues of fire upon his shining eye.   680
The very tree he felled out of the sky
will rise again from ash, in red reaction.
A little present from the god of wine! And one good turn
of this, a turn of that, and many happy returns—until
that big black eye is blind. That way he learns
the price you have to pay, the fee
for drunken satisfaction. After that,
we're up! we're off! to ivy-covered halls
where Dionysus dwells. We'll leave behind
his single-minded self, self-centered mind—   690
and we'll be free—if there can *ever* come
a happiness from hell.

Enter ODYSSEUS *from the cave.*

ODYSSEUS   For god's sake hold your tongues, you animals,
and seal your lips. I forbid you so much as to blink
or clear your throats or breathe, for fear you'll wake
the Cyclops up, before his eye is disciplined with fire.

CHORUS   We're shutting up. We're swallowing our words.

ODYSSEUS   Let's go inside in force, now,
stand together unforsaking.
There's a red-hot hand of poker   700
in there, ready for the taking.

CHORUS LEADER Before we go, could you explain
               exactly how we are to hold the stake
               while burning out his eye?

LEADER OF CHORUS A I think my standing too far from the door
                    would not be so effective.

LEADER OF CHORUS B I think I'm suffering from leg cramps.

LEADER OF CHORUS A I think I got a sprain myself,
                    I can't think how.

ODYSSEUS You sprained your leg while standing there?

LEADER OF CHORUS A Apparently. And now there are   710
                    some ashes in my eye.

ODYSSEUS My cohorts are turning to cowards.

CHORUS LEADER So it's cowardice to want to save
               my neck? to want my teeth intact?
               I'd rather be a coward then, in fact—
               for people hurt you when you're brave.

               I know an Orphic spell that I could train
               on the firebrand, till it rises of its own   720
               accord, marches to the Cyclops' skullbone—and then
               pow!—it bursts the bastard into flames.

ODYSSEUS I always thought you might be of this kind.
          It's true: you are untrue. My friends
          will be my only surety, at last,
          before this awful beast.

          And you—who find no arms to lend—
          can help with some encouragement at least.

                              Exit ODYSSEUS *into the cave.*

CHORUS LEADER As long as his own mercenaries
               run our risk for us, we'll do the cheerleading.   730
               Death to the Cyclops! Let the sucker burn!

CHORUS   Hooray for heroes! Stick it to him good!
            Tighten the screws on the son of a bitch!
            Burn his lookout station down! That's right,
            that's right! incinerate the sinner! Ram your point
            straight home! Not one more guest for dinner! Atta boy,
            Odysseus! Drive it in, and pull it out, you'll turn the
                tables on
            his awful appetite. Skewer him deep, past lash and brow;
            impale his every view. But turn his lights out
            as you go: don't let him get   740
            a lash at you.

            Enter the CYCLOPS *from the cave, his face all bloody.*

CYCLOPS   Aiii! Aiii! My eye!!! The sun is turned to cinders!

CHORUS LEADER That's a pretty song. Sing it again
            for us, dear Cyclops, would you?

CYCLOPS   Woe is me! I've been assaulted! Traitors!
            Vermin! You will not escape unscathed!
            I'll stand here in the entranceway
            and block your passage with my arms!

CHORUS LEADER O Clopsy-Wopsy! What's that tune you're bellowing?

CYCLOPS   My god, without my eye, how can   750
            I look? They've ruined me!

CHORUS LEADER You don't look good. In fact you are
            uncommonly unsightly.

CYCLOPS   Uncommonly uncomfortable, as well.

CHORUS LEADER What happened, did you black out in the fireplace?

CYCLOPS   No, by heaven! No-man did this to me!

CHORUS LEADER So you did this to yourself?

CYCLOPS   No, no, I tell you, No-man stabbed my eye.

CHORUS LEADER I see. You say you are not blind.

CYCLOPS Says you. I say I cannot see.

CHORUS LEADER But how could no one make you blind?   760

CYCLOPS You're making fun of me.
        But where is No-man now?

CHORUS LEADER He's nowhere, as you see.

CYCLOPS That goddamn guest destroyed me
        when he drowned me in his drink.

CHORUS LEADER It's true, a little port in a storm
        can be a downright danger.

CYCLOPS For mercy's sake just tell me:
        have the strangers left? or are they still inside?   770

CHORUS LEADER They're standing here, quite quietly,
        beneath the overhang, though they are not hung over.

CYCLOPS To my left or to my right?

CHORUS LEADER Your right.

> The CYCLOPS *moves from the entranceway.*
> ODYSSEUS, *his men, and* SILENUS *slip silently out of*
> *the cave.*

CYCLOPS Where?

CHORUS LEADER Right next to the cliff. Have you got it in hand?

> The CYCLOPS *runs into the cliff.*

CYCLOPS I got it in the head. I think my brain is broken.

CHORUS LEADER I see they've made a break for it, themselves.

CYCLOPS I thought you said that they were over here.

CHORUS LEADER But I meant here.   780

CYCLOPS Where do you mean?

CHORUS LEADER This way, your left.

CYCLOPS You're mocking me again, I'm desperate
and you are toying with me.

CHORUS LEADER I'm not lying to you now, I swear. He's right in front of
you.

CYCLOPS You fiend, where on earth are you lurking?

ODYSSEUS Far enough away from you
to keep Odysseus' person safe.

CYCLOPS Odysseus, is it? So No-man has a new name.

ODYSSEUS No. But *some* man had, the day   790
my father called his son Odysseus—
he can be odious as well, if he's compelled,
as you have seen. You owe your fate completely
to your own ignoble appetites. My victories in Troy
mean nothing, if I let you get away
with murdering my friends.

CYCLOPS There was an ancient prophecy that said
I would be blinded by you, in this way.
It also prophesied a punishment for you: 800
to roam around the sea for what
would seem an endless age.

ODYSSEUS So now you are a sage. I say the future you predict
is history already. Take all your time warps and your
prophesies,
and go to blazes. I, for one, am going to the beach.
A boat awaits, to take us home
from this infernal Sicily.

Exeunt ODYSSEUS *and his men by Ramp B.*

CYCLOPS   Oh no, you don't. I'll break this rock apart
          and throw down boulders, till your boat and you
          and all your friends are smithereens.   810
          I may be blind, but you are all at sea—
          I may be single-minded: you are all adrift.
          You think a son of earth was what you dropped—
          but I'm Poseidon's son as well, and I can lift.
          You twisted time to your own ends—
          but I can still negotiate a twisted space:
          I'll feel my way to No-man's land. My blindness
          knows its place: it has no boundaries, it doesn't stop.
          I'll take an under-tunnel to the mountaintop.

                                   Exit CYCLOPS *into the cave.*

CHORUS LEADER   Forget his malices and his miseries. What future   820
                could so big a blindness tell? His selfishness
                is ancient history. Whereas, now, we—
                we are the model of modernity—that's why
                we're saved: to multiply, at last, in luxury!

                By change's wind and by the future's wave,
                let's sail, O brave Odysseus!
                Just forward us to Bacchus, and

                we'll be the best of slaves.

                                   Exeunt CHORUS *and* SILENUS *by Ramp B.*

NOTES

Minor uncertainties in the Greek text and slight alterations of the Greek for the sake of fluent English are not noted. The reader is referred to the introduction and the translator's foreword for discussion of the translation.

For a Greek text with facing literal translation, see David Kovacs, *Euripides* vol. 1, in the Loeb Classical Library (Cambridge, Mass., 1994). For the Greek text only, accompanied by a learned commentary and introduction, see Richard Seaford, *Euripides Cyclops* (Oxford, 1984).

1–41 / 1–35 *prologue* The opening speech, recited in plain conversational meter, sets the scene for the action that follows. Silenus explains how he and his sons, the chorus of satyrs, find themselves slaves of Polyphemus in his savage home in Sicily.

6 / 3 *the jealous goddess Hera made you crazy* Hera was presumably jealous over Zeus' affair with Semele, Dionysus' mother; the story of Dionysus' madness is recounted by Apollodorus, *Library of Mythology* 3.5.1.

13–17 / 7–9 *enormous Enceladus ... shared the war-spoils* Enceladus was one of the Giants (sons of Earth) who rose up against the Olympian gods and were defeated. The spoils stripped from Enceladus prove that Silenus didn't dream up the encounter.

19 / 10 *The torments can't be counted* On the number imagery, see translator's foreword.

20 / 11–12 *riled those pirates out of Tuscany* For the story, see the introduction.

42–84 / 36–81 *First choral song* The chorus of satyrs, who have entered by one of the two side ramps from the mountain pastures where they have been herding Polyphemus' sheep, sing a full-fledged choral ode (as opposed to the marching song, in anapestic meter, that is more typical of the choral entrance, or *parodos*). Accordingly, they would have performed relatively more intricate dance steps as they herded the animals into their pens.

45–46 / 37 *partied all the way to sweet Althaea's house* Althaea was Dionysus' daughter; nothing is known about the party.

74 / *to strike up drinking songs* The Greek text at this point has the cry "Iacchos, Iacchos," a cult name of Bacchus used as an ecstatic exclamation.

83–402 / 82–355 *First episode* This section (technically, an episode is a passage in dialogue meter framed by two choral songs) begins with a scene involving Silenus and Odysseus, much of it in the line-for-line exchange called stichomythy. At line **197** / 174, Silenus exits, and the Chorus Leader continues the dialogue with Odysseus until Silenus' return at line **210** / 188. The arrival of Polyphemus at line **227** / 203 inaugurates a complex, four-way conversation among the Cyclops, Silenus, Odysseus, and the Chorus Leader, in which Silenus blames Odysseus for stealing Polyphemus' wares; the passage culminates in a pair of set speeches or *agôn*, in which Odysseus entreats the Cyclops to spare him and his men, and the Cyclops replies with a sophistic diatribe in defense of his bestial appetite. The episode ends with the Cyclops herding Odysseus and his sailors into the cave, visually recalling the end of the prologue in which the satyrs usher the sheep inside.

110 / 104 *son of Sisyphus* In some versions, Sisyphus, later condemned to push a rock up hill forever in the underworld, was Odysseus' father.

162–63 / 146–47 *Is there some magic way to make more wine flow in?* These two verses are missing in the manuscript; the supplement is anybody's guess (this one follows Kovacs).

188–89 / 166 *lovers' leap in old Leucadia* Leucadia was an island near Ithaca with steep limestone cliffs on its western side.

240 / 213 *I think I see Orion* The constellation of Orion, a famous hunter, was (and is) imagined as bearing a club.

303 / 273 *judge on Judgment Day* The Greek text has Rhadamanthus, one of the judges in the underworld.

388 / 343 *sea-salt* "Sea-salt" is Kovacs's supplement.

403–17 / 356–74 *Second choral song* With the stage momentarily empty of actors, the Chorus sings a brief ode (*stasimon*) in which it reveals horror at Polyphemus' cannibalism.

417 / 374 *to the rotisserie...* A verse is missing from the Chorus at this point in the Greek original.

418–532 / 375–482 *Second episode* Odysseus emerges from the Cyclops' cave to re-count the horrors he witnessed inside, largely in the kind of set piece conventionally called a messenger speech. He then discusses with the Chorus Leader his plan to blind Polyphemus.

487 / 439–40 *a lick or two* The Greek text is uncertain here.

533–79 / 483–518 *Third choral song* This choral interlude begins with a brief anapestic song (the marching meter), followed by a lyric exchange between the Chorus and Polyphemus, who exits drunk from his cave; in this part, the Chorus sings a stanza, the Cyclops responds with another, and the Chorus concludes with a third, all in a meter that is more like that of personal poetry than choral song. The style is that of the bawdy songs that were characteristic of the Greek symposium or drinking party (there is an amusing caricature of such a gathering at the end of Aristophanes' comedy *The Wasps*).

537 / 587 *Singing from within* An ancient (and rare) stage direction, preserved in the Greek text.

580–677 / 519–607 *Third episode* This scene begins with another series of stichomythic (line-for-line) exchanges involving Odysseus, Polyphemus, and Silenus, in which the symposiastic spirit takes the slapstick form of horseplay around the wine jar, culminating in a pederastic assault by the Cyclops on Silenus. The episode ends with Odysseus' return into the cave.

582 / 519–20 *this Dionysus you've been drinking* Since Dionysus was associated with wine (among other things), one might refer to wine poetically by the god's name (usually in the form Bacchus).

651 / 581 *those Graces* Goddesses associated with beauty and charm.

652 / 582 *this charmer of a Ganymede* Ganymede was a Trojan youth beloved by Zeus and thus might symbolize a male (usually a boy) who was sexually attractive to an adult man. Drunken ribaldry was characteristic of the classical Greek symposium in its more vulgar forms.

670 / 601 *Morpheus* The Greek has Hypnos, like Morpheus a personification of sleep.

678–92 / 608–24 *Fourth choral song* A brief interlude while the stage is vacant.

693–731 / 625–55 *Fourth episode* A brief scene between Odysseus and the Chorus, which reveals its cowardice. The Chorus is momentarily divided into two half-choruses, each presumably represented by a leader who speaks in the meter of dialogue.

718 / 646 *Orphic spell* An incantation like those connected with the cult of Orpheus, which involved secret mystical rites and belief in an afterlife.

732–41 / 656–62 *Fifth choral song* This very brief song fills the interval in which the stage is empty, between Odysseus' entry into the cave and the emergence of the blinded Cyclops.

741—828 / 663–709 *Exodos (fifth and final episode)* The blinded Cyclops is teased by the Chorus Leader, and after this horseplay Odysseus, his men, Silenus, and the Chorus exit by the ramp leading toward the sea. The meter is that of dialogue throughout (the Chorus has no separate exit march).

820–24 / 707–8 *Forget his miseries...multiply in luxury!* This passage is slightly amplified in respect to the original; see On the Translation.

GLOSSARY

ACHERON: One of the many rivers of Hades.

ACHILLES: Son of Peleus and Thetis, greatest of the Greek heroes of the Trojan War.

ADMETOS: Son of Pheres, husband of Alcestis, and king of Thessaly.

AEACUS: Son of Zeua and king of Aegina, an island in the Saronic gulf southwest of Athens; known for his justice and piety. Hesiod records his marriage to Psamanthë.

AEGEAN: Sea lying between mainland Greece and Asia Minor.

AEGEUS: Ancient king of Athens, who gives his name to the Aegean Sea, but is primarily known as the father of Athens' founding hero, Theseus. After Medea's escape from Corinth, she becomes Aegeus' concubine and, in one version, the mother of another son by him, Medus. When Theseus arrives in Athens, Medea tries to do him in; but Aegeus recognizes him, and Medea and her son are forced to flee Athens and Greece for good.

AEROPE: Daughter of Catreus, king of Crete, wife of Atreus, and mother of Agamemnon and Menelaus.

AETNA: Volcano in eastern Sicily, traditionally imagined as the forge at which the Cyclopes manufactured Zeus' thunderbolts; in *Cyclops*, the Cyclopes dwell on its slopes.

AJAX: Son of Telamon, king of Salamis and brother of Teucer; greatest Greek hero at Troy after Achilles, he was shamed when the armor of the slain Achilles was awarded to Odysseus and killed himself.

AKASTOS (ACASTUS): Son of Pelias and king of Iolcus; brother of Alcestis.

ALCESTIS: Wife of Admetos and daughter of Pelias.

ALKMENE: Princess of Thebes; the mortal woman who was, Herakles' mother by Zeus.

ALTHAEA: Daughter of Dionysus and, in a least one version of the story, of Deianira, wife of Herakles.

AMMON: The Egyptian god Amen-Ra, equated by the Greeks with Zeus. His shrine, located at the oasis of Siwa in the Libyan desert, was the seat of a great oracular shrine.

APHRODITE: Goddess of love and sexuality, born from sea-foam (*aphros* in Greek) fertilized by the blood of her father, Uranus (Sky), after he was castrated by his son Zeus. She was invoked primarily by brides, married women, and prostitutes, who sought from her the power to seduce men. Her literary persona embodies beauty and feminine wiles.

APOLLO: Son of Zeus and Leto, Artemis' twin brother, the multifaceted god of prophecy, music (poetry), healing, purifications, and light. A god of healing, he fathered Asklepios the physician. Often depicted carrying a bow and arrows, he was invoked as the averter of all kinds of evils. From his temple at Delphi his prophetess, the Pythia, disseminated his oracles to the Greek-speaking world; his oracle at Patara in Lykia was almost equally renowned.

ARES: God of war, and father of a fabulous horde of warlike sons.

ARGO: Jason's ship, the world's first. Built with the goddess Athena's help and manned by intrepid pre–Trojan War heroes, it sailed where no Greek had gone before, from Thessaly to Colchis and home again, in quest of the Golden Fleece.

ARGONAUTS: The crew of the Argo.

GLOSSARY

ARGOS: City in southern Greece; its name frequently also designates
the region around it, and even the whole of the Peloponnesos.
The western part of Argos was arid and so the country was
proverbially called "thirsty"—an epithet in the translation of
Alcestis playfully transferred to the hard-drinking Argives.

ARTEMIS: Daughter of Zeus and Leto and twin sister of Apollo a virgin
huntress and mistress of wild creatures, in which capacity she is
often depicted in the wild, surrounded by a maiden chorus.
This mighty goddess honored virginity above all and oversaw
numerous rites of passage (sometimes bloody and cruel) from
childhood to adulthood of both maidens and teenage boys. In
this capacity her duties extended to aiding brides the first time
they gave birth.

ASKLEPIOS: Son of Apollo by Koronis, and culture-hero of medicine
and the healing arts generally. For his *hybris* in restoring men to
life with his simples and herbs, Zeus blasted him with lightning.

ATHENA: Motherless daughter of Zeus, from whose head she is said to
have sprung fully armed; she was a warrior goddess, the patron
deity of Athens, and associated with crafts and cultivation of the
olive. The cult of Athena was important in Sparta, too, where
she had a famous "bronze temple."

ATHENS: Chief city of Attica, where Athenian tragedy and comedy
received their first performances at the festivals of Dionysus.

ATREUS: Son of Pelops and father of Agamemnon and Menelaus. He
avenged his brother Thyestes' seduction of his wife Aerope by
killing all of Thyestes' children (except Atreus) and serving
them to their father at a banquet.

BACCHUS: Another name for Dionysus.

BISTONES: Wild Thracian tribe ruled by Diomedes.

BLACK SEA (or Pontus):   The sea connected by straits to the northeast
corner of the Aegean Sea; of strategic and commercial importance for Athens, a portion of whose grain supply came from its
fertile hinterlands.

BOIBIAS: Lake in Thessaly, at whose southern shore Pherai was situated.

CALCHAS: Seer who accompanied the Greek expedition against Troy.

CALLISTO: A member of Artemis' band of maidens, made pregnant by Zeus, was transformed into a bear. See note on *Helen* 369.

CALYPSO: Seanymph; she dwelled on an isolated island, where she detained Odysseus for seven years during his voyage home to Ithaca.

CAPE MALEA: Promontory off the south of the Peloponnesos; its crosswinds and lack of harbors made it proverbially perilous for sailors.

CASTOR: See DIOSCURI.

CEPHALLENE: Large island to the west of Ithaca.

CEPHISUS: River that flows around Athens.

CHALYBES: Asian tribe, renowned in antiquity for their metallurgical skill and the hardness of the iron they worked.

CHARON: Ferryman of the dead.

CLASHING ROCKS: "Symplegades" in Greek, are also known as the Cyanaean ("Blue-black") Islands, which like boundary stones marked the entrance to the Black Sea at the east end of the Bosporus and also marked the division between Europe and Asia, stnding between barbarians (non-Greek speakers) and Hellenes. In legend they moved together (hence "clashing"), a threat to passing ships, but became fixed after the Argo successfully sailed between them on her maiden voyage.

COLCHIS: The well-watered plain lying beneath the Caucasus Mountains at the eastern end of the Black Sea. Though Greek traders lived there in the late fifth century B.C., it had a largely non-Greek population and paid tribute to the Persians. For the Greeks of that time, it still represented an eastern limit of the traveled world. Medea is referred to as "the Colchian."

CORINTH: A prosperous Greek trading city and maritime power situated on the narrow isthmus that joins the Peloponnesus to mainland Greece. In historical times, there was a long-standing rivalry between Corinth, a Spartan ally, and Athens.

CRETE: The largest of the Greek islands, locate at the southern end of the Aegean sea.

CUPID: Latin rendering of the Greek god Eros, a winged prepubescent boy who personified sexual desire (*erôs*) and regularly accompanied Aphrodite. He carried arrows, with which to strike unsuspecting victims. (See also LOVES.)

CYCLOPS (plural CYCLOPES): The Cyclops of legend is Polyphemus, whose story is first told in the *Odyssey*. Cyclopes were one-eyed (or "wheel-eyed") giants who lived, according to Homer (followed by Euripides in *Cyclops*), in caves, innocent of agriculture and seafaring as well as of political institutions. Another tradition (found in *Alcestis*) identified them as the forgers of Zeus' thunderbolts. In Euripides' version, they were killed by Apollo for providing the thunderbolts with which Zeus killed Apollo's son Asklepios.

CYPRIS: See KYPRIS.

CYPRUS: The third largest island in the Mediterranean, located south of Turkey, with Syria and Lebanon to the east. A major wave of Greek settlement is thought to have taken place following the Bronze Age collapse of Mycenaean Greece in the period 1100–1050 B.C., reflected in the story of Teucer's foundation of Salamis. Cyprus occupies an important role in Greek mythology, not least as the birthplace of Aphrodite and Adonis.

DANAUS' SONS: The Greeks; see note on *Helen* 233.

DELPHI: Seat of Apollo's oracle on the slopes of Mount Parnassus.

DEMETER: Goddess associated with the cultivation of grain; she was a daughter of Cronus and Rhea, hence a sister of Zeus. When her daughter Persephone was abducted by Hades, in her frantic search she abandoned her care of the crops, threatening the survival of life on earth. She and her daughter were worshipped together, most prominently in connection with the Eleusinian mysteries, an initiation rite conducted at their sanctuary near Athens.

DIOMEDES: Legendary king of the tribe of the Bistones in Thrace, and son of the war god Ares. Famed for his hatred of strangers, he was the owner of a four-horse team of man-eating horses. He died in combat with Herakles.

DIONË: Mother of Aphrodite; in Hesiod, one of the daughters of the sea god Oceanus (pointing perhaps to Aphrodite's birth from the sea-foam); she was later treated as one of the Titans.

DIONYSUS: Son of Zeus and the mortal Semele; associated with wine and festivity. Among his entourage were Silenus and the satyrs. He was also the patron deity of the theater in Athens.

DIOSCURI: Castor and Polydeuces (in Latin, Pollux), brothers of Helen; deified and at some point identified with the constellation Gemini, they were venerated as saviors of those lost at sea. For this role, see notes on *Helen* 1486–87, 1487–88, 1631–73.

EARTH: A primeval deity (Greek: Gê, Gâ, Gaia), ancestral mother of the races of gods and men and of all living things, the firm foundation of the universe.

EIDO: Childhood name of Theonoë; see note on *Helen* 8–9.

ELEKTRYON: Son of Perseus and father of Alkmene; grandfather of Herakles.

ENCELADUS: One of the Giants; in the battle with the Olympian gods, Enceladus fought against Athena. He was buried under Mount Aetna and nourished its fires with his incinerated corpse.

EPIRUS: Territory of ancient Greece, bounded to the north by Illyria and Macedon, to the east by Thessaly, and the Adriatic (or Ionian) Sea on the west.

EUBOEA: Large island off the eastern coast of Attica.

EUMELOS: Son of Admetos and Alcestis.

EUROTAS: River of Sparta, sometimes used as a metonym for Sparta.

EURYSTHEUS: King of Tiryns in Argos, who imposed upon Herakles the canonical twelve labors for which that hero was famous.

FATES (Moirai): Conceived of as three spinning sisters. According to legend, Apollo outwitted the Fates and procured the deferment of Admetos' death by the simple stratagem of getting them drunk.

FURY: Corresponds in these translations to a number of Greek names (*erinys, alastor, miastor*). Tireless demonic avenger, often pictured operating as a band of Furies as embodiments of the bloody curses and unappeasable wrath of the grievously wronged. Furies issue from the underworld, gorge upon the enabling, polluting blood of victims, and torture transgressors, their families, and even their cities with terrible afflictions—disease, madness, barrenness, crop failure, and the like. Highest on their list of deserving offenders are perjurers and the slayers of kin.

GAIA: See EARTH.

GALANEIA: "Calm sea"; in Euripides the daughter of Pontos, the sea-god himself; elsewhere Galene, one of the daughters of Nereus.

GANYMEDE: Trojan youth loved by Zeus, who had him borne up to Mount Olympus on an eagle and made him the immortal cupbearer of the gods.

GIANTS: Monstrous sons of Uranus (Sky) and Earth, who rebelled against the hegemony of the Olympian deities.

GOLDEN FLEECE: The fleece of a magical golden ram on whose back Phrixus, son of Athamas, king of Boeotia, escaped from death at the hands of his wicked stepmother Ino and was carried to safety in Colchis. In gratitude to the gods, Phrixus sacrificed the ram and gave its fleece to Aeëtes, king of Aia and Medea's father. Jason and the Argonauts undertook to bring the Golden Fleece back to Greece.

GORGON: Female monsters, usually three in number, with golden wings, huge tusks, bronze claws, and serpents for hair. One of them, Medusa, was mortal, but her face turned to stone anyone who looked at it. She was beheaded by Perseus, using a mirror given to him by Athena, who placed the severed head at the center of the *aegis*, a kind of goatskin shield that is one of her regular attributes.

GRACES: Three minor goddesses associated with ideals of beauty and charm.

GREAT MOTHER: Cybele, a Phrygian fertility goddess adopted into Greek cult and identified with Greek deities such as Rhea and (particularly in *Helen*) Demeter. Her oriental cult had orgiastic elements, and she was often depicted in a chariot drawn by lions.

HECATE: The menacing, nocturnal goddess associated with Artemis, Persephone, and the Moon. Accompanied by ghosts and hell-hounds and holding torches aloft, Hecate guarded the sacred entrances to the underworld, especially at crossroads. Through her, witches and sorcerers gained possession of their infernal, arcane knowledge.

HADES: Lord of the underworld, frequently equated with his own kingdom. (Etymologically, his name means "unseen," and his realm is therefore the home of the unseen, and unseeing, dead; the sunless kingdom.)

HARMONY: Harmonia ("fitting together") was the daughter of Aphrodite (Love) and Ares (War). As the wife of Cadmus, the mortal founder of Thebes, she became the mother of Ino and the grandmother of the wine-god Dionysus.

HELEN: Wife of Menelaus, king of Sparta; in the story that underlies the Trojan saga she ran off with Paris, a son of Priam, king of Troy, when he visited Sparta, and was thus the immediate cause of the Trojan War. *Helen* develops a counter-tradition in which Helen never went to Troy, but was replaced by a phantom that possessed all her seductive beauty and fooled both Trojans and Greeks into believing Helen guilty.

HELENUS: Trojan seer.

HELIOS: The sun, personified as the most powerful of the planetary
deities, who during the day drives his chariot westward across
the sky, and at night travels back through the underworld to the
place of his rising. As a nocturnal sojourner, he is associated
with the occult, and it is this dimension of his divine personality
that makes him the father of Aeêtes, Medea's father.

HEPHAESTUS: Lame son of Hera, whose particular province was the
blacksmith's art; in one tradition, he had his forge in the
Sicilian volcano Mount Aetna.

HERA: Olympian goddess, daughter of Cronus, wife (and sister) of
Zeus; queen of the gods and goddess of marriage. Depicted in
many stories as jealous over Zeus' philandering, as in the case of
Zeus' fathering of Dionysus on Semele.

HERAKLES: Son of Zeus by the mortal woman Alkmene, and the most
renowned of all Greek heroes. Indentured to Eurystheus, king
of Tiryns in Argos, he was compelled to undertake the twelve
labors and a life of struggle and toil against the bestial and the
barbarous, which made him the supreme culture-hero of the
Hellenic world.

HERMES: Son of Zeus and Maia, Zeus' herald, and god of heralds,
travelers, merchants, and thieves. He protected travelers and
children, and guided the souls of the dead to the world below.
An ingenious inventor and trickster, he invented the first lyre by
stretching strings across the hollow shell of a tortoise. Characteristically seen with a snake-wound staff (the caduceus), cap,
and winged sandals, his image in the form of a talisman pillar
with a head and an erect penis stood at doors throughout Athens.

HERMIONE: Daughter of Menelaus and Helen.

IDA: Mountain near Troy, site of the judgment of Paris.

ILIUM: The city or citadel of Troy.

INO: Daughter of Cadmus and Harmony, stepmother of Phrixus, aunt
and nurse of the wine-god Dionysus, she became the sea nymph

Leukothea, who in Homer's *Odyssey* rescued raft-wrecked Odysseus off the shores of Phaeacia.

IOLCUS (IOLKOS): Port town in Thessaly at the foot of Mount Pelion, from which the legendary Argo set sail. It was Jason's hometown, ruled by his Uncle Pelias at the time of the Argo's voyage but in the action of the *Medea*, by Pelias' son Acastus. It was also the birthplace of Alcestis.

ITHACA: Island off the west coast of Greece, the home of Odysseus.

KARNEIA: A yearly festival of Apollo Karneios, celebrated at Sparta and elsewhere during the period of the full moon in August.

KERBEROS: Fabulous three-headed dog who guarded the gates of Hades.

KORE: "The maiden," see PERSEPHONE.

KYKNOS: Son of Ares slain by Herakles.

KYLLENE: A mountain in the Peloponnesos, site of the birth of Hermes.

KYPRIS (KYPRIAN, CYPRIS): Epithet of the goddess Aphrodite, who was reputed to have been born from the sea off the island of Cyprus and who had a famous shrine on that island.

LACEDAEMON: The territory around Sparta, also used as a synonym for Sparta itself.

LEDA: Daughter of the Aetolian king Thestius, and wife of King Tyndareus of Sparta; mother of Helen, Clytemnestra, and Castor and Pollux (Polydeuces). Zeus, in the form of a swan, seduced her on the same night that she lay with her husband, resulting in two eggs from which the four offspring hatched. Which children were sired by Tyndareus, the mortal king, and which by Zeus is disputed in our sources, but the division is almost always two mortal, two half-divine.

LARISA, LARISSA: Town of Thessaly.

LEUCADIA: Island near Ithaca, famous for its white limestone cliffs.

LIBYA: Greek name for a wide swath of northern Africa to the west of Egypt.

LOVES: English for *erôtes*, the plural of Eros. Often the ardor that attends sex (Aphrodite) is conceptualized as a plurality.

LYDIAN: Adjective of Lydia, a region of western Asia Minor, and a plentiful source of slaves for the Greek market.

LYKAON: Son of Ares, god of war; he challenged Herakles to single combat and was killed.

LYKIA: Region situated on the southern coast of Asia Minor.

MAIA: Eldest of the Pleiades, the seven daughters of Atlas and Pleione, and mother by Zeus of Hermes.

MARON: Priest of Apollo at Ismarus; when Odysseus raided the city on his way home from Troy, he spared Maron, who in gratitude gave him a casket of excellent wine.

MENELAUS: King of Sparta and husband of Helen; son of Atreus, he was along with his brother Agamemnon, king of Mycenae, one of the chief leaders of the Greek forces at Troy.

MEROPS' CHILD: Identified in the Greek text as a Titan and in a late lexicon given the name Cos, but otherwise unknown.

MOLOSSIANS: Greek tribe of Epirus, regarded in *Alcestis* as a part of Admetos' kingdom of Thessaly.

MORPHEUS: Minor god personifying sleep; used instead of the "Hypnos" of the Greek, another personification less familiar in English.

MOUNT PELION: Mountain on the northeast border of Thessaly, at the foot of whose southwest slope lies the harbor town of Iolcus. In a cave near the mountain's peak, the mythical centaur Chiron, tutor of heroes (including Jason), lived and taught. From its slopes the timbers of the Argo were cut.

MUSES: Daughters of Zeus and Memory who were the divine patronesses of poetry and music, learning, and the transmission of wisdom from one generation to the next.

NAIADS: Nymphs who inhabited springs or brooks.

NAUPLIA: Port city south of Argos and Mycenae in the Peloponnese.

NAUPLIUS: King of Euboea (alternatively of Nauplia) and father of Palamedes, a Greek warrior at Troy executed on false charges by his fellow Greeks. Nauplius exacted revenge as the victorious fleet returned. See note on *Helen* 1132–35.

NEREIDS: Sea nymphs, the daughters of Nereus.

NEREUS: Marine deity, son of Earth and Sea; sometimes called the Old Man of the Sea, he is a figure of knowledge and righteousness whom Euripides associates with Egypt, and makes the grandfather of Theoclymenus and his sister Thonoë.

NESTOR: Aged king of Pylos who took part in the battles at Troy, in which his son Antilochus was killed.

ODYSSEUS: Protagonist of Homer's *Odyssey*, where he is the son of Laertes (rather than of Sisyphus, as was sometimes alleged) and ruler of Ithaca. He was renowned for his wiliness as well as for his strength and courage (the strategem of the Trojan Horse was attributed to him). In Homer's *Iliad*, he is the leader of the Ithacan troops at Troy; the *Odyssey* describes his adventures on his voyage home.

OENOMAUS: King of Pisa in the Peloponnese, father of Hippodameia. Having been told that his son-in-law would kill him, he killed many of Hippodameia's suitors after defeating them in a chariot race; he was himself killed by trickery in a race with Pelops, who then claimed his daughter in marriage.

OLYMPUS: Mountain in northern Greece, imagined as the home of Zeus and the gods of his generation (hence their designation as Olympians).

ORION: A giant hunter, transformed after his death into a constellation.

ORPHEUS: Poet and musician of myth and legend who was reputed to charm trees, rocks, and wild animals by the beauty of his music. According to myth, he descended to Hades in order to bring back his dead wife, Eurydike, and he was associated with mystical rites and the promise of salvation. Orpheus was a member of Jason's crew and, according to Apollonius of Rhodes, sang at Jason's and Medea's wedding.

ORPHIC: Pertaining to Orpheus, a mythical singer associated also with mystical rites, magic, and survival in the afterlife; hence Orphic spells and songs.

ORTHRYS: Mountain about thirty-five miles south of Pherai.

PAIAN: God of healing, frequently associated (and sometimes identified) with Apollo.

PAN: A wild, ithyphallic, Arcadian shepherd god, half-goat, half-man-shaped, who played the syrinx (panpipes), presided over flocks and the hunting of small game, and was also credited with striking animals and men—herds, armies, and individuals—with "panics," sudden, inexplicable fears that propelled them into flight or other uncontrollable movement.

PARIS: Son of Priam and Hecuba, whose abduction of Helen while a guest at the house of Menelaus caused the Trojan War. Helen had been promised to him as a reward by Aphrodite in return for awarding her the prize for beauty in the famous judgment of Paris.

PEIRENE: A copious spring whose waters flowed into an open well in the center of Corinth, from which citizens drew their water.

PELEUS: Banished from his home island of Aegina, he in time became king in Phthia, a kingdom in southern Thessaly. Through the agency of Zeus, he married the divine Nereid Thetis, and their child was Achilles.

PELIAS: King of Iolkos (Iolcus) and father of Akastos and a number of daughters, including Alcestis. Fearing because of a prophecy that his nephew Jason would kill him, he sent Jason on a seemingly impossible mission to retrieve the Golden Fleece. After the Argonauts' return, he was killed by his daughters, whom Medea tricked into thinking they could rejuvenate him by adding his butchered limbs to a magical stew.

PELION: High mountain range in eastern Thessaly, sloping abruptly down to the Aegean Sea.

PELOPS: Eponymous hero of the Peloponnese, buried and worshipped at Olympia, he was the father of six sons, including Atreus, father of Agamemnon and Menelaus, the men who led the Greeks to Troy. See also TANTALUS.

PERSEPHONE: Daughter of the goddess Demeter, wife of Hades, and goddess of the underworld.

PERSEUS: Greek hero, ancestor of Alkmene and Herakles.

PHRYGIA: The region in which Troy was located.

PITTHEUS: The clever ancient king of Troezen and Theseus' maternal grandfather.

POLYPHEMUS: A Cyclops, and son of Poseidon; although the Cyclopes are solitary cave dwellers, Polyphemus appears to be the chief among them in Homer's *Odyssey*.

POSEIDON: Olympian god whose chief domain was the sea; he was also associated with earthquakes. In Homer's *Odyssey*, he is represented as the father of Polyphemus and the cause of Odysseus' subsequent wanderings.

PRIAM: King of Troy at the time of the Trojan War; slain after the capture of the city by the Greeks.

PROTEUS: An "old man of the sea" in the *Odyssey*, a shape-shifter with prophetic powers whom Menelaus compels to give advice about his return home. Euripides, following Herodotus, makes him the king of Egypt, to whom, because of his upright character, Helen has been entrusted for safekeeping.

PSAMANTHË: "Sandy," one of the Nereids, the fifty daughters of Nereus; wife of Aeacus and subsequently (only in Euripides) of Proteus.

SALAMIS: Island in the Saronic Gulf, just off the coast of Attica; city in Cyprus said to have been founded by Teucer after being banished from his home island.

SATYRS: Woodland deities, human in form but often imagined as having the ears, horns, tail, and legs of goats. They were associated with Dionysus' retinue, and sometimes (as in *Cyclops*) represented as sons of Silenus. They formed the regular chorus in satyr plays, hence the name.

SCAMANDER: Most important river of the Trojan plain.

SCYLLA: A terrifying, sea-dwelling she-monster first described in Homer's *Odyssey*. As Odysseus' ship passed by, each of her six doglike heads snatched one of his crew. In some later accounts she is the daughter of Hecate. By Classical times her watery lair was located in the Straits of Messina at the entrance to the Tyrrhenian (Etruscan) sea.

SICILY: Large, triangular island south of the boot of Italy. In classical times, it was inhabited by native populations in the interior; several Greek cities were located on its shores, including one near the slopes of Mount Aetna. The Cyclopes were imagined as residing there in mythical times.

SILENUS: Fat, satyrlike, boozy companion of Dionysus, sometimes represented as Dionysus' foster-son and father, in turn, of the satyrs.

SIMOIS: River on the Trojan plain.

SIRENS: Daemonic female singers pictured as bird-women. See note on *Helen* 162.

SISYPHUS: King of Corinth, noted for his cunning; in some traditions he is represented as Odysseus' father. He was punished in the underworld by having to roll a heavy stone endlessly uphill.

SPARTA: Major city of the southern Peloponnese; royal seat of Menelaus and his Spartan wife, Helen.

SUNIUM: Promontory in the south of Attica (the territory around the city of Athens).

TAENARUM: Promontory on the south of the Peloponnesus, west of Cape Malea.

TANTALUS: Son of Zeus and, as father of Pelops and grandfather of Atreus, founder of the Argive royal line. He is said to have killed Pelops and served him to the gods at a banquet. When they discovered this transgression, the gods restored Pelops to life, and the gods punished Tantalus in the underworld by placing him in a pool of water that receded when he tried to drink it, and beneath branches laden with fruits that, whenever he tried to reach them, were blown beyond his grasp by a breeze.

TELAMON: King of Salamis and father of Ajax and Teucer, whom he banishes after Ajax's death.

TEUCER: Son of Telamon, king of Salamis; archer and companion of his half-brother Ajax at Troy. Banished by his father for returning home without his brother, Teucer founds a new Salamis on the island of Cyprus.

THEMIS: Titan goddess, daughter of Earth, but closely associated in myth with Zeus. Her name means "right" or "customary law"; she is the divine personification of what is laid down as naturally right and holy to do, and her main function is to punish transgressors of her law.

THEOCLYMENUS: Son of Proteus and Psamanthë, and after his father's death king of Egypt.

THEONOË: Daughter of Proteus and Psamanthë, gifted with prophetic knowledge; called Eido as a child. (In the *Odyssey*, Eidothea is the name of Proteus' daughter who gives Menelaus advice about how to capture her father and make him reveal prophecies that will ensure Menelaus' escape.)

THETIS: Sea deity, daughter of Nereus and mother of Achilles by the mortal Peleus.

TRITON: Sea god, son of Poseidon and Amphitrite, sometimes imagined as having the tail of a sea serpent and tooting on a large conch.

TROEZEN: A city in the northeast corner of the Peloponnese, overlooking the Saronic Gulf toward Athens. The two cities shared ancient ties of kinship and friendship, and it was to this place that the Athenians sent their wives and children when they abandoned their city to the Persians before the battle of Salamis, in 480 B.C.

TROY: City (or its territory) near the Hellespont, where the Greeks fought the Trojans and their allies in a ten-year campaign to avenge the abduction of Helen.

TYNDAREUS: King of Sparta, husband of Leda, and putative father of her children, a distinction he shares with Zeus.

ZEUS: Ruler of the Olympian gods, he forcefully overthrew the Titan generation of gods to become the most powerful of all the gods in the Greek pantheon. His special domain was the sky, where he wielded the thunderbolt; his brothers Poseidon and Hades ruled the seas and the underworld, respectively, and his sister Hera became his consort, although he remained a famous and prolific bedmate of gods and mortals. He was believed to favor the just and was the patron deity of guests and strangers. Thus, he is often invoked in drama as the protector of suppliants, the arbiter of oaths, and the terror of wrongdoers.

FOR FURTHER READING

EURIPIDES

Peter Burian. "Euripides." In Michael Gagarin and Elaine Fantham, eds., *The Oxford Encyclopedia of Ancient Greece and Rome*. New York and Oxford: Oxford University Press, 2010, pp. 129–41. A brief, broadly based introduction.

Desmond J. Conacher. *Euripidean Drama: Myth, Theme, and Structure*. Toronto: University of Toronto Press, 1967. Still the most useful play-by-play study of Euripides.

Donald J. Mastronarde. *The Art of Euripides: Dramatic Technique and Social Context*. Cambridge: Cambridge University Press, 2010. A new assessment of the entire Euripidean corpus, employing a variety of perspectives.

Ann N. Michelini. *Euripides and the Tragic Tradition*. Madison: University of Wisconsin Press, 1987. A study of Euripides and the history of Euripidean criticism.

James Morwood. *The Plays of Euripides*. London: Bristol Classical Press, 2002. Brief, personal discussions of all the surviving plays.

Judith Mossman, ed. *Euripides*. Oxford: Oxford University Press, 2003. A collection of influential critical essays, including chapters that focus specifically on *Alcestis* and *Medea*.

ALCESTIS

Jennifer J. Dellner. "Alcestis' Double Life." *Classical Journal* 96 (2000): 1–25. A fascinating exercise in "tragic economics," examining the systems of exchange (barter, bargaining, reciprocity) that pervade the play and are finally stopped by Heracles' "free gift" of the original object of exchange with death.

Charles Segal. *Euripides and the Poetics of Sorrow: Art, Gender, and Commemoration in "Alcestis," "Hippolytus," and "Hecuba."* Durham, NC: Duke University Press, 1993. This contains three chapters on *Alcestis*, dealing with insight and authority with aspects of genre, gender, and mortality in this play.

Niall W. Slater. "Nothing to Do with Satyrs? *Alcestis* and the Concept of Prosatyric Drama." In G. W. M. Harrison, ed., *Satyr Drama: Tragedy at Play*. Swansea: The Classical Press of Wales, 2005, pp. 83–101. A persuasive recreation of the play's original performance and reception from the perspective of spectators confronting a nonstandard tragicomic play in place of the expected satyr drama.

MEDEA

Anne Pippin Burnett. "Connubial Revenge: Euripides' *Medea*." In *Revenge in Attic and Later Tragedy*. Berkeley: University of California Press, 1998, pp. 192–224. A study of *Medea* in the context of the revenge tragedy tradition.

James J. Clauss and Sarah Iles Johnston, eds. *Medea: Essays on "Medea" in Myth, Literature, Philosophy and Art*. Princeton: Princeton University Press, 1997. An excellent series of essays discussing the figure of Medea from the earliest appearance of the myth to Roman imperial times.

Helene P. Foley. "Tragic Wives: Medea's Divided Self." In *Female Acts in Greek Tragedy*. Princeton: Princeton University Press, 2001, pp. 243–71. Makes a strong case for a Medea divided between two selves—one private and female, the other public and male—and shows how the triumph of the male self raises questions both about the possibility of women's independence and the nature of heroic masculinity.

HELEN

Eric Downing. "Apate, Agon, and Literary Self-Reflexivity in Euripides' *Helen*." In M. Griffith and D. J. Mastronarde, eds., *Cabinet of the Muses*. Atlanta: Scholars Press, 1990, pp. 1–16. A sophisticated and rewarding study of the play of appearance, deception, and paradox in the language of the play.

Ingrid E. Holmberg. "Euripides' *Helen*: Most Noble and Most Chaste." *American Journal of Philology* 116 (1995): 27–49. A sympathetic interpretation of the drama, emphasizing the complex relation of the Euripidean Helen to that in the *Odyssey*.

Charles Segal. "The Two Worlds of Euripides' *Helen*." *Transactions and Proceedings of the American Philological Association* 102 (1971): 553–614. Still the fullest introduction to both the literary and philosophical aspects of this play.

CYCLOPS

Carol Dougherty. "The Double Vision of Euripides' 'Cyclops': An Ethnographic 'Odyssey' of the Satyr Stage." *Comparative Drama* 33 (1999): 313–38. Discusses the play's allusions to the *Odyssey* and how they allow the Athenian audience both to experience the exoticism of Odysseus' travels and to scrutinize their own culture.

George W. M. Harrison. "Positioning of Satyr Drama and Characterization in the Cyclops." In George W. M. Harrison, ed., *Satyr Drama: Tragedy at Play*. Swansea: Classical Press of Wales, 2005, pp. 237–58. An insightful and comprehensive close reading that opens into a larger discussion of the genre of satyr drama. This volume also offers several other important articles about *Cyclops*.

David Konstan. "The Anthropolgy of Euripides' *Kyklôps*." In John J. Winkler and Froma Zeitlin, eds., *Nothing to Do with Dionysus?* Princeton: Princeton University Press, 1990, pp. 207–27. The most useful interpretative essay on this play to date.

CPSIA information can be obtained
at www.ICGtesting.com
Printed in the USA
BVHW050859110921
616356BV00003B/8

9 780195 388718